Questions

AND

Answers

VOLUME II

Questions

AND

Answers

VOLUME II

By

GUY N. WOODS

Gospel Advocate Co.
P.O. Box 150
Nashville, Tenn. 37202

Published by Gospel Advocate Co.
P.O. Box 150, Nashville, TN 37202
www.gospeladvocate.com

ISBN 0-89225-277-4

To

Earnest and sincere students of the Word everywhere is this book affectionately dedicated.

Foreword

In response to a great many requests since the publication of QUESTIONS AND ANSWERS—OPEN FORUM, a second volume is now being offered to our readers.

While the format is much the same as that followed in the first volume, Volume 2, as its title indicates, was planned to provide material not included in the first. We have also carefully avoided matters dealt with in QUESTIONS AND ANSWERS by Lipscomb and Sewell, in order that this publication might complement those books and not duplicate them.

These questions and answers cover a vast variety of subjects set out in the sacred writings, and they range widely over many themes which at one time or another challenge the attention of all serious students of God's Word. The answers herein given are the views of the author and not necessarily any other; they are the result of a half century of study, observation and research, using the best tools available. Difficult matters often obscure are frequently dealt with, and the answers, in consequence, will be sometimes controversial. It is not expected that every reader will agree with each sentiment expressed; it is sincerely hoped that all who examine these pages will be stimulated to additional study and investigation in the search for truth, since it is the truth, and the truth alone, which frees from the bondage and thraldom of sin. (John 8:31,32.)

People are disposed to ask questions only when they sincerely believe that it is important to have correct answers; in proportion as people lose respect for the authority of God's Word, their interest in, and their desire for right answers diminishes. The author earnestly hopes that this book, involving much effort, will be helpful in enabling those who read it to understand "the way of God more accurately." (Acts 18:24-28.)

Guy N. Woods
P.O. Box 150
Nashville, TN 37202

Introduction

The first volume of QUESTIONS AND ANSWERS by Guy N. Woods has proved to be one of the most popular books of the past decade among New Testament Christians. It is expected that the second volume will be equally well-received, coming as it does from one of the most able, lucid and scholarly writers of this or any other generation.

Guy N. Woods is uniquely qualified to write concerning Bible questions which are interesting, challenging, difficult, complex, or obscure. If he had spent all of his life in anticipation, preparation and study for the writing of this one book, he could not have prepared more thoroughly than he has already done through the normal course of events throughout his lifetime. A man of broad learning and background, brother Woods has been able to focus all of his diverse training and experience in the direction of analyzing and expounding the inspired scriptures. He is, above all, a "man of the Book."

For many years he was the author of the *Gospel Advocate Adult Quarterly* which operated upon a cycle of covering the entire Bible every seven years. It is likely that during this period he had occasion to examine and to comment upon every verse in the Bible.

He served for approximately 30 years as the moderator of the Open Forum at the Freed-Hardeman College Bible Lectureship. Over the years almost every conceivable question asked of preachers in meetings, classes, discussions and debates has been raised and answered in the forum. I have often marveled at the enormous breadth of information which he possessed and which he was able to communicate with instant recall, yet in the simplest and most coherent fashion. Under his direction the forum became the most popular feature of one of the most popular lectureships conducted among our brethren.

Further, brother Woods has engaged in more public debates on various religious issues than any other living person. He has met the leading exponents of error both in and out of the church, from Roy E. Cogdill of the non-cooperation persuasion to Ben Franklin of the charismatic movement, and from D.L. Welch of the oneness Pentecostals to D.N. Jackson of the association Baptists. His early preaching transpired in the years when congregations were often challenged and when they were often set for the defense of the gospel and, as a consequence of his preparation and ability, he was called both far and wide to contend earnestly for the faith. These polemic excursions gave him a keenness of insight far beyond his years in recognizing error, inconsistency and false reasoning, enabling him to vindicate the truth and to refute false teaching.

For more than 40 years he has served as a staff writer of the *Gospel Advocate*. In this capacity, he has been compelled, by the nature of the case, to set down his convictions in writing which has had the effect of stimulating far more serious study and precise expression than mere oral presentation. He has a systematic and logical approach both in speaking and writing which is unexcelled by any man I have ever known. In addition to his articles and editorials in the *Gospel Advocate*, he has distinguished himself as the author of sermons, commentaries, published debates, and linguistic studies.

Early in life he acquired a legal education. Although he has never followed the profession of law, this training has tended to sharpen his analytical powers and to train him in the rigorous discipline of painstaking research and investigation.

Many have known Guy N. Woods, the preacher, the writer, the lecturer, the scholar, or the debater, but not all have known him in his personal attributes and characteristics. It has been my privilege to have known and been associated with brother Woods for more than 25 years. I knew both his mother and his father, gentle, good and godly people of faith and courage. His brother, Earle, is a faithful preacher of the gospel. Educated at Freed-Hardeman College, brother Woods was strongly motivated by the late N.B. Hardeman. It is out of these influences that his fundamental character has been shaped. His personal conduct bespeaks quiet dignity, refinement, kindness, gratitude and industriousness. He is by any worthwhile standard a most remarkable individual.

All of these traits and experiences have, in my judgment, converged into the depths and riches out of which this book emanates. It is truly the product of a lifetime of preparation and study, and an exceptional lifetime at that. The name of Guy N. Woods will take its place in future generations alongside those of McGarvey, Hardeman, Brewer and others, whose contributions to the Cause of Christ have endured long after the principals themselves have "crossed over the river to rest in the shade of the trees."

Alan E. Highers
Henderson, Tennessee
December 15, 1984

"Was there forgiveness of sins under the Old Testament covenant?"

The "forgiveness" offered by means of the sacrifices of the Old Testament were both provisional and temporal. Provisional in that they were efficacious only as they typified the ultimate sacrifice at Calvary; and temporal, in that there was a recognition of obligation and consequently an awareness of the imperfect character of the offerings in the fact that they had to be repeated year by year. "For the law having a shadow of the good things to come, not the very image of the things, can never with the same sacrifices year by year, which they offer continually, make perfect them that draw nigh. Else would they not have ceased to be offered? because the worshippers, having been once cleansed, would have had no more consciousness of sins. But in those sacrifices there is a remembrance made of sins year by year. For it is impossible that the blood of bulls and goats should take away sins." (Hebrews 10:1-4.)

The apostle thus makes it clear that the people were aware that the "blood of bulls and of goats" could not absolve them of sin and their conscience did not permit them to disregard these offerings each year. The penalty was lifted—pretermissed is Paul's word for it, (Romans 3:25)—passed over, but not canceled, the sacrifices being typical of the death of the Lamb of God who alone can take away the sins of the world.

"Why is the 37th verse of the 8th chapter of Acts omitted from the American Standard Version of the New Testament?"

Because it does not appear in most ancient Greek manuscripts on which the American Standard translation is based. It is for this reason that most scholars believe that it is an interpolation. J.W. McGarvey, said to have had the most profound knowledge of the Bible of any man of his day and whose dedication to the authority of the scriptures is unquestioned wrote, "In regard to scarcely any reading are the textual critics more unanimously agreed, or on better manuscript evidence, than the rejection of this verse as an interpolation." He believed that the "interpolator obtained the idea which he inserted from such passages as Romans 10:8,9; 1 Timothy 6:13; and Matthew 16:16, which show that such a confession was taken by the apostles; and it is not improbable that this apostolic custom was still prevalent when the anterpolation was made."

It will be seen, therefore, that its omission from many ancient manuscripts by no means proves that the confession was not a part of the original divine plan. (1) Romans 10:9,10 reveals that a confession, made with the mouth, was a part of God's plan to save. The confession does not depend for its validity on this passage. (2) The response which the eunuch made to Phillip's request shows that not only was some confession expected but was required as a condition precedent to the baptismal act. "If thou believest with all thine heart, thou mayest . . ." requires response. (3) The statement appearing in the KJV in verse 37 is not wholly without manuscript evidence; it must have been in at least one valid document in the second century because Irenaeus, whose active ministry was from about 170 to 210 A.D. wrote, "When the eunuch himself was persuaded, and thought proper to be baptized immediately, and said, I believe that Jesus Christ is the Son of God." Cyprian, born near the beginning of the third century, quotes the verse substantially as it appears in the current KJV text. It appears, therefore, that the verse was known in the early centuries, the confession was a part of the plan of God to save, and ought always to be included today.

"Occasionally, one officiating at the Lord's table will say: 'Father we thank thee for having shed thy blood on the cross for us.' Please comment."

The statement evidences the fact that the one making it is guilty of gross inattention, pathetic ignorance of the Scriptures, or both. The Father did not die, nor did he shed his blood in our behalf. As all should know, it was the Son whom the Father gave to mankind to die on the cross through whom salvation becomes possible to all. ". . . Christ . . . through the Eternal Spirit offered himself without blemish unto God" in order that he might cleanse our conscience "from dead works to serve the living God." Because he did this, "he is the mediator of a new covenant, that a death having taken place for the redemption of the transgressions that were under the first covenant, they that have been called may receive the promise of the eternal inheritance." "Wherefore Jesus also, that he might sanctify the people through his own blood, suffered without the gate." (Hebrews 9:14,15; 13:12.)

"Also, now and then some brother refers to 'the spilt blood' of our Saviour at the Lord's table. Is this phraseology correct?"

I occasionally hear the statement also and there is a song in one of the books widely used by our brethren which contains a similar phrase. I cringe with pain when I hear it either uttered or sung, because it is unscriptural, tasteless, positively wrong. Our blessed Lord did not spill his blood on the cross, or elsewhere. One spills something only accidentally—never on purpose; and, that which is spilled is wasted, beyond recovery. Webster's New Collegiate Dictionary defines the word *spill* "to cause or allow accidentally or unintentionally to fall, flow, or run out so as to be lost or wasted." Were brethren who use the phrase really aware of its significance they would be shocked to think they have attributed such sentiment to our Lord's atonement. His sacrifice was neither accidental nor unintentional; and certainly his blood was not wasted! It was fully in accord with God's "determinate counsel and foreknowledge" that Christ suffered and died at Calvary. (Acts 2:23.) The sainted T.B. Larimore once wrote: "So far as my limited observation shows, men make more mistakes at the Lord's table, where they frequently talk and pray, instead of simply giving thanks, as the Bible authorizes, than anywhere else in the service of the Lord." This, too, has been my observation of the matter through many years.

"Was John the Baptist ever baptized?"

The Bible does not say. We are therefore without any information regarding the matter. If he were not, it was simply because it was not a part of the will and plan of God that he should be. In view of the fact that it is specifically declared that baptism is a part of God's plan to save today (Mark 16:15,16); it is "for (in order to) the remission of sins" (Acts 2:38); and it is the consummating act of salvation (1 Peter 3:21), it is certain that one may not with impunity disregard this duty today. Whether John himself was baptized is not material to the fact that he taught others to be baptized, and those who refused to do so were in disobedience to God in not being baptized. John preached baptism for the remission of sins (Mark 1:4; Luke 3:3), because God so ordained it; and to reject the act was to repudiate him who commanded it—the Lord himself. The people and publicans, when they heard John preach baptism for the remission of sins, "justified God being baptized with the baptism of John. But the Pharisees and the lawyers rejected for themselves the counsel of God, being not baptized of him." (Luke 7:29,30.) If those Jews who rejected God's counsel by refusing to submit to the baptism John preached, were in rebellion to God for this, how much more the guilt of those who regard as unimportant and refuse to submit to the baptism which Christ commanded. (1 John 2:4.)

"Jesus said, 'For unto every one that hath shall be given, and he shall have abundance: but from him that hath not, even that which he hath shall be taken away.' What does this mean?"

This is one of the conclusions and applications the Lord appended to the parable of the talents. (Matthew 25:14-30.) Among the many matters taught in this useful and interesting narrative is the lesson that we must seize the opportunities which life offers or not only lose the benefits resulting therefrom, but ultimately the opportunities themselves. This is the well-known law of nature that we either "use or lose" the blessings that a wise and beneficent God makes available to us. If we will not properly utilize the blessings which come from his omnipotent hand, even the opportunity to use them will eventually disappear. Many people in the world today, in a frenzied search for affluence and pleasure, have so long squelched the tenderer aspects of their nature, they have destroyed forevermore their capacity to enjoy the higher and nobler things of life. A soul, long starved of spiritual food, ultimately mummifies. Sad indeed is the status of one who, in the mad scramble for worldly things, has sacrificed and eternally lost the finer and tenderer side of his nature. Doubly great is the tragedy when such worldliness and materialism have created an immunity to all spiritual influences, and led the possessor thereof along a path of no return. We should never forget that only that which we do for our Saviour is enduring; that which is done for self and selfish reasons soon perishes.

"Please explain 1 Peter 3:7. In what way is the woman the weaker vessel?"

The passage reads: "Ye husbands, in like manner, dwell with your wives according to knowledge, giving honor unto the woman, as unto the weaker vessel, as being also joint-heirs of the grace of life; to the end that your prayers be not hindered." The verb "dwell" translates a Greek word which, in this context, denotes the marriage relationship. This association is to be "according to knowledge," that is, with due understanding of, and appreciation for the marital relation, each showing proper regard for the other, and both discharging the obligations peculiarly theirs. It is of interest that the word "giving" is the rendering of a word nowhere else occurring in the scriptures (*aponemoo*), and means to assign, to apportion; and "honor," in the text, is the rendering of the same word translated "precious" in 1 Peter 1:19. Christian husbands (such being the only type contemplated by the apostle here), are to regard their faithful wives as precious, and to be careful to assign to them their full honors. The woman is called a "weaker vessel," not because of moral, mental or intellectual inferiority, but solely from the fact that she lacks the physical prowess usually characteristic of man. The husband is to dwell with his wife in due realization of the fact that she is physically weaker, and always to consider her as a fellow-heir of the race of life which awaits all the faithful. (John 17:3.) In characterizing the wife as "the weaker vessel," there is the very clear implication that man is also a vessel, and that both the husband and the wife are instruments in God's hand to do him service. Where the harmony which

16

the apostle enjoins is wanting, prayers are hindered, literally, cut into, interrupted—the message to heaven is short-circuited! Bitterness, bickering and strife in the home make an effective prayer life impossible. Only when peace and harmony prevail may a husband and wife engage in acceptable prayers before the throne of grace.

"Why is it wrong to gamble?"

Gambling is wrong because it is immoral, destructive of character, and eventually fatal to those who persist in it. It is immoral, because it violates God's basic plan designed for man and that is that he is to earn his living by the sweat of his brow. This, of course, does not mean that only those who engage in physical activity to the point of perspiring do God's will; the familiar statement of Genesis 3:19 is metaphorical in nature and designates labor whether physical, mental or intellectual. Gambling is wrong because it is destructive of both body and soul; it's feverish victims become so obsessed they easily succumb to other temptations in order to indulge their desire. And, gambling is fatal because most of those who fall prey to its incitements lose their moral stamina, their strength of character and any desire to earn their living by honest work, as God intended.

Gambling is really a form of theft, because it takes from many and gives without effort to a few. Most often, those from whom money is taken are least able to lose, and usually the loss falls on helpless women and children who must suffer deprivation because of the gambler's obsession. States sometimes legalize some forms of gambling; but this does not make it right in God's sight, or any less serious in its consequences.

One of the most common arguments to justify gambling (there are those so brainwashed they really think the action is a proper one), allege that there is an element chance in all that we do and that in a very real sense all of us are gamblers. The argument is often advanced that farming, operating a business or investing money involves risk and is therefore a form of gambling. This is fallacious and false reasoning. True, businessmen and farmers assume risks in their planning but this is an exchange of effort, mental or physical, in order to produce tangible and useful benefits for others as the fruit of their labors. Gambling differs from this in the very real sense that artificial risks are created and the results simply take from the many in order to benefit the few. No goods, labor or services, as in legitimate efforts, result. In the nature of the case, gambling is wrong because it is a form of greed which takes from others without offering anything of value in return. Remarkably, some, even including religious organizations, allege that gambling is proper when the proceeds are given to useful and worthy purposes. This is the age-long fallacy of doing evil that good may come. The law may legalize it; some churches and civic organizations may practice it; nonetheless, gambling is subversive of the human spirit, harmful to the best interests of all who engage in it, and sinful in God's sight.

"Does love for man take precedence over the laws (commandments) of God? Is love 'the highest moral principle,' and to be exercised, though such involve disregard of the divine edicts? Is it true that what is 'right' may indeed differ in any given situation, depending on what the 'loving' response is? Is there an 'intrinsic' conflict between the way of law and the way of love through Christ?"

Such an instance is alleged when Paul is said to have "ignored" our Lord's teaching:

"Jesus said, 'Give to the one who asks you, and do not turn away from the one who wants to borrow from you.' (Matthew 5:42.) But for a special situation in Thessalonica Paul ignored that teaching and gave this moral instruction: 'For even when we were with you, this we commanded you, If any will not work, neither let him eat . . .' (2 Thessalonians 3:10-12.)"

This is hardly an instance of situation ethics! Were we to concede the conflict between Christ and Paul which the author alleges, this passage puts Paul in the position of the defender of law against love. Did not the apostle know that the welfare state, in which every person may do his own thing, without the annoying problem of making a living, is the highest realization of love? And, besides, the world owes "us" a living; and wealth and property ought to be re-distributed, anyway. To demand, as the apostle does, that a man must work before he can eat, is law, on its lowest level, not love! This is situation ethics.

Of course, we concede no such conflict between Paul and Christ. The effort does gross injustice to our Lord and the great apostle. Our Lord's edict, "Give to the one who asks you . . ." must be interpreted in the light of its context and in harmony with his teaching elsewhere. "If ye shall ask anything in my name, that I will do." (John 14:14.) To ask in his name, is to ask by his authority and in keeping with his will. Since he gives in this manner, he does not require of us to act in any fashion contrary to his will. To give indiscriminately is not love. A gun to a would-be murderer, charity to a deceiver, alcohol to a drunkard are not acts of love, but of injury. Further, Paul's injunctions to the Thessalonians, grounded as they were in the well-being of the people to whom he wrote, actually exhibited the principle which Jesus taught. Strange

18

indeed that a writer affecting loyalty to the Scriptures would attempt to array Paul against Christ. The effort borders on blasphemy.

We are informed that

"Jesus himself approved the action of David and his companions when, on a time of special need, they ate the bread which was lawful only for the priests to eat. (Leviticus 24:5-9; 1 Samuel 21:6; Mark 2:23-28.)"

The Pharisees charged the disciples with violating the law of Moses because they gathered a portion of grain on the sabbath day to allay hunger. The charge was false (Deuteronomy 23:25); it was the Talmud, not the law, which did this. Jesus replied by pointing out that on an occasion of special need David ate bread lawful only for the priests to eat. The Pharisees justified David's act; yet, they condemned an act identical in principle on the part of the disciples of Jesus. The allegation of the writer under review is that the disciples of Jesus violated the law, and that Jesus justified it by an appeal to the case of David.

The conclusion does not follow. Jesus cited the case of David, and the shewbread, but he did not approve of David's action, either here, or elsewhere, in this instance. It is an argument *ad hominem*, an appeal to their own reasoning; and, it ran like this: David's action, in this matter was in violation of the law, yet you justify him in it; my disciples engaged in an act which the law permits, yet you condemn them. Jesus taught his disciples to observe all of the law, even its most minute portions, observing that not one "jot" or "tittle" should pass until all was fulfilled. He warned that "Whosoever therefore shall break one of these least commandments, and teach men so, shall be called the least in the kingdom of heaven." (Matthew 5:17-20.) If we are at liberty to regard love as the only "universal and permanently binding ethical rule," as the writer under review alleges, taking precedence over all of the divine edicts of Scripture, every man becomes a law unto himself; reason, not faith, determines the proper course, and the New Morality becomes the order of the day. Paul and Christ are in no sense in conflict, and the allegation is therefore false.

"Were the giants, 'mighty men that were of old, men of renown,' the fruit of co-habitation between angels and earthly women?"

Genesis 6:4 reads: "The Nephilim were in the earth in those days, and also after that, when the sons of God came in unto the daughters of men, and they bare children to them: the same were the mighty men that were of old, the men of renown." Jude writes of "angels that kept not their own principality, but left their proper habitation, he hath kept in everlasting bonds under darkness unto the judgment of the great day. Even as Sodom and Gomorrah, and the cities about them,

19

having in like manner with these given themselves over to fornication and gone after strange flesh, are set forth as an example, suffering the punishment of eternal fire." (Jude 6,7.)

There is a theory that the pronoun *these* in Jude 7 has, as its antecedent, *angels* of verse 6, and that it was the design of the inspired writers to describe the sin of the angels as fornication and the desire for "strange flesh." An attempt to buttress this view is made by citing Genesis 6:4, and by interpreting the phrase "sons of God," to mean "angels of God," and thence to conclude that the Nephilim, the giants, "mighty men of old, men of renown," resulted from the union of angels and beautiful women. In some manuscripts of the Septuagint Version (a translation of the Old Testament from Hebrew to Greek, begun about the third century before the beginning of the Christian era), the reading "angels of God" rather than "sons of God" appears. Moreover, it is alleged that the pronoun *these* in Greek is masculine gender, whereas, Sodom and Gomorrah are neuter, and thus do not agree; and, inasmuch as a pronoun must agree with its antecedent in gender, reference is not to the cities but to the angels.

This theory has a strange fascination for many people, and numerous scholarly writers in the denominational world subscribe to it; but, it is fanciful and false. It should be noted that the word *angels*, in the Septuagint manuscripts alluded to, is not a translation of the original Hebrew text, but an unwarranted interpretation from Alexandrian influences. The pronoun *toutois* (these) has the same form in the masculine and neuter genders, and thus the objection based on the gender of the pronoun is without merit. In determining the antecedent of a pronoun, where two or more are grammatically possible, the nearer is to be selected. *Toutois* refers to that which is nearer in the context. Had the translators intended to refer to the more distant antecedent, they would have used the word *those* instead.

The sin which the angels committed was in leaving their proper habitation and in not keeping their principality. There is no hint in the text here, or elsewhere in the Scriptures, that their sin consisted of co-habitation with women, beautiful or otherwise. It is an immutable and inviolable law of reproduction that everything brings forth after its own kind. This law is announced and repeatedly affirmed in the first book of the Bible. (Genesis 1:11; 12:21,24; etc.) Our Lord implied that angels are sexless beings, and he positively asserted that they never marry. (Luke 20:35.) The "Nephilim" were not angelic beings or monstrous prodigies resulting from the crossing of human beings with the angels, but gigantic human beings, men of great stature and size, and possessed of vast physical strength. The view that the sin to which Jude alludes was the same as that which characterized the cities of the plain—fornication and unnatural sexual indulgence—is false and absurd.

The "sons of God" were those who descended from godly and faithful parents who still recognized Jehovah; the "daughters of men, were women from a godless line of people who had given up the religion of the one true God. The fruit of these unholy unions were the Nephilim, men of great size and of wild, violent natures. They were renowned, not because they were good, but because they were bad; the world has never honored and respected good and godly men. Then, as now, men of corrupt minds and of dissolute lives enjoy the adulation of the ungodly. The world reserves its love for its own kind.

"Explain 1 Peter 3:18-20."

> Because Christ also suffered for sins once, the righteous for the unrighteous, that he might bring us to God; being put to death in the flesh, but made alive in the spirit; in which also he went and preached unto the spirits in prison, that aforetime were disobedient, when the longsuffering of God waited in the days of Noah, while the ark was a preparing . . . (1 Peter 3:18-20.)

Every word in the foregoing affirmation is of the greatest significance. Christ "suffered" (a euphemism for his death in our behalf); he suffered "for" (*peri*, concerning) our sins; he suffered concerning our sins "once" (literally, once for all, *apax*); and the design of his suffering was that "he might bring us to God."

In his suffering (death), though put to death in the flesh, he was made alive in the spirit. "In flesh," and "in spirit" (*sarki, pneumati*), are locatives, indicative of the sphere in which the action took place. "Put to death" and "made alive" are aorist passive participles, pointing to a definite occasion when these events occurred. The meaning is the sphere of death, for our Lord was in the flesh; the sphere in which he was made alive was in the spirit. Thus, death touched him only "in flesh;" far from dying in spirit, in spirit he was made alive (quickened). In what spirit? In view of the fact that "in flesh" and "in spirit" are exactly balanced in the text, it is not likely that one of them is locative and the other instrumental—each measures the extent of the participles to which they are attached. Flesh and spirit are often opposed to each other in the sacred writings: "Manifested in the flesh, justified in the spirit" (1 Timothy 3:16); "judged according to men in the flesh, but live according to God in the spirit" (1 Peter 4:6). The "spirit" alluded to in the passage before us must allude to that inner principle of man which stands in contrast with the flesh. But, why should it be asserted that "in spirit" he was made alive?

It was the purpose of the apostle to show that though our Lord suffered death this, very far from terminating his existence, freed him

21

from the restraints necessarily imposed by the flesh, thus enabling him to pass into a new sphere of existence, in which state he is affirmed to have been "alive."

It was "in spirit," that he "went and preached unto the spirits in prison . . . ," i.e., in this inner principle not subject to death. "Preached" (*ekeruxen*, aorist indicative of *kerussoo*, to publish, proclaim, herald abroad), is a general term denoting a public announcement. The preaching was done to "spirits in prison." They are called "spirits" because they had died and were in the spirit world, when Peter wrote; and, they are said to be "in prison," because they were under restraint as wicked beings. (2 Peter 2:4; Jude 6; Revelation 20:7.) We should carefully note, at this point, that Peter did not say that this preaching was done to disembodied spirits; all that is affirmed here is that such characterized them at the time Peter penned his statement. The passage proceeds to make clear when the preaching was done and through whom the Lord did it.

"When the longsuffering of God waited in the days of Noah, while the ark was a preparing . . ." These "spirits," now dead and in the spirit world, were once in the flesh; they were "aforetime" (*hote*) disobedient; the period of their fleshly existence, and the time of their disobedience was while "the ark was a preparing," i.e., while Noah preached and warned of impending judgment. Christ, through the agency of Noah, his "preacher of righteousness," accomplished this. What one does through an authorized agent, one does oneself. (1 John 4:1.) Hence, Christ preached "in spirit" to "spirits in prison." These spirits in prison were wicked persons who lived while the ark was being built. The preaching which Christ did was through Noah, his servant. Hundreds of years later, when Peter wrote his epistle, these people were in restraint, awaiting the judgment of the last great day.

There are those who, rejecting the view hereinbefore set out, teach that Christ, in his own person and not through the agency of Noah, during the three days' interval between his death and resurrection, actually and literally preached to the disembodied spirits who had lived in Noah's day.

Objections to this position are many and weighty: (1) Those holding thereto are unable to explain why the preaching was limited to the spirits of those who lived just prior to the flood. Inasmuch as God is no respecter of persons, why were these people afforded opportunities not offered to others? (2) Similar difficulty confronts them in attempting to explain the nature of the message alleged to have been preached. (a) If the offer involved salvation from sin, what of the many passages in the scriptures which clearly teach that at death one's destiny is determined; judgment will be based on the manner of life in the flesh; and that an impassable gulf intervenes between the world of the good and the bad beyond death? (b) If the offer did not involve salvation, what did it involve, and why was it made? Attempts to avoid this objection, by asserting that it was done to inform the faithful who had died in the triumphs of faith that redemption, through his death on the cross, had been accomplished, fail, because the preaching was not done to the faithful, but to "the disobedient." (1 Peter 3:20.)

The interpretation, that the preaching was done by Christ, through Noah, is reasonable; it harmonizes with the general teaching of the scriptures touching the state of the dead; it is in keeping with the earlier teaching of the epistle in which it is asserted that the Holy Spirit preached through the prophets. (1 Peter 1:11.) Noah was a "preacher of righteousness" (2 Peter 2:5), and was directed by the Holy Spirit in his preaching (Genesis 6:3). There is no impropriety in asserting that in such preaching Noah was the agent of Christ.

It is alleged that since it is said that Christ went and preached he must have gone in his own person. But, the objection is without validity, because no special significance is to be attached to the repetition of idea. It is a simple pleonism for "he preached," numerous examples of which are in the Bible. Christ "came and preached peace to you that were afar off (Gentiles), and to them that were nigh (Jews)." (Ephesians 2:17.) Never did our Lord, following his resurrection from the dead, preach to Gentiles, in person. All such preaching was done through the apostles, and principally by Paul, so far as sacred history is concerned. Beyond doubt, if Christ came and preached to the Gentiles, through Paul, he could go and preach to the people before the flood through Noah. Such indeed he did, and these passages so affirm. (For a more detailed discussion of the contextual significance of this interesting passage, see *A Commentary on the Epistles of Peter, John and Jude*, by Guy N. Woods, pp. 99-110, published by the Gospel Advocate Co., P.O. Box 150, Nashville, Tenn.)

"To what extent must we forgive?"

Forgiveness is man's greatest need from God, and his highest and noblest achievement toward his fellow men. Our Lord said, "Be ye merciful, even as your Father is merciful." (Luke 6:36.) Inasmuch as our Father has been, and continues to be, merciful to us, we must be merciful to others if we are to please him. It is, truly, the grossest ingratitude, on our part, to expect God to exhibit mercy toward us, when we refuse to show mercy to others. Our willingness to forgive others is the test of our fitness to receive forgiveness from God. "For if ye forgive men their trespasses, your heavenly Father will also forgive you. But if ye forgive not men their trespasses, neither will your Father forgive your trespasses." (Matthew 6:14,15.)

23

Any wrong done us must be, in the nature of the case, of little consequence; if we refuse to forgive the smaller indignity, it is idle for us to expect God to forgive us of the vastly greater sins against him. It has been said that "to return evil for good is devilish; to return good for good is human; but to return good for evil is godlike." It is common for people who need the greatest mercy from God to show the least disposition to forgive those who sin against them. A man in John Wesley's presence once said, "Take care how you offend me, for I never forgive," Wesley replied, "Then I hope you never sin!" Only the merciful may expect mercy from God.

All of us need to know what forgiveness involves; we need to learn how to forgive others; and we need to know how to prompt others to forgive us. It is difficult for us to forgive others without leaving the impression that, in so doing, we are conferring a favor. If a brother sins against us, and later exhibits penitence, often-times we react by saying, "If you'll act right, and conduct yourself properly, I'll consider forgiving you," or words signifying such a disposition. In so doing, we overlook the fact that we must forgive the penitent brother, not in order for him to be saved, but in order for us to be saved—not in order for him to go to heaven, but in order for us to go to heaven! We have earlier noted that our Lord made it clear that he will forgive us only when we are willing to forgive others.

Peter once asked the Lord, "How oft shall my brother sin against me, and I forgive him? until seven times?" (Matthew 18:21.) It will be observed that the question which the fisherman disciple raised goes beyond an initial act of forgiveness, and raises additional queries. Suppose the erring brother repeats the sin, and again exhibits penitence? What limits may be placed on our obligation to forgive him? Seven times? The Jewish rabbis taught that if a brother sinned against you three times, exhibiting forgiveness following each offense, and you, in turn, forgave him, this exhausted reasonable expectation; even if he showed penitence following a fourth sin, you were not further obligated. Three times was enough, they thought.

Peter felt there was something too limited about this Jewish talmudical rule, and he sought greatly to enlarge it. He wanted to be especially generous; he multiplied the Jewish number by two, and then added one for good measure! "Until seven times?" he asked. This, he felt, would surely fulfill all obligation. And, from a purely human viewpoint, it would seem to be sufficient; it is certainly far, very far beyond that which is generally practiced, even by Christians today.

Our Lord answered, "I say not unto thee, Until seven times; but, Until seventy times seven." (Matthew 18:22.) Seventy times seven is four hundred ninety. We may be sure that the Lord did not intend a literal interpretation of this figure; to do so would be to put a limitation

24

on the duty of forgiveness, the very thing he was teaching should not be done. The number was made so great—so far beyond the likelihood of ever occurring—that it seems clear that he was simply teaching that our duty to forgive our penitent brethren is without limitation. We are to forgive as often and as long as our brethren cease their wrong doing and show genuine penitence for their sins. It is obvious, from these words of our Lord, that it is improper for us to keep books on our brethren. Brotherly love is not a matter of mathematics.

"Is it possible that the ark may be, or has been, found?"

Periodically, the news media carry reports of expeditions to Mount Ararat to search for Noah's ark. These efforts, to locate the vessel which bore Noah and his family from the wicked antediluvian world to one washed and purified, have been engaged in for centuries. As early as the eighth century of this era, the site was alleged to have been found, a monastery and mosque to memorialize the event were built and relics of the ark were therein displayed. Eventually, lightning destroyed the buildings and the tradition failed.

Early in 1975, reports were circulated that photographs from one of our orbiting satellites showed an object of the proportions of the ark, protruding from the snow and ice of Ararat; and, despite the fact that officials of NASA say that it is most unlikely that an object no larger than the ark would appear in pictures taken from such heights, the report has spurred further interest in the search, and more than one party are seeking permission from the officials of the country to enter and to pursue the effort.

From *apriori* considerations, it is most improbable that (a) the ark still exists; and, (b) if it does, it can be found. No more emphatic lesson of history has been taught than that divine providence looks with the greatest disfavor on any effort of this kind. Not one genuine object of religious significance is today known to exist! Where, for example, are the tables of stone on which Jehovah wrote, with his own fingers, the law; the rod that budded; the axehead that floated; the brasen serpent; the cross of Christ; or, the original autographs? There must have been definite design on the part of Deity in allowing these items, and hundreds of others of religious interest, to perish; if men are disposed to revere objects of traditional significance, what must they have done with the genuine items? It would require a forest to produce the timber requisite to supply the splinters which have been sold from the cross of Christ; the clothes he wore have often been displayed; and some years ago, in France, a small vial allegedly containing the tears of Mary was exhibited in a church. It seems most unlikely, in view of this penchant of man, that God would suffer any physical objects of the past to remain, to tempt to worship of such.

Moreover, it is not possible, at this late day, to determine where the ark landed. The Scriptures assert that "the ark rested in the seventh month, on the seventeenth day of the month, upon the mountains of Ararat." (Genesis 8:4.) The phrase, "mountains of Ararat," is usually interpreted to mean "Mount Ararat." This is far from certain. The Hebrew here is the plural of indefiniteness, indicating merely that the place was somewhere in the area thus described; and, there is ground for supposing that Ararat, in that day, was the name of Armenia, or perhaps the southern portion thereof. Elsewhere, in the Scriptures, when the name appears, it designates a country—not a mountain range. (2 Kings 19:37; Isaiah 37:38; Jeremiah 51:27.) It seems clear, from this induction, that Ararat designates an area and not necessarily a mountain system.

The ark did indeed land on a mountain peak; but, the site thereof has been lost to human view, and any geographical detail regarding it is veiled in obscurity. The mountain peak on which it landed was evidently in Armenia. But which peak? There are at last three different sites traditionally identified with the historic landing. (1) A mountain now named Ararat, consisting of two peaks, the highest of which is more than 16,000 feet above sea level, in an almost inaccessible area, extremely difficult to ascend, and thus posing problems of the most formidable nature involving the unloading of the ark. (2) An unknown mountain in central Armenia. (3) A peak of the mountain range separating Armenia from Kurdistan. Where such great uncertainty exists, it is impossible to know where the ark landed, nor have we any need whatsoever for such information. It is doubly tragic that many people today are vitally interested in, and will spend great sums to satisfy their curiosity regarding where the ark landed, while at the same time being largely uninterested in the spiritual realities of Christianity, the only ark which can bear us to the heavenly Canaan.

"What must one do to 'obey God'?"

Our Lord, early in his ministry, and to make crystal clear his divine right to enjoin obedience on his followers said, "Not every one that saith unto me, Lord, Lord, shall enter into the kingdom of heaven; but he that doeth the will of my Father which is in heaven." (Matthew 7:21.) To this he later added, "And why call ye me, Lord, Lord, and do not the things which I say?" (Luke 6:46.) To certain Jews who evidenced an interest in his ministry and believed "on" him, he said, "If ye continue in my word, then are ye my disciples indeed; and ye shall know the truth, and the truth shall make you free." (John 8:31,32.) Did the "truth" of which he spoke include the plan of salvation, its nature and purpose? Surprisingly, some among us today think not. Does one "obey God" who, ignorantly or otherwise, substitutes human reasons for divine ones in one's encounter with him? Some think so.

It is axiomatic that edicts, enacted by duly constituted authority, may not be disregarded with impunity. When enactments issue from divine sources and reflect the will of the Creator, loyalty, love and fealty necessitate full and unreserved submission thereto. Rejection of this principle in the governments of men produces criminals, in the government of God, sinners. To this fundamental and basic rule there are, and can be, no exceptions.

There are three things basic to obedience, any one of which omitted, renders invalid the rest. (1) We must do *what the Lord said do;* (2) we must do what the Lord said do, *in the way the Lord said do it;* (3) we must do what the Lord said do, in the way the Lord said do it, *for the reason or reasons the Lord said do it.* To illustrate: (a) Were the Lord to command us to go south, and we go north, we have disobeyed him; (b) were the Lord to bid us to go south to work in the fields, and we go south, but work in a factory, we have disobeyed him; (c) were the Lord to tell us to go south to work in the fields, to earn money to buy a house in which to live, and we go south and work in the fields to purchase an automobile, we have disobeyed him. It should never be forgotten that obedience requires us to do what the Lord said, in the way the Lord said do it, and for the reason or reasons that the Lord said do it.

This fundamental principle has special relevance to a discussion now current touching what constitutes acceptable obedience. It is by some among us alleged that it is possible for one to "obey God" in baptism though wholly in error regarding its divinely designated purpose, and under the mistaken notion that one is in possession of salvation before and without it. Specifically, it is being taught that one may consider oneself to be already saved prior to the baptismal act, and to submit to it for some extra-biblical reason, in conflict with the design set out in Acts 2:38, 22:16, Romans 6:3,4 and 1 Peter 3:21, yet render an acceptable response to God. It is said that there are more than a dozen and a half blessings attributed to baptism in scripture, and that it is unrealistic to expect every one who submits thereto to be thoroughly familiar with all of them. Waiving, for the moment, any discussion of the merits of this assertion, it should be noted that this, if true, affords no support for the view that one may deliberately disregard, in fact and act, the purpose and design which the Holy Spirit specified, but at the same time to "obey God."

Taught with utmost clarity in the sacred writings is that salvation on the one hand, and damnation on the other, is a matter dependent on whether one obeys, or disobeys, God. (1 Thessalonians 1:7-9; He-

27

brews 5:8,9.) This is far, very far, from meaning that the mere intent to obey God is obedience. He who submits to sprinkling, or pouring, for baptism has, as his intent, to "obey God," i.e., he is motivated to this end in his response to what he has been taught (erroneously) to be baptism. Neither intent nor desire will turn an act from disobedience into obedience. Only as we yield our wills to the Lord, and only when we comply with his conditions are we promised pardon.

Baptism, to a penitent believer, stands in relation to salvation as a condition precedent. (Mark 16:15,16.) Every reference to it in the New Testament either asserts or implies this connection. It must follow, therefore, that any action which denies this relationship invalidates the act. Invalidation of any act of God is not obedience—it is disobedience. The command to perform an act authorizes no more, no less and no other, than the thing commanded. Were this not so, exactness and specificity in contracts, legislative acts and judicial decrees would be impossible and such documents would be rendered useless. The Bible, the source of man's only hope, in this world and in the world to come, would henceforth be worthless, no longer capable of supplying the surety we all so much need.

This principle of definiteness in commands is often emphasized in the scriptures, and no where more vividly and clearly than in the case of Naaman. (2 Kings 5:1-14.) The leprous Naaman was commanded to dip, to dip seven times, to dip seven times "in Jordan," in order to be healed of his affliction. Suppose that instead of following the command "to dip," he had applied to the leprous nodules the balm of Gilead; or, if he dipped, dipped six times; or, if he dipped, dipped seven times in the clear waters of Damascus instead of the Jordan; or if he dipped, dipped seven times, dipped seven times in Jordan, but without faith in the act and simply to please his servants, would he have received the marvelous blessing of healing?

Details touching Israel's departure from Egypt on the night of the Passover are numerous and significant. (Exodus 2:2-24.) A lamb (not a yearling) was to be offered, it was to be on the tenth day of the month (not the ninth or eleventh), it was to be killed in the evening (not the morning), it was to be of the first year (not some succeeding one), it was to be a male (not female), the blood was to be sprinkled on "the lintel, and on the two side posts," of the house (not on the roof), the people were to eat unleavened bread seven days (not six). Does any one in his right mind for a moment think that the Israelites, in performing the generic command to offer a lamb, could have altered the specifications of that ancient memorial feast without incurring the divine displeasure? Yea, more, that such alteration would have been regarded by Jehovah as acceptable and obedient acts? Suppose the lamb they offered was two years old, was offered on the ninth day, was killed in the morning and the blood was sprinkled on the roof, and the people had eaten unleavened bread only six days, would they have been in submission to his will?

Were one holding the view that salvation is by faith only (James 2:24-26), and who thinks that baptism is no more than "an outward sign of an inward act," and merely a "door into the church" to respond to an invitation and request immersion and membership, few among us would immerse such a person. Most would insist that these errors should be corrected and the person taught the way of salvation "more perfectly" as conditions precedent to salvation and to the extension of fellowship. There are those who would accept him and his baptism readily, however, if he has been immersed into a denominational church by a teacher who has misled the candidate and who consequently denies that baptism is "for" remission of sins (Acts 2:38), puts the penitent believer "into" Christ (Romans 6:3,4), and is the consummating act of salvation. (1 Peter 3:21.) What sacramental powers operate in the latter instance not characteristic of the former?

It will be said that those who hold to error touching the design of baptism have indeed been misled and are uninformed what the will of the Lord is, but that any motivation, so long as it springs from a vague understanding that baptism is mentioned in the New Testament, is sufficient to validate the act. Are we prepared to extend this reasoning to other areas? Worshipers are required to observe the Lord's Supper on the first day of the week as a memorial feast in commemoration of the suffering and death of the Lord of glory. The emblems, the loaf representative of his body, and the fruit of the vine which portrays his shed blood, are the elements of the Supper. May one, ignorant of the divine design of the Lord's Supper, nonetheless partake of it acceptably, sincerely believing that the elements thereof have been miraculously and mysteriously changed into the actual body and blood of the Lord? If one may render suitable obedience in baptism while disregarding the design, why not in the Supper of the Lord?

Baptism, in the case of a penitent believer, is the response of faith in Christ, results from hearing God's word (Romans 10:17), and has as its design the remission of past, or alien, sins. (Acts 2:38; 3:19.) None among us would dare affirm that the antecedent—faith—may be omitted, but since it is faith that prompts to obedience, is not the omission of the consequent— the design—equally fatal, indeed, is not faith itself wanting in such an act? If the response to which faith leads is defective, is not the "faith" which prompts it defective also? When Philip preached Jesus to the Ethiopian eunuch (Acts 8), on the lonely road from Jerusalem to Gaza, he emphasized the necessity of baptism, as the response to faith, drawing from the eunuch the desire to be baptized immediately. If the eunuch, ignorantly or otherwise, had rejected it, he would have rejected Christ in so doing, since to reject the teaching of Christ is to reject Christ himself. (John 8:31,32; 12:48; 1 John 2:4.)

We do not serve the cause of the Saviour, nor do we contribute to the well-being of those in error, by minimizing the importance of a full and faithful response to the Lord's commandments. Hebrews 11 is inspiration's magnificent hall of fame. In that resplendent setting, the great and good of earth appear in majestic array, imperishably enshrined in the sacred chronicles, because the faith they held prompted them to render unquestioning obedience to the God they loved and served. We walk in the steps of that faith only when we wholly submit our wills to him whose we are and by whom alone is there salvation.

"Does one ever have the right to do wrong?"

A writer, in a magazine designed to circulate among members of the churches of Christ and whose purpose is to provide "assistance in the how of teaching, leading and building up of the church," argues that one may properly disregard specific laws of God and men when a "situationally higher principle" comes into view.

"For example," he wrote, "under normal conditions it is right to obey the speed limit. But when an exceptional moral principle is introduced to the situation (an injured person in the car) it becomes right to exceed the speed limit and possibly wrong not to." Waiving the legal aspects of the question (e.g., exceptions involving emergencies, emergency vehicles, when a vehicle becomes an emergency one, etc.), we shall examine the brother's argument as he presents it.

(1) The laws of the land, including speed laws, are ordained of God. (Romans 13:1ff.) Paul solemnly warned, "Whosoever therefore resisteth the power (civil authority), resisteth the ordinance of God: and they that resist shall receive to themselves damnation." (13:2.) God ordained civil power because it is absolutely essential to man's well-being. It is not possible for man to survive in a state of society without civil law. Anarchy is the alternative.

(2) These laws have taken shape over a long period of years; they were forged in the furnace of experience, and have been honed by use so that they represent the best and most practical regulations our legislative bodies are able to devise. Our speed laws, particularly in school zones, and residential areas, were specifically designed for the safety and protection of all, whether drivers or pedestrians.

(3) To disregard these laws is to put in jeopardy other people. Our situational brother contends that it is an exhibition of the law of love, to violate the law of man (and, consequently, the law of God) in behalf of an injured person. Does the law of love justify the risk of grave injury or death to others? There are instances where injured people, being

30

rushed to the hospital by intemperate driving, have experienced another accident and suffered further injuries. Does love prompt such risks? Our brother's argument is invalid. His illustration involves the violation of law and love!

The brother further argues, "Biblical examples of this point include Rahab, who lied to protect the men of Israel in her home (Joshua 2:1-7) and who was catalogued among the 'Heroes of the Faith' (Hebrews 11:31) for doing so." This conclusion is grossly erroneous. Rahab was commended, and chronicled among the heroes of the faith, not because she lied, but because her faith in God's plan and purpose prompted her to take the grave risks which she did. She rightly regarded opposition to God as vastly more dangerous than possible discovery by her countrymen of the acts involved, and she thus exhibited great faith. This faith earned for her a niche among the great people of the past—not her falsehood. There is no more reason to suppose that this aspect of the incident was approved of God than the treachery of Jael (Judges 4:17-24), or the vow of Jephthah (Judges 11:1-40) in keeping with a remarkable characteristic of Scripture to report truth, whether favorable or unfavorable to those involved, the historian merely recorded the fact of Rahab's falsehood without evaluating it.

Matthew Henry very aptly says, "We are sure that God discriminated between what was good in her conduct and what was bad; rewarding the former, and pardoning the latter. Her views of the divine law must have been exceedingly dim and contracted. A similar falsehood, told by those who enjoy the light of revelation, however, laudable the motive, would of course deserve a much heavier censure." He who is the very embodiment of truth; who by the truth makes men free; and, whose mission into the world was to dissipate error with truth, cannot look with favor on an effort designed to disregard it. Moral law has, as its end, the welfare of the race; and, genuine happiness here, and hereafter, is dependent on man's adherence thereto. It is supreme folly for man presumptuously to say that it is in order to set aside these laws on the ground that his judgment is superior to God's will in specific situations. The claim, however sincere the motive, is rebellion against God at the highest level.

"Please harmonize 1 Corinthians 7:15 with Matthew 19:9 and 1 Corinthians 7:39."

There is no semblance of conflict between the first one and the last two references, because they deal with different aspects of the marriage question. Matthew 19:9 sets out the one condition under which an innocent party may remarry during the lifetime of a former marriage-partner; 1 Corinthians 7:39 designates the one condition under which a Christian widow may remarry following the death of her companion. Both passages deal with the question of remarriage; whereas, 1 Corinthians 7:15 involves only the abandonment of a husband or wife by a former partner—not remarriage. "Yet if the unbelieving departeth, let him depart: the brother or sister is not under bondage in such cases: but God hath called us in peace." It is interesting to observe, and essential to the proper understanding of the word "bondage" in this passage to note that it translates the Greek word *dedoulotai*, third person singular, perfect indicative passive of *douloo*, enslaved, subservient, bound by the will of another. It is often used, in feminine form, in Greek literature, of a female slave, one in a servile condition, abjectly submissive to the will of another. It follows, therefore, that the contention by some today that this word is descriptive of the marriage relationship and that an abandoned party is on this account free to remarry is, in effect, to say that a married woman is in a state of slavery! The conclusion is nonsensical; the discussion is with reference to duties and obligations in the relationship—not the relationship itself. Paul's teaching in 1 Corinthians 7:15 is not in conflict with the Lord's teaching in Matthew 19:9; it simply conforms to, and complements it.

"Is it correct to speak of 'erring Christians'?"

I long ago quit doing so. The word "Christian" is made up of the word "Christ," and "-ian," a suffix meaning "of" or "related to" and in biblical usage when attached to the word "Christ," a follower of the Lord. Thayer, the Greek lexicographer, defines the word Christianos, "a Christian, a follower of Christ." It follows, then, that the phrase, "erring Christian," is a contradiction of terms. To err is to turn aside from; to follow is to take the leadership and direction of another; thus, it is not possible both to follow and to turn away from, at the same time. It is correct to speak of an erring and disobedient "child of God;" it is not proper to refer to an "erring Christian."

"Did Moses literally see the face of God?"

It is written in Exodus 33:11, "And Jehovah spake unto Moses face to face, as a man speaketh unto his friend." This verse must be understood in the light of Exodus 33:20, where it is said that when Moses asked to see the face of God, the answer came, "Thou canst not see my face; for man shall not see me and live." Centuries later, the apostle John was to write, "No man hath beheld God at any time." (1 John 4:12.) It must follow, therefore, that the words, "Jehovah spake unto Moses face to face," mean that God addressed the great Israelite leader directly, positively, without equivocation. The words are designed to show that God dealt with Moses with that degree of friendliness and familiarity characteristic of friends. Paul and Moses were privileged to have special "revelations" and "visions of the Lord," (cf. 2 Corinthians 12:1-4), and these were indeed advances on the usual approach fallen man might make to God, but the opportunity to appear in his holy presence for them and us must await the day of full realization and in a sinless world, since God dwells "in the light which no man can approach unto," and "whom no man hath seen or can see." (1 Timothy 6:16.) However near we may be able to bring our lives to the divine standard, it must remain that while we are in this life we are sinful creatures and wholly unfitted for association with him of whom it is said, "Thou art of purer eyes than to behold evil, and canst not look upon iniquity." (Habakkuk 1:13.)

"Is it wrong to use instruments of music in the home?"

The answer to this question is dependent on the manner in which, and the purpose for which the instrument is used. It is a violation of God's will to use an instrument in worship and praise to him at home, "in church," or anywhere else. He is the object of worship; he, alone, then, is privileged to determine what pleases him. In this, the Christian age, there is no hint in the sacred writings that God wants the praise he commands intermingled with music mechanically made. It should never be forgotten that such activity, in Christian worship, is wholly unauthorized in the Word of God. Our Lord never commanded it, no apostle ever sanctioned it, no New Testament writer ever specified it, no apostolic church ever practiced it. It is no answer to this to assert that it was used in Old Testament worship; so also was the burning of incense, and animal sacrifices and the observance of the Sabbath day. We live under a dispensation from which such practices, along with instrumental music in worship, are excluded. (Colossians 3:17.) The presence of instruments of music in the home, and their accompaniment of classical, folk and other secular types of songs violates no law of God; but the worship of God in songs of praise must not be corrupted by unauthorized practices the use of instruments of music would involve. Every Christian home ought to engage regularly in prayer and praise to God, and in such fashion as to receive his approbation. Faithful Christians will always seek to do only that which they are certain is pleasing to the God they love and serve.

"Paul forbids fraternal association with a withdrawn person, 'with such a one no not to eat.' (1 Corinthians 5:11.) What is a faithful Christian wife to do when her husband is withdrawn from?"

It seems clear that Paul was not alluding to a relationship involving husband and wife in the passage cited. The laws of God are never in conflict; all truth is harmonious with itself, and the principles under which God ordains we are to live are never contradictory. Wives have duties to their husbands— whether they are Christians or not—and these duties harmonize with their obligations as Christians, as well. Marriage relationships were designed of God to take precedence over all other relationships; any situation later arising must be understood in the light of this fact. The Christian wife should therefore continue to live with her husband and use her influence to bring him to repentance. 1 Peter 3:1, though not directly applicable to this matter, nonetheless indicates the principle involved.

"If instrumental music in Christian worship is wrong, why do some song leaders use a tuning fork? What is the difference between using an instrument to get the pitch of a song, and to continue it?"

A tuning fork is not an instrument of music. An instrument of music is that "upon which a succession of pleasing tones" may be made. It is, of course, impossible to make a "succession" of varying tones, pleasing, or otherwise, on a tuning fork. It is the function of a tuning fork to "measure the pitch of musical tones," not maintain them, and it is therefore impossible to make music with a tuning fork. The tuning fork gives the leader the pitch of the first note and is silent when the worship begins. This is one great difference between a tuning fork and organ or piano—the tuning fork knows when to quit! It is already in the pocket of the song leader before the worship begins! Attempts to justify instrumental music in worship in this fashion are shallow and without merit. The only way any act of worship may be justified is by showing that it is authorized in the scriptures. Those who use instrumental music in worship are obligated to demonstrate that God is pleased with its use— not man. Were it possible to show that there is a parallel—which there is not—between a tuning fork and an instrument of music such as an organ or piano, this would not prove that instrumental music in worship is scriptural. It would only demonstrate that both the tuning fork and the instrument of music in worship are wrong. We have clearly shown the difference between the two.

"How may it be proved that Revelation 1:10 refers to the first day of the week?"

John wrote, "I was in the Spirit on the Lord's day . . ." The meaning is that the apostle was under special guidance by the Spirit—the third person of the godhead—on that day. It is called the Lord's day, the first day of the week, in contradistinction to the Sabbath day, the seventh day of the week, just as the memorial feast of our Lord is called the Lord's Supper to distinguish it from the feasts of the Old Testament order. It was on the Lord's day—the first day of the week—that the early disciples, under the direction of the apostles met (Acts 2:42; 20:7; 1 Corinthians 16:2), and it is our duty and obligation to do so today. It was on this day that our Lord rose from the dead. (Matthew 28:1; Mark 16:2,9; Luke 24:1; John 20:1.)

Many authentic statements come down to us from early ages attesting to this practice of meeting on the first day of the week, in following the example of the first and original disciples. Ignatius, less than 10 years following the death of John the apostle wrote that they were "no longer observing the Sabbath, but living in the observance of the Lord's day, on which also our life has sprung up by him and by his death." Justin Martyr (A.D. 140) said, "On the day called Sunday is an assembly of all who live either in the cities or in the rural districts, and the memoirs of the apostles and the writings of the prophets are read." He then proceeded to describe the items of worship, mentioning the Supper, prayer, and contribution. Irenaeus (A.D. 178) penned these words: "The mystery of the Lord's resurrection may not be celebrated on any other day than the Lord's day, and on this alone should we observe the breaking off of the Pascal Fast." We may therefore conclude with a writer in *Smith's Bible Dictionary* (4 vol. ed., by Hackett), that "The general consent both of Christian antiquity and modern divines has referred it (the Lord's day) to the weekly festival of our Lord's resurrection, and identified it with 'the first day of the week on which he rose . . .'"

"Do the sacred writings have any clear teaching on attending all of the services and study sessions of the church as planned by the eldership?"

The view, that there is but one essential service of the church—the meeting in which the Lord's supper is served—is a persistent and widespread one. Many thousands of disciples in congregations throughout the world regularly attend services on Lord's day at the morning hour, but are never present at the evening service, or any other. Proceeding on the assumption that this meeting alone is obligatory, they attend it and do not bother to concern themselves with other activities of the church, with the satisfying feeling that they have rendered a sufficient measure of devotion to the Lord in this one hour for all of the week following. Content to do only what is required, and under the impression that this meeting exhausts such requirements, they attend no other. This attitude, and the resulting disastrous effect on the church, is limited to no one section of the brotherhood. It is a problem of far-

35

reaching proportions, a major obstacle in the progress of the church today.

Were those thus influenced correct in the conclusion that the Lord's day morning service is really the only one that cannot be ignored with impunity, the disposition shown must be greatly displeasing to the Lord whose presence they disregard at all the other meetings of the church. (Matthew 18:20.) It is based on a willingness to do, and to be satisfied with less than what one can do for the Lord! The fact that it is possible for one to plan a course in life that deliberately short changes the Creator reveals a worldly and hardened heart. In the parable of the Plowing Servant (Luke 17:7-10), the Lord taught us that when we have done what we ought to do we are still unprofitable servants. If, having rendered service in keeping with a designated obligation, we are still regarded as unprofitable servants, what may be said of the individual who has not done as much as he could?

This parable is a striking and impressive reminder of the fact that we are not our own; we have been bought with a price. Of the legality of the Lord's title to us there can be no doubt. This right of ownership extends to the Christian, to what he is, and what he has, and what he can do. The Lord is entitled to all the service we are capable of rendering, and it is the ultimate in presumption for any creature of his to question the fact.

The faithful servant does not ask, What do I have to do? With him the only question is, What may I do? He who seeks to put the kingdom of God first in heart and life will not advance fallacious arguments by which to justify indifference and little faith in God. To seek the kingdom of God first (Matthew 6:33), is not to seek it last, or for that matter, second. It requires one to give it top priority in all the affairs of life. When one's personal interests conflict with duty to God, the former must always yield to the latter. To fail to follow such a course is to be guilty of the sin of the rich man of Luke 16.

Those who attend church services irregularly evidence the symptoms of lukewarmness, indifference, selfishness and love of the world more than the love of God. The practice is an exceedingly dangerous one because it leads to greater hardness of heart and further departures from the way of righteousness. He who resorts to fallacious and false reasoning to justify absence from the services of the church, or who attends them out of an irksome sense of duty, and to still the voice of an accusing conscience, will soon have little difficulty in discovering other convincing (?) arguments which to him, at least, justify further neglect and unfaithfulness. "Take heed, brethren, lest there be in any of you an evil heart of unbelief, in departing from the living God. But exhort one another daily, while it is called Today; lest any of you be hardened through the deceitfulness of sin." (Hebrews 4:12,13.)

"Would you please identify the 'man' and the 'son of man' spoken of in Hebrews 2:6? Do verses 7 and 8 refer exclusively to the character of man?"

"What is man that thou art mindful of him? or the son of man, that thou visitest him? Thou madest him a little lower than the angels; thou crownedst him with glory and honor, and didst set him over the work of thy hands: thou didst put all things in subjection under his feet. For in that he subjected all things unto him, he left nothing that is not subject to him. But now we see not yet all things subjected to him." (Hebrews 2:6-8.) The "man" of this passage is *mankind* (the human race). Those expositors who seek to make the "man" of this text Jesus Christ our Lord are in error as may be easily seen not only from the context of the Psalm from which the statement is quoted but also from the argument which the apostle develops here. Earlier, the Psalmist had dwelt on the magnificence of God's works as seen in the starry heavens and expressed wonder and amazement that he who created the worlds should be concerned for man and interested in his actions on this tiny planet. To "visit," in biblical phraseology, is to look upon with favor, and to bless. Man's importance in God's scheme is thus seen in the fact that in rank he stands only a little lower than the angelic hosts, and has ever been the recipient of God's richest blessings.

God gave to man dominion over all other created things but, because of the fall, man is now often at the mercy of the lower creation he once divinely superintended. (Genesis 1:28; Hebrews 2:7,8.) This is but another in the long list of things which man lost in succumbing to the seductions of the evil one.

"What happened to all the disciples of John after Christ's baptism came into effect?"

They simply became the disciples of Jesus and were automatically made a part of the one body—the church. It is absurd to assume that all of those who had the baptism of John before the Christian dispensation were required to be "re-baptized" in order to receive the remission of sins. John's baptism was a baptism of repentance "for (in order to)" the remission of sins. (Mark 1:4; Luke 3:3.) The only baptism the apostles had was John's baptism. John was the harbinger—the forerunner—of the Christ; it was his work to prepare the people for the coming of the Lord and this preparatory work consisted of (among other things) baptism for remission of sins. To assume otherwise is to conclude that the apostles were in their sins on the day of Pentecost! Moreover, it is affirmed by the sacred historian that those who responded to Peter's command to repent and be baptized for the remission of sins were by the Lord added "to the church" (King James Version), "unto them" (American Standard Version). One does not add something to nothing; it follows, therefore, that the body of disciples which became the nucleus of the New Testament church on the day of Pentecost consisted of John's disciples plus those garnered by the Lord and the apostles prior to the day of Pentecost. These formed the New Testament church when the Holy Spirit came on that memorable Pentecost day. Simply put, the church began to exist at 9 a.m. on Sunday on the first Pentecost following the resurrection of Christ. The twelve who were baptized by Paul in Ephesus (Acts 19:1ff), were people who had been baptized "unto John's baptism" after the inauguration of the new institution and when only the baptism of the great commission was valid. All who were baptized prior to the cross when only the baptism of John was available had acceptable baptism and were not re-baptized.

"What law did the people obey after Christ's death until the church came on Pentecost?"

It is a legal principle observable in the laws of all nations and all ages that when one law supercedes another, the effects of the superseded law continue until the new law takes over. Effects of the law of Moses would have continued for a year if such had been necessary. (Hebrews 10:1-4.)

"Is there any scripture authorizing singing while partaking of the Lord's supper? Please analyze the following scriptures: Matthew 26:30 and Mark 14:26."

Not only is there no scripture for singing while observing the Lord's supper, the act itself is a gross perversion and corruption of both acts of worship. Neither may properly be engaged in while the other is being done and the effort itself is a travesty on New Testament worship. Worship, in order to be acceptable, must be directed to God, performed in the right spirit and from proper motives and in harmony with the expressed will of God. (John 4:24.) It is utterly impossible to engage in singing and partake of the Lord's supper at the same time and follow these divine guidelines.

When we sing, we ought to follow the lyrics as sincerely as if we were actually composing them at the time and in sincere and heartfelt dedication to God; when we partake of the Lord's supper our attention ought to be fixed undeviatingly on the sacrifice of the Lord, and his return for the saints (1 Corinthians 14:15; Ephesians 5:18,19; Colossians 3:16); each action requires the whole concentration of the worshiper and neither ought to be diluted by other thoughts or acts. Since the rules of divine worship cannot be adhered to by mixing the different items of worship it is clear that those who wish to engage in such have abandoned the basic scriptural reason and have substituted an emotional approach. The Christian Church creates the same emotional situation by soft and pleasing organ tones while observing what they style the Lord's supper, an action no more unscriptural, in my view, than to sing while the supper is being served. It would be no more out of order for the congregation to sing while the preacher preaches than to sing while the supper is being observed.

Matthew 26:30 and Mark 14:26 (parallel passages) simply chronicle the fact that following the events of the upper room and prior to departure the disciples sang a hymn. This followed the Passover feast and the institution of the supper, not accompanied it! Indeed, there is strong evidence to conclude that following the observance of the Passover and the institution of the supper and prior to the singing of the hymn which immediately preceding the termination of the meeting the entire sermon of the Saviour recorded in John 14,15, and 16 was delivered.

Quite obviously there is nothing either here or elsewhere in the Scriptures to support the practice of singing while the supper is being observed.

"In the light of what Christ said in John 16:23,24, would it be wrong to sing songs such as 'Tell It To Jesus,' 'My Jesus As Thou Wilt,' and 'Just a Little Talk With Jesus,' and others which seem to advocate making our requests made known to Christ instead of the Father?"

No. It is a misinterpretation of John 16:23,24 to draw from it the conclusion that Jesus there forbade any address to him. It is of course very true that our prayers are to be addressed to the Father "in the name" of Christ, i.e., by his authority but the words of the foregoing passage were not intended to prohibit any address to him. It was the Lord's design, in this instance, to indicate to his followers their relation to him and to the Father when he was no longer with them. He said in effect this: "You shall not, as you presently do, bring your questions to me; henceforth, you shall make your needs known to the Father by my authority and he will hear and answer." For instances of such direct address to Christ as is involved in these songs, see Acts 7:60 and 9:6. There are many other examples of this in the New Testament.

"Is it scriptural to have three or four men to serve as leaders of a congregation subject to a business meeting, but with full authority in matters of judgment and discipline, etc., when there are no men qualified to serve as elders?"

It is certainly expedient to do so and that which is expedient is scriptural. In the absence of qualified men who have been duly and properly appointed to serve as elders some leadership is requisite to the proper conduct of the affairs of the congregation and this method is most generally followed. I would question the "full authority" of such since they act only by the will and concurrence of those whom they serve. Such an arrangement ought to be regarded as temporary and special effort should be made to form such an organization for leadership as the New Testament authorizes. Most congregations have men who can qualify as elders and all ought to have. We must be careful not to set up an impossible standard for others while excusing ourselves! With but one or two exceptions the qualifications set out in the New Testament for elders ought to characterize every mature man in the church! With the exception of being the husband of one wife which of the others may we exclude as unnecessary for all male members of the congregation?

"Is the *Emphatic Diaglott* a reliable work for a 'non-Greek' student to use?"

This work is what is known as an "interlinear," i.e., it contains a Greek text and a literal translation into English so arranged that a student who knows little or no Greek can recognize the corresponding Greek and English terms involved. Such a work is of little or no value as a translation since it is not only baldly literal but also reflects the order and idiom of the Greek text rather than English. For example, Luke 12:35, which reads in the American Standard Version, "Let your loins be girded about . . ." appears in the *Emphatic Diaglott* as "Let be of you the loins having been girded . . ." Its author was Benjamin Wilson, evidently a materialist, because this doctrine is often made to appear in the text. This will account for the fact that it has always been a favorite of "soul sleepers," and that its present publisher is the Watchtower Bible and Tract Society, the publishing company of Jehovah's Witnesses. It is perhaps adequate when used as an interlinear. Other interlinears are Berry's, Marshall's, Nestle's and the *Englishman's Greek New Testament*, with critical apparatus.

"Does the Lord approve of any fund raising for the local church other than the offerings of Christians?"

No. All examples and precepts to this end, in the New Testament, show clearly that the Lord's way of meeting financial needs of the church is by the contributions of its members. (1 Corinthians 16:1,2; 2 Corinthians 8 and 9.) Activities involving family life and responsibility may be met in any legitimate fashion. These are not church activities.

"I recently heard a sermon preached in which it was said there will be a physical body resurrection. He said our human flesh and bones will be resurrected. What is the truth?"

Paul, in the great resurrection chapter (1 Corinthians 15), clearly teaches that our present bodies will be raised from the dead. "It is sown in weakness; it is raised in power;" the antecedent of the pronouns is the same in each case. The "it" that is sown is the "it" that is raised. A change occurs in which that which is mortal puts on immortality and that which is corruptible puts on incorruption, but this does not alter the fact that there is to be a resurrection, a word signifying "to come forth again." We are to be like our Lord and he possessed a body bearing some characteristics of that which he had before his crucifixion. (Luke 24:39; 1 John 3:1ff.) More than this we cannot know until the day of realization.

"Should I forgive a man even though he does not repent?"

Our Lord said, "If thy brother sin, rebuke him; and if he repent, forgive him." (Luke 17:3.) Jesus forgives only those who repent (Acts 2:38), and he expects no more of us. It is, indeed, impossible to forgive one who does not repent since forgiveness is the acceptance of a relationship which existed before the sin. Unless the rebellious brother desires this relationship it is impossible to establish it. We must ever be ready to forgive and we must entertain no malice or bitterness in our hearts. But, we can forgive only when penitence is shown. Those who question this conclusion (and there are always those who thus do, not knowing the true significance of forgiveness), remember that the Lord's order is (1) if a brother sins against you, *rebuke* him; (2) if a brother repents, *forgive* him. (Luke 17:3.)

"Hebrews 10:25 says: 'Not forsaking our own assembling together . . .' Would the severe language following this verse apply to the 'recreational absentee'? What about the custom of 'dropping in' somewhere en route to the lake for communion or, having the communion in the back of a pickup with 'two or three gathered together'?"

The casual, disinterested manner so often characteristic of members of the church today, touching the worship of God, evidences the fact that many of us are far removed from the devout and consecrated disposition of the disciples of the early church. To many today the Lord's supper partakes of the characteristics of the Catholic Mass and is observed with much the same ritual and ceremony. Those whose hearts are bent on recreation, whose interests are largely material and worldly, might as well dispense with the worship entirely insofar as pleasing the Lord is concerned. By the wildest stretch of the imagination, he who hurriedly observes the "emblems" so that he may immediately pursue his pleasures is devoid of the spirit of the Master and wanting in the basic elements essential to New Testament worship. Some time ago I saw an advertisement in a Texas paper bearing in bold headlines the words, "Fisherman's Mass." Our "recreational" brethren who make worship a sideline can find empathy with these people! If we expect to please the Lord and to enjoy his approbation at the last day, we must give his affairs precedence here, and his day (the Lord's day) ought to be spent in worship, meditation and Bible study rather than in fishing, hunting, boating and the myriad other ways in which the world about us attracts. These practices will be of small comfort when we stand before the Judge of all the earth in that Last Great Day. (Romans 14:12; 2 Corinthians 5:10.)

"In the light of 1 Timothy 2:8-12, would it be scriptural for a Christian wife and mother to lead in prayer and/or be part of a chain prayer in a devotional in her home with her husband and/ or her Christian sons present?"

It seems clear to me that the context is with reference to public devotions and that it may not therefore be properly extended to embrace those occurring in the family circle. A correct exegesis of the phrase "in every place," where men (as distinguished from women) are to lift up "holy hands" must be understood to mean in every place where public worship is engaged. This conclusion is supported by the admonition given to the sisters to array themselves in modest apparel and to evidence such deportment as is proper in the presence of others. It is obvious that what would be proper dress in the bedroom alone with her husband would not qualify as modest in the assembly. For these reasons it appears to me that the passage has primary applications to public meetings. It should be noted that thus far we have dealt only with the question: Does 1 Timothy 2:8ff have general or specific application?

"In view of 1 Timothy 2:9 on modest apparel not being limited to the worship assembly of the church, can 1 Timothy 2:8,11,12 be limited to the public worship assembly? Would these restrictions apply to a devotional and the saying of thanks at a meal in the home? If she could lead in prayer in her home under these circumstances, would she need to cease when her sons became Christians or when they reach a certain age? If so, at what age?"

In my view, the effort of this querist to parallel modesty and the participation of women in prayer in private devotion is defective because modesty is a basic requirement that finds application in every circumstance (though what might be modest dress in one set of circumstances would not be in another as hereinbefore indicated), but if our interpretation of 1 Timothy 2:8ff is correct, there is no other passage which may properly be cited to support the view that women may not actively engage in devotions in their own family circle. It is a grave sin to make laws where God has not—to speak where he has not spoken. Parents (not simply the fathers) are to bring their children up in the nurture and admonition of the Lord (1 Timothy 5:3,4), and widowed mothers would certainly need to pray with and for their children in audible and intelligible fashion. In the light of many affirmations of scripture I do not see how this point can be successfully controverted.

Are not then the queries of our brother touching the ages of children largely moot? So long as children are at home, they are under the care and discipline of both father and mother and it would appear to me that the age question is without significance. I think it is absurd to contend that a Christian mother cannot teach her children the Bible nor audibly pray in their presence. This conclusion extends neither to public prayer nor teaching in the assembly. Both are prohibited. We should learn to distinguish between things that differ and to refrain from drawing from scripture what is not there.

Having so said, I should like to add that in my opinion this issue may easily be resolved in doubtful cases by the simple expedient of having the husband or son lead the devotion and all others to follow. I am wholly unable to understand the significance some seem to attach to the importance of uttering prayers—an act by no means necessary in order to pray. For a quarter of a century I preached almost continuously in meetings and months and months would pass in which I never uttered an audible prayer, such being done by those in charge of the meetings in which I preached, and yet I was privileged to pray in every one of those services! So-called chain prayers are without biblical precedent and are wholly unnecessary. Outside the family circle, the prohibitions of 1 Timothy 2:11,12, are clearly applicable.

"Would you please address yourself to and comment on the proposition, 'Does God change his mind?' To support the affirmative position the following scriptures are cited: Genesis 6:5; 18:12; Exodus 32:10; 1 Chronicles 21:10; 2 Kings 20; Jeremiah 18:8; Luke 18:8; 2 Corinthians 12:8; James 5:16; and the verses immediately following each reference. To support the negative position the following scriptures are cited: Numbers 23:19,20; 1 Samuel 15:29; Job 23:13; Psalms 23:11; 119:89-91; Proverbs 19:21; Ecclesiastes 3:14; 7:13; Isaiah 31:2; 40:28; 59:1; Hosea 13:14; Malachi 3:6; Romans 11:29; Hebrews 6:17,18 and James 1:17."

The first group of passages establishes the fact that God's decrees are not irrevocable, his will is not absolutely inflexible, and his judgments are not arbitrary. On the contrary, his actions exhibit love, concern and pity for man, and are designed to deal with him in a way commensurate with both justice and mercy. He who "tempers the wind to the shorn lamb" will certainly show equal compassion for him who is made in his image, and in whom he finds his greatest pleasure.

The warnings and the promises of Jehovah are often conditional in nature and thus depend on the actions of those to whom they apply. this is frequently affirmed in the sacred writings and where not expressly declared is nevertheless implied. Through the ancient prophet he said, "At what instant I shall speak concerning a nation, and concerning a kingdom, to pluck up and to break down and to destroy it; if that nation, concerning which I have spoken, turn from their evil, I will repent of the evil that I thought to do unto them. And at what instant I shall speak concerning a nation, and concerning a kingdom, to build and to plant it; if they do that which is evil in my sight, that they obey not my voice, then I will repent of the good, wherewith I said I would benefit them." (Jeremiah 18:7-10.) Sodom's threatened destruction would have been averted, despite the threat thereof, if ten righteous people could have been found there. (Genesis 18:22-33.) The condition, though not stated, was implied.

The second group of passages teaches us that on God's side he does not change, i.e., his character is not vacillating, wavering, undependable, as is so often true of men. Promises and actions by him, when not dependent on man's response, are utterly and absolutely unchangeable, and cannot be altered by men or demons. (Numbers 23:19.) God does that which he promises and he does not change to satisfy the whims of weak and sinful men. (1 Samuel 15:29.) His faithfulness is beyond question and on him we may with complete confidence rely. (Job 23:13.)

When man sinned in Eden God's divine purpose regarding him was altered and this prompted him to "repent," i.e., change his mind (so the verb signifies) regarding his original plans touching man. Inasmuch as a radical change had occurred in man in his relationship to God there was consequently a change in the relationship of God to man, and so God changed his course regarding man. In the centuries which followed the original transgression this change often took place with a corresponding and a necessary change in God's attitude toward, and relationship to man. But, this does not indicate any modification of the character of God, who changes not. (Malachi 3:6.) Men may, through no fault of ours, fail us, but God who is unchangeable will evermore be faithful to our trust, and can never disappoint us. (Romans 8:31-39.)

In the GOSPEL ADVOCATE, this question was raised.

"If a man divorced his wife without cause and married another, would the wife, being an innocent party, be free to marry if her former husband and not she obtained the divorce?"

I answered "Yes."

A brother wrote,

"I disagree with your answer as Matthew 19:9 says, 'And I say unto you, Whosoever shall put away his wife, except for fornication, and shall marry another, committeth adultery: and he that marrieth her when she is put away committeth adultery.' The above scripture teaches me that the person who marries the woman that was divorced even though she was innocent would commit adultery."

He has grossly misapprehended the teaching of our Lord in this passage. (1) He has ignored the exception which the Lord put into the verse. He strikes out the words, "except for fornication," in order to deny what the Lord, by implication, affirmed. It should read, in his view, "Whosoever shall put away his wife *even in the case* of fornication and marries another, commits adultery and he who marries her thus put away commits adultery." (2) He disregards the grammar of the passage which makes the exception clause, *except for fornication*, modify the entire statement including the final clause, "He that marrieth her when she is put away committeth adultery." (3) He rules out any occasion when an innocent party may properly and scripturally remarry. He is therefore in grave error in the conclusion drawn.

45

To put the matter in proper perspective let us assume the following instance: Jane and John, both single, neither having been previously wedded, marry. John, of weak character, soon tires of Jane and abandons her though she is a good wife, and a faithful Christian woman. As soon as he can conveniently do so, he contracts another marriage. Not free to remarry, his relationship with the second woman, though legal, is adulterous. Jane, meantime, has remained free of marital relationship, and would have received John back at any time prior to the adulterous marriage into which he entered. Being a Christian woman, she does not recognize the state's legal grounds for divorce, willing only to accept the Lord's ground—fornication. By unscripturally contracting marriage with the second woman John is now guilty of the act constituting the exception clause of Matthew 19. Jane meets Bill, a fine Christian man never before married. May she scripturally marry him? Of course she may. To deny to her this is presumptuously to pass judgment on the validity of the Lord's edict and take from her what the Lord granted.

Jesus said, "Whosoever shall put away his wife, *except for fornication*, and shall marry another, committeth adultery and he that marrieth her when she is put away committeth adultery."

If the objection is raised that Jane did not divorce John but John (the guilty party) divorced Jane, it should be remembered that divorce is a civil, legal action having nothing whatsoever to do with determining the moral and religious principles involved. It is the Lord's edict, not man's, that governs. "But," it may further be objected, "Jane and John were not living together at the time when the fornication occurred." Who said they had to be? To inject this condition into the exception clause is to speak where the Lord has not spoken, is to legislate for him! Suppose, for example, that Jane, while married to John, had suffered mental illness and required residence and treatment in a mental hospital for five years. During this interval John cohabited with another woman. Would Jane, because she was not living under the same roof as John, be denied the right to put him away "for fornication"? He who so affirms has abandoned reason, revelation and good sense!

The implications of scripture touching marriage and divorce are crystal clear. The New Testament teaches that when one of the parties of the marriage bond becomes guilty of fornication the other (the innocent one, not the guilty) may scripturally put away the offending party and remarry. Luke 16:18 does not countermand Matthew 19:9, it simply supplements it.

"In this area there is almost an orgy of the male members who consistently engage in osculatory behavior in their greetings of some of the sisters. I may be too prudish; it may be a holy form of greeting, but when repetitiveness of this is engaged in there are some who wonder if it is not Freudian to some degree."

More simply stated our brother is saying that some of the brethren where he worships are kissing the sisters as a form of greeting and others in the congregation are made to wonder if the action is truly holy or if sexual overtones are not involved.

It is impossible of course for us at this distance to pass judgment on the motives which prompt this action and to determine the condition of heart from which it springs. If there is "almost an orgy of it," as our brother asserts, it would appear that the practice is open to question.

We learn from the early "church fathers" that kissing, as a mode of greeting, fell into disuse for the reason that it was abused, and as in the case above, disposed to put those who practiced it under suspicion in the congregation.

It should be noted that kissing, as a mode of greeting, did not originate with the early church nor was it commanded by the Holy Spirit. Kissing, in oriental lands is a centuries-old tradition; instances of it abound from the days of patriarchy. When mentioned in the New Testament the kind of kiss is emphasized, i.e., a "holy" kiss, a kiss "of love." (Cf. 1 Corinthians 16:20; 2 Corinthians 13:12; 1 Thessalonians 5:26; 1 Peter 5:14.) Thus, emphasis, in the New Testament, is on the word holy which must have characterized the motivation when engaged in. There was to be total avoidance of anything lustful or licentious in it. Then, the kiss as a mode of greeting, was engaged in by all; the Holy Spirit sanctified it and raised it to the level of propriety which should characterize Christians.

A cheerful word, a handshake, even a smile are acceptable modes of greeting today. Any greeting, engaged in by the followers of the Lord, ought to be meaningful, sincere and without affectation. Kissing, unrestrained, leads to promiscuity and it is therefore not common to our culture or day.

"Please reconcile Matthew 10:19,20 with Acts 23:5."

In the former passage the Lord promised the twelve that when they appeared before civil authorities they were not to be concerned about what they were to say in their defense since the Spirit of the Father would provide them with proper words on such occasions. When Paul was brought before the Jewish council in Jerusalem and the order was issued for him to be smitten (slapped), his sense of fairness and justice was outraged that he should be punished, not only before the guilt was established but also before evidence was heard and he sharply rebuked the officer who thus acted saying, "God shall smite thee, thou whited wall: and sittest thou to judge me according to the law, and commandest me to be smitten contrary to the law?"

Witnesses to the proceedings were amazed that Paul would thus speak to a dignity and said, "Revilest thou God's high priest?" The apostle apparently apologized, saying: "I knew not, brethren, that he was high priest: for it is written, Thou shalt not speak evil of a ruler of thy people." But that there was no impropriety in the rebuke is evident in the fact that the apostle did not retract it! Far from being an outburst of intemperate passion it was a measured and proper statement of what would occur to one who would deal so unjustly with another. It reminds of a similar incident in the Lord's public ministry when he is said to have looked "with anger" on men equally wicked. (Mark 3:5.) It is very possible that the apostle did not recognize him who issued the command in view of eyesight deficiency; and, on being informed that it was the high priest who had thus spoken, acknowledged that the rebuke, though just, would not have been offered against one of high office. It should be noted that this Ananias was a usurper and held the position without legality. Brother McGarvey offers the following incisive comment on this incident and equates it with the Lord's promise in Matthew 10:19,20: "Had Paul known that Ananias was the high priest and had he been left to himself without the guidance of the Holy Spirit promised on such occasions (Matthew 10:17-20), he would have withheld the rebuke; and the world would have been the loser; for rebukes like this help to strengthen the moral sense of men. He knew not Ananias personally, for he was not the Ananias of the Gospels, but a new usurper of the high priesthood; and it is certain that on this occasion he wore no robe or badge to indicate his office, or Paul could not have failed to know his position. The fact that he presided on this occasion did not show it, because the high priest was not always present at meetings of the Sanhedrin, and especially at meetings called unexpectedly, as this one was. This Ananias was one of the worst men who ever wore the robes of a high priest. His career of crime and extortion, fully set forth in various chapters of Josephus, finally ended in assassination." Thus, there was no inconsistency in the apostle's action and the teaching of our Lord in Matthew 10:19,20.

"Ought men to be used to serve the Lord's table, lead in prayer and otherwise participate actively and publicly in the worship who attend only on Lord's day morning?"

The answer is No! The querist indicates in the letter that these are people who simply do not have sufficient interest to attend other services of the church, choosing to engage in worldly and material affairs rather than to attend services on Sunday evenings and on Wednesday nights. Those who take part in the services are to serve as examples (1 Timothy 4:12), to follow that which is good (1 Thessalonians 5:15), and to forsake not the assembly of the saints (Hebrews 10:25-28). How can we hope to influence others to be faithful if those in public view in the church are not themselves faithful? If we truly love the Lord we will be present in all of the services possible.

"What is the meaning of Revelation 21? Is the new heaven and earth meant to be the church while it is here on earth or the church after it is in heaven?"

Limitations of time and space render it impossible to give an exposition of an entire chapter.

The reference of the inspired writer to "a new heaven and a new earth," in Revelation 21:1 is, in my view, a description of the state of the redeemed at the end of the age. He has thus far shown us the steady spread of evil in the world, the end of Satan and his wicked reign and the general judgment when men are to be rewarded in harmony with their conduct on earth. The narrative is completed with the detailed description of the enjoyment of the righteous in the world to come. The weary struggle is over, the old order is gone and the bliss of heaven is seen prophetically by the ancient seer.

Evidence of this I believe to be decisive. (1) The Shekinah, or divine presence, hovered over the ark of the covenant in the earthly tabernacle. In the age to come, God will make his tabernacle among men and dwell with them. (Revelation 21:3.) (2) In that blessed land there will be no sorrow, no tears, no death, no weeping, no pain; God himself will wipe all tears away. (Verse 4.) Only when death is no more will this glorious state prevail. (3) Rivers of tears, bitter anguish and sorrow, lonely nights of pain, are often the lot of the Lord's finest and thus the description cannot be of this age, and must therefore be of the next. There will be no night there, with its lonely shadows, no sea to separate, no gates to shut its inhabitants out of any portion of the celestial city. Only in heaven will these joys be experienced.

"In Matthew 24, is this dealing only with the destruction of Jerusalem or is it a double prophecy of the destruction of Jerusalem and of the end of the world?"

In the beginning of Matthew 24, three questions are raised: (1) When shall these things be? (2) What is the sign of thy coming? (3) When will the end of the world come? Chapters 24 and 25 are devoted to these matters and questions are there answered. Matthew 25 is devoted largely to the third question and thus involves events associated with our Lord's second coming and, in particular, the judgment. (Matthew 25:31-46.) Thus, Matthew 24 answers questions 1 and 2, "When shall these things be?" and "What is the sign of thy coming?" By "these things," the Lord's questioners had in mind the dismantling of the stones of the temple not one of which the Lord said would remain on another. This came to pass in the destruction of the temple in the fall of Jerusalem in A.D. 70.

It has long been my view that the answer to the first question continued through verse 35 and that it is not until the Lord begins to speak in verse 36, that he deals with the second coming. A careful analysis of the chapter seems conclusively to show this. It will be seen that through verse 35, the Lord often mentioned signs by which observers would be able to trace the course of events which he describes; however, beginning at verse 36, no signs are given because "of that day and hour knoweth no one, not even the angels of heaven, neither the Son, but the Father only." (Matthew 24:36.) For it we are to be ever watchful, not being able to discern by signs its advent.

"Who does the rejoicing in Luke 15:10 when a sinner repents, God or angels?"

That angels, along with all the glorious host of heaven, rejoice when a sinner repents and turns to God, I have not the slightest doubt. In the passage cited however, emphasis is given, not to angels who rejoice, but to One who rejoices in their presence— the father himself. It is often said that there are three parables in Luke 15, the parable of the lost sheep, the parable of the lost coin and the parable of the lost son. Actually, there is but one parable in this remarkable chapter, but with three applications and designed to show God's love and concern for every class of humanity. Some are lost like the coin—with no awareness whatsoever of their condition. Others are lost like the sheep— aware of their lost condition, but do not know the way to the fold. And, many others are lost like the son was lost—lost, aware of it, and fully informed of the way back to the Father's house. These illustrations of our Lord embrace the whole of humanity and reflect to us the needs of each class. A recognition of this is absolutely essential to effective evangelism.

The owner of the sheep, having returned it safely to the fold, called for the neighbors to join with him in the joy he felt. The owner of the lost coin called for her female friends (the word is feminine gender) to share her joy in the discovery of the coin that had been lost. That the neighbors, in both instances, were pleased, I doubt not; but, who rejoiced the more, the owners or the neighbors? How wonderful it is to know that the deliverance of one soul from the snare of Satan is not only duly recorded in heaven but that it also provides an occasion of rejoicing on the part of God himself!

"The name 'Jehovah' is not revealed in the original manuscripts as a name for our God. Jesus Christ never called the Father by that name. Where then does the name come from? Is it acceptable worship to address God by that name?"

Our querist has been strangely and gravely misinformed. Many names, both personal and attributive, are ascribed to Deity in the Old Testament, the most personal and the most distinctive of them all is the name Jehovah, a transliteration of the tetragrammaton, *yahweh*. When Moses was being commissioned of God to deliver Israel from the thrawldom of Egypt, he felt keenly the need of identification of the source of his authority and thus inquired of God, "Behold, when I come unto the children of Israel, and shall say unto them, The God of your fathers hath sent me unto you; and they shall say to me, What is his name? What shall I say unto them? And God said unto Moses, I AM THAT I AM: and he said, Thus shalt thou say unto the children of Israel, I AM hath sent me unto you. And God said moreover unto Moses, Thus shalt thou say unto the children of Israel, Jehovah, the God of your fathers, the God of Abraham, the God of Isaac, and the God of Jacob, hath sent me unto you: this is my name for ever." (Exodus 3:13-15; see also Exodus 6:2-8; 33:27.)

The New Testament, in the original tongue, is in Greek—not Hebrew, and thus the references to Deity involve the Greek *theos, kurios*, the Most High, and others, and not the literal Hebrew words appearing in the Old Testament. Other terms, descriptive of Deity, occurring in the Old Testament, are Jehovah-Jireh, "Jehovah seeth" (Genesis 22:14), Jehovan-Nissi, "Jehovah is my banner" (Exodus 17:15), and Jehovah-Shalom, "Jehovah is peace" (Judges 6:24). Any of the names of Deity may properly be used in addressing him.

"The early disciples were instructed to 'honor the king.' (1 Peter 2:17.) Does this mean that civil authorities are to be honored regardless of their conduct of office or their manner of life?"

Civil government is essential to any well-ordered society. In recognition of this fact the scriptures often direct the followers of the Lord to live in harmony therewith as good citizens. (Romans 13:1ff.) However, neither in the passage inquired about, nor elsewhere do the sacred writers designate any particular form of government to which Chris-

51

tians are to be subject, nor are they taught to busy themselves in an effort to establish any certain form or type of government as being more conducive to their well being.

Those writers were aware that the saints would have no choice in the kind of secular power under which they live, and thus they concerned themselves solely with the conduct to characterize them regardless of the form of government to which they owe allegiance.

It is noteworthy that the form of government which obtained when Peter's words above cited were penned was dictatorial, totalitarian, and tyrannical, and the men who dispensed the laws thereof were, for the most part, exceedingly corrupt, depraved and dissolute. Notwithstanding, Peter's readers were to honor the civil authorities, not because of their manner of life, but because of the office they held. We owe the same respect to those in high places today though we may deplore their public and private personal conduct. We are to honor them always, but we are to obey them only when their edicts are not in conflict with the sovereign and supreme law of God. This is vividly demonstrated by Peter, author of the words inquired about, when he boldly disregarded the order of a Jerusalem tribunal when forbidden to preach any more in the name of Jesus. His answer forevermore provides the rule in such cases: "Whether it is right in the sight of God to hearken unto you rather than unto God, judge ye: for we cannot but speak the things which we saw and heard." (Acts 4:19,20.)

"In 1 Peter 3:1,2, the apostle wrote, 'In like manner, ye wives, be in subjection to your own husbands; that, even if any obey not the word, they may without the word be gained by the behavior of their wives.' Does this mean that it is possible to convert people without teaching them the gospel?"

No, obviously not! (Romans 1:16.)

Those to whom Peter wrote were formerly pagans; in some instances both husband and wife would obey the gospel; in other instances, only the wife. It is this latter situation which the apostle contemplates here. The "word" in the phrase, "if any obey not the word," is the gospel. "Obey not" is translated from a term denoting antagonism and stubbornness as well as disobedience. It means, literally, not to allow one's self to be persuaded. The text, as it appears in our translation, makes Peter to say that men may "without the word" be gained, i.e., they may be led to the word of truth without the word of truth. Such an idea is self-contradictory, is opposed to the plain teaching of the scriptures elsewhere (James 1:18; 1 Corinthians 4:15), and does not correctly represent what the inspired writer really wrote.

The Greek article does not appear before the noun "word" in the phrase, "may without the word be gained . . ." Here, "word" does not refer to the word of truth—the gospel—as it does in the former phrase, but to the exhortations, the persuasions and entreaties of the wives. These husbands had heard the gospel and were fully familiar with its demands and requirements. But, they had thus far been stubborn, rebellious, disobedient, resisting all efforts on the part of their wives and others to bring them to obedience. Peter admonished the wives of these men to desist from further importunity, lest such should descend to nagging; and instead, by godly conduct and discreet behavior to encourage their husbands to do that which they already clearly understood to be their duty. Properly translated, the passage reads: "If any obey not the word, they may without a word (i.e., from the wife) be gained by her godly behavior." This is an instance where silent eloquence is much more powerful and effective than vigorous and vehement debate! "Be gained" in the passage is a significant and important statement. In it is suggested that every soul saved is a gain to the Lord, to the church, and to itself.

"Does the phrase 'the elect lady' in the salutation of 2 John 1, refer to a church or to an individual?"

This has been a subject of controversy for centuries and to this day much diversity of opinion exists as to the meaning which should be given the words, "the elect lady and her children" whom John addressed in this brief epistle.

One view of the matter is that the phrase should be construed as a proper name, a conclusion reached from the following considerations: The words "elect lady" are translated from *eklekte* (elect) and *kuria* (lady), from which it is assumed by those who regard the address as a personal one that John meant to designate the woman by one of the following terms (1) *Eclecta*, (2) *Cyria*, or (3) *Electa Cyria*, and still others by the words "the lady Electa," or "the elect Cyria," depending on which of the terms is to be regarded as the proper name. Cyria is the English spelling of the Greek *kuria*, and etymologically means "lady." This however alone considered is not significant, inasmuch as most Bible names mean something, as Jacob (supplanter), Israel (one who prevails with God), Jesus (Saviour.) On the assumption that either *eklekte* or *kuria* is to be regarded as a proper name it would seem to be the latter rather than the former, since the choice, on the basis of this interpretation, would be between "the lady Eclecte," and "the elect Cyria," and women are not elsewhere called ladies in the New Testament, though the word women often appears. In 1 Peter 5:13, there is a reference to an elect sister where obviously an individual, though not named, is

53

designated. It should be observed that the marginal reading in the American Standard Version supports the view that the sister addressed by John was named Cyria.

Others have thought that a church is thus figuratively designated by the words, "the elect lady," under the allegory of a woman, in keeping with the mystical use of Revelation 12. This view seems most improbable. To arrive at this conclusion one must translate the Greek word *kuria* as "lady," interpret the word "lady" to mean church, and then to construe the word "children" in the phrase "the elect lady and her children" as the members of the church. Only in the most highly figurative portions of sacred writ is the church ever alluded to as a woman, and it does indeed seem unlikely that the apostle, in this brief treatise, would have used the word thus metaphorically. Moreover, other serious difficulties arise: If the "lady" were the church, who were the children of the lady addressed by the apostle? The church has no existence apart from those who constitute its membership. The elect lady had a sister who also had children. (v. 13.) On the assumption that the elect lady was the church and her children the members of the church, who was the sister, and what did she and her children represent? From all the facts involved it appears to this writer that the preponderance of evidence leads logically to the conclusion that the terms under consideration are to be literally interpreted; that the elect lady was some faithful sister known to John and that she may have borne the name Cyria.

"Who were the Nicolaitans whom Jesus said he hated? (Revelation 2:6.) What was the 'synagogue of Satan' alluded to by John in Revelation 3:9?"

The origin of the ancient sect of Nicolaitans is shrouded in obscurity, and it is not possible at this late date to know where, and by whom this heretical movement first began to plague the early church. Conjectures are many; it is, for example, assumed by some that its members were followers of Nicolaus, one of the seven mentioned in Acts 6, the assumption being that this disciple apostatized from the faith and became the founder of this pernicious sect. But, of this there is no reliable proof available to us today. It seems likely that the view originated because of the similarity of the names Nicolaus and Nicolaitans.

Others have taught that the name Nicolaus (a Greek word) is equivalent to the Hebrew Balaam but this, too, is far from certain. It does appear from allusions of John in the Revelation that the doctrine of the Nicolaitans (Revelation 2:6), of Balaam (v. 14), and of "that woman Jezebel" (v. 20), were alike to the extent that all taught that under Christ people are free from the moral law and are at liberty to practice what they please from idolatry to adultery. They urged that it was not possible to know the mastery of sin in life without experiencing it and they actually taught the disciples to abandon themselves to lives of fleshly lusts. Among the arguments offered to sustain the view it was alleged that sin is of the body only and that the spirit is not involved in any evil or vile conduct. It is remarkable that this is the contention of some defenders of the doctrine of the impossibility of apostasy today. It is by them contended that only the spirit is regenerated; after conversion, it is the body that sins; the body is of the devil and will remain so until the resurrection and the spirit is not responsible for the acts of the body! This reasoning is fallacious and pernicious in tendency. The truth is, the body is merely the agent or instrument of the spirit; our Lord taught us that it is out of the heart those actions arise which corrupt and defile the man. (Matthew 15:18-20.) The churches in Ephesus and Pergamum were especially beset by these heretics when John penned the Revelation. The doctrine was denounced by Peter (2 Peter 2:1ff), and by Jude (7-13). It should be noted that the text does not say that Jesus hated the Nicolaitans; it was their works, not the people whom he hated. The oft-repeated statement, we should hate the sin but love the sinner, is certainly correct. How vastly different would matters be in the church were this aphorism always followed!

The synagogue originally signified the place of Jewish worship and later the congregation that met there. It appears that a group of people in Philadelphia, one of the seven cities of Asia Minor which had a congregation to which our Lord addressed a letter, met in a synagogue and professed to be worshipers of the true God but who were so evil and wicked in their teaching and practice that John regarded them as a synagogue of Satan! Though they professed to be of God they were really of the devil. They claimed to be Jews and were doubtless of Jewish ancestry but they had lost their right to this title by their ungodly conduct. Originally, the name signified those who were the Lord's chosen people but by their rejection of Christ they lost this honored privilege. It is significant that Christians are the only true Jews today: "For he is not a Jew who is one outwardly; neither is that circumcision which is outward in the flesh: but he is a Jew who is one inwardly; and circumcision is that of the heart, in the spirit not in the letter; whose praise is not of men, but of God." (Romans 2:28,29.)

"Does Matthew 18:15-17 deal with procedures for private differences between brethren, or does it also demand a private rebuke for a false teacher whose errors have been presented publicly?"

It is disturbing that many brethren these days have no hesitancy in taking texts out of their contexts, and using them utterly without regard to the purpose that prompted the statements, thus reaching conclusions wholly foreign to that intended. Such is very obviously the case here.

Even the most casual examination of Matthew 18:15-17 will show that our Lord had under consideration offences of a personal nature, occasions where one brother has suffered injury of one kind or other at the hands of another brother in the congregation, it has not the slightest reference to, nor may it be properly applied to those instances where erring brethren have propagated false doctrine to the detriment of the cause of Christ itself: "Moreover if thy brother shall trespass against thee, go and tell him his fault between thee and him alone: if he shall hear thee, thou hast gained thy brother. But if he will not hear thee, then take with thee one or two more, that in the mouth of two or three witnesses every word may be established. And if he shall neglect to hear them, tell it unto the church: but if he neglect to hear the church, let him be unto thee as an heathen man and a publican."

(1) The offence involved is a "trespass" (*amarteesee*, sin) by one brother against another brother. (2) The offending brother is to be visited by him whom he has harmed and rebuked *(elegdson auton)*. It is significant that the Greek word here is not the usual term for rebuke *(epitimoo)*, but one which means to rebuke for the purpose, and in the manner leading to conviction. (3) If this brings the sinning brother to repentance, fellowship is restored and a brother "gained." (4) However, if the brother is stubborn and will not make right his wrong, "one or two" brethren are to be taken along on the assumption that their intervention may bring him to his senses. If this attempt also fails, the issue is to be brought before the church, and the matter publicly considered. And, if this, too, does not influence the brother to confess and correct his wrong-doing, he is to be withdrawn from and thenceforth regarded as a heathen and a publican. Heathens and publicans were looked upon as wicked and corrupt men, out of fellowship with the saints, and under the disapproval of God. Such was this erring and impenitent brother so long as he persisted in his impenitent way.

It is obvious, therefore, that this passage is applicable only to those instances, involving personal offenses, where one brother has sinned against another brother. Often, elsewhere, in the New Testament, when brethren were guilty of other types of wrongdoing, vastly different means were followed in dealing with them. Who, for example, could seriously believe that Paul, the apostle, should have contacted the incestuous man of 1 Corinthians 5:1, before penning his instructions to the church regarding its obligations in the matter? Are we to suppose that he was in violation of our Lord's admonitions in Matthew 18:15-17, when he warned Timothy of Hymenaeus and Philetus because of the errors they were propagating regarding the resurrection? (2 Timothy 2:15-18.) And, what of his rebuke of Phygellus and Hermogenes who were responsible in turning all of the saints "in Asia," against him? Ought he to have talked with these errorists before making their actions publicly known? (2 Timothy 1:15.)

It is gross misapprehension of Matthew 18:15-17, to offer it as a rule of procedure in dealing with instances where false doctrine is being advocated to the disruption of the cause and to the destruction of the souls of men; and those who thus do fall into grave sin themselves. The disposition to apologize for, or to protect anyone who is teaching error, makes those who do so parties to the effort itself and the Lord will deal with them accordingly at the last day. Paul's admonition to the church in Rome settles the matter for those who truly respect God and his word: "Now I beseech you, brethren, mark them which cause divisions and offences contrary to the doctrine which ye have learned; and avoid them." (Romans 16:17.)

"What must I do to be saved?"

"Now when they heard this, they were pricked in their heart, and said unto Peter and to the rest of the apostles, Men and brethren, what shall we do? Then Peter said unto them, Repent, and be baptized every one of you in the name of Jesus Christ for the remission of sins, and ye shall receive the gift of the Holy Ghost." (Acts 2:37,38.)

Here, for the first time under the Christian dispensation, did men inquire of their duty; and here, too, is the first time the question is answered as it applies to the reign of Christ. Whatever may have been the correct answer applicable under former dispensations, it is indisputably certain that Peter gave the only answer applicable to his day and ours. Circumstances combine to make this passage truly significant. Peter, the speaker, had been invested with "the keys of the kingdom." (Matthew 16:19.) The prophets had foretold that the "word of the Lord" should "go forth from Jerusalem." (Isaiah 2:2,3.) They, too, had designated that this would occur in "the last days." All prophetic utterances touching the establishment of the kingdom pointed to this day, and here culminated the events that were to result in the first promulgation of the gospel of Christ. This, were there no other reasons, invests the passage with profound significance.

It is obvious that the Pentecostians were asking what to do in order to obtain remission of sins. This, at least, was Peter's impression of the matter, a conclusion we may arrive at by combining the question asked with the reward promised—viz., "Men and brethren, what shall we do . . . for the remission of sins?" Peter's answer was designed to supply this information. Thus, if we regard Peter's reply simply as the answer to this query, we learn that they were commanded to do two things "for the remission of sins": (1) Repent; (2) be baptized. (It should be recalled that those who propounded the query were already believers.) If Peter had stopped with this and said no more, his answer would have been complete and the world would know that it is the duty of sinners "pricked in their heart" to repent and be baptized "for the remission of sins." But the inspired speaker saw fit to accompany the commands with an explanation. He qualified the command to be baptized with the words "in the name of Jesus Christ" to show that it is by Christ's authority that men are to be baptized. "In the name of Christ" means simply by the "authority of Christ," since one can act in Christ's name only when authorized so to do. Thus, Peter's answer involved the following: (1) repent; (2) be baptized on the authority of Jesus Christ himself. Christ, therefore, through Peter, authorized believers to repent and be baptized for remission of sins. This conclusion may be arrived at in another way: Strike out that portion of the passage which has been the occasion of so much controversy—viz., "for the remission of sins." This done, Peter's answer to the question, "Men and brethren, what shall we do?" is simply this: "Repent, and be baptized in the name of Jesus Christ." Thus the conclusion is the same, whether we regard Peter's answer as a duty expressed without regard to the consequences which follow, or whether it be taken (as Peter did) as the answer to the question of what one must do to obtain remission of sins.

From these considerations it is certain that, so far as our duty or salvation is concerned, Peter's words in this passage definitely establish the essentiality of both repentance and baptism to the end proposed—viz., the remission of sins. It is scarcely necessary to point out that repentance is not for remission of sins alone, nor is baptism when unattended by faith and repentance. Peter did not say, "Repent for remission of sins"; neither did he say, "Be baptized for remission of sins." Repentance and baptism, in this passage, are accordingly joined, and, therefore, equally related to their object: remission of sins.

Denominational theologians, however, contend that baptism does not stand in the same relation to remission of sins as does repentance. While conceding that repentance, in this passage, has as its object "the remission of sins," they, nevertheless, insist that baptism is "because of" remission. To this contention there are at least two insuperable objections:

(1) Whatever be the design of baptism in this passage, repentance bears the same end or aim. If baptism be "because of" remission, then so is repentance. To command men to repent because of remission is absurd, since it is universally granted that repentance is a condition precedent to remission. But let it be admitted that repentance is for (in order to) the remission of sins, and no amount of illogical juggling of words will hide the fact that baptism is for the same purpose and in exactly the same sense.

58

(2) Moreover, the denominational theory contradicts an obvious fact in the case. The Pentecostians were asking what to do to be saved, not something to do because they were already saved. The conclusion is irresistible: Peter, in response to the query there raised, made repentance and baptism conditions precedent to the remission of sins.

So skillfully did Peter interweave the answer to the query that it is beyond the cavils of men so to arrange the passage or pervert it to make it mean other than that originally intended. To illustrate: Draw a pencil through the controverted statement, "for the remission of sins." We have, then, this statement: "Repent, and be baptized every one of you in the name of Jesus Christ." Why did Peter utter these words? Obviously, in answer to the question: "Men and brethren, what shall we do?" Do for what? Surely to escape the consequences of their act 53 days before. How did Peter answer them? "Repent, and be baptized every one of you." Thus, whether Peter's answer be contemplated as a solution for the grave difficulty in which the Pentecostians found themselves, or whether it be considered simply as the answer to the question, "What must we do to obtain remission of sins?" the answer is the same: "Repent, and be baptized." They were not told to repent for one purpose and be baptized for another. Repentance and baptism in this passage stand in precisely the same relationship. The rule of grammar operative in such cases is as follows: Coordinate connectives connect similar grammatical elements, and place them in equal ranks; or, more simply, "Whenever two things are connected by the copulative conjunction 'and' and something is affirmed or predicated of them, however much they may differ in other respects, they are perfectly equal as to the thing predicated or affirmed." Repentance and baptism are, of course, different acts; but in this sentence their object is the same, and they are entirely equal as to the thing predicated or affirmed, which, in this case, is remission of sins.

"Does 1 Timothy 2:11-15 teach that childbearing is a condition of woman's salvation?"

No.

Women are forbidden to teach or to have dominion "over the man." The reason assigned by inspiration for this prohibition is, "For Adam was first formed, then Eve; and Adam was not beguiled, but the woman being beguiled hath fallen into transgression: but she shall be saved through her childbearing, if they continue in faith and love and sanctification with sobriety." In consequence of the deception which Eve suffered the serpent to exercise upon her and in punishment therefore, she was told, "In sorrow shalt thou bring forth children" (Genesis 3:16), and this burden has been borne by women from that hour to this.

59

Notwithstanding woman's participation in the fall, "she shall be saved through her childbearing," if they (women in general) continue in faith, in love and in sanctification with sobriety.

Various explanations have been offered: (1) Eve, though deceived, and not permitted to teach unrestrainedly, would be saved by being the mother of all living, and hence, the mother of Christ, the Saviour. This is a contrived effort and without support in the passage, though the conclusion which follows it is true. (2) She shall be saved from the dangers of childbearing. This would apply the passage exclusively to Eve; whereas it will be seen that the application extends to all women. (3) She shall be saved by bearing children. This would make the ability to bear children a condition precedent to salvation, thus excluding many women from the possibility of going to heaven. Such a view is obviously false. (4) She shall be saved by discharging her function, which is childbearing. But, this view would make woman's mission in life solely childbearing—an also obviously false conclusion.

The change in number of the pronouns, from singular to plural, in the passage is significant and sheds light on the meaning. "She (the woman) shall be saved . . . if they (women in general) continue in faith . . ." Thus, the meaning would appear to be: Eve, representative of womankind, was deceived in the transgression and because of this her sex bears restrictions in teaching; this, however, will not keep women from being saved provided they practice the precepts of faith, love and sobriety, i.e., live the Christian life!

"Explain 1 Timothy 1:8-10."

"But we know that the law is good, if a man use it lawfully, as knowing this, that law is not made for a righteous man, but for the lawless and unruly, for the ungodly and sinners, for the unholy and profane, for murderers of fathers and murderers of mothers, for manslayers, for fornicators, for abusers of themselves with men, for menstealers, for liars, for false swearers, and if there be any other thing contrary to the sound doctrine; according to the gospel of the glory of the blessed God, which was committed to my trust."

To forestall the possibility that his opposers would say that the apostle was without respect for the law which the Jews revered greatly, Paul emphasized the proper function of law in these verses. To use it lawfully is to (a) recognize its purpose; (b) its limitations; (c) its termination as a constitution at the cross. (Colossians 2:13-17.) The principles, i.e., the moral character of law, are ageless; they did not originate at Sinai, when the law was given (Exodus 20:1ff), nor did they end when the law, as a constitution, ended at the cross. The principles of the law are embraced in the gospel and Paul clearly shows their application to all in these verses.

The law has no terror for righteous people; on the contrary, they respect and honor it. It is indeed not designed for righteous people today, i.e., to make them righteous; this is done only through obedience to the commandments of the Lord. (Psalm 119:172; Matthew 7:21; Acts 10:34,35; 1 John 2:4; 5:3.) Law, any law, all law is designed to control the lawless (those refusing to be bound by any law), the ungodly and sinner (those in rebellion to the law of God), the unholy and profane (those without respect for God's commandments), for murderers, for immoral people, for slave-traders, for liars and perjurers, and for all others who are in violation of the commandments of God.

We thus learn that the purpose of the law was to restrain and keep in check men in rebellion against God and their fellowmen. The "sound doctrine," which Paul taught, and which Timothy was to impress upon the people in Ephesus was in harmony with God's law, being a part of it, and thus those who accepted it walked in harmony with all of God's will, whether of a moral or of a positive nature.

Here as often elsewhere in the New Testament, we note that the early church had its problems with false teachers even as we do today. The price for a pure faith and an unsullied practice is undeviating adherence to the "sound doctrine" which Paul enjoined Timothy to teach.

"We were asked this question in our Sunday morning Bible class: How do we figure that it has been about 6000 years since God prepared the earth for man? The answer given was something like this: By adding the ages of the antediluvians Adam, Seth, Enos, etc., at the birth of their first sons, we know the number of years before the flood . . . Will you please answer these questions for me: (1) Is it possible to count the time from the creation of man in this manner? (2) Is Ussher's chronology used in such counting of time? How dependable is Ussher? (3) Is there any conflict between this method of counting time and the claims of science regarding the age of man? I will be very grateful for any help you can give us on this subject."

The age of the earth and man. Above the center reference column at the top of the page of the first chapter of Genesis in some Bibles of the King James' translation is the notation 4004 B.C., indicating that the events therein arranged occurred 4004 years before the birth of Christ. This is based on the chronological system of an English Bishop (a preacher of the Church of England) by the name of Usher (sometimes spelled Ussher) who, in the year 1650 A.D., sought to establish a biblical chronology from the flood up to Adam by adding up the ages of the patriarchs, as given in the genealogical table of the fifth chapter of Genesis, at the births of their first sons. This table follows:

Adam	130
Seth	105
Enos	90
Cainan	70
Mahalaleel	65
Jared	162
Enoch	65
Methuselah	187
Lamech	182
Noah	500
Shem	100
Total	1656

Whence it was assumed that at the time of the flood man had been on the earth exactly 1656 years! Dates, grounded in the Usherian system, were printed in early English Bibles and have often been copied into others since; and, so familiar is the notation to some people there has actually been an assumption that this constitutes a portion of the inspired record. All of the more recent translations omit it.

In considering this difficult question, it is well to keep in mind that the inspired text contains no data on which the events of Genesis 1 may be dated. In a majestic affirmation, simple, sublime and satisfactory, we are informed that "In the beginning God created the heavens and the earth." When this beginning was, we are not told. We should not be disturbed by the wild and extravagant claims of so-called scientists who allege an extremely advanced age for this earth and thereupon attack the reliability of the Bible.

"How dependable is the Usherian system of chronology before the flood?"

It assumes that Hebrew genealogical tables were designed on the same premises as those characteristic of more recent ages when a study of them reveals that they neither are, nor were intended to provide full, detailed and complete records. It is quite clear that such was the case in the genealogical charts of our Lord which consists of three tables, divided into 14 generations each, and obviously not complete yet entirely satisfactory and without grounds for criticism by our Lord's most inveterate enemies. (Matthew 1:1-17; cf. Luke 3:23-38.) Often, in Old

62

Testament usage, one said to be a son of another may, indeed, be several generations removed from the ancestor.

Jewish writers and other ancient authorities, with these tables before them, and fully informed regarding their evidential value in this matter, have reached different conclusions regarding the antiquity of man. Josephus, the famous historian of the first century, provides data which would make the period from the flood to Adam 2256 years; the Septuagint (Greek Translation of the Old Testament, approximately 280 B.C.), 2262 years while the Samaritan Pentetuech has only 1307 years. Moreover, other systems of chronology differ widely from Usher's. Hales, a well-known chronological authority, arrived at the date 5250 B.C., for the origin of man, but made no attempt to establish a date for the earth's beginning; Jackson, another eminent writer in this field, differs from Hales and Usher; and the common Hebrew reckoning of 3760 B.C., for the creation, and on the basis of which they have established their calendar, varies from all of the foregoing by hundreds of years.

Sufficient grounds do not exist on which it is proper to affirm an extremely advanced age for man on the earth. Conservative scientists concede this.

"I am disposed to attribute to man an antiquity of about 10,000 years. It seems likely that the general consensus of chronologists will ultimately fix on a date which shall be below rather than above 10,000 years as the nearest approximate to the age of our race." (Zahm, *The Bible, Science and Faith*, p. 311.)

"The very beginnings of our race are still almost in sight." (Winchell, *Sketches of Creation*)

Chronological details, from the times of the Exodus until the end of the Apostolic Age, obtain in great abundance, and are subject to corroboration from history both sacred and profane. And, from the exodus to the flood, sufficient data exists on which to form definite conclusions regarding the period of the events described. But, from Adam to the flood our information is incomplete and the effort to formulate a system of chronology is at best imperfect. It is for this reason that the most conservative scholars place little confidence in the systems of Usher, Hales, etc., before the deluge.

Science, properly conceived, is "systematized knowledge" (*New World Dictionary*); and, there is no conflict between it and the Book which is the sum of all spiritual truth. Truth, wherever found, is not in conflict with itself. We must, however, distinguish between science and scientists just as we differentiate between the Bible and biblical people (preachers). True science is no more responsible for the wild claims of the former than the Bible is answerable for the affirmations of the latter. As a matter of fact, when scientists presume to speak about the origin of life, matter, the world, etc., they are out of their proper sphere of observation, analysis and experimentation with existing phenomena. The Bible is an infallible, inerrant, inspired (God inbreathed) document, containing all the information necessary to furnish us unto every good work. How tragic to reject it for the vapid opinions of men!

"What is modest apparel?"

Among the questions I am most often asked in meetings conducted throughout the land is with reference to proper apparel. Godly women shrink from wearing clothes, acceptable by worldly standards, but questionable for Christians; and, what constitutes suitable adornment is a matter of no little concern to many.

In Paul's epistles, occasional references are made to this matter; and, in 1 Timothy 2:9,10, specific instruction thereon is given: "In like manner, that women adorn themselves in modest apparel, with shamefastness and sobriety; not with braided hair, and gold or pearls or costly raiment; but (which becometh women professing godliness) through good works." As men are to exhibit proper dignity in worship (the theme of the apostle immediately preceding the foregoing quotation), "in like manner," women are to conform to the standards of modesty and decorum characteristic of faithful people. Their dress is to consist of "modest apparel," i.e., garments preserving their modesty. The word translated "apparel" here is *katastole*, literally, a long flowing robe, reaching down to the feet, but here used figuratively to indicate not only modesty in dress but also in conduct. It was often used by Greek-speaking people of the first century to indicate demeanor, whether in look, manner, or dress.

Sisters are to dress "in shamefastness and sobriety; not with braided hair, and gold or pearls or costly raiment; but (which becometh women professing godliness) through good works." Shamefastness is that disposition which prompts one to shrink from all that is immodest and indelicate either in appearance or conduct; sobriety is soberminded-ness, a well-balanced state of mind which results from the exercise of self-restraint. These characteristics are, figuratively, to be their garments rather than "braided hair, and gold or pearls or costly raiment." The "braided hair," to which the apostle alludes consisted of strands of gold woven into the hair, the effect of which was to cause the entire headdress to glisten with brilliance in the light. Ancient historians, in describing this practice, have written that so vain were many women of the first century who affected this sort of coiffure they often resisted sleep for several nights, to the point of exhaustion, lest they cause disarray to their vaulted hair-do!

The "gold," the "pearls," and the "costly raiment" mentioned by the apostle were the usual ornaments of the proud, the vain and the worldly.

Such displays the apostle regarded as unseemly in the house of God. If the Holy Spirit looked with such opposition on those modes of dress, what must be his attitude toward the glaring and tasteless types of dress now often seen in church gatherings? Truly faithful Christian women will seek to avoid any mode of dress or actions which raise questions regarding their modesty and purity of heart. Chrysostom, born about the middle of the fourth century, in commenting on the passage herein being examined, asked the congregation in Antioch: "And what then is modest apparel? such as covers them completely and decently, and not with superfluous ornaments; for the one is decent and the other is not. What? Do you approach God to pray with broidered hair and ornaments of gold? Are you come to a ball? to a marriage-feast? to a carnival? There such costly things might have been seasonable: here not one of them is wanted. You are come to pray, to ask pardon for your offences, beseeching the Lord, and hoping to render him propitious to you. Away with such hypocrisy! God is not mocked. This is the attire of actors and dancers, who live upon the stage. Nothing of this kind becomes a modest woman, who should be adorned with shamefastness and sobriety." The illustrious Chrysostom's remarks are pertinent and true. They ought carefully to be taken to heart by us all.

"Give a simple and brief refutation of atheism."

Atheism is the denial of the existence of a supreme being. It is an unreasonable, irrational and absurd doctrine for many reasons, among them the following: (1) It assumes to be true that which no man can possibly know. To know that God does not exist would require one (a) to know all there is to know; (b) to have forever lived; (c) to have lived forever in every place in the universe and out of it! One possessed of less than all knowledge; or, if so possessed, not to have lived forever; or, though eternal and omniscient, not omnipresent, may not have lived at the right time, or have been at the right place, or have possessed the proper knowledge to establish the contention that deity does not exist. It would indeed require God to know that God does not exist—an obvious absurdity.

(2) Moreover, atheism is incapable of providing a sane and satisfactory explanation of the origin of the world and of man. It must assume that the amazingly intricate and at the same time orderly composition of the universe and of man is the result of blind chance, wholly uninfluenced or directed by any intelligent source and operating solely from forces resident in them. How can intelligent men reasonably reach such a conclusion? How long, for example, would it take a succession of monkeys, idly toying with the keys of a typewriter to compose the book of Romans, Longfellow's poems, or the U.S. Constitution? Would it be

possible for a man with unlimited time and patience to throw blobs of paint at a canvas until, by chance, he had duplicated the world famous painting, The Last Supper? Am I to suppose that my watch, an extremely complicated and delicate instrument is, nonetheless the result of chance, the mindless and fortuitous assembly of various parts which, through accident and not design, came together to produce an accurate and dependable timepiece, and that the slow evolutionary process which produced it though imperceptible is continuing and that in the ages to come it will become a Volkswagen? Absurd though such is, is it not much, much easier to believe than that the earth and the heavens and all that in them is, exist by chance and not by design? In the light of these facts it is not surprising that David identified as a fool one who asserts that there is no God. (Psalm 14:1.)

"At a recent service I attended the speaker made a point which bothered me. As I understood him, he was saying it is not scriptural to make a benevolent contribution through the church treasury earmarking it for a specific work. The impression was left that the church should not be thus used to gain income tax deductions. But to a non-profit organization such as an old folks' home, orphan home, etc., it is tax deductible whether by an individual or through the church. How can that be using the church? A private source indicated the point in question was that the specification on the donation represented telling the elders what to do with the contribution thus usurping their authority. Since I am one who has, at times, given above my regular contribution to a stipulated cause, I am desirous to understand wherein I am doing wrong. I have been unable to get my questions answered and it was suggested that I write you.

"It is readily agreed that special contributions should be above the regular contribution else the eldership would have no base on which to plan the local program. However, if earmarking constitutes a usurping of the eldership's authority regarding special contributions, what about sending contributions to the eldership overseeing a missionary's funds? If we do not earmark such contributions how do they know not to put it into their general fund?

"It has never been my intention to usurp or disrespect the authority of the eldership. I firmly believe they have a specific God-given authority by which I am to abide. It has been my desire to do benevolent work for God's glory, however, not my own. How can I do that if not through the church? A contribution sent via personal check (for tax records) in my name results in my name being listed as contributor not the church. Keep in mind that we are talking about a contribution to a Christian work which would be tax deductible to the individual whichever way it is contributed. If I am wrong in the method I have used heretofore could you suggest a scriptural method which still gives God the glory, and his church? Since I need the check as proof of my contribution the credit goes to me even when I suggest it is for the credit of such and such a congregation."

I believe that it is eminently scriptural to earmark such special contributions when we have contributed as we have been prospered into the regular treasury of the church. This is indeed the proper way to support special projects when an eldership will cooperate since it enables one to give above and beyond the Lord's day contribution obligation and still "through the church." In my view, the brother's reasoning is correct. See Acts 11:29 for a specific example.

"Discuss law and grace."

"For the law was given through Moses, grace and truth came through Jesus Christ." (John 1:17.)

The grace we are privileged to receive through Christ is vastly superior to the blessings of the old covenant even as Christ, through whom this grace comes, is infinitely superior to Moses, by whom the law came. (Deuteronomy 5:1,2.) The "law" mentioned here is that which was given from Sinai. This law was by Paul regarded as the opposite of grace in that it created obligations it could not help discharge thus making apparent man's need of God's grace which may be received only through Christ. (Galatians 3:10; 4:4; Romans 8:2-4.) The law was helpless to justify, and it served only to bring the Jews to Christ. (Galatians 3:8-27.) Only in Christ is there deliverance from the guilt, and power and the presence of sin. The blessing of salvation we appropriate (not merit, earn, purchase, or deserve) through obedience to his will as expressed in his commandments. (Matthew 7:21; Acts 10:34,35; 1 John 2:4; 5:3.)

Law is "a rule of action," and grace is unmerited favor. It involves grievous error to assume, as many today, do, that all there was of the Old Testament order was law, and all there is of the New Testament system is grace. Paul's purpose was to show the origin of law and of grace, and not to limit their operations. It was the unmerited favor of God which allowed sinful man to approach him through Jewish modes of worship and it is by means of "the law of the Spirit of life in Christ Jesus" that we are made free from the law of sin and death in this, the

Christian age. (Romans 8:2.) The commandments of the Lord are the rule of action by which we are answerable to God today and in keeping them we neither earn nor merit salvation but evidence our faith in, and our dependence on, him who saves. To say that if we must comply with the commandments in order to be saved is legalism is both false and foolish; to urge that justification is received in the act of believing and not on condition of keeping the commandments is contradictory since the act of believing is as much a human act as is either repentance, confession or baptism. To those who asked, "What must we do, that we may work the works of God?" Jesus answered, "This is the work of God, that ye believe on him, whom he hath sent." (John 6:29.) Any view of either grace or faith which minimizes the obligation of the sinner to obey the commandments is a perversion of biblical teaching and pernicious in its tendencies. Peter's words to this point are clear and unequivocal: "Of a truth I perceive that God is no respecter of persons: but in every nation he that feareth him, and worketh righteousness, is acceptable to him." (Acts 10:34,35.) To work righteousness is to keep the commandments. (Psalm 119:172.)

"Do animals have souls?"

The word soul is used in the Scriptures to mean (a) persons (1 Peter 3:20); (b) the life-entity of man (Psalm 78:50); (c) the immortal nature (Acts 2:27). Animals have "spirit" i.e., life (Ecclesiastes 3:19), but not a soul in the senses above described.

"Is there any proof that Paul preached in Rome?"

Yes, see Acts 28:16-31.

"Is it right to divide members of the congregation into teams, reward the teams with 'points' for the greatest activity in Christian service, and provide the winning team with a spaghetti supper?"

Often members of the church are far more influenced by gimmicks than by conscience. Denominational churches have followed this procedure for years. Is it not sad that it takes an appeal to the stomach to induce people to serve Christ, who no longer feel the compulsion of love?

"Is 'born of the Spirit,' in John 3:5, the same as the 'gift of the Spirit,' in Acts 2:38?"

No. By being born of water and the Spirit (believing and being baptized, Mark 16:16), one enters the kingdom. The Samaritans, having so done (Acts 8:4,12) were saved and in the kingdom, thus had been "born of the Spirit," but they had not received the Spirit prior to the imposition of the hands of Peter and John (Acts 8:16). One is born of the Spirit when baptized into Christ.

"Were John's converts re-baptized on the day of Pentecost, or following?"

No. Acts 19:1-5 involves people who received John's baptism after the great commission became effective. It is absurd to say that the apostles were in their sins until the day of Pentecost. John's baptism was "for" (unto) the remission of sins. (Mark 1:4.)

"What is the difference between the nation of Israel and the nation of the Jews? To whom was the promise of the Messiah made?"

Israel is the name which God gave to Jacob, and to that illustrious patriarch's descendents. (Genesis 35:9-15.) The word "Jew" derives from "Judah," one of Jacob's sons. Thus, all "Jews" were Israelites, being descended from Jacob, but not all Israelites were "Jews," since the name *Jew* originally referred to the descendents of Judah only. Often, during the period of the divided kingdom, the northern realm was called "the kingdom of Israel," and the southern division was called "the kingdom of Judah." The promise of the Messiah was to all of Abraham's seed—regardless of race—both spiritual and natural, whether Jew or Gentile, whether descended from Jacob or not.

"When do we become a part of the bride of Christ?"

The church is the bride of Christ. (2 Corinthians 11:2; Ephesians 5:23-32.) We become a part of the bride of Christ when we obey the gospel, and the Lord in the process of saving us adds us to the church. (Acts 2:47.) Revelation 19:7 is not in conflict with this conclusion since the reference there is to the Oriental custom of the bridegroom coming for his bride.

"Is it possible for man to think of anything which God has not first thought of?"

Jehovah, through his faithful prophet Jeremiah, said, "And they have built the high places of Topheth, which is in the valley of the son of Hinnon, to burn their sons and their daughters in the fire; which I commanded not, neither came it into my mind." (Jeremiah 7:31.) Ob-

69

viously, God has never entertained wicked, depraved and corrupt thoughts often in the minds of men.

"What is the law of sin and death alluded to in Romans 8:2?"

Despite the fact that good and great men have thought otherwise, I believe it to be the law of Moses. It is to me unaccountable that the apostle would use the word "law" in verse 2 in a sense entirely different from that in verse 3, where the reference is by all admitted to be the law of Moses. The law of Moses was a law "of sin and death," because it exhibited sin in the lives of men and led to death and because no one except Christ could meet its requirements. Paul affirmed this fact in his own case. (Romans 7:9-11.)

"What does it mean to 'know' God?"

One does not know God who does not conform to his will. We may believe intellectually that there is a God; we may affirm the truth of his existence, the facts of his attributes, the reality of his works in nature. But only those who have wholly committed their wills to his know him in his saving power. "And this is life eternal, that they should know thee the only true God, and him whom thou didst send, even Jesus Christ." (John 17:3.) If it be asked which commandments constitute the test here submitted, the answer is, all of them! Any commandment we are disposed to break because of our unwillingness to bend our wills to his provides the occasion which demonstrates lack of full knowledge of him. This is the "one thing" which we "lack" and which, like the young ruler's riches, will close the door of heaven in our faces.

The Gnostics boasted of their superior knowledge and spiritual insight and maintained their acquaintance with the Lord despite the fact that they kept not his commandments. With reference to all such the apostle solemnly declares, "He that saith, I know him, and keepeth not his commandments, is a liar, and the truth is not in him." (1 John 2:4.) The verbs in the Greek text are in the present tense. He who keeps on saying, I know him, and yet keeps not on keeping his commandments, is a liar, and the truth is not in him. Far from actually and really knowing God, those who refuse to do his will are, in addition to being disobedient characters, liars and without truth. The words, "He is a liar" are more emphatic than "we lie," of John 1:6, and "we deceive ourselves," of 1:8. His status is not simply that of one who is guilty of a single falsehood, or one who is innocently deceived; his acts of falsehood have become embedded in his character and he is, essentially, a liar. Such a one is demonstrating the nature and character of his father, the devil, who is a liar from the beginning. (John 8:44.) It was evidently no uncommon thing for men, at the time John wrote, who had adopted the pernicious doctrine of the Gnostics to affirm that they, though willfully guilty of sinful acts, were not thereby corrupted. Some of these men maintained that they were no more polluted by sin than gold is by the mire into which it might fall.

As shocking as the foregoing theology is, it has its modern counterparts. Those false teachers, while denying any contamination from sin, did admit the fact of sin in their lives. There are those today who deny both the sin and the contamination. A prominent denominational preacher, in a tract entitled, "Do a Christian's Sins Damn His Soul?" wrote: "We take the position that a Christian's sins do not damn his soul. The way a Christian lives, what he says, his character, his conduct, or his attitude toward other people have nothing whatever to do with the salvation of his soul . . . All the prayers a man may pray, all the Bibles he may read, all the churches he may belong to, all the services he may attend, all the sermons he may practice, all the debts he may pay, all the ordinances he may observe, all the laws he may keep, all the benevolent acts he may perform will not make his soul one whit safer; and all the sins he may commit from idolatry to murder will not make his soul in any more danger . . . The way a man lives has nothing whatsoever to do with the salvation of his soul." Such theology, whether ancient or modern, is precisely in principle what John condemned when he affirmed that those who say they know him, yet do not keep his commandments, are liars.

"Are songbooks authorized? We see no mention of the early Christians using a 'songbook' in their worship and if they did use a 'songbook' it is evident that the music was not written along with the words as we have it today in our modern songbooks, because the present method of writing music was not invented for centuries after the church was in operation. Therefore, is not worshiping with a book with the music written along with the words an innovation and not commanded just as much as singing when the whole tune is being played on an instrument? With an instrument my ear guides me in singing and with the written music my eye guides me so that I sing in harmony with others who are also singing. I can find no more authority in the New Testament for using songbooks with music written, than there is for musical instruments."

We are glad to give attention to this brother's question, not because it is likely that any of our readers would experience difficulty in distinguishing between the use of mechanical instruments in worship and the use of songbooks, but because this letter affords us an opportunity

71

to teach an ever-needed lesson on what constitutes authority. We are not disposed to enter into the question he raises as to the type of book in use in the apostolic age nor the manner in which the music was written. It is enough for us to know that the early church utilized the use of "psalms, hymns and spiritual songs" (Ephesians 5:19), and a collection of these constituted a "book" (see dictionary definition of a book), whether such is specifically mentioned in the New Testament, or not; and, by whatever name it was known at the time. Our brother would not seriously object, we think, to the conclusion that a collection of psalms would be a psalmbook, of hymns, a hymnbook, of songs, a songbook! Thus, the mere fact that no mention is made of such does not justify the conclusion that none existed; and, when he writes, "Therefore, is not worshiping with a book with the music written along with the words an innovation and not commanded just as much as singing when the whole tune is being played on an instrument?" his *therefore* is *non sequitur*; the conclusion he would draw does not follow from the premises.

His reasoning follows this pattern: That which is not mentioned in the New Testament is unauthorized in Christian worship today. Songbooks are not mentioned in connection with Christian worship in the New Testament. Therefore, songbooks are unauthorized in Christian worship today. Our brother's fallacy is glaringly apparent. His erroneous conclusion stems from the unwarranted assumption that because a thing is not specifically mentioned in the New Testament it is, for this reason alone, not authorized. He is eminently correct in his conclusion that unauthorized matters may not properly be injected into religious worship. He errs, however, in concluding that a thing not mentioned is necessarily unauthorized. This defect in reasoning is by no means an uncommon one. The failure to distinguish between specific mention of matters, and authority often leads to misapprehension and misrepresentation. For example, Brother A concedes that the details of a practice in question are not designated in the New Testament, but insists that the practice is permissible; Brother B immediately concludes from Brother A's concession that Brother A believes it is proper to engage in matters not authorized in the New Testament. Brother B's reasoning is obviously fallacious. A matter may be authorized, though not specified in the New Testament. The command to perform a duty, authorized (though it may not specify) the details necessary to its discharge. Baptistries are not specified in the New Testament; they are, nevertheless, authorized, since the command to perform the act (in this instance, immersion) justifies the means essential to its performance. The New Testament makes no mention of church-owned meetinghouses; insofar as the record reveals, no apostolic church ever was seized of real estate, the practice thereof, so common today, terminating this side of the apostolic age, by some hundreds of years. Nonetheless, we may confidently affirm that it is scriptural for churches to own meetinghouses today, since the obligation to assemble authorizes the means essential thereto. Our querist is thus in obvious error in his assumption that because songbooks are not specifically mentioned in the New Testament they are unauthorized innovations.

But, if songbooks, though not mentioned, are authorized in the scriptures, why may we not regard mechanical instruments of music in worship in the same fashion? Granting that such are not mentioned in Christian worship, since some matters may properly be engaged in, though not specified, why is it not allowable to use organs, pianos, and other mechanical kinds of musical instruments on this basis? This is the crux of our brother's question.

We answer that the use of songbooks in the worship, and the use of instruments of music therein, fall into two entirely different categories. Songbooks and singing (an authorized act) are co-ordinate, they are of the same rank or order. Songs are essential to singing; singing is commanded (Ephesians 5:19); it is, therefore, impossible to discharge our obligation without psalms, hymns and spiritual songs. A collection of these, we have seen, constitute a psalmbook, a hymnbook, a song-book. Instruments of music and singing are not of the same rank, or order; it is necessary to have a song in order to have singing; singing is enjoined; therefore, songs are essential; it is, however, not necessary to have an instrument in order to sing; the instrument is not co-ordinate to singing. As a matter of fact, the instrument injects a foreign element into the worship—playing. One does not sing by playing; thus, the playing becomes an addition and an innovation.

We may illustrate it thus: The elements of the Lord's supper instituted by our Lord are bread and the fruit of the vine. In none of the accounts thereof is there mention of the vessel to be used in connection with the bread. We nevertheless affirm that it is scriptural to use a plate on which to place the bread in the observance of the Lord's supper, inasmuch as it serves merely as a means to discharge the obligation. Its use in no way alters, modifies, adds to, or takes from, the service enjoined. Suppose, however, that one should insist that with the bread flesh should be added on the allegation that to some people this would aid them in more properly visualizing the body of the Lord than the bread alone! In such a case the flesh (meat) would be, and would be correctly regarded as, an unwarranted and unauthorized addition, an innovation. The principle involved is this: A command carrying with it the means or method of procedure is specific; and, the means or method indicated is essential to the performance of the command. A command not specifying the means is generic; and, the means are to be supplied in the most expedient manner possible. Unfortunately, there is the disposition evidenced occasionally to invade the realm of expediency and presume to establish rules regulating matters in this area. All such should be solemnly warned of the fact that it is as wrong to make laws as it is to break them!

"In Matthew's gospel are certain events on which I would appreciate your thoughts. In the garden before his arrest Christ prayed, 'If possible let this cup pass' (Matthew 26:39); was there no other way? While hanging on the cross the land was blanketed with darkness for three hours. Was that to hide his intense, horrible suffering from his mother and perhaps other relatives?"

There was no other way. We may be certain that had there been, a loving Father would have chosen the alternative and thus have enabled his only begotten Son to avoid the burden, the shame and the suffering of the cross. Matthew 26:42 clearly evidences the fact that the Lord wanted an alternative only if the Father's will could otherwise be realized, "He went away again the second time and prayed, saying, O my Father, if this cup may not pass away from me, except I drink it, thy will be done." His nature was both human and divine. Humanity was his mother; deity his Father; as he faced the final hour the realization of the awesome load he bore weighed heavily on his soul and his humanity cried out for some way, if possible, to avoid it. The agony of soul he experienced indicates his immeasurable suffering before the event and when to this is added the actual pain of the cross it is no wonder that the sacred writers so often refer to his suffering in our behalf in those tragic hours.

Though he shrank from the horrors he faced he would not avoid them at the expense of the atonement, saying, in effect, "I wish to accomplish the grand design of my Father's plan whatever the cost to me." Only by freely giving himself up to die was salvation for mankind made possible.

Beyond the fact, we can know nothing about the darkness which shrouded the land in those awful hours. Light is a synonym of truth and darkness symbolizes error. For the moment, the forces of evil had triumphed and our blessed Lord hanged helplessly on the cruel cross of Calvary. It is no wonder that the sun refused to shine upon such an event, and that darkness, representative of the state of mind of those who condemned the Saviour, should for the time prevail. The Jews had chosen to reject Jesus; unwilling to walk in the light of truth, they were now forced to walk in literal darkness in token of that fact. Great though the darkness was in which they, walked in Judea, greater still was the darkness of soul which now characterized them in condemning to death the Lord of glory. Israel today walks in darkness because her people still refuse the light. Expectation of a future state of glory for national Israel is a delusion though widely believed and proclaimed; the "hope of Israel" is only in Christ, and Israel's house remains desolate because they have rejected him. (Matthew 23:37-39.)

"I hesitate to write you because I know that you are very busy, but a problem has existed in our congregation for some time that is causing a great deal of consternation and while there seems to be no real danger of division, it has considerably frustrated many attempts to get a harmonious work program going. If you or some other capable man could either find time to write me a letter or put an article in the ADVOCATE on this in the very near future it would be greatly appreciated."

Our brother describes a situation here often characteristic of congregations these days. A brother, or group of brethren, espouse a theory, industriously propagate it, set brethren at variance with each other; and, if division in the body of Christ is not the result, all "attempts to get a harmonious work program going" are frustrated, and the cause of our Lord in the community is rendered impotent. Paul pinpointed the disposition thus: "If any man teach otherwise, and consent not to wholesome words, even the words of our Lord Jesus Christ, and to the doctrine which is according to godliness; he is proud, knowing nothing, but doting about questions and strifes of words, whereof cometh envy, strife, railings, evil surmisings." (1 Timothy 6:3,4.) We do not know the identity of the man of whom our brother writes, and do not imply that such must be his motive in this instance; but, he should carefully examine his heart to see that such does not characterize him. It is a fearful thing to divide the body of Christ, either actually or substantially, and for all such a terrible judgment awaits. What is the problem of which our brother writes?

"We have an influential brother in the congregation who prides himself with his understanding of, and insistence upon the technical use of words. He insists that the word 'church' does not, in the New Testament, mean 'called out' but always refers to an assembly or an organization (can apply to an organization on paper only and not necessarily in existence). Such passages as Matthew 16:18; Ephesians 1:22,23; Colossians 1:18,24, etc., that I have taught applied to the church universal, he says has no reference to the individual saints at all but refers to only an organizational form existing in the mind of Christ. He says that 'my church' of Matthew 16:18 indicates 'kind,' 'type' and refers not

to people but organization, stating that Ephesians 4:11-16, refers not to individuals in the church (assembly) but offices in the local organization. That such an organization and offices can exist even if there were no humans to fill them. That the word church never refers to God's people in the universal sense, but that where such a thought is indicated the term 'kingdom' is always used."

We have not lately seen a more obvious misapprehension of one of the most fundamental matters of New Testament teaching than is exhibited in the foregoing quotation. We see not how it is possible for one to make any sort of investigation of the lexical significance and New Testament usage of the word church and arrive at the conclusion that it "does not, in the New Testament, mean 'called out.'" It means precisely this!

Our English word church is translated from the Greek *ecclesia*, occurring about 120 times in the Greek New Testament, and compounded from the preposition *ek*, of, or out of, and the verb *kaleoo*, to call; hence, the called out. This word (*ecclesia*), as is characteristic of many others in the New Testament, had originally a secular significance which made it especially suited to sacred usage it was henceforth to have. It means "any public assembly of citizens summoned by a herald" (Moulton and Milligan, *The Vocabulary of the Greek New Testament*, p. 195), "an assembly of the people convened at the public place of council for the purpose of deliberating. (Acts 19:39.)" (Thayer.)

It is, therefore, clear that the basic significance of the word *ecclesia* (from which is translated the word church) is (a) an assembly, (b) "summoned," or "convened." That this was its Septuagint significance is, likewise, clear, from the fact that Stephen designated the congregation in the wilderness— Israel called out of Egypt—by the term. (Acts 7:38.) "It is an assembly of the called, or those who are brought together by one leader, or profession." (Campbell, Appendix, *Living Oracles*, p. 77.) The word, in the New Testament, designates the body of Christ, i.e., all the saved (Ephesians 5:23-25); and, those assembled in one place—the congregation ("an assembly of persons," Webster). Its general usage is sometimes limited by a geographical phrase as, "the church of God which is at Corinth." (1 Corinthians 1:2.) The church is, then (a) a body of baptized believers (1 Corinthians 12:13), (b) who have been called out from the world by the gospel (2 Thessalonians 2:13,14), (c) over which Christ rules as head (Ephesians 1:19-23), and in which the Spirit dwells (1 Corinthians 3:16).

Erroneous is also the view that the passages cited in the quotation (Matthew 16:18, Ephesians 1:22, Colossians 1:18,24, etc.) do not refer to the body of saints called out from the world, but "to an organizational form existing in the mind of Christ." The church is the body of Christ.

76

(Ephesians 1:22.) The "body" is made up of individual saints. (1 Corinthians 12:20.) Therefore, the church is made up of individual saints, called out from the world, and which often meet in called assemblies. "For as the body is one, and hath many members, and all the members of that one body, being many, are one body: so also is Christ . . . Now ye are the body of Christ, and members in particular." (1 Corinthians 12:12,27.)

If, to this, the objection is raised that the "one body," under consideration here, was the local congregation at Corinth, we direct attention to the following: Paul, from Ephesus (and beyond the Aegean Sea), addressed the Corinthians thus: "The bread which we break, is it not the communion of the body of Christ? For we being many are one bread, and one body: for we are all partakers of that one bread." (1 Corinthians 10:16,17.) Those of Ephesus, along with the saints of Corinth were all partaking of "one bread," and were all members of "one body." They did not, of course, eat from the same piece of bread on the Lord's day; nor, were they members of the same congregation; yet, they ate from the one bread which portrays the Lord's body, and were members of that same spiritual body, though living in widely separated areas.

It is incredible that one should conclude that Ephesians 4:11-16, refers "not to individuals," but "offices in the local organization," and that such may "exist even if there were no humans to fill them." The design of the ministry there mentioned was "the edifying of the body of Christ" (verse 12), thus requiring both "edifiers," and the edified! The concept that there are offices of any kind in the church of the Lord is a pernicious one, and has been the occasion for much strife and contention. (1 Timothy 3:1 has no word for office in the Greek text.) The so-called offices of the church are functional, not official; men are elders because (a) they have been selected for such work; and (b) are actually performing it. If either of these characteristics is wanting, there is no scriptural precedent to establish a claim to such on the ground of official position. The "influential brother" is far from the truth when he alleges that "the whole body" of Ephesians 4:16, which may be "edified" and "grow up in him," i.e., Christ, does not refer to individuals.

Equally distant from the truth is the allegation that the word "kingdom" is used to denote the universal aspect, rather than "church." The word kingdom emphasizes the governmental characteristics of the Lord's cause; the word church its relationship to the world—the called out.

The brother whose position is under review evidently does not reject the idea of a local assembly, he denies that the word "church" ever designates the Lord's people in the aggregate:

"He believes where 'church' is used, not indicating organization, it always means local assembly such as a local city council." With him,

77

the word "church" is either a group of people actually assembled; or, merely an organizational concept which Christ had in mind, and not the entire body of believers throughout the world. Numerous instances of its usage, in the New Testament, will not fit into either of his concepts. In addition to those cited (i.e., Matthew 16:18; Ephesians 1:19-23; Colossians 1:18,24), we direct his attention to the following: "But ye are come unto mount Sion, and unto the city of the living God, the heavenly Jerusalem, and to an innumerable company of angels, to the general assembly and church of the firstborn, which are written in heaven." (Hebrews 12:22,23.) The Lord's people under consideration here are described as the "church of the firstborn," literally, firstborn ones, identified as "the general assembly," in "the heavenly Jerusalem." This may not be classified as his "organizational form existing in the mind of Christ," because it was a "general assembly," made up of firstborn ones; it was not a local assembly, in a congregational sense, inasmuch as it was composed of all those whose names are "written in heaven." This includes all the saved. (Philippians 4:3.)

The church sustains the relationship of a bride to Christ. (2 Corinthians 11:2; Ephesians 5:25-27.) Obviously, Christ is not merely married to a local congregation; but to the entire body of believers. This bride, for which Christ shall return, will be composed of all the saved, though some of these may, from economic necessity or other reasons, be isolated, and no part of a local assembly. When one moves away from a local congregation, into a mission field, does our brother believe that he is no longer in the body of Christ? If yes, will he indicate to us how one may get into Christ's spiritual body except by baptism? (1 Corinthians 12:13.) He evidently believes that one is not a member of the church when thus isolated:

"He feels that even though the 'type' or 'kind' of organization is universal it is applicable only to the local assembly and that the church is no larger than the local assembly . . . That the local assembly being the largest unit in the organization and thus, while members of other congregations are brothers in Christ, they are of different assemblies and can in no way participate in any activity that the officers of another assembly propose . . . That a Christian is not a member of the church unless he is a part of a local congregation, assembly."

Our brother has thus espoused the Baptist view of the church, as to organization or structure. Said J.M. Pendleton: "The *Baptist Church of the United States* is a phrase which ought never to be used—which can never be used with propriety. There are thousands of Baptist Churches in the United States, but they do not constitute one great Baptist Church of the United States." ("Three Reasons Why I am a Baptist," p. 133.) It is on the ground which our brother alleges ("while members of other congregations are brothers in Christ, they are of different assemblies and can in no way participate in any activity that the officers of another assembly propose"), that the Baptists defend the doctrine of closed communion. Does our brother object to the comparison, on the ground that the Lord originated the supper, and not "the officers" of an assembly? We answer: The Lord authorized every function in which Christians may properly participate in the congregation. The observation, "A Christian is not a member of the church unless he is a part of a local congregation (assembly)," hardly needs notice, and collapses of its own weight before those who have any well-defined concept of New Testament teaching concerning the church. We hardly think John, while exiled on Patmos and "in the Spirit on the Lord's day," was not in the church, or body, of Christ, wherein are all spiritual blessings, including salvation! (Ephesians 5:23; Revelation 1:10.)

"The word 'church' . . . sometimes means the general spiritual body over which Jesus is the head and in which every Christian is a member. (Matthew 16:18; Colossians 1:18,24; Ephesians 1:22.)"—F.D. Srygley, "The New Testament Church," p. 7.

" 'Church' . . . is also very often applied to the whole body or aggregate of the faithful."—Alexander Campbell.

"It should be noticed that the term church, or congregation is here applied so as to include all the disciples in these three districts, the region of our Saviour's personal labors. It is a secondary use of the word, the whole body being contemplated as if congregated together."— J.W. McGarvey, "New Commentary on Acts," at Acts 9:31.

" 'Church' is used in the strictly local sense in Acts 8:1,3 . . . and in the general spiritual sense in Matthew 16:18."—Boles, "Commentary on the Acts," pp. 153,154.

ADDENDA

Nothing we have written or said at any time justifies the conclusion that Christ does not exercise headship over the congregation. Being the head of the body he, of course, is the head of all that which constitutes the body. The body of Christ, in scriptural parlance, is, however, the sum of the saved—the church in the aggregate—and is one. (Ephesians 4:4.)

"What is your opinion of the Hardeman-Boswell Discussion?"

The greatest debate ever held on the use of mechanical instruments of music in worship, was conducted in the huge Ryman Auditorium, Nashville, Tenn., May 31-June 5, 1923. The disputants were N.B. Hardeman, representing the churches of Christ; and Ira M. Boswell, of the Christian Church. There were five sessions of the debate; each session was of two hours' length; and from six to seven thousand people were in attendance at each of the sessions.

79

F.B. Srygley, who wrote the introduction to the published debate, says, "There was, perhaps, more interest shown in this debate, especially by those who do not use the instrument of music in worship, than has been shown over the discussion of any other religious question which has ever been held in the city of Nashville."

Dr. Boswell, who attempted to defend the use of such instruments in Christian worship, represented the highest type of scholarship available to those whom he defended. He came to Nashville with a great array of scholarly evidence, the design of which was to show that the Greek word *psallo*, translated "make melody" in Ephesians 5:19, includes the idea of an instrument.

Brother Hardeman gave a brief resume of the word, traced its history through the centuries and showed that it once signified the twanging of a bowstring, then the twitching of a carpenter's line, later the touching of the strings of an instrument; and, finally, in the New Testament, *to sing.* He conceded that, metaphorically, the instrument is in the word. Then said he, "But the question tonight, and the only one for consideration, is: What, under the New Testament, is the instrument that accompanies the singing? The apostle Paul, in his peerless announcement, settled that once for all. He says we are to sing unto the Lord and *'psallo'* with the heart—not with the fingers, not with the plectron, but with the heart; and, therefore, the heart is the instrument that accompanies the singing." (Page 43.)

The effect of this, in the Boswell camp, was nothing short of catastrophic. Rendered utterly useless was the vast array of Lexicographical evidence designed to prove what no one questioned—that *psallo* had, in ages past, embodies a number of meanings, one of which included the plucking of the strings of an instrument. With irresistible logic Brother Hardeman said, "The word *psallo*, like the word *baptizo* carries with it always the idea of pluck or twang an instrument. No question about that. The point at issue with us is: What is the instrument as used in the New Testament? The word *'baptizo'* doesn't carry the precise instrument with it. It might be a baptism of the Holy Ghost; it might be immersion of suffering; it might be a baptism of fire. The precise element used in baptizing must be learned from the context. Just so with reference to *'psallo.'* The idea of pluck or twang the instrument is in the word, but the precise instrument that is necessary to the fulfillment of it in each case depends on the context. If you refer to the hair, the hair becomes the instrument; if you refer to the bowstring, the bowstring is the instrument. But in the New Testament, when you refer to singing, God said the heart is the instrument; and that is the position, if you please, that the word demands tonight." (Pages 57,58.)

From this logical and irresistible approach Boswell retreated in obvious and conscious defeat. Pathetically, he continued to use his prepared material to prove what no one doubted; and he continued to disregard, because he could not answer, Brother Hardeman's sole contention—the instrument is not in the word, the word does not designate the type or kind of stringed instrument, which must always be supplied; and, in the New Testament Paul declares that the instrument is the heart.

In corroboration of this, Brother Hardeman produced lexical evidence of the highest type that the word *"psallo,"* in the New Testament means simply *to sing*. (So Thayer, Bagster, Sophocles, etc.) Even more significant, the 47 scholars who gave to the English-speaking world the most influential translation ever published (perhaps, ever shall be) in our tongue (the King James' translation), excluded the idea of a literal mechanical instrument, rendering the word, "make melody." Nearly 300 years later, the 100 scholars who gave the world the Revised Version, generally conceded to be the most accurate translation into the English tongue ever made, saw no reason to dissent from their illustrious predecessors. And, commented Brother Hardeman: "Most of these belonged to churches which use mechanical instruments; and yet when they rely upon their scholarship, they translated *'psallo'* to sing to make melody in our hearts!"

The impact of this debate in Nashville and Middle Tennessee was far-reaching. Today the Christian Church, in this area, has drifted farther and farther away from the Bible and toward *modernism* until its constituents have lost practically all regard for, and knowledge of, the Restoration movement, while more than 100 churches of Christ in the Nashville area alone, continue to advocate a pure faith and faultless practice in all matters religious.

The "Hardeman-Boswell Discussion" is an indispensable handbook to those who would acquaint themselves with the issues involved in the use of instrumental music in the worship.

"Discuss the 'jot' and 'tittle.' "

Jesus said: "Till heaven and earth pass away, one jot or one tittle shall in no wise pass away from the law, till all things be accomplished." (Matthew 5:18.) The law was designed to escort the Jews unto Christ: "Wherefore the law was our schoolmaster to bring us unto Christ, that we might be justified by faith. But after that faith is come, we are no longer under a schoolmaster." (Galatians 3:24,25.) The "schoolmaster" (Greek, *paidagoogos*) was not an instructor, but a person, usually a slave or freedman, to whom the boys of a family were committed, whose duty it was to conduct them from and to the schoolroom, exercising at all times superintendence over their conduct and safety. Without doing violence to the apostle's argument, we may paraphrase thus: "Wherefore the law was our (the Jews') school bus driver to bring us (the Jews) to Christ." Having escorted the Jews to Christ, it had accomplished its purpose and was removed. (Colossians 2:14-17.) Before it had done this, heaven and earth would sooner pass than its most insignificant portion. Though these words were spoken of the law which came from Sinai, the principle is applicable to all of his word.

The "jot" is the Hebrew letter *yod*, the smallest in the Hebraic alphabet. The "tittle" (Greek, *keraia*) is the hornlike projection, or apex, which is used to distinguish Hebrew letters, which greatly resemble each other. Several of the Hebrew letters (*beth* and *caph*, *cheth* and *he*, *resh* and *daleth*, for example) differ only in the slightest degree, the difference being indicated by the use of the "tittle"; and to disregard these slight, but highly significant, markings is to alter radically the meaning of many words and sentences. As an example, consider the Hebrew words *chalal* and *halal*. These words differ only in their first letters. *Ch* in Hebrew is expressed by one letter, even a *h*, the only difference being a very slight break in the left limb of the latter. To appreciate how slight the difference is between these letters, take a pencil and draw a short line from left to right, make a right angle, and extend the line downward until it is about one-fourth longer than the line it meets at a right angle. Next, place your pencil just under the point where you first began to extend the horizontal line, leaving only the very smallest space; draw it to a point equal in distance to the perpendicular line on the right. This is the Hebrew *h* (*he*, pronounced *hay*). To make the *ch* (*cheth*), draw another letter identical with that just drawn, and *close up the slight opening*. This is the difference between these two letters. The point used to close up the space is the tittle. (Any good dictionary, under the word "Alphabet," will list the Hebrew characters. The *he* is the fifth letter; the *cheth*, the eighth.) Such is the difference between the words *chalal* and *halal*. A variation too trifling to notice in our alphabet; and yet let the line be broken where it should be continuous, and "Thou shalt not profane the name of thy God" becomes "Thou shalt not praise the name of thy God"! (Leviticus 18:21.)

The Hebrew daleth is a horizontal line and a perpendicular line meeting at a right angle, the horizontal line being drawn a bit heavier than the other. The letter *resh* is very similar, differing only in the lines meeting in an arc, instead of a right angle. Yet let the latter be changed into the former, and Exodus 34:14, which reads, "Thou shalt worship no other God," becomes "Thou shalt not worship the only God." The *beth* and *caph* differ only in that one has square corners and the other slightly rounded ones; yet if the latter is changed into the former, 1 Samuel 2:2 reads, "There is no holiness in the Lord," instead of "There is none holy as the Lord." The Old Testament abounds with instances of such. This demonstrates how indissoluble are the thoughts and the words of the Sacred Writings, and that whatever affects the one, imperils the other. The adage, "The bottles are not the wine; but if the bottle perish, the wine is sure to be spilled," finds apt illustration here.

"Explain Nehemiah 8:8."

For 51 years the people of Judah languished in Babylon, while their land lay desolate from the ravages of war and the depredations of their conquerors. When Babylon was no more, contingents of them were allowed to go back to begin the work of restoration. Among the leaders was Ezra, a scribe. Determined to bring vividly to the consciousness of the people their obligations to Jehovah, he arranged for a public reading of the law, an account of which may be seen in Nehemiah 8:1-8. Numerous ones assisted him in the reading, and the manner in which it was done is thus designated by the sacred historian: "So they read in the book in the law of God distinctly, and gave the sense, and caused them to understand the reading." (Nehemiah 8:8.) Here is a perfect pattern for all who propose to preach and to teach the word. (1) They read; (2) they read in the book in the law of God; (3) they read distinctly; (4) they gave the sense; (5) they caused the people to understand the reading.

(1) To read well is indeed a rare achievement. Any teacher or preacher who reads well, instantly attracts attention and holds the interest of his hearers. To be able "to add to the beauty of" the text "the rhythm of the voice" is a goal well worth striving for. The great Jewish rabbis insisted on their pupils reading aloud, because such reading is a powerful aid to mental retentiveness. Reading aloud helps the listener to understand the text. A monotonous, singsong, artificial reading deprives the word of its meaning and prompts the mind to wander fruitlessly away.

(2) They read in the book in the law of God. However skilled the reader, if that which is being read is ephemeral and worthless, no value is derived. He who presumes to bring to people the bread of life sustains a solemn obligation to be able to discern between bread and a stone. While people perish is not time to dally with the trivia of life.

(3) Ezra's compatriots not only read, and read from the law of God; they also read distinctly. Impressed with the weighty responsibility that was theirs, the words of the text were pronounced soberly, pointedly, distinctly.

(4) Further, they gave the sense—they explained the significance of that which they read, and expounded the vital truth which God had given. To be able to open up the truth of God's word and bring from it treasures both new and old is surely life's greatest achievement. Much

of the Scripture we may grasp without help. Every fundamental duty of man is set forth with such clarity that the intelligence which establishes responsibility is all that is necessary to understand it. These facts, like air and light and water, are available to us, and may be had without help. But just as there are many things in the material realm which can be seen only with a telescope or microscope, so there are depths and beauties and powers and blessings only an experienced interpreter can point out. Occasionally we find a book which makes portions of the text sparkle with great brilliance where before our unaided eyes caught only a feeble gleam. Every once in a while this writer reads interpretations of the text which open up vast fields of hitherto undreamed possibilities in the Sacred Volume.

(5) Finally, Ezra's readers caused the people to understand the reading. Here is the apex, the ultimate goal, the only design of all teaching and preaching. Unless this be achieved, the time is lost, the effort useless. Much of that which parades under the guise of teaching is far short of it. We teach only when people learn. Unless instruction is actually imparted, and edification results, whatever the effort may be designated, it is not teaching. Learning is an essential correlative to teaching. When one is absent, the other is nonexistent.

"Is the Bible no longer reliable?"

The following heart-breaking letter describes a situation which is becoming increasingly prevalent over the land.

I find myself faced with a situation that is very confusing and frustrating to me. I have been a Christian and a member of the church of Christ for about 30 years. I have never had any doubt about what I have been taught and what I believe until now. I purchased a set of commentaries, published by the Gospel Advocate Company, about 15 years ago and have used them in my Bible study.

Now my preacher and elders are telling me some things in the Bible have changed because of growth in knowledge. My preacher talks of the direct operation of the Holy Spirit. They believe that Christians reach a point in life, if they are walking in the light, that you do not have to pray for the forgiveness of sins. They say because of the continual cleansing of the blood of Jesus, we cannot fall from grace, but since we cannot be perfect Jesus will make up the difference. I do not really understand all of this, but I know it does not agree with what I believe the Bible teaches.

Does the Bible change as time goes on and people supposedly learn more?

Our elders told us we can believe as we do and they can believe as they do and we can still worship together. Is this possible? Is it doctrine that is in question? They are teaching what they believe as truth. We have two young boys. Should we allow them to be taught, by the church, something different than what we believe? Do you still believe the Bible says the same as it did when you wrote your commentary on Peter, John and Jude? These things my church leaders are teaching are causing me much anguish. I would appreciate any comments you would care to make. I need help in this situation.

My heart overflows with sympathy for this precious sister who is desperately seeking to save her faith, and that of her children, from attacks on truth by the very men who ought to be her first line of defense against every form of unbelief—her preacher and elders! She has been a Christian for 30 years; throughout this long period she has implicitly believed the sacred writings and has entertained no doubt whatsoever regarding the truth of the matters of which she writes; and, now, she finds these matters under assault by those allegedly guardians of the faith and proclaimers of the truth! The preacher and the elders.

By what means do they attempt to justify their abandonment of things once surely believed among us? We are now in possession of information which enables us to know that some things we once believed to be taught in the scriptures are not true: specifically, with reference to grace, forgiveness, justification and the security of those affecting salvation, they have informed the sister. Their claim is positively, palpably, clearly and unmistakably false.

It is very likely that what they are trying to say is that advances in textual criticism now admit of a more accurate text than was possible when the King James' translation was produced. Were such so, this would have absolutely nothing to do with what the scriptures teach regarding the mode of operation of the Holy Spirit, the manner and extent of his indwelling, and the means by which he influences people either in, or out, of the church today; the doctrine of grace, or the conditions of forgiveness and the possibility or non-possibility of falling away from the grace of God, inasmuch as these matters do not involve questions of textual criticism but interpretations of unquestioned texts. Were their lives to depend on it, these men could not produce any evidence whatsoever tending to show that the views long held by our people are no longer valid. And, with reference to the accuracy of the text on which the older translations rest, there is a want of candor (a better word would perhaps be honesty) in the allegation that textual studies have brought to light considerable information regarding the meaning of much of the New Testament. This is simply not so. Increased knowledge in that field has to do largely with spelling, order of words, confirmation of texts and other principal inconsequential matters; in not one instance—not one—has new light been shed on any fundamental matter involving either directly, or indirectly, our salvation here, or hereafter. Not infrequently, brethren today seek to defend "modern speech" translations with the allegation that the means available today to produce translations are vastly superior to those of earlier days. On what one must do to be saved? On how to worship God acceptably? On how to live the Christian life? Our scholarly brethren who write learnedly about our "growth in knowledge" ought to be candid in their appraisal of such matters and to see to it that they do not unjustly reflect on translations which will be responsible for populating heaven more than all "modern speech" versions put together.

The preacher of whom the sister writes "talks of the direct operation of the Holy Spirit." It is my observation that one's respect for what the New Testament says diminishes in exact ratio to the extent that one believes the Spirit operates apart from the word of truth. Such a view is essentially a repudiation of what the Spirit has said through the word. It is not surprising that with such a view of the Holy Spirit prevailing that "the preacher and the elders" should seek to impute error to those who have not experienced the "growth in knowledge" they affect.

The preacher and elders are also in gross error regarding 1 John 1:7-9. It is indeed true that those who "keep on walking in the light" the blood of Jesus "keeps on cleansing from all sin," but to walk in the light means to conform to the teaching of the New Testament which requires (a) confession, (b) evidence of penitence and (c) prayer. (1 John 1:9; James 5:16; 2 Corinthians 2:6-8.) Any sin consciously committed will be forgiven only on the basis of a penitent heart and a petition to God. The teaching, that there is imputed to us the righteousness of Christ and that this makes it impossible for us to fall away from the grace of God so as finally to be lost is pure and unadulterated Calvinism and the preacher and elders who advocate these views have abandoned New Testament teaching for denominational theology. It is not "growth in knowledge" which prompts such views; their espousal is possible only when true knowledge is forsaken for error. There is nothing new or knowledgeable about such views; Baptist preachers, even those of most elementary knowledge, have been preaching them for the past 100 years.

The doctrines being taught as described by our distressed sister are grave and dangerous. She is fully justified in being concerned whether her sons should be subjected to it. She writes from a mid-Western city with several faithful congregations and numerous sound gospel preachers. She should immediately identify herself with a congregation where the scriptures are respected, the truth is taught, and error is denounced—not embraced.

Yes, I believe the Bible to be just as true now as when I wrote the commentary on Peter, John and Jude. And, it will be just as true, and just as reliable from now to the end of the age as it was when first penned; and by its infallible standard will we be judged. To its teaching we must adhere without deviation if at the end of the age we are to receive its promises. "All flesh is as grass, and all the glory thereof as the flower of grass. The grass withereth, the flower falleth: but the word of the Lord abideth for ever." (1 Peter 1:24.)

"Define the words 'death,' 'perish,' and 'destroy' as used in the Bible."

A brother writes that he would appreciate an article "on the meaning of the words that are translated *death, perish*, and *destroy*" in the sacred writings, and suggests that such a study would be of benefit to those who "from time to time must confront 'Jehovah's Witnesses,' 'Christadelphians,' and others who have been taught that the wicked will not be punished eternally."

Our correspondent is correct in the assumption that much of the effectiveness of these people and other materialistic religious groups in the propagation of their peculiar and distinctive doctrines stems from gross misuse of these words and other similar terms. It is characteristic of the people of these sects to talk long and learnedly regarding death, destruction, perdition, and the soul, assign an arbitrary meaning to them, and to their Hebrew and Greek originals, and thereupon deduce the doctrine of no eternal retribution for the finally impenitent. Such efforts are frequently productive of much deception, since the average person, unschooled in the use of these terms in the Bible, and particularly the words from which they are translated, is unable to follow them in their devious excursions into the field of semantics.

It is the allegation of such theologians that the ultimate penalty of all disobedience unrepented of at the termination of one's earthly sojourn is death; and, death, they define to be simply and solely non-existence. Clearly, if one ceases to exist, one is not subject to constant and continuous suffering through eternity. It is very true that the penalty proscribed for those dying in sin is the "second death" (Revelation 2:11; 20:14; 21:8); as eternal life is assured the faithful, so its opposite, eternal death is the inevitable destiny of the wicked (Galatians 6:8); but, it is far from true that the death thus threatened is no more than, or consists of, non-existence. Such a conclusion may be reached, as we shall later see, only by an abandonment of reason and

87

revelation, logic and language and by the adoption of an arbitrary lexicon and glossary. This is, indeed, precisely what materialists have done. There is not the semblance of support of their positions in proper lexicography or the Bible; and, our experience in dealing with those of this persuasion is that they ordinarily exhibit little regard for either when their pretensions are exposed to light.

Death, etymologically and in contextual significance, is separation; such is its basic meaning; whether figuratively or literally used this aspect is always dominant. The word, in the New Testament, is *than-atos*, and this, too, is the rendering of the Hebrew words *muth* and *maveth* by the Seventy in the Septuagint (Greek) translation of the Old Testament scriptures. Mr. Thayer, in his Greek Lexicon, says: "Prop. the death of the body, i.e., that separation (whether natural or violent) of the soul from the body by which the life on earth is ended." Thus, physical death involves separation of soul and body; figurative uses include spiritual death—the separation of the individual from God; the second death, separation of the individual from the fullness of joy to be experienced by those in possession of eternal life.

It is most significant that the phrase, eternal life, occurring nearly four dozen times in the New Testament, never suggests mere existence, but always the inexpressible joy of association with God and all that is good; so its opposite, eternal death, never denotes mere non-existence, but always separation from, and the loss of, heaven and all that it means. Our Lord promised us an hundredfold here; and, in the life to come eternal life; if, therefore, life is no more than existence, as materialists urge, he offers us less in heaven than we have here, since we have both existence and a hundredfold here, but only existence there! (Mark 10:29,30.) As eternal life is synonymous of unending happiness, so eternal death denotes ceaseless misery. This is, indeed, clearly suggested in words which declare characteristics of the place prepared for the wicked: "And they shall be tormented day and night for ever and ever." (Revelation 20:10.) Consciousness is an essential element of torment or misery. It is not possible to torment an unconscious or a non-existent person. The torment is to last forever; therefore the one tormented must endue forever. Only those who are conscious can be tormented. The torment is to continue forever. Therefore, the consciousness of the one tormented must be forever. From this irresistible conclusion there is no escape. If one is to regard reason as a safe guide and if any confidence may be placed in the affirmations of sacred writ whatsoever, it is idle to deny these considerations.

There appears to have been a studied effort by the Holy Spirit to establish the duration of punishment in a manner beyond cavil. The adjective used to denote the duration of the enjoyment of the righteous in heaven is the same as that which designates the period which shall characterize the wicked in the hell of fire. "But these shall go away into eternal (*aioonios*) punishment: but the righteous into eternal (*aioonios*) life." (Matthew 25:46.) It is idle to seek an avoidance of this by the ridiculous device of attempting to distinguish between punishing and punishment. These variations are verbal and grammatical; they do not differ in sense. As a matter of fact, Webster's New World Dictionary defines punishment as "a punishing or being punished;" and the Collegiate Dictionary gives, as its first definition, "act of punishing." In neither is there the remotest support for the view that punishment is a state of non-existence resulting from annihilation. Nor does the Greek word (*kolasis*) lend the least encourage to such a position. Thayer points out that the word denotes correction, penalty, punishment; and Moulton and Milligan, in their monumental work on the Greek Papyri, cite an instance where the following sentence occurs: "For the evil-doers among men receive their reward not among the living only, but also await punishment and much torment." Here, the word for punishment is *kolasis*, the same as that which describes the status of the wicked following the judgment.

But, do not the scriptures affirm that the wicked shall *perish, be consumed,* suffer *destruction*? Yes. Do not these words denote annihilation? No! *Perish,* in the Old Testament, is translated from the Hebrew *abad,* often occurring in the Hebrew scriptures to describe that which is ruined, dispersed, laid waste, destroyed. It also means to stray, to wander, to be lost. David said, "The wicked *shall perish* at the presence of God." (Psalm 68:2.) The verb *shall perish* is third person plural, masculine gender of the word *abad* in the *kal* conjunction. It occurs, in the same conjugation, in Deuteronomy 4:26, where Moses warned Israel that she would "utterly perish (*abad*) from off the land whereunto ye go over the Jordan to possess it; ye shall not prolong your days upon it, but shall utterly be destroyed. And Jehovah will scatter you among the peoples, and ye shall be left few among the nations . . ." Though Israel would "utterly perish," and "be destroyed," from off the land whither she was journeying, this did not mean that the people were to suffer annihilation and become non-existent; on the contrary, they were to be scattered among the nations about them. Ruin, destruction, dispersion would be theirs; they would, however, continue to exist, and to suffer the consequences attending their subjugation by the heathen. This, indeed, is a vital lesson of history often cited by the sacred writers to impress us with the importance of faithfulness. Israel perished from off earthly Canaan because of her wickedness, and infidelity to God; we are often warned that similar conduct will result in our exclusion from the heavenly Canaan. And, as Israel did not cease to exist, though separated from the land of promise, but continued to suffer greatly for her folly, so will those who come short of the glory of God, and are thereby excluded from the heavenly realms, continue to exist and to endure the torments of the damned forever and ever.

Greek words, often cited by materialists from the original text of the New Testament, are *apollumi, apooleia* and *olethros,* rendered by such terms as damnation, destruction, perdition, etc., in translation. None of these terms, or any others they might cite, support the view of annihilation. More than two dozen times *apollumi* is translated by the word lose or some form thereof. The sheep of the parable (Luke 15:3-7), was *lost,* but had not ceased to exist. Jesus came to seek and to save the lost (a form of the same word denoting, in other passages, that which is damned, destroyed, etc.), but the world of sinful men he came to save had not ceased to be. "Jehovah's Witnesses," Adventists, Christadelphians, and all other annihilationists err greatly in their attempts to assign to these terms the significance of non-existence.

If death is simply and solely becoming non-existent; and, if all the punishment awaiting the wicked is annihilation, it follows that the martyrs who suffered death by fire experienced the same suffering as that which awaits the most wicked. Birds, beasts, living things which die in fire suffer the same "punishment" as that of the wicked corrupt outcast. Moreover, it is possible, under such an hypothesis, for one man to administer eternal punishment to another, since one can, and sometimes does, destroy the life of another by fire. Yet, Jesus said, "And be not afraid of them that kill the body, but are not able to kill the soul: rather fear him who is able to destroy both soul and body in hell." (Matthew 10:28.) Here, the *soul* and *body* are clearly distinguishable; one is susceptible of destruction (ruin) at the hands of men; the other, only by the Lord. It follows, therefore, that when one man burns another there is that which escapes the destruction of the body.

"What is fellowship? To whom may it properly be offered, and from whom should it be withheld? Is its sphere limited to one local congregation, or is it a relationship in the body of Christ, and as extended as the church itself?"

The word "fellowship," is the translation of the Greek word *koinoonia,* defined by the lexicographers as "the share which one has in anything; participation," instances of such are in Philippians 2:1, 3:10; 1 Corinthians 1:9, 10:16; 2 Corinthians 8:4, 13:13; and Ephesians 3:9; "a common interest and intimacy of association," Acts 2:42; 2 Corinthians 6:14; Galatians 2:9; Philippians 1:5; 1 John 1:3,6,7; "Collection, contribution," 2 Corinthians 8:4, 9:13; Romans 15:26; Hebrews 13:16. These instances fully reflect the usage of the term in noun form in the New Testament. These passages reveal that there is fellowship with the Holy Spirit, with the sufferings of Christ, in a common faith in the church, with the body and blood of Christ in the communion; a sharing of responsibility toward those in need, and a warm and intimate union with the Father and the Son, in a common relationship which includes all faithful Christians.

An induction of the verses where this word appears clearly evidences its sphere and scope, and shows that it extends far beyond the limits of any local congregation and embraces all who are in the body of Christ. Paul, in a distant mission field, was in fellowship with the church in Philippi (Philippians 1:5), and the churches of Macedonia are specifically said to have sustained this relationship with Judean saints. (2 Corinthians 8:4; Romans 15:25). All Christians are to be partakers of the same mind as God and Christ, and of all the blessings issuing from them. That which can be offered, may also be withheld; any effort, therefore, to limit or restrict fellowship to the confines of one congregation is a form of "closed communion," resulting from fallacious reasoning and improper deductions not supported in the premises.

Were this incredible concept correct, the saints would be compelled to stand helplessly by and watch the people of God seduced, deluded and led astray by a heretical teacher, so long as he did not place membership in the congregation he seeks to deceive! The church could not mark him (Romans 16:17), identify him before the congregation (3 John 9), nor expose him as a false and designing teacher to be avoided (2 Timothy 3:8, 9.) The argument confuses membership with fellowship; and it derives from the false assumptions that it is (1) the exclusive prerogative of elders to exercise discipline in the church, and (2) the limits of such action is the local congregation.

It is not correct to conclude that "the other party" of 1 Corinthians 5 was not disciplined by the church in Corinth because she was not a member of the congregation, and therefore not answerable to the elders, but because she was not a Christian and never had been! This, Paul made clear, when he wrote: "For what have I to do to judge them also that are without? Do not ye judge them that are within?" (vv. 12,13.) The object of discipline, the apostle points out, is "Any man that is called a brother ..." (v. 11.) The distinction is thus not between a brother "within" and an erring brother "without" the congregation, but between a brother and an alien sinner never in the family of God. It seems especially incredible to the writer of these lines that any one could seriously believe that the "wicked person" of this chapter could have effectively removed himself from the disciplinary action of Paul and the church in Corinth by simply announcing that he no longer considered himself a member of the church in Corinth!

Let it be carefully noted that it was the church in Corinth, in her collective capacity—and not her elders, as such, who was by apostolic edict to deliver the erring one over to Satan. (1 Corinthians 5:3-5, 13.)

The elders would, of course, participate as members of the congregation in this action, but not in their "official" capacity, as elders. If to this the objection is offered that the church was to do this through its elders, this conclusion may easily be seen to be erroneous in the fact that each member had tolerated the unseemly condition prevailing, had, indeed, sought to justify it and was thus at fault from having failed individually to "put away" the "wicked person." The alternative to this conclusion is that only the elders were to avoid eating with the apostate brother, and any other social and fraternal relationship with the guilty one, while the rest of the congregation might merrily continue their brotherly contacts with the incestuous man with impunity!

The persuasion that one may avoid discipline by withdrawing one's membership from the congregation is in conflict with the scriptures because it assumes that fellowship is no more than a congregational relationship, and that it terminates at the congregational level. Were this so, an ungodly person, faced with imminent discipline, might simply announce his withdrawal from the congregation and thenceforth defy the church to act. Does any reader seriously think that one may thwart the plan of God for his church in this cavalier fashion? The analogy of the irrevocable relationship of a child to his father is indeed apropos; the father may disinherit his offspring, but the child can never escape the fact of biological relationship. The attempt to compare the situation to "an eighteen-year-old child" who decides to abandon the family and is no longer subject to the "rules and regulations" of the family is quite obviously not analogous because God—not the family (the church)—makes the rules and one cannot take himself out of the divine jurisdiction! Human institutions, such as the Masonic Lodge and the Odd Fellows fraternity, may extend their rules only to those who submit thereto; one in the body of Christ may no more renounce his sonship than he can resign from the human race! Apostates are not rebaptized when they repent. The only way out for the wicked person is when the Lord spews him out of his mouth at the Last Great Day. (Revelation 3:16.) Moreover, non-attendance, teaching and conduct of either a moral or doctrinal nature does not place the guilty party beyond the influence of other Christians in the community. The apostolic decree is, "Now we command you, brethren, in the name of our Lord Jesus Christ, that ye withdraw yourselves from every brother that walketh disorderly . . . (2 Thessalonians 3:6.) The "disorderly" are the *atakoos,* from *a* privative, and *tassoo,* to place, thus, out of place,— the position of one who is not walking in step with the people of God in the community. To equate the position herein set out with the doctrine of "once saved, always saved," is surely something more than absurd. This injunction, to all the saints in Thessalonica, included "every brother" out of step, whether acknowledging membership in the congregation, or not.

Finally, where is the remotest hint in the sacred writings that one, faced with discipline, may avoid it by withdrawing from the congregation? (The transfer of membership, in good standing and with the approval of the congregation is not remotely related to the type of withdrawal hereinbefore considered.) The conclusion the brother draws that this would mean that elders would have jurisdiction over those walking disorderly in other congregations is a non sequitur, because (a) disfellowshiping is a function of each member of the congregation (elders merely determine that disfellowship is necessary and appropriate, and the notice to the congregation they serve to this end is merely the announcement of intention to withdraw—not the withdrawal itself); and (b) it is indeed the function of Christians to declare nonfellowship with any person, anywhere who is walking disorderly, when such action is necessary to protect the purity and the integrity of the church. Strange indeed is the reasoning which would justify a warning to the members of congregation "A" in Nashville that John Doe, a factious member of "A" is teaching false and dangerous doctrine and should be avoided, and not be able to warn the congregation of the efforts of Richard Roe in congregation "B" who is propagating the same fatal doctrines.

We believe that the attempt to justify avoidance of discipline in this fashion is wrong, hurtful to the cause of Christ, and if accepted, will put an end to any effective discipline in the churches of Christ, the effort itself being sinful, the attempt to avoid discipline by this evasive act adds sin to sin—sadly providing another reason for disciplinary action.

David Lipscomb and E. G. Sewell edited the GOSPEL ADVOCATE for fifty years. In response to the question, "Is it right for an elder, and a minister of the word, to fall out with a part of the members of the church to which he belongs and withdraw his name from the congregation," brother Lipscomb wrote, "There is nothing more plainly taught in the Bible than that the church, the individual congregations at Corinth, at Thessalonica, at Ephesus, constituted the body of Christ, and the individual members were parts of this body. To withdraw from this body was to withdraw from Christ. The idea that a man can be a member of Christ, can be in Christ, and yet in no congregation or body of Christ is an idea that has no foundation in the Bible." Brother Sewell, when asked if a member who requested permission "to withdraw from the congregation" because the majority of the members had turned against him and his wife, replied, "We have no scriptural example of anything like the above. Where one individual complains of a whole congregation, we very naturally suppose that he is wrong himself. It very rarely occurs that a whole congregation will array itself against all the efforts of one of its own members. We have not known an instance of the kind. The probabilities are that the above-named member is either morbidly sensitive and suspicious of his brethren or he is in some way radically wrong himself and they do not wish to encourage him in his wrong course. . . . If in such a case a member withdraws, he withdraws from the church of God and ought not to be recognized as a Christian by any congregation till he mends his ways. And, moreover, when a member gets wrong and all gospel means fail to get him right, the congregation where he belongs, instead of allowing him to withdraw from them as in good standing, ought to withdraw from him for walking disorderly."

"Election—is it conditional or unconditional?"

Calvinist Confessions of Faith teach that all things, whether good or bad, whether great or small, whether involving angels or men, were, from all eternity, unchangeably determined, and must therefore unalterably come to pass. These religious standards declare that the election of some, and the damnation of others, are without regard to faith and obedience on the one hand, or unbelief and disobedience on the other. It is alleged that this election and reprobation are irrevocable, unconditional and personal, and that the Scriptures so teach. Two passages, in particular, are frequently cited in support of the foregoing conclusion.

"Elect . . . according to the foreknowledge of God the Father. . . ." (1 Peter 1:1,2.) "For whom he foreknew, he also foreordained to be conformed to the image of his Son. . . ." (Romans 8:29.) "Elect" is from *eklegoo,* a word signifying to choose or to select. A verb form of the word is translated "choose" in John 15:16, "chose" in Ephesians 1:4, and "have chosen" in John 13:18. "Foreknowledge" is from the Greek *prognosis,* which means previous determination, or purpose. Those to whom Peter penned his epistle were indeed chosen people, selected by a definite exercise of the divine will, and in keeping with a purpose earlier formed. Was this purpose or plan *conditional* or *unconditional?*

First Peter 1:1 reads in full: "Peter, an apostle of Jesus Christ, to the elect who are sojourners of the Dispersion in Pontus, Galatia, Cappadocia, Asia, and Bithynia, according to the foreknowledge of God the Father, in sanctification of the Spirit, unto obedience and sprinkling of the blood of Jesus Christ." An election is indeed affirmed here; but, it differs widely from that characteristic of the Calvinist creed. Here, election is said to extend to those who are sanctified by the Spirit and who believe the truth. That which is sanctified is set apart, separated to special purpose. We thus learn that it is the function of the Holy

Spirit, in election, to separate the sinner to the sphere where, through obedience and sprinkling of the blood of Christ, he is constituted a chosen or elected one. This the Spirit accomplishes by revealing, through the Word of truth, the means whereby one obeys the Lord and is therefore enabled to appropriate to one's self the benefits of the blood. Moreover, if election occurs through "sanctification of the Spirit," which leads to the belief of the truth, such election cannot take place until such sanctification and belief occur. It must follow, therefore, that since one does not believe from all eternity, one is not elected from all eternity!

It should be observed that 1 Peter 1:1 asserts the *fact* of election in the purpose and plan of God; the *manner* by which such is achieved is through "obedience" and the "sprinkling of the blood of Christ." "Unto obedience" indicates the human side of salvation; "sprinkling of the blood of Jesus Christ," the divine. The prepositions in the Greek text of 1 Peter 1:1 are significant and edifying: Election is "according to" (*kata*) the purpose and plan of God; it is "in" (*en*) the sphere of the Spirit's influence; and it is "unto" (*eis*), i.e., it is designed to produce obedience. In election, the Father chooses, the Spirit sanctifies, and the Son, by his blood, redeems. The alien sinner appropriates the blessings of election through "sanctification of the Spirit, and belief of the truth."

Even more directly Paul emphasizes these matters in 2 Thessalonians 2:13,14: "But we are bound to give thanks to God always for you, brethren beloved of the Lord, for that God chose you from the beginning unto salvation in sanctification of the Spirit and belief of the truth: whereunto he called you through our gospel, to the obtaining of the glory of our Lord Jesus Christ." From this clear statement of election we learn: (1) God "chose" us. (2) He chose "from the beginning." (3) The choice was made "in sanctification of the Spirit and belief of the truth." Those thus chosen were "called" by the gospel. (4) The gospel is addressed to all men. (Matthew 28:18-20; Mark 16:15,16.) (5) All who believe and obey the gospel are saved. (6) But, God chooses (elects) those who are saved. (7) Therefore, God chooses or elects to salvation all those who obey the gospel!

The thoughtful reader will easily discern that election extends to *character,* and not to *individuals.* God has ordained, "from the beginning," that those possessed of a certain disposition or character are elected to salvation; those who submit their wills to him, in obedience to the gospel, possess this disposition; therefore, those who obey his will are elected.

The theory of an arbitrary selection without regard to character is repulsive to reason and revelation. (1) It conflicts with all scriptures which plainly assert the conditionality of salvation (e.g., Matthew 7:21; Luke 13:3; Acts 17:30; 2 Thessalonians 1:7-9; 1 John 2:4). (2) It pictures God as a cruel and arbitrary sovereign acting by caprice and not by the

95

principles of justice and righteousness. (3) It nullifies all human responsibility, and reduces man to the status of a puppet, unworthy of commendation for any good he may do, and deserving of no condemnation for any evil he practices. (4) All promises, warnings, invitations, threatenings, and admonitions to the faithfulness to the Word of God, become meaningless, and without significance. (5) Such a concept makes God the author of sin, and utterly destroys the free agency of men.

Some years ago this writer engaged in a public discussion in Lovington, New Mexico, with a gentleman who subscribed to, and who attempted to defend, the Calvinist view of an arbitrary election devoid of human responsibility. *We charged that according to his view one might as well curse as to pray; might as well go to a saloon as to church insofar as one's ultimate salvation is concerned.* We urged that he either deny or confirm this charge. The former he *could not* do without surrendering his position; the latter he *would not* do because of its repulsive implications. He was impaled on the horns of a dilemma, and could do neither. To admit that one must avoid profanity and pray; or, that church attendance must characterize one is to concede the essentiality of human response—a principle his creed required him to deny!

Paul's affirmation in Romans 8:29 is in complete harmony with the foregoing conclusions. Some, God "foreknew," i.e., recognized or approved them before hand. These, he "foreordained"—appointed them to "be conformed" to the "image of his Son." To be conformed to the image of Christ is to accept Christ as the pattern of our lives, and to live in harmony with his will. This, we do by obedience to his commandments. Thus, God *foreknows, foreordains, chooses* and *elects* those who submit their wills to Christ. To submit one's will to Christ is to be obedient to his commandments, and to live by his word. All who thus do are elected to salvation; no others are.

"Would you please comment on the implications of the fact that 'infants who die before reaching the age of accountability are safe'? It seems to me that more than half of the human race will be saved simply due to so many infants dying before coming to accountability. Revelation 7:9 pictures an enormous number of saved."

Infants dying in infancy are indeed *safe* and are not in need of salvation never having been lost. That which has never been lost needs not to be saved; infants have never been lost; hence, infants need no salvation. Of such is the kingdom of heaven. (Matthew 18:3.) The purity which characterizes one on entering the kingdom is that inherently true of infants who have never been defiled by the contamination of sin, and are thus without the need of redemption. *Accountability* is that state where one has attained to sufficient mental capacity to discern between good and evil. It is not the discernment which constitutes accountability; some never make such distinctions; it is the capacity to do so which determines it. Every infant dying will enjoy the bliss of heaven forever never having been under the guilt of sin. The number will indeed be great but it will be in addition to those described in Revelation 7:9 which includes not a single infant since these are those who have come out of the great tribulation "and have *washed* their robes and made them *white* in the *blood* of the lamb." (v. 14.) How we should rejoice that "There is a fountain filled with blood drawn from Immanuel's veins; and sinners plunged beneath that flood lose all their guilty stains."

"Is it scriptural to conduct 'children's church' at the same time as the regular worship hour?"

If by "children's church" is meant an arrangement set up permanently to segregate the younger from the older and to duplicate the services the answer is *no*. Such a procedure is without divine sanction; for it there is neither precept nor example in the scriptures. It is a long step toward the situation prevailing in some Christian churches where the "Junior church" has junior elders and deacons and where the "Lord's Supper" is observed. It violates the divine edict of the church coming together "in one place," and the motivation is convenience. It is in no sense parallel to the "nursery arrangement" prevailing in most congregations since this is (a) a temporary arrangement (b) designed for training and disciplinary purposes and (c) a part of the regular service where the women in charge may and should participate.

"What is the difference in humming and singing in the worship?"

To sing in biblical parlance is to utter scriptural sentiments in step with musical inflection. To hum is to utter sound without articulation. Singing is authorized in the scriptures; humming is not. (Colossians 3:16; Ephesians 5:18,19.) Inasmuch as all acts of worship are to be done "in the name of the Lord" (Colossians 3:17), this effectively eliminates humming at least for those who respect the authority of God's word. (1) The motivation is wrong because it is designed to appeal to the emotion rather than to the sense; (2) it makes aesthetics the standard of conduct in worship rather than the scriptures; (3) it makes man and not God determine what shall be offered; and (4) it is not possible to discharge the divine injunction to sing by humming. And, to add humming to the observance of the Lord's Supper is to compound the error and is as wrong as it would be to accompany it with instrumental music.

"Should a woman lead in prayers in a devotional service where men are present?"

No. First Timothy 2:8-14, properly construed, clearly forbids the practice. Nor is it ever necessary since one does not have to *lead* in order to *pray*. Multitudes of people in thousands of our congregations throughout the world pray acceptably every Lord's day without *leading*. Is it in keeping with the spirit of New Testament Christianity on the part of either men or women to *demand* the right to lead publicly in prayer? It was just such ostentation on the part of the Pharisees which the Lord so severely castigated (Matthew 6:5), and we may be sure that he does not look with approval upon those who manifest this disposition in the church today.

"In a congregation where there are no elders or deacons is it scriptural to appoint deacons before elders? I understand that deacons are servants but can a congregation have scriptural deacons without elders?"

Yes, we think it is scriptural for a congregation having men who can qualify as deacons, but without men possessing the qualifications of elders, to appoint deacons. It seems to us absurd to conclude that men who meet the qualifications of the scriptures as deacons should be regarded as incapable of serving because *other* men are *not* possessed of the qualifications of elders. Such a conclusion in effect adds an additional qualification to those set out by the Holy Spirit in 1 Timothy 3:8-13, i.e., a deacon, notwithstanding his other qualifications, may be appointed only if elders have been scripturally designated. Since when does one's obligation to the body of Christ, *in any area,* depend, in the slightest degree, on the performance or nonperformance, as the case may be, of *others?* Might it not with equal reason be affirmed that since *bishops and deacons* are together mentioned in Philippians 1:1, that it is therefore unscriptural to appoint elders if there are no deacons available? Or, that since a *fully* organized congregation has not only elders and deacons but also an evangelist that without an evangelist neither the elders *nor* deacons may scripturally serve?

It is not a valid objection to this to say that an eldership consisting of two men can no longer scripturally function when one dies; or, that an elder whose wife becomes unfaithful is thereby rendered incapable of serving. In the former instance, authority is vested in an *eldership*, not in an individual person; and in the second, the duties and responsibilities of the eldership are no longer possible to the man involved. Our question does not deal with the *failure* of men to act scripturally, but to their *right* to do so! Does not the disposition to object to the appointment of deacons where, for the time being, it is not possible to have elders, grow out of the fear that the deacons will seek to serve as elders? Our question deals with *scriptural* deacons which characteristic would preclude this possibility. One might with equal reason object to the selection of a preacher in a congregation without elders on the ground that the preacher might seek to usurp the authority properly belonging to elders only. That such sometimes occurs is due to the improper functioning of the preacher and not to the impropriety of a congregation having a preacher and no elders. The church in Jerusalem had deacons before it had elders (Acts 6:1-4); and in the period immediately following Pentecost the apostles performed the duties later assigned to elders. Bales (*The Deacon and His Work*, p. 15), says that "we do not know that there were no elders in the church in Jerusalem at that time," and that "it cannot be proved that these men (the seven) were deacons." We think he is wrong on both counts. There is not the remotest hint, in the New Testament, that elders oversaw the Jerusalem church, since the apostles discharged this responsibility as well as shepherded the flock, at the time the events of Acts 6 occurred; and if they existed in those early days, of which there is no trace, they were without portfolio! Later, elders were appointed, there. Because David Lipscomb said it so well, we transcribe his view of whether the seven were deacons: "While the name *diakoon,* or servant, is not used in Acts 6, the verb *diakonein,* to serve, is mentioned, and *diakoneo* the service rendered is spoken of. To say that a man served, or did service, is about as definite as to say that he was a servant. That is what is done in Acts 6. A deacon then, is a servant of the church. These men served the church; they did service. Hence, they have been called deacons or servants—I suppose, justly." (*Queries and Answers* by Lipscomb, page 126.)

"May a non-Christian baptize another into Christ? If a non-Christian may perform baptisms, would it also be proper for women to baptize men?"

One will search the scriptures in vain in seeking qualifications for those who baptize. Does it not then logically follow that since no qualifications are given that qualifications are required? To controvert this conclusion one must assume that in spite of the fact that God has not spoken thereon, man may do so, and thus demand conditions not divinely originated. But, were not all those who baptized in Bible times faithful disciples and does not this establish a precedent we may regard as binding as a definite edict? If it were granted that in all instances mentioned faithful disciples baptized it would then be necessary to show, from other considerations, that only those of this category might properly perform the act. Other reasons, not related to the matter of qualification, might explain the fact. Those not Christians in the apostolic age were either unbelieving Jews or pagans: the former were so antagonistic toward Christianity they would not encourage by any act, this movement; and the pagans, being idolatrous devotees, were so repulsive in practice there was no association between them and the Lord's followers.

But, were all who baptized always faithful disciples? John, a biographer of Jesus, tells us that Jesus baptized more disciples than John, "although Jesus himself baptized not, but his disciples" (John 4:1,2), by which it is meant that the Lord did not himself immerse people but acted through his disciples thus, in effect, baptizing more than John did. Among those who baptized for Jesus was Judas Iscariot, eventually his betrayer. Were all those, by him immersed, without valid baptism? Were those Judas baptized re-immersed by some faithful disciple? Of course not. Here is indisputable proof of the fact that the validity of one's baptism does not depend on the character, or lack of it as the case may be of the baptizer. How very thankful all of us should be that such is true. Were our acceptance before God dependent on the genuineness of heart characteristic of the one who baptized us, or his baptizer, or his, and so in unbroken sequence to the apostolic age, who of us has any assurance of ultimate redemption in heaven whatsoever? Who knows but that a hypocrite was somewhere in our past thus constituting a defective link in the chain, rendering all subsequent parties, *including ourselves* without acceptable baptism!

As these lines are written the crisis in Iran continues. Suppose that one of the hostages, knowing that baptism is for, in order to, the remission of sins, and fearful for the future, should ask one of his Iranian captors to immerse him in a bathtub in the embassy, who can seriously doubt that the effort would be pleasing to the Lord? The vital aspect of the matter is the conformity of the candidate to the expressed will of the Lord and not the character of the baptizer that determines the acceptability of the act. Would a person presented a New Testament by an infidel and who learns from it what to do to be saved *and does this* be any less saved because the means by which salvation came was through the hands of an unbeliever? The case of Apollos and the re-baptism of the twelve at Ephesus has no bearing on this question since these people had erroneously submitted to a baptism that was itself invalid having been superseded by Christian baptism. (Acts 18:24-28; 19:1-5.)

The only baptism Thomas and Alexander Campbell, their families and several of their close associates had was administered by Matthias

Luce, a Baptist preacher, who was asked to perform the act for them on the simple New Testament confession made by the eunuch. (Acts 8:37.) Luce first demurred, then consented, saying that though contrary to Baptist usage he believed such to be right and he immersed them.

May a woman scripturally immerse one into Christ? The question is both moot and impractical; moot, because it is purely an academic question, and impractical because seldom indeed would there be an occasion for such today. Were I without scriptural baptism and knowing such to be my duty, I would prefer that a Christian brother, known and loved by me, should immerse me; were one not available, my next choice would be a faithful godly man though unknown; were neither of the foregoing available, I would want to be baptized by *any* man who would agree to do so in harmony with New Testament teaching. As an alternative I would ask a woman to immerse me. Such a course I have not the least doubt the Lord would approve.

"What is the difference between the soul and the spirit of man?"

Though it is characteristic of most people today to use these terms interchangeably the scriptures very definitely differentiate them. "For the word of God is living, and active, and sharper than any two-edged sword, and piercing even to the dividing of soul and spirit, of both joints and marrow, and quick to discern the thoughts and intents of the heart." (Hebrews 4:12.) Since the sacred writers provided for "the dividing of soul and spirit," in those instances where they differ, so ought we and so we must if we are to entertain biblical concepts of these words.

The word "spirit," when denoting the human entity (from the Greek word *pneuma*), is a specific term and designates that part of us which is not susceptible of death and which survives the dissolution of the body. (Acts 7:59.) It is infused in us directly from God and is not a product of human generation. (Hebrews 12:9.) "Soul," from the Greek word *psuche,* however, is a generic word and its meaning must be determined, in any given instance, from the context in which it appears. Were I, in conversation with you, to use the word *apple* you are at once able to conjure up in mind the fruit by this name and you are not dependent on my usage of the word to ascertain its meaning. But, were I to ask, "Define the word *bark* for me," you could not possibly know whether I mean by it the sound a dog makes or the outer covering of a tree! However, should I say, "Bark is thicker this winter than usual," you are able with ease to gather the meaning of the term from the context in which I have used it.

Similarly, were you to ask, "Define the human spirit for me," I can at once and correctly say to you, "It is the immortal nature—the portion of us derived directly from God, and not subject to death." But, when you ask, "What is the biblical significance of the word *soul?*" I must respond by asking, "What passage of scripture do you have in mind in your reference to the soul?" since it is used in *four* different senses in the sacred writings:

1. As a synonym for *person:* "And there were added unto them in that day about three thousand souls." (Acts 2:41.) "Wherein few, that is, eight souls, were saved through water." (1 Peter 3:20.)

2. To denote the animal life which man possesses in common with the beasts of the field and which is lost in death: "He spared not their soul from death, but gave their life over to the pestilence. . . ." (Psalm 78:50.) By this it is simply meant that they were suffered to die. Their soul was their physical life.

3. The intellectual nature in contrast with the higher spiritual nature and the lower physical nature. "Now the natural man receiveth not the things of the Spirit of God. . . ." (1 Corinthians 2:14.) The "natural man" of this passage being literally, *the soulish man,* since the adjective "natural" translates a form of the Greek word for soul, which may be expressed in English as *psychical.* Thus, this usage is supported by etymology and required by the context. See, especially Paul's teaching in 1 Corinthians 1:18-28 and 2:6-16.

4. As a synonym for the never-dying spirit: "Because thou wilt not leave my soul unto Hades, neither wilt thou give thy Holy One to see corruption." (Acts 2:27.) Here it is obvious that the word soul signifies the immortal nature; that entity of the Lord which was not to undergo death.

It will be seen from this induction of biblical teaching that there is no pat and easy answer to the question, What is the soul? since any proper reply must take into account the significance intended by the inspired penman who used it. It is not unusual for shrewd materialists (among whom are "Jehovah's Witnesses," Adventists, and Christadelphians) to induce an uninformed person in these matters to affirm that "the soul never dies," and then to produce numerous statements from the Old Testament that the soul does indeed die, the conclusion then being pressed that man is wholly mortal, his entire being subject to death. The argument is a fallacious one and the conclusion is false because it results from the assignment of a specific meaning to a generic term where such was not the intent of the Old Testament writer. The spirit of man is not subject to death (Genesis 25:8; 35:18; Psalm 90:10; Acts 7:59; 2 Corinthians 5:1, 6-8); it is the spirit leaving the body which constitutes death (James 2:26); and, in any instance when death is affirmed of some part of us, it does not embrace the spirit—the immortal nature.

"Watchtower Magazine published the following statement, 'Regarding a future "coming" Jesus himself made it plain that he would not be in the flesh, visible to humans.' Please comment."

This, like every other *distinctive* doctrine of "Jehovah's Witnesses" is positively and palpably false. He himself said, *after* his resurrection from the dead, that "a spirit hath not flesh and bones, as ye behold me having" (Luke 24:39), thus establishing for those who saw him the fact that he was not simply or only a spirit. It is noteworthy that his phrase is, "flesh and bones," not flesh *and blood* since his resurrection body had undergone that transformation from a mortal to an immortal body of which Paul writes (1 Corinthians 15:53), in his detailed discussion of the *body* in which the saint will come forth at the last day. Despite this clear affirmation of the scriptures the article from the "Watchtower Magazine" says that Christ was resurrected *as a spirit!* (January 15, 1980, page 31.) Equally erroneous is the statement that Jesus "would not be . . . visible to humans." John wrote, "Behold, he cometh with the clouds; and *every eye shall see him,* and they that pierced him; and all the tribes of the earth shall mourn over him. Even so, Amen." (Revelation 1:7.) Sad indeed that these people have espoused these glaring errors.

"What is the significance in the fact that orthodox Jews do not use instrumental music in their worship today?"

The querist is correct in designating those Jews who do not use instrumental music in their worship as *orthodox* inasmuch as liberal and "reform" bodies among them have adopted its use in their services with consequent bitterness, alienation, strife and eventual division. It is remarkable that the history of its introduction into Jewish synagogue worship is much the same as that which plagued the churches of Christ in the decades nearest the beginning of the twentieth century. There are clear parallels between the synagogue worship and the worship of the New Testament church; originally, neither used instrumental music in worship and both have been beset by elements bent on innovation and change. It should be kept crystal clear that our Lord never authorized its use in Christian worship, no apostle ever sanctioned it, no New Testament writer ever commanded it, and no apostolic church ever practiced it. It came from the bosom of mother Rome along with the counting of beads, the burning of candles and the worship of images.

"Is a physical description of Christ, said to be in the archives at Rome, written by a Roman officer to Tiberias, considered a forgery?"

Yes, along with such other hoaxes as "Pilate's Court" (sometimes published under other titles as "The Archaeological and the Historical Writings of the Sanhedrin and the Talmuds of the Jews," the "Archko Volume," "Letters of Pontius Pilate," etc.), the book of Enoch, the Testament of the Twelve Patriarchs, the Assumption of Moses, the Narrative of Joseph of Arimathaea, the Gospel of Nicodemus, the Acts of Paul and Thecla, the Gospel of Thomas, The Gospel of the Nativity of Mary, the Letter of Abgarus to Christ, and The Reply of Christ to Abgarus, and many others.

"Is it permissible to use a pitch pipe in worship service?"

It is entirely in order to use a pitch pipe or tuning fork to obtain the proper pitch for a song about to be led, but this is prior to the beginning of the worship in song and not "in" it. This, significantly, is the difference between a tuning fork and a piano in relation to the worship; the tuning fork knows when to quit—before the worship starts!

"I have a question concerning 1 Corinthians 7:5. Does this mean that a husband and wife may not refuse each other sex relations unless they have agreed to use the time for prayer and fasting?"

It should be observed that verse 6 immediately following reads: "But this I say by way of concession, not of commandment." Ordinarily, the circumstances described in 1 Corinthians 7:1-4 would require that the admonition of verse 5 be followed by both husband and wife; however, exceptional situations might exist where this could not well be and so the apostle, *by inspiration,* recommended this course without unconditionally enjoining it because of the possibility of such exceptions. Where such exceptions do not obtain it is sinful for either to suspend the rule.

"Discuss the ministry of angels."

The ministry of angels in God's great redemptive plan is clearly and unmistakenly taught in the sacred writings. Of these divine messengers the writer of Hebrews penned these interesting and significant words: "Are they not all ministering spirits sent forth to minister for them who shall be heirs of salvation?" (Hebrews 1:14.) Not all of the areas of their activity are indicated but some of them are and in these ought we to find immeasurable satisfaction and inexpressible joy. Who of us that truly love the Lord have not been thrilled far down in the very depths of our souls in singing of this boundless blessing in the following words of a magnificent old hymn:

O come, angel band, come, and around me stand;
And bear me away on your snowy wings
To my immortal home, to my immortal home!

This concept is not a fanciful one nor is the hope it engenders imaginary. Lazarus was "carried by the angels into Abraham's bosom" (Luke 16:22), and no reason exists why the Lord would do this for the pitiless begger but not for all others who die as Lazarus did in the Everlasting Arms. Was not this narrative penned for the purpose of depicting the destiny of the classes represented by Lazarus and the rich man? If to this the objection is raised that the account is parabolic and not intended to be interpreted as an actual event, this must be shown to be so from the report itself which no man can do; and, in either event— whether a parable or a historic incident—the affirmation of the Spirit that angels carried the spirit of Lazarus into the next world means *something* and if it does not mean that angels do indeed bear spirits away from their bodies at death the statement is misleading and without significance to those to whom it purports to apply. We may therefore properly conclude that the human spirit, having been faithful to God, when free of the body in death is borne by angels into the Hadean realms, and that this is but one of the ways in which angels minister to (serve) the heirs of salvation.

There is indeed a much closer relationship between this world and the one that awaits us than this materialistic and skeptical age would like to admit. Though the river of death intervenes, on the farther shore there awaits us a "great cloud of witnesses" vitally interested in the spiritual progress of those whose race is not yet run. (Hebrews 12:1, 2.) The two worlds are so close but one step is required to make the journey and but a moment of time to experience the transition. It is not impossible to conclude that in the passing *both* worlds are *for the moment* in the view of the dying saint. Stephen *saw* Jesus standing at the right hand of the Father (Acts 7:56); was this but the fevered delusion of a distraught and dying man? Materialists so conclude, but with which conclusion we are not in agreement.

Moses E. Lard, one of the most brilliant stars of a glorious firmament of truly great men in the Restoration movement, relates an incident in his Quarterly which we condense from "The Old Path Pulpit," by F. G. Allen, himself one of the ablest preachers and writers of his day. A sailor, now in the sunset years of his life, and in retirement, took up abode in Missouri, where he and his aged companion found deep satisfaction in obeying the Lord and serving him after the New Testament pattern. For some years they served the saviour faithfully, delighting

105

in the service and worship of God, being dearly loved by all the saints. Ultimately the infirmities of age brought him low and friends and brethren gathered about him for his last hours. He talked much of the heavenly home and of the journey he was soon to take. His last words were to his faithful and devoted wife. "Mary," he said, "we have lived a long time together; we must now separate. We have often talked of our Father's house and wondered how it is over there. This will soon be fully known to me because I shall soon be there. I cannot communicate with you from that farther shore but put your hand in mine and when I am passing through the portals if the sea is calm, the sky is clear and the port is open, I'll send you a sign." She put her hand in his, the hand with which she had so often smoothed his troubled brow and lightened for him the burdens of life now wrinkled in honored old age, and waited with breathless silence the end. He breathed but a few times more as the spirit prepared to take its flight in death. At last when the silent witnesses thought there was to be nothing more, he gave her hand a gentle pressure and all was over. The sea was calm, the sky was clear, the port was open, and all was well. She had received the promised sign!

"Discuss the enclosed tract."

Occasionally I am mailed a tract such as this prepared by those who oppose homes for the fatherless and widows among us containing quotations from the GOSPEL ADVOCATE and its publications of earlier years with the allegation that the views then expressed by those writers are in conflict with those currently subscribed to by us and that their statements could not now appear in these pages. The most recent copies have come from Weakley County, Tennessee. Among the men quoted are B. C. Goodpasture, H. Leo Boles, Foy E. Wallace Jr., E. A. Elam, and Guy N. Woods.

It is quite true that some of the statements from the tract are not *now* acceptable to us, not because we are in disagreement with the positions originally expressed, but because of the compiler's distortions, omissions and perversions of the original statements these men made. For example, brother H. Leo Boles is quoted as saying, "Christians are to do good to all, and helping those in distress is a good work. We do not find any example of a church that has sent to help those not Christians." Here, the tract writer terminated the quotation; but, in the article brother Boles wrote, he continued by saying, "It seems that if one Christian could help those in distress who are not Christians, a church could do the same." Why did our anti-brother suppress this statement? To have done so would destroy his intention to insinuate in the tract that Boles supported the "saints only" theory they advocate!

Foy E. Wallace, Jr., is quoted as editorializing, "If it were permissible to have a Bible college as an orphans' home in the work of benevolence, we quite agree that it would also be permissible to have a missionary society in the work of evangelism," but what he really said was, "If it were permissible to have a Bible college as *an adjunct to the church* in the work of education and an orphans' home in the work of benevolence, we quite agree that it would also be permissible to have the missionary society in the work of evangelism." The compiler omitted the words "as an adjunct to the church," knowing quite well that none of us who defends the homes believes that they are "adjuncts to the church." The reader will draw his or her own opinion why this undisclosed deletion was made: or, why the tract did not reveal the fact that in the *same* paragraph brother Wallace set out the conditions under which a church might support an orphan home.

E. A. Elam is quoted as follows: "How to do what is called 'mission work' is taught as clearly and plainly in the New Testament as anything God ever commanded. The church sent out preachers, supported them and received their report," the implication being that brother Elam wrote to condemn cooperative evangelism *by churches*—the sending of funds from one church to another church. But, the two sentences which are omitted and which clearly reveal why brother Elam made the previous statement are, "No convention was necessary. The convention perverts the way of God in these particulars." He wrote to oppose support of institutions usurping the work of the church as do missionary conventions—not the sending of funds from one church to another in cooperative evangelism. And, that it is a gross misrepresentation of brother Elam to represent him as opposed to churches contributing to orphan homes is clear from the fact that in the *same* issue from which the quotation is taken brother Elam wrote, "Our readers will please not overlook the fact that the Tennessee Orphan Home is needing funds with which to make improvements. We are contemplating building a new house on the farm, also making improvements that are much needed in the Home in Columbia. A liberal contribution will be appreciated just now." In the same year (1921), another article appears from his pen entitled, "An Appeal For Fanning Orphan School," in which there is a report included from A. N. Trice addressed to "Mr. E. A. Elam, President of the Board of Trustees of the Fanning Orphan School," and listing numerous contributors including the Highland Avenue *church,* Russell Street *church* and Foster Street *church* in Nashville.

The tract has a "quotation" from me in which I am alleged to have written, "No organization is needed to accomplish the work the Lord has authorized to do." What I actually wrote was, "No organization is needed to accomplish the work the Lord has authorized *the church* to do." Caring for orphans was by the Lord assigned to the *home* institution, not the church institution; a missionary society is wrong because it does what God assigned to the church to do; thus, the two are not parallel in their relation to the church. It is the responsibility of the home to provide child care; it is the function of the church to preach the gospel. (James 1:27; 1 Timothy 5:16; Ephesians 3:21; 1 Timothy 3:15.) No other organization is needed to accomplish the work which God gave *the church* to do and so the statement reflects precisely what I have believed and do now believe to be true. By suppression and misrepresentation do the advocates of negativism seek to divide and to turn away the Lord's people from the work God has assigned them to do. Limitations of space preclude further exposure of the gross misrepresentations and implications of this "tract" and honest people will have no difficulty in judging its motives and merits.

"Please explain Isaiah 2:4."

"And he will judge between the nations, and will decide concerning many peoples; and they shall beat their swords into plowshares, and their spears into pruning hooks, nation shall not lift up sword against nation, neither shall they learn war any more." It should be observed that these words of the prophet follow the announcement of the building of the Lord's house—the church—"in the latter days." The law was to go out from Zion and the word of the Lord from Jerusalem. Verse 4 is descriptive of conditions to prevail "in the house of the God of Jacob," so vividly pictured in this prophecy and fulfilled on the day of Pentecost following our Lord's resurrection. (Acts 2:1ff.) It is a prediction of harmony between "the NATIONS" (Jew and Gentile), of the removal of the barrier—the middle wall of distinction—between them in Christ, and the peace resulting. The figure of the spears being turned into pruning hooks and the swords into plowshares is a common one in the sacred writings. Isaiah 2:1-5, Ezekiel 34:20-26 and Ephesians are parallel and explanatory of each other. Gone is the enmity formerly existing between Jew and Gentile in Christ.

"Is it correct to say that the scriptures teach by (a) direct command, (b) apostolic example and (c) necessary inference? What is meant by necessary inference?"

Yes. Acts 2:38 is an example of a direct command, 1 Corinthians 16:1,2 of an apostolic example and 1 Timothy 3:2 of a necessary inference. (We necessarily infer that since a bishop *must* be the *husband* of one *wife* a woman cannot serve as a bishop!)

An inference is a conclusion logically drawn from premises preceding. A necessary inference exists when only one possible conclusion may be properly drawn from the preceding premises. One might infer that Nicodemus came to Jesus *by night* because of fear but this is far from being a necessary inference since there are other equally plausible conclusions to be drawn why he came "by night." Our Lord plainly taught that the subjects of baptism are those who are taught the word, and who believe. (Matthew 28:18-20; Mark 16:15,16.) We necessarily infer that infants are not subjects of baptism since they cannot be taught and are unable to believe.

"Is the case for a common church treasury dependent on a necessary inference in 1 Corinthians 16:1,2?"

No. The obligation here is a direct command. (1) It was an obligation to be discharged on "the first day of the week." (2) It was to be put into a common treasury. If to this the objection is raised that the words "lay by him in store," suggests only that it was an action to be discharged at home, such vanishes in the face of the fact that (3) the reason for the common treasury was to eliminate the need of a "gathering" when Paul arrived. This points irresistibly to a "common treasury" in Corinth. Contributions at home would have required the "gathering" Paul sought to avoid by means of the common treasury. Recognized here is the common meeting of the church on the first day of the week (Acts 20:7), and the obligation to give as prospered on that day.

Our querist adds the reason for "these questions is that I heard a brother say that Paul's preaching in an upper room would be a necessary inference that we should meet only in upper rooms today." The brother is in error. There is no such necessary inference as he alleges since we have numerous examples of preaching on land and on the sea, in buildings and outside of them, on the castle steps in Jerusalem, and many other places too numerous to mention.

"Recently I have heard of several congregations whose Sunday morning attendance has outgrown the seating capacity of the building and they have scheduled a second worship service. Is this dividing the assembly?"

No. It is really not correct to refer to this practice as a *second* worship service since those who participate attend only the one. It is not the best possible way, but in the interim before a building of greater capacity can be erected it is expedient so to do. No, such does not constitute a division of the assembly since there is but one in progress at the time. The alternative to two or more such services, pending the erection of a larger auditorium, would be to discourage attendance down to capacity! We think the Lord would not be pleased with this.

"What is the supreme virtue?"

"And the greatest of these is love." (1 Corinthians 13:13.) There is significance in the fact that the greatest eulogy of love ever written—the thirteenth chapter of First Corinthians—occurs in a letter torn by factions and divided in sentiment regarding many matters. An overview of the book is necessary in order for a proper appreciation of the problems which beset that New Testament church. A wide diffusion of spiritual gifts there had resulted in strife, envy and unseemly pride. Those thus possessed had disregarded the divine purpose of the spiritual gifts of tongues, healing, interpretation, prophesying, and others and had allowed themselves to act unworthily toward their brethren. Those who spoke with tongues, for example, regarded themselves as being more richly endowed than those who prophesied. This pride produced envy and jealousy on the part of those who regarded themselves as possessed of less spectacular manifestations. Paul penned the epistle, not to belittle the gifts which were essential to that day, but to show that all such were useless in the permanent building up of the body of Christ without the supreme virtue—love.

It is not possible for a heart filled with love to entertain bitterness and hate. Those who truly love each other do not engage in bickering and strife; such emotions have no place either in the heart or life of those disciples who follow the example of the loving Saviour.

During the war between the states at the close of a day of fierce fighting there was a lull in battle. When the thunder of heavy artillery and the clatter of musketry were no longer heard the quiet and peace of a summer evening fell on the embattled forces. Only a narrow river separated the opposing armies. Suddenly, a company of Union soldiers began to sing "The Star-Spangled Banner." As the last notes of the stirring song died out on the evening air, a company of Confederates on the other side of the river struck up the rousing strains of "Dixie." The men of the North sang, "Rally Round the Flag," and the Southerners answered with "My Maryland." Back and forth they challenged each other with the patriotic airs of their respective causes. Finally, there rang out on the night air the sad, sweet words of the song, "Home, Sweet Home." Immediately, both camps took up the refrain and sang it together. In one moment the bitterness of war was drowned in the memory of a father and a mother, a sister and a brother, a wife or a sweetheart, back home. A common love, for the moment, at least, blotted out their differences and they became one as the blessed memories of home and loved ones surged through their breasts. When our hearts

110

are permitted to overflow with love for God and for his children all envy, strife and bitterness vanish into forgetfulness.

"Does 1 Corinthians 1:7 teach that spiritual gifts would continue until the Lord returns?"

No. It should be noted that the reference by the writer is to the *church* in Corinth and not to each individual Christian since no one of them possessed every gift. In the church, however, every spiritual gift common to that day was exercised, being "behind in no gift." In support of this, see 2 Corinthians 12:13. Neither the church, as an organized unit, nor its members would remain on earth until the judgment day (the revelation of the Lord Jesus Christ), but there they would appear and God would approve them in confirmation of the faithfulness they now exhibited. Spiritual gifts were for the confirmation of the word and ended when that word was fully revealed. (Mark 16:15-20; Hebrews 2:1-4; 1 Corinthians 13:1-13.)

"Since Jesus was victorious over Satan in his resurrection from the dead, how do we explain such passages as 'But Satan hindered us,' 'the devil as a roaring lion, walketh about, seeking whom he may devour,' and 'When they hear, Satan immediately comes and takes away the word.'" (1 Thessalonians 2:18; 1 Peter 5:8; Mark 4:15.)

Our Lord, by means of death—his own—destroyed him, who had in his possession the power of death, the devil. The Evil One, in the beginning of the race, exercised his powers of bringing death upon all mankind by causing our first parents to sin. (Hebrews 2:14,15.) It is significant that the sacred writer, in describing this action of the devil, uses for the word *power* not *exousia* (lawful action), but *kratos* (power seized by trickery). Christ, the firstfruits of them that sleep, brought life and immortality to light through the gospel. Henceforth Satan is bound by its restraints. (Revelation 20:1-4.) This is far from meaning that his influence is no longer felt, or that he has lost the power of temptation; not until the end of the age will mankind have been able wholly to triumph over him. He "hinders," goes about as "a roaring lion," and steals the word out of the hearts of the shallow-minded, but he can be, and should be resisted by those "stedfast in the faith." (1 Peter 5:9.) This victory we achieve by faith. (1 John 5:4.)

"In the parable of the Prodigal Son, who is represented by the father? The elder brother? The prodigal?" (Luke 15:11-32.)

The principal lesson taught here and in the narratives of the lost coin and the lost sheep (there are many incidental ones) is the concern

111

which God, our Heavenly Father, feels for the lost. Because there are several classes of lost people the several illustrations of the chapter were utilized. Some are lost as the *coin* was lost—lost and do not know it. Others are lost as the *sheep* was lost—lost and know it, but do not know the way to the fold. Others are lost as the *boy* was lost—lost, know it, and know the way back. Each of these categories of lost people requires a different approach and a message especially adapted to it. There is much ineffectual evangelism today from a failure to recognize the lessons taught in this beautiful story.

The three persons involved represent God and his people, the two sons, people of vastly differing moral levels. The elder son is a picture of Judaism at its Pharisaical best, without blame in its adherence to the demands of traditional religion. The younger son, not now possessed of the strictness characteristic of his brother, and perhaps never having been, is representative of those afar off from Jewish ritualism and the moral standards it imposed. When finally he came to himself his submissiveness to his father's will was far greater than that of his brother whose principles protected him from abandonment, but which also were allowed to blind him to love, forgiveness and full fellowship with one long lost.

"What is the 'third heaven'?"

The word "heaven" is used in at least three different senses in the sacred writings. Occasionally it describes the atmosphere about us where birds fly (Luke 9:58), in other instances where the sun, the moon and the stars are (Psalm 19:1-6) and in some occurrences the abode and throne of Jehovah. (Deuteronomy 4:39.) Thus, the "third heaven" to which Paul alludes in 2 Corinthians 12:1-4 is undoubtedly that region which surrounds the throne of God—the ultimate home of the soul.

"What is Paradise?"

"Paradise," etymologically, is a "pleasure garden," and is used in the scriptures to denote a place of great blessing. As in the case of the word "heaven," the context must be noted in order to determine its meaning since it is used, as is the word heaven, to signify several places of bountiful and great blessing. For example, the original paradise was the garden of Eden, the blissful abode of our first parents (Genesis 2:28); it is applied to that bourne of the blessed dead who rest from their labors (Luke 23:43), and it is also used to describe the heavenly city. (Revelation 2:7.) Because it denotes the *state* of things existing it is thus variously applied in the Bible.

"My sister, a non-Christian, believes that Matthew 17:10-13, teaches that John the Baptist was really Elijah reincarnated into another body. Please explain this to me in words understandable to me and back it up with proper Bible texts."

Four hundred years before our Lord came to the earth it was predicted that Elijah would appear. (Malachi 4:1,6.) The Jewish scholars erred in expecting an actual and literal return of the fiery prophet and the disciples were also confused at this point. The Lord clarified the matter for them by explaining that John the Baptist fulfilled the prophecies touching the coming of Elijah. (Matthew 17:13.) John, by his stern and fearless denunciation of wickedness in high places, reflected the same disposition and accomplished much the same work as did Elijah, and thus demonstrated the same power and spirit. But, he was not Elijah, in his own person, and said so! When the priests and Levites from Jerusalem questioned him, they asked "Who art thou?" and they persisted in their inquiry, particularly asking, "Art thou Elijah?" John answered, *"I am not."* (John 1:19-21.) Thus to affirm that John was actually the person of Elijah returned to the earth is to controvert the Baptizer himself. Moreover, Elijah, the great lawgiver, appeared with Moses on the Mount of Transfiguration where the reference is obviously to the ancient prophet and not to the Harbinger of the Christ. (Matthew 17:1-4.) John was an Elijah in will, disposition, and work, but he was not the literal Elijah *and said so!* There is no support here, or elsewhere, in the scriptures, for the doctrine of reincarnation.

"Jesus said of the man born blind, 'Neither did this man sin, nor his parents: but that the works of God should be made manifest in him.' Is our Lord saying that this man was born blind so that the Lord could give him his natural sight to show those Jews who were so bitter against him that he was truly the Son of God?" (John 9:3ff.)

The view existed among the Jews (and still exists even among some who profess to be children of God today) that affliction, trial, illness, indeed, all misfortune, result from specific wrongdoing either on the part of the person involved or one's parents. Jesus, in Luke 13:1-5, deals with this assumption and refutes it. Taught here is the fact that neither the man, nor his parents had sinned so as to lead to the affliction of which he was healed; it occurred in the ordinary course of human events and was now to afford the Lord an opportunity to exhibit his amazing power and marvelous grace to suffering humanity, in consequence of which the man would be blessed, the cause of Christ honored and the glory of God enhanced. The Lord thus *used* the occasion to the honor of

God's name; it is a gross misapprehension of the incident to assume that the man was *created* with an affliction in order that he might be healed in the circumstances described.

"Why did Paul call himself an 'apostle' since the New Testament speaks of twelve apostles (Matthew 10:2-4; Luke 6:13; Acts 1:21-26)? Is it possible there was a thirteenth apostle?"

It is not correct to conclude that there was any intent to maintain the number *twelve* in the company of apostles following the establishment of the church on Pentecost. It is indeed true that the number *twelve* is a common one in the sacred writings but so also is the number *seven* and there is as much reason to urge that there should be no more nor less than *seven* deacons (since this is the number of the first ones, Acts 6:1-5) as to urge that there were no more nor less than twelve apostles. Exegetical ingenuity to maintain the number is seen in the effort to deny the validity of the action by Peter and the disciples in the selection of Matthias on the ground that the selection of Paul as an apostle evidences the rejection of the previous effort by Peter regarding Matthias. But of such there is no hint in the Spirit's account and it is expressly said that Matthias was numbered with the eleven apostles. (Acts 1:26.)

The word "apostle" means *one sent forth.* The broader use of the term, following the day of Pentecost and the establishment of the church, is seen not only in its application to Paul but also to Barnabas *and others.* In his salutations to the saints in Rome, Paul wrote: "Salute Andronicus and Junias, my kinsmen, and my fellow-prisoners, *who are of note among the apostles,* who also have been in Christ before me." (Romans 16:7.) (See, also, Acts 14:14.) It is obvious therefore that the original number was not adhered to. If to this the objection is raised that in the Revelation there is reference to "the twelve apostles of the Lamb," it should be noted that this appears in a highly figurative setting where the language throughout is symbolic. The walls of the city have *twelve* foundations, the elect are sealed from the *twelve* tribes, there are *twelve* thousand from each. Quite obviously these designations are not to be literally construed.

What appears to be absolutely decisive of the matter is the reference of Paul to "false apostles" who had been active in the church in Corinth. If the word *apostle* embraced no others but the original twelve and Paul, the claim to the apostleship by these pretenders would have been self-condemning. (2 Corinthians 11:13.)

114

"To what extent, if any, is it right for a Christian to be employed in the production or sale of alcoholic beverage?"

To no extent, whatsoever. The Bible abounds with clear and emphatic statements showing it is wrong for one to put a stumbling block in another's way and it is expressly stated that one is not to make available to his neighbor *drink!* (Romans 14:13; Habbakuk 2:15.) So grave are the consequences threatening one who toys to *any* extent with intoxicating drink of *any* type that those who would encourage such use become guilty parties to their destruction. Those of us who have felt the crunch of broken bones and heard the moans of loved ones suffering because of drunken drivers on the highways (and we number in the hundreds of thousands in this country), can make but little distinction between the drunk who drives the car and the character who provided the drink which made him drunk. To piously plead that this is the misuse of the fiery liquid offers little consolation to the tens of thousands who die each year in these wrecks, and the multiplied thousands who suffer agonizing pain as a direct result of them. It is certain that if the stuff were neither made nor sold there could be no such "misuse" of it.

"To what extent, if any, is it right to use in a leadership position, a member of the church who consumes alcoholic beverage, or is employed in its production? How can a man whose business or occupation is neither good nor honorable according to New Testament teaching (Ephesians 4:28; 1 Thessalonians 5:21, 22; Romans 12:17; 14:21) be considered 'of good report' (Acts 6:1-3), or worthy to be set over the Father's business, whether it be serving tables or otherwise?"

No one in the church is without some influence and those in positions of leadership or who appear before the congregation in presiding at the Lord's table, in leading in prayer, or directing the singing, in teaching classes, and other such functions ought always to set an example in both public and private life which may be safely followed by all. To this end Paul admonished Timothy to be "an ensample to them that believe, in word, in manner of life, in love, in faith, in purity." (1 Timothy 4:12.) It is impossible for one, in any measure, to follow the instruction of Paul and to be a purveyor or a user of intoxicating liquors. The fact that there are those in ever-increasing numbers imbibing liquor in the church today who attempt to justify its use, despite the moral, scriptural, religious, economic and sensible grounds against it, evidences its strange, hypnotic power to brainwash, to deceive and to delude those enslaved by it.

"Discuss the doctrine of 'transferred righteousness.'"

It is of Abraham affirmed that his faith was "reckoned" (credited) to him "for righteousness." (Romans 4:1-9.) Periodically, there are those who from this assume that it was the sacred writer's intent to teach that there was *transferred* to the patriarch the righteousness which God possesses and that such is a preview of the action involved in the salvation of all of us today. Specifically, that each person, in consequence of the exercise of belief in Christ, has transferred to himself or herself the *actual* or *same* righteousness which the Lord possesses. Those thus concluding believe that the "righteousness" obtained in this fashion is summed up in the Christian character, is secured *solely* by belief, and by *no* other acts of obedience. Some brethren, having espoused this view, are by no means averse to using the phrase "by faith only" to indicate the manner or means by which the blessings of salvation and the hope of eternal life are made available to us today. There is by them ascribed to faith—the act of believing—a peculiar efficacy they are unwilling to admit to repentance, confession or baptism.

The errors involved in such reasoning are numerous and the conclusion drawn therefore fallacious. It requires only the most elementary logic to observe that were the premises true once Christ's righteousness has been received the individual thus possessed *is as good as he and will thenceforth be privileged to appear before God on the basis of merit rather than mercy!* Obviously, our Lord will not in judgment be required to justify his faithfulness in few or many things in the record books of life and, the foregoing conclusion being true, neither will those equally possessed of his character. What then of the Seer's description in Revelation 20: "And I saw the dead, small and great, stand before God; and the books were opened: and another book was opened, which is the book of life: and the dead were judged out of those things which were written in the books, *according to their works.*" Why according to *their* works if no works of any kind are involved in the reception and possession of the Christian life? If they have had transferred to themselves the righteousness Christ possesses why won't they be accepted on the same basis he is—*actual merit?*

Those espousing this utterly impossible view err with reference to the significance of the phrase, "righteousness of God"; "righteousness" and "imputation." *Righteousness of God* (or *of Christ*), is not the righteousness which they possess but which they "impute" (credit to) to those who comply with their will and thus which originates with them. Righteousness which is acquired in the process of salvation is exactly equivalent to justification. To make righteous is simply to justify (i.e., acquit), of charges formerly existing. Abraham was "justified" by being regarded as in a right relationship with God. The basic meaning of the

116

word in the Greek text *(dikaioo)* is to pronounce or declare one just. Thus, one in a righteous, or justified state, is simply regarded as no longer alienated from God. Because we are expected to maintain the state of non-alienation between us and the Lord there is an extension of the idea of approval in the obedience required. In this sense we *work* righteousness. (Acts 10:34,35.) This is consistent with the basic meaning of the word since such working is essential to the continuance of the state of acquittal between us and God!

There is immeasurable difference between the theory of the transference of Christ's righteousness (the Lord's own inherent purity) to the sinner, as some today teach and the biblical doctrine of the imputation of righteousness—the acquittal of those formerly alienated from God. Paul's point in Romans 4:1-8 is *not* what Abraham received in the imputation of righteousness—this is crystal clear from the meaning of the word—but *how* it came, whether by meritorious human works or by appropriation in compliance with the will of God. The former is denied, the latter affirmed and shown to be true in the fact that his faith was *reckoned* (put to his account) for righteousness. That is, the illustrious patriarch accepted, without question, and in spite of his natural inability to beget a child, that the promise of God of an heir was true *before* anything else was expected of him, and this act of believing was put to his account as an act of obedience. Nonetheless, it is by the sacred writer expressly declared that he was justified "by works," the works, of course, being obedience to Jehovah's commands. The phrase is, literally, *out* of works (not as a *means*), since it is God who justifies—declares one just—but only when faith is proved to be valid. (James 2:26.) Adam Clarke clearly perceived the truth of this important term when, after listing numerous passages in which it appears, commented that "in all of these texts the word 'justify' is taken in the sense of 'the remission of sins' through faith in Christ Jesus; and does not mean making the person 'just' or 'righteous', but treating him as if it were so, having already forgiven him his sins." (Vol. 6, page 43.)

More detailed but equally clear and correct in the views presented is the following transcript from the usually judicious and scholarly MacKnight in his comments on Romans 3:28: "In this verse 'works of law' are all those works which the law enjoins, performed in the perfect manner required by law. Wherefore, when the apostle tells us, that 'by faith man is justified without works of law,' his plain meaning is, that men are justified gratuitously by faith, and not meritoriously by perfect obedience to any law whatever. But many interpreting this passage differently, have argued, that, in the affair of justification, men's faith only is regarded, and no regard whatsoever is had to their works, as if they attributed man's justification to some efficacy in faith which is not in works. This, however, hath no foundation in scripture. For while it teaches, that men are 'justified by faith without works of law,' it at the same time teaches, that men are 'justified freely through God's grace' consequently it excludes faith equally with works, from any meritorious efficiency in the matter. And with respect to 'instrumentality' faith cannot be thought more necessary for preparing us to receive justification as a free gift than works; seeing in that light, 'faith' is itself the greatest of all good works, being the principle from which every good work proceeds. Hence it is called 'the work of faith.' (1 Thessalonians 1:3), and 'the work which God hath commanded.' (John 6:29.) But, it hath been said that faith alone is necessary to men's justification, because thereby they lay hold on the righteousness of Christ, and receive it by imputation. To this it is sufficient to answer, that no such operation of faith is taught in scripture. Neither is it said that 'Christ's righteousness is imputed to believers.' What the scripture saith is, that the believer's faith 'is imputed, or counted to him for righteousness.' (Romans 4:3.) In short, to connect justification with 'faith,' and to separate it from 'works,' is to put asunder what God declares he hath joined together, and what is joined in the nature of things. For faith without good works is 'a dead faith, or no faith at all,' as the apostle James expressly affirms. (James 2:26.)" (*Apostolical Epistles*, Vol. 1, page 211.)

The doctrine of imputation which alleges a transference of Christ's goodness to the sinner derives from a gross misapprehension of the scriptures and is untenable both etymologically and theologically. In saving us the Lord forgives us of sin, absolves us of guilt, and acquits us of being sinners. A man, convicted of crimes against the state may be pardoned and henceforth no longer a criminal but this is far from saying that the pardoning process also makes of him an active and useful member of society. This he must do by conformity to the standards and norms of such society. Similarly, God cancels out our guilt and treats us as if we had never been guilty but we must thenceforth live in keeping with the divine precepts essential to the Christian character. It was this which Paul affirmed when he penned the following words to Titus: "For the grace of God that bringeth salvation hath appeared unto all men, teaching us that, denying ungodliness and worldly lusts, we should live soberly, righteously, and godly, in this present world; looking for that blessed hope, and the glorious appearing of the great God and our Saviour Jesus Christ; who gave himself for us, that he might redeem us from all iniquity, and purify unto himself a peculiar people, zealous of good works." (Titus 2:11-14.)

"What are the basic fruits of faith?"

Whether one's religion results from genuine conviction or from mere convenience depends entirely on whether it springs from unquestioning

118

acceptance of God and all that he has said, or is prompted by subjective, emotional or purely selfish reasons with little regard from him who is its Author. Faith is "the assurance of things hoped for," i.e., the full realization that the Lord, in whom we believe, is himself faithful and thus is certain to fulfill every promise he has made and for which we yearn; it is the "conviction of things not seen," hence containing all the evidence any reasonable mind requires, though not before the senses, as to its credibility. (Hebrews 11:1.)

The testimony on which our faith rests is worthy of our belief because it meets the demands of all reasonable rules of evidence and ought therefore to be accepted for the same reason that ancient documents, bearing on their face no indication of fraudulent content or questionable origin and coming from the proper sources are deemed to be genuine and true and to be accepted as such unless there are other considerations of such weighty significance against their reliability they must be rejected. Of current interest is the appearance of the "Hitler Diaries," now alleged to be a hoax from having failed to meet the test of genuineness in not being sufficiently old, in not coming from the proper repository and in bearing on their face indications alleged to demonstrate their fraudulent character. The holy scriptures, on the contrary, fully met these requisites of admissibility and would thus be acceptable as evidence in any court in the land on these grounds. More, vastly more, grounds, however, obtain in support of the admissibility of the sacred writings than any rules of evidence human wisdom may construct because their credibility rests not on the wisdom of men alone but on the direct testimony of Deity who gave them, and who *cannot* lie!

Conviction of the truth of his word not only produces strong assent, it also prompts its possessor to assert it kindly, courageously, and unhesitatingly to others. Paul wrote, "We also believe, and *therefore* speak. . . ." (2 Corinthians 4:13.) One's dedication to the divine message and desire to influence others to similar commitment and acceptance is in direct ratio to the assurance felt in the heart as to its truth, desirability, and reliability.

The principles that follow are clearly and unmistakably taught in the scriptures; they have been subjected to a trial of fire on thousands of battlefronts for hundreds of years and they have proved to be absolutely invincible in every contest—they simply cannot be overthrown. These propositions are grounded in the infallible testimony of God himself; to question them is simply to impeach the Creator. Do we believe, truly believe, his word? Let us test the matter by noting our reaction and response to the following propositions.

1. The Bible is God's final message to man. In this, the Christian age, the New Testament meets our every need (2 Timothy 3:17,18); it

is inerrant, infallible, all-authoritative, verbally inspired and contains all we need to know in order to obtain salvation here and hereafter.

2. The conditions of salvation are faith (Hebrews 11:6), repentance (Luke 13:3), confession (Romans 10:10), and baptism, in water, for (or unto) the remission of sins (Acts 2:38). The "baptism" to which they of the first century were required to submit consisted of a burial in water. (Romans 6:4; Acts 10:45.)

3. Those who did so obtained pardon and the Lord, in the process of saving them, added them to his church. (Acts 2:47.)

4. Those thus added were called Christians (Acts 11:26), they met regularly on the first day of the week for worship and in their Lord's day meetings sang the praises of God unaccompanied by instrumental music (Ephesians 5:18,19; Colossians 3:16); they partook each first day of the Lord's supper (Acts 20:7) and they contributed of their means as they were prospered (Acts 2:42; 1 Corinthians 16:1,2).

5. The church to which the Lord added them is identified in collective capacity, as "the churches of Christ," i.e., churches owned by Christ; and whose members honored him by bearing his name. (Romans 16:16; Acts 11:26.) Only those who obeyed him were said to be "in" him (Ephesians 1:3), and therefore in possession of salvation (Romans 6:3,4).

6. The church of which we read in these scriptures began on the day of Pentecost following the Lord's resurrection (Daniel 7:13,14; Mark 9:1; Acts 1:8; 2:47), and thus antedates, by hundreds of years, the oldest denominational body ever established.

The Bible being true, the foregoing propositions necessarily follow and from them the following conclusions must be drawn:

1. New Testament Christians are not Catholic, Jewish or Protestant; the religion to which they subscribe originated in the teaching of Christ and his apostles, and they may move neither to the right nor to the left of the inspired and divine directions by them given. Denominationalism, of whatever variety, is human in origin, contrary to the spirit and teaching of New Testament Christianity, harmful to its best interests and directly responsible for the divisions among religious people which the scriptures repeatedly condemn.

2. Creeds, confessions of faith, church disciplines, and dogmas wrought out in church councils, synods and conferences are unnecessary accretions, wholly divisive in nature, and serve only to perpetuate and create further schisms and warring factions among men.

3. Sprinkling and pouring for baptism, infant church membership, instrumental music, church choirs, the worship of images, holy water, penance, auricular confession, and a great host of other current practices in religion, are the fruits of apostasy, and began to be practiced only when men were no longer satisfied with the scriptures as a suffi-

cient rule of faith and practice and turned to the doctrines and commandments of men. (Matthew 15:1-9.)

4. The New Testament church began in Jerusalem by the direction of the Lord in A.D. 33; any organization which started at any other time, at any other place, and by any other authority cannot be identified with the church for which the Saviour died. (Acts 2:47; 20:28.) The scriptures make no mention of a Roman church, an English church, a Lutheran church, a Baptist church, a Methodist church or any other church which began, as all of these did, hundreds of years this side of the apostolic age. No human organization, however worthy its aims, respectable its membership or imposing its properties, can substitute for the church of our Lord.

5. Good citizenship, respectability, morality cannot save a single soul from sin and only those who believe and obey the Lord are promised salvation. (Mark 16:16.) Salvation cannot be obtained by faith alone (James 2:24), repentance alone, baptism alone (1 Peter 3:21), grace alone or works alone (James 2:20). The end of those who do not fully obey the gospel is everlasting destruction. (1 Peter 4:16-18; 2 Thessalonians 1:7-9.) Believing this, and doing something about it involves genuine faith.

"Discuss the difference between faith and knowledge."

The disposition to regard faith as a form of emotionalism has long been with us and in former days the wide swings of subjectivism such a concept inevitably produces was considered to be normal and expected. Those thus possessed even sang about it: "Tis a thought I long to know/ oft it gives me anxious thought/ do I love the Lord, or no/ am I his or am I not?" Feelings were thus suffered to take the place of facts and that which resulted, though often styled faith, was far, very far from it. Genuine faith derives from facts presented to the mind and from which proper and correct deductions are then drawn. (John 20:30, 31.) Feelings which necessarily follow are the *effect,* not the cause, of faith.

More recently, a much more sophisticated form of subjectivism has appeared wherein faith and knowledge are compartmentalized, put in sharp contrast, and each made to exclude the other—the allegation being that a proposition which one holds by faith one cannot know by deduction—a conclusion reached by taking one definition of the word "know," putting it in opposition to the word "faith" thus making them mutually exclusive. To do this is to err with reference both to faith and to knowledge!

True, "to know" means "to have direct cognition of," that is, to be responsive to sensory stimuli; but, it can also mean "to be aware of" through evidence presented to the mind, and this is what faith is. (Hebrews 11:1.) Indeed, the two terms are often used interchangeably, differing in such use only in the fact that *to know* emphasizes the impact of the senses on the matters involved whereas, *to believe* produces no less assurance but bases the sentiment resulting on the trustworthiness of the testimony which leads reason to faith.

The word "know" is often used in the sacred writings to denote that disposition ordinarily spoken of as "believing." "But as for me I *know* that my redeemer liveth, and at last he will stand upon the earth. . . ." (Job 19:25.) This Job *knew*! That is, the confidence he felt in the truth expressed was such that he could and did say he knew it. He had no sensory evidence of it. He had neither seen, tasted, smelled, felt nor heard with bodily organs that which he affirmed. Yet, he knew it! (Cf. 2 Corinthians 5:1; 2 Timothy 1:12.) Such is common biblical usage.

To say that a man cannot hold by faith a truth that he holds by reason also is effectively to say that there is no place for logic in proving propositions involving faith. The Restoration movement provides an effective answer to this erroneous conclusion; an open Bible and irresistible logic, in the hands of faithful men, battered down countless doors of error in all of its forms in truth's ongoing sweep over the world, and continues to serve its adherents as effectively today. Paul, in Acts 14:17, inferentially argued God's goodness, as demonstrated in rain and fruitful seasons freely bestowed, this being a "witness" to his existence and benevolence—a logical conclusion (by inspiration) drawn from the premises mentioned. Rather than to say, "If reason establishes the way man has no need for faith," it should be said, reason enables one by the use of faculties divinely given—a logical and intelligent mind—to arrive at faith. There is no such thing as "blind" faith. Faith itself is possible only when reason recognizes the trustworthiness of the testimony which produces it.

"Discuss the foreknowledge of God."

The doctrine, that God did, from all eternity, "by the most wise and holy counsel of his own will, freely and unchangeably ordain whatsoever comes to pass," is a basic tenet of all Calvinistic creeds. Some consequences which logically follow such a view were, at least in times past, readily and unhesitatingly embraced, notwithstanding their objectionable characteristics, by those who, because of an erroneous concept of biblical teaching regarding divine foreknowledge, accepted the creedal statement, in full. It is insisted by those who subscribe thereto that God "for his own glory" ordained to salvation a portion of humanity, while ignoring and passing by others, through no merit or action on the part of the former and because of no default or failure on the part of the latter, each action of God being by arbitrary decree.

If God did, from all eternity, "freely and unchangeably ordain whatsoever comes to pass," it is impossible for a human being to violate the divine will. Any action which man may do, be it good or bad, is the result of such ordination; and, in the last analysis, is really the act of God! If a man takes the life of another in cold blood, God has not only so ordained it, he has ordained it unchangeably and from all eternity. The theory admits of no human responsibility whatsoever. Was there ever a more false and foolish doctrine taught? It is true that the compilers of this creed sought to avoid some of the obvious consequences of this affirmation by adding, "Yet so is thereby neither is God the author of sin." But, why not? If God has ordained everything, then he has ordained every act that man performs—good or bad—in which case every act of man is traceable directly to God, and for it God, not man, sustains the responsibility. The effort to avoid the conclusion sought by the defenders of this view fails because the conclusion is not only not in the premises, it is in palpable conflict with them. Millions of people today for either religious or philosophical reasons accept the fatalistic conclusion this theory provides.

This distasteful doctrine results from the erroneous notion that divine foreknowledge necessarily includes foreordination. It starts with the mistaken premise that because God knows and sees the end from the beginning he must therefore have planned the end from the beginning. It concludes with the view that the fact of foreknowledge supports, indeed, makes necessary, immutable decrees.

Strange that multitudes of people at least nominally subscribe to this doctrine; stranger still that others who reject the basic premise of unconditional election nevertheless argue for some of its tenets because of a vague or mistaken conception of what the foreknowledge of God involves. For example, there are those who insist that 1 Peter 1:19,20 teaches that the plan of salvation antedated the fall and was provided for man before creation. (A detailed discussion and exegesis of this passage by this writer will be found in *A Commentary on the Epistles of Peter, John and Jude*, published by the Gospel Advocate Co.) It is sufficient for our present purpose simply to point out that "world" in this passage is from the Greek "cosmos," an orderly system, hence, age or dispensation. This "dispensation" was that which preceded the Christian age, announced by Moses, and revealed to him on Sinai. Thus long after the fall in Eden the plan was given and the types which prefigured it were made known.

The projection of a plan to save fallen man into the period prior to the Fall raises immediately and inevitably the question of the free agency of Adam and Eve. If God had already provided a plan to save them from a sin they were certain to commit, in what possible way could they have avoided its commission? If our Lord were indeed a lamb slain before creation for the expiation of the sin of Adam and Eve, how could their action have been other than it was, since not only it but its consequences had already been arranged and provided for in the councils of eternity? In such a view of the case, since our first parents were but passive actors in a drama written and sealed before they had existence, ought not they to be commended for their obedience in dutifully supporting a scheme ordained for them in eternity and which they could not possibly have changed without falsifying God's immutable plan? This conclusion is so obviously and palpably false we may be sure that the premises which lead to it are highly suspect and therefore fallacious. They follow from the failure to make the proper distinction between foreknowledge and foreordination—the difference between knowing of an action and planning it.

Isaiah wrote, "Thus saith the high and lofty One that inhabiteth eternity, whose name is Holy." (Isaiah 57:15.) Since the dwelling place of deity is eternity, time as we know it does not exist with God. He occupies the entire spectrum of time and eternity; with him all is present whether it be with us past, present or future. All things are ever before him; he is without either past or future limits; all of that of which we measure in time is ever before his eyes. He lives in eternity and sees it all; we live amid the restrictions of time and "see" only that which is occurring; but his knowledge of all things past, present and future is no more the occasion for the things that happen than our knowledge of the present causes everything to happen! We should be careful to distinguish between causative knowledge and the awareness which sees but does not originate, whether it be with reference to God or man. Adam and Eve were under no compulsion to do wrong nor were they bound by some immutable and eternal decree to follow a course already determined for them.

They were free, wholly free, to choose right or wrong; they chose to do wrong and thus violated the will of God and were justly deserving of the condemnation which they received.

"Explain 1 Corinthians 1:11-13."

It seems quite likely that Paul wrote First Corinthians in the early part of A.D. 57 and near the end of the three-years' period of his labors in Ephesus. He had established the church in Corinth approximately five years before; and the immediate occasion of its writing appears to have been the arrival of a family, or some portion thereof, of a Christian woman of Corinth named Chloe. From her, or from members of her household, the apostle learned of conditions prevailing in the church in Corinth and requiring his immediate attention.

He wrote: "It hath been signified unto me concerning you, my brethren, by them that are of the household of Chloe, that there are contentions among you. Now this I mean, that each one of you saith, I am of Paul; and I of Apollos; and I of Cephas; and I of Christ. Is Christ divided? was Paul crucified for you? or were ye baptized into the name of Paul?" (1 Corinthians 1:11-13.) The contentions in Corinth grew out of partyism; and the partyism was the result of extreme favoritism toward preachers! So pronounced were these preferences factions had arisen and alienations had resulted. Though Paul was among those thus "honored," he rejected and repudiated the situation as being wholly foreign to the will of the Lord.

"Is Christ divided?" he pointedly asked, literally, "Is Christ parcelled out in small portions?" Did the Corinthians think that it was possible to rend the body of Christ into small bits and divide it among the several factions existing? This is the implication which obtains wherever division occurs in the body of Christ. Though Paul was one of those elevated to the head of a party, he refused to accept it with the inquiry, "Was Paul crucified for you?" Had the apostle died on the cross for those who sought to follow him there would be some appropriateness in the situation; but, he was not crucified for them and they were therefore in grave error in seeking to identify themselves by his name. He further inquired, "Were ye baptized into Paul's name, they might, with propriety, wear his name. They had been baptized "into the name of Christ" (Matthew 28:18-20); only Christ's name—Christian—might they therefore properly wear.

Lessons of great present and practical value emerge from this interesting and significant incident. We are able clearly to see that baptism "into the name of the Father and of the Son and of the Holy Spirit" is absolutely essential to becoming a Christian. The pattern of the apostle's argument is this: Had you been baptized into the name of Paul you would be a Paulite; had you been baptized into the name of Cephas you would be a Cephasite; had you been baptized into the name of Apollos you would be an Apollosite. But, you were not baptized into Paul's name, therefore, you are not a Paulite; you were not baptized into Cephas' name, therefore you are not a Cephasite; you were not baptized into Apollos' name, therefore, you are not an Apollosite. You were, however, baptized into the name of Christ, therefore, you are a Christian and you may properly wear no other name religiously except that of Christ—Christian! There is one step more in this logical and obvious chain: If you have not been baptized at all, you have no right to any name religiously—not Paul's, not Cephas', not Apollos', not Luther's, not Calvin's, not even Christ's!

Here, too, is clear evidence of the fact that the disciples of the first century church were taught not only to accept Christ as their only head religiously but also to reflect this fact to others by wearing only his name. Luke, the inspired historian of the early church, wrote that the disciples "were called Christians first in Antioch." (Acts 11:26.) It is significant that these disciples not only claimed to be Christians, it was by this divinely given name they were known. It is in this name—the name Christian—that we glorify God. (1 Peter 4:16.)

"In a congregation where there are two elders and one of them resigns may the other continue to serve as the sole elder of the congregation?"

No.

For a number of reasons it was the will of the Divine Mind that the oversight of the church (congregation) be vested in an *eldership* consisting of two or more persons. In every instance where reference is made in the sacred writings to men serving in this capacity a plurality is mentioned. 1 Timothy 5:17: "Let the elders that rule well be counted worthy of double honor. . . ." Titus 1:5: "Appoint elders in every city." Hebrews 11:2: "The elders had witness borne to them." James 5:14: "Call for the elders of the church." 1 Peter 5:1: "The elders therefore among you I exhort." Paul and Barnabas appointed "elders" in every church in Asia Minor where they preached. Oversight of the congregation and the necessary powers involved in the discharge of this duty (Hebrews 13:7,17), is not in *an elder* as distinguished from the body of elders but in *the eldership*. It follows, therefore, that when elders are divided in sentiment the congregation is without scriptural leadership in the matters involved. It is imperative in such cases that the eldership get its house in order since it is impossible to have a *united* congregation and a *divided* eldership.

"The Bible says that a man can put away his wife for fornication only. (Matthew 19:9.) However, many brethren say that a wife can also put away her husband for fornication, without giving scriptures for authority for switching it around."

The Bible abounds with instances such as this where the principle applies equally to men and women. "He that soweth sparingly shall reap also sparingly; and he that soweth bountifully shall reap also bountifully." (2 Corinthians 9:6.) Should we from this infer that the principle stated is applicable only to the male of the species since it does *not* read, "*She* that soweth sparingly . . .? Jesus said, "*He* that believeth and is baptized shall be saved." (Mark 16:16.) Are women excluded by the fact that it does not read, "*She* that believeth and is baptized shall be saved?" Peter, having become fully convinced by the events at Caesarea that the Gentiles were to become fellow-heirs with the Jews, remarked, "Of a truth I perceive that God is no respecter of persons: but in every nation *he* that feareth him, and worketh righteousness is acceptable to him." (Acts 10:34,35.) The "he" of this passage is generic in usage and is as applicable to women as to men. Such is also true of Matthew 19:9.

"In a recent issue of the GOSPEL ADVOCATE were two fine pieces by women. I have trouble seeing the difference in a woman teaching mixed groups in a paper and in a Bible class or preaching."

First Timothy 2:11,12 forbids a woman to teach "over a man." That there is a difference in teaching a man and teaching *over* a man is very clear from the fact that Priscilla, wife of Aquila, did indeed, and with the obvious approval of the Holy Spirit participate in the teaching of Apollos. (Acts 18:24-28.) Moreover, it would have been equally acceptable for Aquila and Priscilla to have written the instructions to the young evangelist which they gave orally. In teaching *over* a man there is the exercise of authority which 1 Timothy 2:11,12 forbids; this is certainly involved in preaching (see Titus 2:15), and to some extent also in the teaching of Bible classes, since the teacher both directs and controls in some measure those participating. In reading material sent out, the reader exercises his own will and pleasure in the perusal and is in no sense subject to, nor under the domination of, the author.

"Is it permissible to have quartet singing during the worship hour on the Lord's day?"

All children of God are to participate in worship. Singing is one of the items of worship. All children of God must sing in worship in order to be pleasing to God. (Acts 2:42; Ephesians 5:18,19; Colossians 3:16.) The practice of quartet singing in Lord's day worship is without precedent in the apostolic age and should therefore be shunned by all who wish to have the Lord's approval today. Only by complete conformity to New Testament teaching and practice may we be assured of that approval.

"Please explain 1 Peter 3:19-21."

The passage and its context reads: "Because Christ also suffered for sins once, the righteous for the unrighteous, that he might bring us to

God; being put to death in the flesh, but made alive in the spirit; in which also he went and preached unto the spirits in prison that aforetime were disobedient, when the longsuffering of God waited in the days of Noah, while the ark was a-preparing, wherein few, that is, eight souls, were saved through water; which also after a true likeness doth now save you, even baptism, not the putting away of the filth of the flesh, but the interrogation of a good conscience toward God, through the ressurrection of Jesus Christ."

Christ preached; the spirit which motivated him in this preaching was the inner principle of life not subject to death. Those to whom he preached are identified by Peter as "spirits in prison." They are called "spirits" because they were in a disembodied state when Peter wrote; and they were "in prison," i.e., under restraint as wicked beings. Peter does not say that those who were the objects of this preaching were in a disembodied state *when the preaching was done;* such describes their status *when he wrote.* These now in the spirit world were once in the flesh; they were disobedient; the period of their disobedience was while the ark was being built; and it was during this interval that Christ preached to them. This he did through Noah—he being the principal and Noah his agent, in the same way that he baptized through the disciples (John 4:1) and preached through the apostles to the Gentiles (Ephesians 2:17). The wicked world rejected the Lord's preaching through Noah and perished. Noah's family were saved "through water"; the water bore up the ark and carried them away from the corruption of the old world. This deliverance is a type of our salvation from the world of sin in water baptism. It should be observed that Peter does not say that Noah and his family were saved *in* water, nor *from* water; they were saved *through* water—through this water God exercised his saving power. In this there is a "true likeness" in the manner in which baptism saves today, not of course as a Saviour, but as an instrument through which God exercises saving power.

Lest the reader should conclude that baptism must then be some sort of a ceremonial rite in which physical defilement is removed the apostle points out that it is not "the putting away of the filth of the flesh," it is not to be confused with a bath for the body or the ceremonial cleansing of the flesh but "the interrogation of a good conscience toward God." A good conscience is not proof of salvation (Saul of Tarsus had this while persecuting the church of the Lord—Acts 23:1) but it prompts one to desire to do fully God's will; and since baptism is a condition precedent to salvation, one thus possessed will earnestly desire to be baptized. (Mark 16:15,16; Acts 2:38; 22:16.) Baptism derives its significance "through the resurrection of Christ" which it symbolizes. Baptism "doth now save" only because our Lord was raised from the dead.

"I noticed in one of the GOSPEL ADVOCATE Quarterlies that the time is referred to as A.M. 1. Please explain this and how it is used in reference to B.C."

In order that all the space possible may be given to explanation and exposition of the sacred text, the writers of the comments frequently use abbreviated forms and contractions in order to shorten words and phrases, and so reduce the space required. This practice is limited to those instances where long usage has established such contractions, abbreviations and forms as standard procedure.

The most common ones follow:

(1) A. M., the abbreviated form of the Latin phrase, *anno mundi* (an'no mun'di), which means "in the year of the world," and is used to fix the date of any given incident from creation. For example, "A.M. 1500," would signify, "fifteen hundred years after creation." Adam Clarke regularly uses this manner of reckoning, listing it at the head of all chapters in the Old Testament. His chronology is based on the system devised by Archbishop Ussher which few students would regard as absolute, particularly prior to the flood.

(2) A. D., the abbreviation for *anno Domini* (an'no dom'i-ni), "in the year of (our) Lord," i.e., the Lord Jesus Christ. This is used to designate the period specified within the Christian era, as A. D. 1959, nineteen hundred and fifty-nine years after the beginning of the Christian era. This date, however, is slightly misleading, because of the present system of chronology. Students of the birth of Christ are often perplexed to note that he was actually born *four years* before the time from which we count his birth. The reason is that centuries passed after his birth before anyone attempted to calculate dates *from* the birth of Christ; and, then, when the monk—Dionysius—did so in A. D. 256, he made a mistake of four years in his calculations. He placed the birth of our Lord in the year of Rome 754. But, it is known that Herod the Great who issued the decree for the slaughter of the male children at Bethlehem died in April of the year of Rome 750. Christ was born shortly before this event—and thus four years earlier than that designated by Dionysius. He was, therefore, five years old at the close of A. D. 1. Many years passed before the error was widely discovered; and, inasmuch as the dates were scattered in records throughout the world, the matter was allowed to stand, being rectified, at least in part, by the designation of B. C. 4 or 5, for the actual birth of Jesus.

(3) B. C., designates the phrase, "before Christ." Thus 1500 B. C., means fifteen hundred years before the birth of Christ.

(4) Numerous other devices are used to shorten words and phrases to conserve space, common to all writers: viz., abbreviation of the Latin *videlicet*—namely; i.e., for the Latin *id est*—that is; etc., *et cetera*—and

129

so on or and so forth; mms—manuscript; D. V., abbreviation for the Latin *Deo volente*—God willing or by God's will; *ibid.*, for the Latin *ibidem*—in the same place; cf.—compare.

Every desk or study table should have a good dictionary of the English language. Judiciously used, it will be found to contain a vast gold mine of invaluable information to those who would be good students of the word. One of the major causes of poor and inadequate study is the failure fully to apprehend the meaning of English words. The wisdom of the ages is buried in marvelous translations in our mother tongue. Surely there is no endeavor so glorious for the mind of man as the industrious mining of this priceless ore.

"What is death?"

"The body *without the spirit* is dead." (James 2:26.)

Death then, is that condition which is obtained when the spirit, the conscious entity of man derived directly from God (Hebrews 12:9), is no longer in the body. Many questions which clamor for solution must await the day when faith ends in sight and hope in realization. We may, however, from the allusions which the sacred writers make to man's passing, reach some very definite conclusions regarding the characteristics of this experience awaiting us all at the end of life's day. Word pictures which they draw of our passing allow us to catch a glimpse of what we may expect when it is ours to walk into the gathering twilight as the sun of life sinks for the last time on the hills of earth.

Paul, aware that the moment of his passing was not far distant, said, "I am now ready to be offered, and the time of my departure is at hand." (2 Timothy 4:6.) The word "departure" in this passage is translated from the Greek *ana-lusis,* definitions of which Thayer lists as follows: "An unloosing (as of things woven), a dissolving (into separate parts). Departure (a metaphor drawn from loosing from moorings preparatory to setting sail) . . . or, according to others, from breaking up an encampment. . . ." Forms of this word occur in both 2 Timothy 4:6, and Philippians 1:23, passages descriptive of death. Death is, then,

(1) The unraveling of a garment, the separation and disentanglement of the threads of a woven cloth. As a piece of cloth, by unraveling, returns to the element out of which it was made, so the individual, in death undergoes the separation of body and spirit the combination of which is life. Separated, the body returns to the dust out of which it was made and the spirit wings its way into the unseen realm there to await the resurrection and judgment.

(2) "A dissolving into separate parts," an *analysis* wherein there is a division into constituent parts or elements. This figure is opposite in

130

describing the results which attend the flight of the spirit from the body thus "dissolving into separate parts" the elements which constitute man.

(3) Death is a "departure" and is used of the "breaking up of camp," and the loosing of moorings as a ship prepares to hoist its sails and launch out into the great deep. (a) The activities which characterize the taking down of a tent figuratively picture in impressive fashion the experience of death. Death is truly a journey; and, the lonely traveler of the sandy reaches of Eastern world was not without his shelter. Any journey was necessarily preceded by the taking down of the tent. It is significant that the body is styled a *tent* in the sacred writings: "For we know that, if our earthly house of this tabernacle were dissolved, we have a building of God, an house not made with hands, eternal in the heavens." (2 Corinthians 5:1.) Here the word "tabernacle" is from the Greek word *skeenee,* tent.

(b) Moreover, it is the loosing of the anchor or ropes which hold a ship to the shore in order that it may move out into the deep. This is a common figure of our passing. Poets, preachers and painters have often seen in the sailing of a ship a pictorial representation of death. In this day of air travel many people have never experienced the thrill of seeing a great vessel going out to sea. There is something wonderfully majestic and magnificent in the departure of a giant ocean liner. The bustle of boarding, the tears of parting, the heady excitement of a new adventure and the throaty roar of the ship's whistle announcing departure, kindle interest to thrilling heights. As the mighty vessel glides out to sea and slowly fades from the sight of the watching throng, the shout ascends: "There, she goes!" And, it is not long until other watchers, on another shore, catch a glimpse of her appearance in the glimmering haze, and cry: "There, she comes!" So it is with those who loose from life's moorings and sail away on the billowing waves of death. Though they pass for a moment from our eyes, others on distant and sunwashed shores wait and watch with joy for their coming.

"Twilight and evening bell, and after that, the dark:
And may there be no sadness of farewell, when I embark.
And though from out our bourne of time and place, the flood
may bear me far;
I hope to see my Pilot face to face, when I have crossed the
bar."

(4) A state of peaceful, dreamless sleep. "But I would not have you to be ignorant, brethren, concerning *them which are asleep,* that ye sorrow not, even as others which have no hope." (1 Thessalonians 4:13.) Here, the word translated "sleep" is from the Greek *koiman,* to put to sleep, whence we derive our word cemetery—from the Greek *kometerion,* "a sleeping chamber, burial place." The word "sleep" is a euphe-

mism for the word *die,* and is often so used in the scriptures. We are not from this to assume, however, that death, in every respect, is comparable to sleep; it is not. The cessation of consciousness, characteristic of sleep, is not a concomitant of death. Death is like sleep in that it is a ceasing from activity, a season of rest and repose. In response to the question, "Is death the last sleep?" Walter Scott truly said, "No, it is the last and final awakening."

"What is verbal inspiration?"

It is the view that the Bible is an inbreathed, inspired, divine document which, as originally given, is absolutely inerrant, infallible and, therefore, true.

(1) Such is the claim which it makes for itself: "All Scripture is given by inspiration of God . . . for instruction in righteousness: That the man of God may be perfect, thoroughly furnished unto all good works." (2 Timothy 3:16,17.) "For the prophecy came not in old time by the will of man: but holy men of God spake as they were moved by the Holy Ghost." (2 Peter 1:21.) "But I certify you, brethren, that the gospel which was preached of me is not after man. For I neither received it of man, neither was I taught it, but by the revelation of Jesus Christ." (Galatians 1:11.)

(2) More than 2,000 times the Scriptures assert the fact that they issued from God. "The Spirit of the Lord spake by me, and his word was in my tongue." (2 Samuel 23:2.) "And the Lord said unto me, Behold, I have put my words in thy mouth." (Jeremiah 1:9.) "I have given unto them the words which thou gavest me." (John 17:8.) "Take no thought beforehand what ye shall speak . . . but whatsoever shall be given you in that hour, that speak ye." (Mark 13:11.) What shall be thought of one who affects to believe the Bible, yet asserts that it has a fallible human element to be sifted by "sanctified common sense" from the divine, in the light of these affirmations?

(3) Nothing short of *verbal inspiration* will meet the demands of the case which the Bible presents. History affords manifold instances of the difficulties which men face in determining the meaning and intent of documents which were written by seasoned and scholarly writers, men who wrote under the conviction that their words would be subjected to the most minute and searching examination, and who were, nevertheless, unable to avoid the litigation they had diligently sought to circumvent. Such is a common occurrence in the matter of wills, though written by legal experts; the Constitution of the United States of America, though penned by the ablest statesmen and lawyers which the land afforded, has been and remains a source of greatest difference of opinion regarding its meaning; and the translators of the King James'

and American Standard Versions, though among the world's ripest scholars, were unable to select words to convey the mind and meaning of the Holy Spirit in every instance wholly satisfactory to all students today. It is significant that the authors of the Constitution of our land, the ablest legal minds of the day, and the most profound scholars of the time could not have received a divine message and then *in their own words* have delivered it to the world in such unambiguous fashion that the meaning was always and everywhere apparent. But, if such men could not have done this, are we to suppose that a group of ignorant fishermen, insignificant and uneducated peasants of Palestine, shepherds and herdsmen, could have succeeded where they failed?

(4) The Law which issued from Sinai, a limited, temporary and confessedly inferior law in the light of the one to follow, was handed to Moses from the hand of God, written by Deity, on tables of stone. Are we to conclude that, though this law was, by its manner of deliverance, protected from the possibility of error, the law of Christ was vouchsafed to the world through the weak and fallible minds of uneducated, untrained and unscholarly fishermen, tax collectors, etc.? It is admitted that the only way we have of ascertaining the truth and accuracy of the word of God is through the record by which it has been delivered to the world. Must we rely on the judgment of such men who wrote according to the wisdom which they possessed, and this without divine guidance?

(5) Near the close of the Revelation, a solemn warning against any addition, subtraction or modification is appended: "For I testify unto every man that heareth the words of the prophecy of this book, if any man shall add unto these things, God shall add unto him the plagues that are written in this book: and if any man shall take away from the words of the book of this prophecy, God shall take away his part out of the book of life, and out of the holy city, and from the things which are written in this book." (Revelation 22:18,19.) It will be observed that here the *words* are of such divine significance that they can neither be added to, nor subtracted from. Are we to conclude that the description of heaven is set out in the Revelation in a fashion more sure than the conditions essential for us to comply with in order to get there in other portions of the Bible?

On the occasion of the birthday of the New Testament church—on the first Pentecost following our Lord's resurrection—the apostles, though without formal education in the schools of higher learning, spoke fluently and intelligibly in languages hitherto unknown to them. Who would be so naive as to believe that the words which they uttered were of their own choosing and that they addressed themselves to the multitude in languages unknown to them but which they spoke without divine dictation? When Peter, the spokesman of the occasion, delivered the words of Acts 2:39, regarding the inclusion of the Gentiles, he had no conception of the significance of what he was saying; and was later to require a miracle to convince him of the truth of that which he here spoke. This fact argues irresistibly for verbal inspiration; indeed, no other conclusion is possible. Our Lord said to the apostles, "But when they shall lead you, and deliver you up, take no thought beforehand what ye shall speak, neither do you premeditate: but whatsoever shall be given you in that hour, that speak ye: for it is not ye that speak, but the Holy Ghost." (Mark 13:11.) Observe that the apostles were not to *think* what they were to speak; this would be supplied them by the Spirit. There is but one way in which one can speak—that is to utter words! The Holy Spirit would perform this through the apostles. The words, "for it is not ye that speak, but the Holy Ghost," mean *it is not you who give utterance to these ideas in words, it is the Holy Spirit which gives utterance to these ideas in words through you.* (1 Corinthians 2:13.)

This is verbal inspiration.

"In Romans 8:16 the Holy Spirit is referred to as 'itself.' Does this lend support to the view that the Holy Spirit is simply and solely an influence and not a distinct Person?"

No. The King James translators rendered the phrase *auto to pneuma* "the Spirit itself" to indicate the grammatical relationship subsisting between the pronoun and its antecedent. Because the *pneuma* (Spirit) is neuter gender *in form,* the translators, to maintain the accord in English which exists in the Greek text, rendered the pronoun "itself"; this does not mean that the Person so designated is neither masculine nor feminine; quite the contrary, the Holy Spirit is clearly indicated to be of masculine gender by the pronouns in the following passage: "Howbeit when HE, the Spirit of truth, is come, HE will guide you into all truth: for HE shall not speak of HIMSELF; but whatsoever HE shall hear, that shall HE speak: and HE will show you things to come." (John 16:13.) In this remarkable affirmation it was the Spirit's intent to make clear that his actual gender is masculine from the fact that the word *ekeinos* is used. Thus, the consideration which led the KJ translators to render the pronoun "itself" resulted from grammatical grounds rather than actual ones; the American Standard translators more properly looked at the actual gender of the Spirit and translated it "himself." The Holy Spirit is not simply or solely an influence; he is a Person wielding an influence and this is done through means—the revelation of truth which he made through the writers of the Scriptures. (1 Corinthians 2:9-13.)

134

"What was the purpose of John's baptism? Were those who submitted to John's baptism rebaptized on the day of Pentecost or thereafter? Explain why those of whom we read in Acts 19:1ff were required to be baptized again."

John was the "harbinger"—the forerunner—of Christ whose work was to prepare a people for the Lord (Isaiah 40:3, Matthew 3:3), and this work consisted (in part) of inducing people to repent and be baptized (Mark 1:4; Luke 3:3). Those who thus did became a part of that body which, on the day of Pentecost, constituted the New Testament church. None of these was rebaptized. To assume otherwise is to conclude that even the apostles were in their sins until that day; and, there is no indication whatsoever that any were baptized on that day except those addressed by Peter as having been a part of the movement, either actually or substantially, who had previously condemned the Christ and who encouraged his death. (Acts 2:36.) Moreover, it is specifically stated that those who responded to Peter's command to be baptized "for the remission of sins" were added to "the church" (KJV)," "unto them" (ASV). One does not add something to nothing; it follows, therefore that the body of disciples which became the nucleus of the New Testament church on the day of Pentecost consisted of John's disciples, plus those garnered by the Lord and his associates prior to the day of Pentecost. These became the infant church when the Spirit brought life to the body at 9 a.m. that morning.

The twelve who were baptized by Paul at Ephesus (Acts 19:1ff), were those who had submitted to John's baptism *after* the day of Pentecost, *after* the baptism of the Great Commission became effective, *after* the beginning of the Christian dispensation. All of those, including the apostles, who were baptized "unto John's baptism," *prior* to the cross and the establishment of the church, when only the baptism of John was available, had acceptable baptism and were not rebaptized."

"Does grace rule out all law?"

"And Peter opened his mouth, and said, Of a truth I perceive that God is no respecter of persons: but in every nation he that feareth him, and worketh righteousness, is acceptable to him." (Acts 10:34,35.) Righteousness is a condition precedent to approval before God. What is it? How is it obtained?

Righteousness denotes that state or condition wherein one is in a *right* relationship with God. Our English word "righteousness," derives from the word "right," which, in turn, suggests that which is straight (as, for example, a straight line), and so designates a relationship with God which he approves. A "righteous man" is, therefore, one who is straight, i.e., *lined up properly* with God! The Psalmist said, "All thy commandments are righteousness," and John affirmed that "every one also that doeth righteousness is begotten of him." (Psalm 119:172; 1 John 2:29.)

A simple, brief definition of righteousness is, therefore, right-doing; to be righteous, *is to do right.* "He that doeth righteousness is righteous, even as he is righteous." (1 John 3:7.) Of a certain type of character it is affirmed that he is righteous. Who is he? He that doeth righteousness. No other is. He who does righteousness is righteous; but, he who is righteous is one who does right; therefore, he who does right possesses righteousness. Conversely, an unrighteous person is a perverse one; a perverse one is an individual in a twisted (as opposed to straight) relationship with God. It is, hence, clear that righteousness is that state or condition wherein one is approved of God; but God approves of those only who do right (keep his commandments); therefore, to possess the approval of God and the righteousness which he requires one must do right, *by keeping his commandments.*

Here, indeed, is unmistakable evidence of the falsity of the denominational doctrine of transferred righteousness. It is by some alleged that in the process of conversion Christ transfers to the sinner the righteousness which he possesses, and thenceforth the sinner is clothed in the righteousness of Christ, i.e., the righteousness which Christ himself exhibits. The idea is repugnant to both reason and scripture. It is absurd to assume the one person is good because another is. It is, of course, true that through the merits of Christ's death, our guilt is cancelled and we are thenceforth permitted to go free, but this is far from declaring that we thereupon become positively good in the absence of *good works.* There is a vast difference in not imputing *guilt* (this, the Lord does for those he justifies); and in conferring merit (this, he does not) in the process of salvation. There is no instance in classical literature where the Greek word translated "righteousness" means to have been made actually righteous. The primary import of the term indicates a change in *position* and not of *condition.* A pardoned criminal is no longer guilty of the charges which brought him before the court; but he is thence by no means a valuable citizen with a long record of civic goodness back of him simply because he has been pardoned. Righteousness is right-doing. *To be righteous one must do right.*

But, was not Abraham's faith reckoned (imputed, counted) to him for righteousness? (Romans 4:9.) Indeed so. In the absence of further duties at the moment, God accepted Abraham's faith as an *act* of righteousness *itself.* (James 2:20-22.) Did not David speak of "the blessedness of the man, unto whom God imputeth righteousness without works"? (Romans 4:6.) Again the answer is in the affirmative. But he gravely errs who assumes that David in this instance promised positive purity of life merely because one believes. Moreover, the works contemplated here (as the context clearly shows) were the works of the law. Further, the man to whom God imputes righteousness is one whose "iniquities are forgiven, and whose sins are covered" (Psalm 32:1,2; Romans 4:6-8); he is one who actively complies with God's plan on the basis of which he justifies. We must distinguish between a righteousness imputed to (credited to, put to one's account, chalked up to), man because he has a right relationship with God through obedience to his will, and the righteousness which Christ (through his own submission to the will of his Father), is alleged to transfer to the sinner. The former, the New Testament teaches; the latter is Calvinism. But, was not Christ made "righteousness" for us? (1 Corinthians 1:30.) He became the *means* of righteousness; it is through him that we receive the "gift of righteousness" (Romans 5:17), but this is accomplished through compliance with his will and not through some mysterious bestowal of merit. It is of course through him that we are privileged to become righteous; but for him, no plan would exist through which approval before God might be attained. We must never forget, however, that it is through compliance therewith that we are enabled to be straight with God.

Law is "a rule of action." To insist that there is no place for *law* in the realm of grace is logically to deny that there is any occasion for human compliance to any rule of action (including the divine rules) in order to receive justification, thus excluding not only baptism on the ground that it is an act of man but also belief which is no less such an act, and also to controvert the testimony of the Holy Spirit Himself who designated "the law of the Spirit of Life in Christ Jesus" as that by which we are made free from "the law of sin and death." (Romans 8:2.) No amount of theological contortion can evade the fact that only those who fear God, and work righteousness are acceptable to him (Acts 10:34,35), and it is fatal to the soul's welfare so to do. The "works of God" (John 6:29; James 2:20-26), are works ordained of God as the avenues of his grace and to urge that the grace of God excludes compliance with his will as conditions precedent to its appropriation is simply to deny to man the channels through which God's grace flows and thus to close the door of grace itself!

"Why did the Lord pronounce a curse on the fig tree for not having fruit when, as Mark reveals, it was too early for the fruit, if not yet being 'the season of figs'?" (Mark 11:13.)

Shortly before our Lord's tragic death at Calvary he was enroute to Jerusalem from Bethany and, being hungry, approached a fig tree "having leaves," and finding no fruit "thereon" he spoke to the tree in the presence of accompanying disciples, "No man eat fruit from thee henceforward for ever." On a later morning the disciples walking with Jesus noted that the fig tree was shrivelled and withered to its roots; and Peter, recalling the earlier declaration of Jesus, commented, "Behold, the fig tree which thou cursedst is withered away."

Superficial and unsympathetic readers have occasionally charged Jesus with being unjust and unreasonable in his pronouncement but this results from an unawareness not only of the circumstances which prompted it but also from an unspiritual and materialistic disposition which blinds them to the higher motivation of the Savior in this and in other actions of his above and beyond the ordinary. The Palestinian fig tree has this unusual and exceptional characteristic: fruit normally appears before the leaves! Thus, a tree *with leaves* would suggest to those familiar with this peculiarity that the fruit was there also, since it normally appeared before the leaves. These events occurred about this time of the year (March); ordinarily, fruit did not mature before early June; but, it was no more unreasonable to expect fruit at the early date than it was leaves; the tree had the leaves; it was proper to expect that fruit was there also. The leaves heralded the fruit; in its absence, they became pretentious and false in their presentation, and brought down upon the tree the righteous wrath of the Lord.

The lesson for us in this is clear and unmistakable. Jesus looks with extreme disfavor upon those whose lives are pretentious, deceptive and hypocritical. Fruitfulness should precede all else; fame, a good name, an enviable reputation must all be posterior to fruitbearing in life.

"Is it a common practice for congregations that move to larger buildings to sell their old buildings to denominations? Is it a scriptural practice?"

It is not an uncommon practice for congregations to dispose of buildings no longer useful to them by selling them to some secular or religious groups, though it is by no means a universal practice. Often, brethren are able to utilize older property by integrating it with new construction and adapting it to Bible school purposes or other needs of the congregation. Sometimes, such property is given or sold to a smaller group of Christians desirous of continuing the worship of God at that place. In other instances, however, and especially when the congregation is moving to a more desirable location and into larger and better suited facilities the foregoing practices are not feasible, and the only alternative is to sell the property.

Is such a practice scriptural? Yes. A church building is an expedient; i.e., it simply expedites the Lord's work—enables it to achieve its obligations more effectively by providing more comfort and convenience for those who carry it on. But, it is not an essential element of such work and ought never to be regarded as such. We should never forget that every responsibility of the Lord's church may be discharged without any church building at all. There is, indeed, no indication whatsoever that any New Testament church ever held a deed to any property at all! There are many reasons why this was so but into which we shall not now enter since such is not pertinent to this discussion; but, it is important to take note of this fact in any discussion involving church buildings. That such are eminently scriptural follows from the fact that the command to assemble (Hebrews 10:25), implies a place to meet and such other arrangements as are conducive to the most fruitful and effective work at such a place. Church buildings certainly fall into this category. But, inasmuch as no New Testament church ever owned property, so far as the record extends, this points up the absurdity of making rules and regulations about their use not otherwise limited by the teaching of truth, the practice of New Testament worship, and conduct in harmony with moral principle set out in the scriptures.

Some congregations, of necessity, met in private homes (Romans 16:3-5; 1 Corinthians 16:19), but this did not create some sanctity or sacredness not otherwise characteristic of houses in which Christian people live. Similarly, when a building is no longer useful to the church, the Lord's money in it should be taken from it and put into property which will enable it to accomplish more for the Lord and to advance his cause more effectively than before. Admittedly, there is great sentimental attachment to a building in which we have long worshipped God and where those who preceded us worshipped and served, but such is also true of private property that has to us hallowed memories and associations we hold dear. Every house in which Christian families live is, in a very real and true sense, *a house of worship* because in it prayers and thanksgivings regularly ascend to God; and houses built by Christians and inhabited by them were built for worship as surely as are church buildings, even though the worship in the one cannot be exchanged for the other. Such property, though dear to our hearts, we do not regard as of such sacred significance that it must not be sold to those who might later misuse it. All such considerations are of secondary significance as they relate to the Lord's work and must give place to the proper answer to this question: *What course will best serve and advance the Cause for which the Saviour died?*

"In what sense was the kingdom of heaven at hand in Luke 21:31?"

If this verse stood alone in the sacred writings in its affirmation that the kingdom of heaven is "at hand," and were it contemplated apart from its general context and the parallel passages, it might be assumed that the words "at hand" have the same significance as in Matthew 3:2, where there is an allusion to the near approach of the kingdom on Pentecost. (Acts 1:6-8.) Matthew and Mark, along with Luke, refer to the same event and the meaning, whatever it is, must be regarded as the same in each instance. (Matthew 24:33, Mark 13:29 and Luke 21:31.) Further, all three writers make the statement, or one very similar, in connection with the parable of the fig tree, indicating that each intended that the words "at hand," "it is near" and "it is nigh thee," must be understood in the same fashion. Of additional significance is the fact that, in Matthew and Mark the pronoun "it" of the King James Version is more accurately rendered "he" in the American Standard translation, thus making the statement to read "he is nigh," an obvious reference to our Lord, and to his coming. Hence, Luke's statement, "the kingdom of God is nigh," must be understood as the coming of the Lord in his kingdom.

The parable of the fig tree was designed to teach the disciples how they might recognize the series of events which would evidence the truth of that which he affirmed and also enable them to know what events would precede his coming. As the leaves of the fig tree portended the coming of summer, so "all these things" earlier mentioned would precede the coming of the Lord in his kingdom. It should be carefully noted that "all these things" are to be regarded as distinct from his coming since it was yet future and thus his coming was no part of "all these things" which they were seeing. So also the statement, "This generation shall not pass away, till all things be accomplished" (Luke 21:32), does not include the coming of the Son of man in his kingdom but matters to occur before this event. How long, the text does not say, nor did the Lord know. (Matthew 24:36.) More specifically, all of these things to which the Saviour pointed as tokens of events yet to occur in the generation of those then living *did not include* the coming of the Lord and thus this event was not to be expected before that generation passed. It is, therefore, crystal clear that "the coming of the Lord" and his coming "in his kingdom" are references to his appearance at the end of this age when he shall come in power and great glory as indicated in Matthew 25:31ff.

"Who, or what, was God's battle-axe? (Jeremiah 51:20.)"

The Babylonians whom God used to punish his rebellious and disobedient people. In Jeremiah 50:23, they are called the "hammer of the whole earth," under the metaphor of a club by which the wicked people were chastised. The verbs in the Hebrew text in Jeremiah 51:20 are in the past tense. The Jews were in Babylonian captivity seventy years— fifty-one of these in Babylon—because of their sins, a punishment

140

which Jeremiah predicted and designated the period of it. (Jeremiah 21:1-7; 25:11.)

"Was Paul talking about himself or using himself as an example to teach the lesson in Romans 7:9?"

His statement is with reference to himself. In his early life, before he came to the knowledge of the truth in Christ, he felt no guilt and his conscience was clear regarding the course he was pursuing, notwithstanding the fact that he was relying on a system which had ceased to exist—the law of Moses. When, at length, he came to the full knowledge of the truth and to the realization that the works of the law could not save him, he discovered how deceived he had been and he experienced the feeling of a man condemned to die. This state he described as wretchedness. (Romans 7:24.) Was there then no hope for him, since the law on which he had relied, had deceived him and had become an instrument of Satan to destroy him? Yes; "I thank God through Jesus Christ our Lord!" Christ, not the law, was his Deliverer and in him he rejoiced.

"Please explain Romans 8:29,30."

> "For whom he did foreknow, he also did predestinate to be conformed to the image of his Son, that he might be the firstborn among many brethren. Moreover, whom he did predestinate, them he also called: and whom he called, them he also justified: and whom he justified, them he also glorified."

Here, as so often elsewhere in the Sacred Writings, it is imperative that the context be considered in order to the proper understanding of the text under study. There are those who have been "called." These are said to have been called by the "gospel." (v. 28.) Those who are called "according to his purpose" are described as the ones who "love God." Those who love God are the ones who keep his commandments. (1 John 5:3.) Therefore, the *called* who are contemplated here are those who have responded to the gospel, and who lovingly keep the Lord's commandments. Those who have so done have perfect assurance that whatever occurs, it will be made to work out to their advantage; no power on or under the earth can defeat the divine plan, because those he foreknew (recognized as his own) he predestinated (determined) that they should conform (in life and in conduct) "to the image of his Son." These, he *purposed* from the beginning to be called by the gospel, to be justified by the atonement and glorified at the end of the age by eternal salvation.

141

It will thus be seen that the *divine purpose* is the premise upon which the apostle's affirmation stands. Following the tragic fall of man in Eden's Bowers, God determined to provide a plan by which to redeem the race, and this plan remained in purpose until perfected in the atonement, the effects of which will not be fully realized until man is glorified in the age to come. The view contemplated is that which existed in the beginning; and, the steps are those which were to follow as the plan became operative. It must, therefore, be obvious that it was not the intent of the apostle to describe actual or arbitrary proceedings but such as were to follow logically in the ultimate discharge of the plan. The verbs *called, justified* and *glorified* are all in the past tense; the "glory" awaiting the *called* is at the termination of this age (Romans 8:18) and thus could not have already occurred at the time Paul penned the statement; vast portions of the race had not been born, and could not then have answered the call; therefore, the description is of *ideal* (and not actual) persons—those possessed of the character which conforms to the image of the Son—who respond to the call of the gospel (2 Thessalonians 2:14) and who thus put themselves among those who "from the beginning" have been chosen "to salvation through sanctification of the Spirit and belief of the truth." (2 Thessalonians 2:13.)

It will aid greatly in the understanding of this sublime and momentous passage if, in the light of the foregoing facts, we see, in one grand panorama, God's great scheme of redemption from the moment it began to appear until it is consummated in the glorification of the redeemed on golden shores when sin and Satan have been destroyed and the world is no more. There, amid the hosts of heaven, the work is done, redemption is a fact and the purpose of God has been fully realized. Thus viewed, the steps, in reverse order, will then appear as the answers to the following questions are noted: Whom did Jehovah glorify? Those whom he justified. Whom did he call? Those whom he purposed to be conformed to the image of his Son. Whom did he purpose so to conform? Those whom he foreknew. Whom did he foreknow? Those whom he called. By what means did he call? The gospel. To whom did he direct the gospel? To the whole world; to every creature. (Matthew 28:18; Mark 16:15,16.) To whom were the blessings of the gospel given? To those who obeyed it. (2 Thessalonians 1:7-9; 1 John 2:4.) These then (and only these) are those for whom all things work out for good in this life and, in the life to come, will be identified as those who were called, justified and glorified. Finally, how may we be assured of being among those whom the Lord foreknew, predestinated, called, justified and will utlimately glorify? By obeying the will of the Father, and by seeing to it that we are conformable in life to the image of his Son.

"Does God's Word teach anything about cremation of the body after death?"

Cremation is the final disposition of a human body by reducing it to ashes with fire. Passages sometimes cited to oppose the practice are Amos 2:1 and 6:10 but a correct exegesis indicates that it was not the method of disposal of the bodies under condemnation but, in the first, the callous desecration of the body of the king of Edom by Moab; and, in the second, the deplorable conditions during the siege of Samaria. The burden of disposing of the dead fell directly upon members of the family; when a near relative came to claim the body, some other person cried out but asked that the name of Jehovah—under whose judgment they suffered—not be mentioned. So wicked were they the name of Jehovah was objectionable!

From these instances no proper conclusion may be drawn regarding the propriety of the disposal of human bodies by cremation. This practice is not unknown in the sacred writings; its occurrence, however, is rare and exceptional. The men of Jabesh-Gilead burned the bodies of king Saul and his sons to keep them out of the hands of the Philistines (1 Samuel 31:12), and some offences were punished by burning (Genesis 38:24; Leviticus 20:14). These and similar cases provide no guidance in the *normal* disposition of those from whom life is gone, nor do ancient customs of the burying of the dead in the earth, in some countries well-nigh universal, establish a precedent for us today. In other nations and lands cremation is the prevailing practice.

Some have assumed that the doctrine of the resurrection of the body has served to restrict the act in Christian lands but, if so, it is not a valid objection on this ground as we shall later see. More likely it was avoided because of its widespread practice in non-Christian religions. Such objections would be more philosophical than scriptural; an act may to some be repugnant on grounds other than biblical ones.

Life is the union of body and spirit; death the condition resulting from their separation. Once the spirit has flown, the body is lifeless and begins its return to its original elements. Whether the return is the slow disintegration of the body through the processes of decay or is achieved in seconds by fire, the result is the same—the return of the body's elements to their original state. In the resurrection, these "building blocks" will be re-assembled; in either instance the effort will be the same. Bodies which have returned to the dust long centuries ago do not today exist in bodily form any more so than do those immediately consumed by fire; in both instances, the elements are in the universe awaiting the call of Deity at the last great day. Undoubtedly, the elements of many bodies have become parts of trees, which in turn have been sawn into lumber and converted into timber, later to be burned;

these too, will be brought forth by the Divine Hand, and reconstituted into the resurrection body. He who by matchless power spoke into existence the elements which make up our bodies will have no difficulty in bringing together again these separated elements when the spirits emerge from the Hadean realm to join them on the judgment day.

We are taught in the New Testament, largely by example, to exhibit proper respect for the dead and to deal with them in dignified and respectful fashion. Cremation, as today practiced, in no way opposes these premises. We believe that the matter is an aesthetic problem, not a biblical one; and that it will be resolved on emotional and philosophical grounds rather than moral ones. It violates no New Testament principle.

"It is being taught by some that 'Spirit' in John 3:5 is a reference to man's spirit and should not have been translated with the capital letter. Is this view correct?"

No. It would be difficult to imagine an error more glaring or one more easily refuted. Strange indeed that any one today should fall into the error of Nicodemus in interpreting our Lord's reference to being born "again" as in part a physical birth; or, should seek to perpetuate the folly of some denominational theologians that the reference to being "born of water" is an allusion to the physical birth, by affirming the same of that referred to as "the Spirit" in the passage. The querist indicates that some in the area whence the question comes are teaching that the spirit (*pneuma*) is the human spirit—the spirit of man—rather than the third Person of the Godhead, the Holy Spirit.

(1) It should be observed that there are not two births contemplated in the passage occurring at different times and differing in character one from the other, but one birth consisting of two elements, (a) "of water" and (b) "of the Spirit," in consequence of which one enters the kingdom of God. To "enter" the kingdom of God is exactly equivalent to being saved from past or alien sins. He who uttered the words of John 3:5, "Except one be born of water and the Spirit, he cannot enter into the kingdom of God" (John 3:5), also said, "He that believeth and is baptized shall be saved" (Mark 16:16). Since things equal to the same thing are equal to each other, it follows that the birth of water and the Spirit occurs when the penitent believer obeys the gospel. It is by all genuine scholars admitted that the allusion to "water" in John 3:5 is a reference to baptism; it must follow then that the part the Spirit plays in salvation involves the begettal act and that this is accomplished in believing the message which the Spirit through his revelation gave.

(2) John wrote, "Whosoever believeth that Jesus is the Christ is born (*begotten,* American Standard Version) of God." (1 John 5:1.) He who

believes (literally, keeps on believing), is begotten (born) of God. To be born (begotten) of God and to be born (begotten) of the Spirit must mean exactly the same thing since it would be absurd to affirm that one is born of God but not at the same time born of the Spirit. He who complies with the conditions of salvation receives the message of the Spirit and is thus metaphorically said to be "born of the Spirit." It is equally absurd to say that one is born of one's own human spirit or, for that matter, of any other's human spirit. It follows, therefore, that "the Spirit" of John 3:5 is the Holy Spirit.

(3) The Lord, in explaining to Nicodemus that the birth from above is not of the flesh, drew out the comparison between the "one born of the Spirit" and the actions affirmed in verse 8, concluding with the words, ". . . so is every one that is born of the Spirit." "So" is an adverb of manner, that is, in the manner indicated is one born of the Spirit. But, only those thus exercised are "born of the Spirit," the limitation being those who have believed and have been baptized; all others, though possessed of human spirits, are excluded—not being born again— so the words "born of the Spirit" in verse 8 are exactly equivalent to "born . . . of the Spirit" in verse 5. Hence, verse 5 refers to the Holy Spirit, and not to the spirit of man.

(4) The distinction between the first and fleshly birth of man, and the second and spiritual birth was further emphasized by the Lord in the words, "That which is born of the flesh is flesh; and that which is born of the Spirit is spirit," i.e., man born of the flesh is what he is by nature; when born of the Spirit he becomes partaker of the divine nature. (2 Peter 1:4.) Thus, that which is of the flesh is fleshly; that which is of the Spirit is spiritual. But, only those born of the Spirit are possessors of the nature resulting from spiritual birth. The birth which produces this nature is "of the Spirit," the Holy Spirit. Therefore, the "spirit" alluded to in John 3:5 is the Holy Spirit.

(5) A second birth is affirmed "of the 'Spirit' " in verse 5. Though *anothen* is variously rendered (it is translated "again" in the King James Version; "anew" in the American Standard Translation and by some others "from above") it is clear from the context that Nicodemus understood him to mean AGAIN thus prompting the query regarding re-entering his mother's womb to be born again. The first birth is of the flesh; it is meaningless to speak of being born out of the human spirit. Generation is of the flesh, not the spirit. But, were it possible, such is logically excluded from the fact that the Lord clearly taught and Nicodemus so understood him to be speaking about a new birth, a second birth, a birth from above in contrast with the first and fleshly birth. Thus, the phrase "of the Spirit" can refer only to the Holy Spirit.

(6) The striking verbal similarity obtaining between John 3:5 and Titus 3:5 is far more than mere coincidence; it is a designed identifi-

cation of the elements common to each. In the former we read,

"Except one be born of water and the Spirit, he cannot enter
into the kingdom of God."

In the latter,

"According to his mercy he saved us, through the washing
of regeneration and the renewing of the Holy Spirit. . . ."

To enter the kingdom and to be saved are equivalent blessings. Since
it is the case that one enters the kingdom by being born of water and
the Spirit and since one is saved through the washing of regeneration
(baptism) and the renewing of the Holy Spirit (from having provided
the means of renewal in revealing the plan of salvation leading to belief
of the truth) and since things equal to the same thing are equal to each
other, it is the case that to be born of water and the Spirit is to believe
the truth and obey the gospel. The "renewing of the Spirit" in Titus 3:5
is exactly equivalent to "born of the Spirit" in John 3:5 and is thus an
inspired commentary on the significance of the passage under study.

"Is it scriptural and, or necessary as Christians to fast in the era in which we now live? Would our prayers be more effective if we fast?"

Jesus, in alluding to the practices of the Jews, warned the disciples
against the ostentation which characterized the Pharisees.

"When ye fast," he said, "be not, as the hypocrites, of a sad
countenance: for they disfigure their faces, that they may be
seen of men to fast. . . . But thou, when thou fastest, anoint
thy head, and wash thy face; that thou be not seen of men to
fast, . . . and thy Father, who seeth in secret, shall recompense thee." (Matthew 6:16-18.)

He thus removed fasting from the realm of public activity and classified it as a matter of private devotion.

The yielding of personal desire, the basic element of fasting, is described in the Old Testament as "afflicting the soul." In that period, as
well as in the days of Christ, the Jews often ignored the spiritual
aspects of fasting, used the practice as a way of gaining favor with God
and, even worse, as a means of appearing pious before men.

That fasting was not intended to be observed under all circumstances, and that its chief purpose was to strengthen us in times of trial
and adversity, and on occasions of sorrow and grief, is evident from an
induction of passages dealing with the subject in the New Testament.
(Matthew 9:14; Mark 2:18; Luke 5:33; 1 Corinthians 7:6; Acts 13:2;
2 Corinthians 6:5.) The disciples of John once propounded this query,

"Why do we and the Pharisees fast oft, but thy disciples fast
not? And Jesus said unto them, Can the sons of the bride-

146

chamber mourn, as long as the bridegroom is with them? but the days will come, when the bridegroom shall be taken away from them, and then will they fast." (Matthew 9:14,15.)

When the joy of the Lord's presence had been turned into sorrow in his absence, the disciples would fast. Does not this teach us that fasting is an exercise designed to strengthen us and to turn our attention away from the desires of the flesh to the nourishment of the soul? And, that it is to be done only in times of adversity, temptation, grief or trial?

Fasting, properly engaged in, can be a source of spiritual blessing, a discipline of the will and an exercise producing inward strength and power. All of us, on occasion, should resolutely put out of our hearts every semblance of wordly desire and fleshly appetite and with prayer and fasting draw very near to God and claim his support and guidance in life. Such an experience would make us all infinitely stronger, richer in faith, and better equipped to live the Christian life. In view of the fact that neither time nor manner of observance is given for fasting, we must assume that these are matters to be determined in each instance and by each person participating.

We may, therefore, properly conclude that (1) Christ did not enjoin fasting upon the church as a public duty; in his reference thereto, he merely regulated a practice already obtaining among the Jews; (2) he taught that (a) it is to to observed, if at all, in private; (b) without revealing it to others; and (c) for the good of one's own soul. Fasting is not an ordinance of the church; it is not commanded in the Christian dispensation, nor are there penalties given for failure to conform therewith; there is no special virtue in it so that all disciples must engage therein; one may find it a blessing, another may not.

"Were people under the old law forgiven of their sins? Some people say that they were not, that their sins were in 'limbo' or something of the sort until Christ."

"For all have sinned, and come short of the glory of God; being justified freely by his grace through the redemption that is in Christ Jesus: whom God hath set forth to be a propitiation through faith in his blood, to declare his righteousness for the remission of sins that are past, through the forbearance of God; to declare, I say, at this time his righteousness: that he might be just, and the justifier of him which believeth in Jesus." (Romans 3:23-26.)

This marvelous passage plumbs the depths of man's depravity and soars to the holy heights of God's great scheme for redemption of the race. It speaks of man's need of a Savior; the redemption that is in Christ; the propitiation that is affected through his blood; his righteous-

147

ness and forbearance; and the justice mingled with mercy that is characteristic of his dealings with man. Here, too, is seen God's attitude toward those who sinned before Calvary, and the manner in which he dealt with those who thus sinned—a fact unfortunately obscured in the King James translation.

The word *aphesis* is the usual Greek word for "remission," and occurs often in the Scriptures, particularly in the writings of Luke. It means the releasing or letting go of something, formerly of debts, and then later came to be used in its higher application of the releasing of sins. A form of this word occurs in Acts 2:38: "Repent, and be baptized every one of you in the name of Jesus Christ for the remission of sins [*eis aphesin harmartioon*]." *Aphesis* is the usual word for "remission" throughout the sacred writings. This word, however, is not the word translated "remission" (King James Version) in this passage. The word thus translated in this passage is the Greek term *paresin*, and occurs *nowhere* else in the Greek Testament! It does not carry with it the idea of releasing or letting go of sins. Thayer defines it as "pretermission, the passing over, letting pass, neglecting, disregarding" of sins. The revisers, recognizing this essential difference in the two terms, did not follow the King James translators. They render the term quite properly, "the passing over." Thus God merely "passed over," for the time, the sins of those who died in faith under the old order, without complete and final absolution thereof. There was thus no absolute forgiveness in former covenants.

> "For the law having a shadow of good things to come, and not the very image of the things, can never with those sacrifices, which they offered year by year continually make the comers thereunto perfect. For then would they not have ceased to be offered? because that the worshippers once purged should have had no more conscience of sins. But in those sacrifices there is a remembrance again made of sins every year. *For it is not possible that the blood of bulls and of goats should take away sins.*" (Hebrews 10:1-4.)

Thus had Christ not died, the rivers of blood that flowed from Jewish altars would never have operated to take away sins. Their efficacy was solely due to the fact that they anticipated the "fountain in Jerusalem for sin and uncleanness," provided by the Lamb of God.

Moreover, the old order of "pretermission," the *passing over* of sins, had operated as long as it well could. Says Thayer in this connection: "Because God had let pass the sins committed previously (to the expiatory death of Christ)—i.e., had tolerated, had not punished (and so man's conception of his holiness was in danger of becoming dim, if not extinct). "To the same end Trench says: "There needed, Saint Paul would say, a signal manifestation of the righteousness of God on account of the long pretermission, or passing over of sins, in his infinite forbearance with no adequate expression of his wrath against them, during all those long years which preceded the coming of Christ; which manifestation of God's righteousness found place, when he set forth no other and no less than his own Son to be the propitiatory sacrifice for sin."

God, therefore, merely *pretermissed* the sins of the old worthies; they were not remitted. The word here used, *paresis,* suggests a temporary passing of sins only, and there is the very definite suggestions that the one who thus passes over, for the time, has the privilege of returning with the original demand, if he wills. Thus did the people of the old covenant stand in relation to God. All had sinned; God mercifully devised an arrangement by which they might hold off the day of accounting; but this arrangement held forth no promise of final and complete absolution. It was in anticipation only; it borrowed its efficacy only by virtue of the fact that it typified the death of Christ on the cross. The creedal statement that Christ stood as a lamb slain from the foundation of the world and that his sacrifice was an effective during the old covenant as the new is thus seen to be without foundation.

"Of what does worship consist?"

The American Standard Version at Matthew 2:8 has a reference to a footnote defining the word worship as follows: "The Greek word denotes an act of reverence whether paid to a creature (see ch. 4:9; 18:26), or to the creator (see ch. 4:10)."

1. Worship, then, involves an *act*. It is incorrect to say that worship is simply and solely an attitude of heart. Inasmuch as worship consists of *acts,* it follows that such acts are as much involved in worship and are as essential to it as the attitude which prompts them.

2. The Greek word for worship denotes an act . . . *paid.* Worship involves an attitude, but an attitude which expresses itself in acts which find acceptance in the will of another. Worship, therefore, necessitates acts. The effort to disassociate acts from attitude in worship was born of the desire to escape the opprobrium of adding unauthorized practices to the worship of God. Knowledgeable people who use instrumental music in worship are well aware of the fact that there is no authority in the New Testament for its use and they seek to avoid the charge of adding to the divine will by the allegation that, after all, worship does not involve acts but attitudes, and therefore the instrument is really no part of the worship.

The effort fails for at least two reasons: (1) We have seen that it is based on the erroneous concept of what worship is; (2) it does not elude, but merely postpones the fatal dilemma. For, this worship which is alleged to be solely a matter of the heart and expresses itself, not by divine law but by the will of the worshiper, is either restrained or unrestrained. If unrestrained, then the will of the worshiper becomes the sole arbiter of the suitability of the act thus leaving the one who worships free to resort to whatever expressions of it one desires. The pompous worshiper behind stained glass windows in a great cathedral, the Salvation Army lass with her tambourine, and the religious snake handler may all properly claim justification for their choices of expression. Acts 2:42 may be disregarded as the expression of the divine pattern, and thenceforth each of us may be governed by our own wishes and preferences in our worship to God.

If, however, no will worship is acceptable but proper worship is restrained (as is the case, Colossians 2:20-23), we may inquire, What is the restraining influence? We are thus brought back to the place where we should have started in any matter involving our duty to God: What does the New Testament authorize us to do in worship? The early church, under the guidance of inspired men, continued "stedfastly" in the apostles' teaching, which included singing, the Lord's supper, the contribution and prayers. These divinely given items are specifically said to have been the means by which the first Christians worshiped. (Acts 2:42; 20:7; 1 Corinthians 16:1,2.) Less than these we cannot offer him and be in conformity to his will; more than these is an unwarranted and officious intermeddling with the will of God.

It follows, therefore, that in this, the Christian age, the use of instrumental music is unauthorized and unacceptable in the worship of God. "It was used in the Old Testament." Yes, along with the burning of incense, the offering of animal sacrifices and the practice of polygamy. These are not patterns we may properly follow today. The shadows of the old order have given way to the substance of the better way and under the clear light of Christianity such matters are conspicuous by their absence. (Hebrews 8:6-13.) Let it be remembered and never forgotten that our Lord never commanded the use of instrumental music in worship, no apostle ever sanctioned it, no New Testament writer ever authorized it and no apostolic church ever used it!

"Why were the twelve men at Ephesus rebaptized? (Acts 19:1-7.)"

A Jew named Apollos, "an Alexandrian by race, an eloquent man, came to Ephesus: and he was mighty in the scriptures. This man had been instructed in the way of the Lord, and being fervent in spirit, he spake and taught accurately the things concerning Jesus, knowing only the baptism of John." (Acts 18:24-28.) Aquila and Priscilla had accompanied Paul as far as Ephesus when the apostle was returning from

Corinth to Antioch (Acts 18:18-21); and, when they heard Apollos speak they at once perceived his error (of teaching the baptism of John *after* it had been superseded by the baptism of the great commission), and they therefore "expounded unto him the way of God more accurately" (Acts 18:26). Apollos readily accepted the correction and served effectively the cause he loved. Some people had been induced to accept John's baptism *after* the day of Pentecost when the baptism of the great commission became effective.

Contacting "certain disciples" he found in Ephesus, Paul said to them, "Did ye receive the Holy Spirit when ye believed? And they said unto him, Nay, we did not so much as hear whether the Holy Spirit was given." (Alford: "We did not so much as hear him mentioned.") Paul's purpose in raising the question of reception of the Holy Spirit by these disciples was to determine whether they had received a *miraculous* measure of the Spirit, since this was dependent on the laying on of an apostle's hand and not on the obedience to the gospel. When they answered that they had not heard that the Spirit was given, the apostle asked, "Into what then were ye baptized? Their answer, that they did not know anything about the Spirit at all, revealed that their baptism was defective, since they could have been scripturally baptized only if they were baptized "*into* the name of the Father and the Son and *of the Holy Spirit.* (Matthew 28:18-20.) If this had been done, they would have "heard" of the Spirit. So the apostle inquired, "*Into* what then were ye baptized?" They answered, "Into John's baptism."

The apostle explained that "John baptized with the baptism of repentance, saying unto the people that they should believe on him that should come after him, that is, on Jesus." John's baptism was prompted repentance; it was not done in the name of Christ; it required faith in one that should come—Jesus Christ. The baptism of John was temporary in nature, designed to be preached and practiced only until the baptism of the great commission became effective, which occurred on its first public proclamation—the day of Pentecost. It was not performed into the name of the Father and of the Son and of the Holy Spirit; and it carried with it no promise of the Holy Spirit.

"And when they heard this, they were baptized *into* the name of the Lord Jesus," an abbreviation for Matthew 28:18-20, "into the name of the Father, the Son and the Holy Spirit." This does not mean that *all* who received John's baptism were required to be baptized over; but only those who received it after its purpose had been served. Those who received it—including the apostles—before Pentecost were not rebaptized. Paul then "laid his hands upon them," the Holy Spirit came upon them miraculously, "and they spake with tongues and prophesied." The number of men involved was twelve. Note that the miraculous measure of the Spirit was bestowed, *not because they had become Christians,* but

151

because Paul, an apostle, *laid his hands upon them*. There are not apostles among us today and hence such actions are limited to the apostolic age.

"Would you please explain to us how you have drawn the conclusion from the Scriptures that Judas was not present at the time the Lord's supper was instituted?"

In the *Adult Gospel Quarterly* the following statement, prompting the foregoing query, appeared: "The Lord's supper was instituted on the evening before our Lord's death on the cross, and immediately following the observance of the passover feast in the upper room in Jerusalem. (Matthew 26:26-30; Mark 14:22-26; Luke 22:14-23.) All of the apostles except Judas (John 13:21-30) were present when it was instituted."

The conclusion is a necessary one when all of the details of all of the writers are carefully considered. It should be noted that no one of the biographers of Jesus relates all of the events associated with the institution of the supper and that a full and accurate account may be had only when each detail by each writer is placed in harmonious relationship to the whole. To this end, the following passages in the order given should be read: Luke 22:14-18; John 13:23-30; Matthew 26:26-30; Luke 22:19,20.

The chronological order of the events of the upper room appears to have been as follows: (1) Jesus and the twelve disciples assembled to observe the passover feast. (2) After the feast began, contention among the disciples regarding their relative status prompted the Lord to teach an object lesson in humility by washing their feet. (3) The Lord took his place at the head of the table and the feast resumed. (4) He began to exhibit much distress and revealed to the group that one of their number would betray him. (5) The perplexed disciples were greatly confused and Peter asked John, who was reclining at the table near the Lord, to inquire of him who it was who would betray him. (6) Jesus identified the infamous disciple to John as the one to whom he would give "the sop." (7) Jesus handed Judas Iscariot the sop following which "Satan entered into him." (8) The Lord thereupon bade the wicked disciple to "do quickly" that which he had already purposed. (9) Judas *went out* "immediately" into the night to consummate his vile and faithless scheme. (10) Jesus then instituted the supper, using the emblems remaining from the passover feast. Following the supper, he delivered the discourse recorded in John 14, 15 and 16. From the upper room he went to Gethsemane.

The *sop* was a morsel of bread or meat dipped into the gravy sauce of the sacrifice. It was not unusual for guests, as a special act of recognition, to be thus served by the host himself. Jesus, by this method, revealed privately to John the identity of the infamous betrayer. The use of the definite article with the word "sop" shows it to have been a part of the paschal supper. Immediately following this Judas left the gathering. Thus, either the Lord's supper was instituted before the passover feast; or, Judas had already departed when the supper was instituted. The former is in conflict with plain statements of the narrative; hence, the latter conclusion follows and Judas was not present when the supper was instituted.

Some months ago we received a lengthy and labored effort from a brother who sought to avoid this obvious conclusion with the allegation that there were *two* upper room meetings the *first* of which was to observe the passover, the *second* to institute the supper; and that the meeting from which Judas departed was the former, being present at the latter! For such a conclusion there is of course not the slightest evidence.

"Please explain 1 John 5:1,2. Why are we told how we know we love 'the children of God'? Are we not capable of knowing this in our own consciousness without any test?"

The passage about which inquiry is made reads:

"Whosoever believeth that Jesus is the Christ is begotten of God: and whosoever loveth him that begat loveth him also that is begotten of him. Hereby we know that we love the children of God, when we love God and do his commandments."

The first clause is often cited by those who subscribe to the doctrine of "faith only" in an effort to sustain the view that all one must do to be born again is simply to believe. But this is a gross mishandling of the passage, disregards the context, and wholly misapprehends the purpose of the writer. It was not the design of the apostle to announce a condition of salvation here, nor are the words addressed to alien sinners. It was his purpose to provide a *test* by which one may ascertain whether one is a child of God. Such someone claims to be. But, is he, really? The test is: Does he believe (with all that such belief involves) that Jesus *is* the Christ," effectively sifted out the heretics of whom the apostle repeatedly warned. Who were they?

Gnostic heresies were widely afloat in the church when John wrote, and the teachers advocating pernicious teaching concerning the person and nature of Christ were deceiving many. Some denied the *deity* of the Lord, others, his *humanity;* the former said that Jesus was not Christ; the latter, that Christ was not Jesus. Thus, to confess that "Jesus is the Christ," was to affirm his deity, his humanity, and his reality, and within the frame of reference in which John wrote, to demonstrate that the one confessing this had not imbibed the poisonous theories of the Gnostics and their cohorts and were faithful children of God.

The reasoning of the apostle in this passage involves a closely knit argument, in logical form a *sorites,* an abridged series of syllogisms in a group of propositions arranged in such order that the predicate of the first becomes the subject of the second, the conclusion uniting the subject of the first proposition with the predicate of the last. The order follows:

1. To believe that Jesus is the Christ is evidence that one is begotten of God.
2. To be begotten of God requires one to love God.
3. To love God requires one to love God's children.
4. Those who love God's children have been begotten of God.
5. Therefore, to believe that Jesus is the Christ requires one to love God's children and evidences the fact that one who thus does is begotten of God.

Two reasons are assigned by the sacred writer, by which we may determine whether we love the children of God: "Hereby we know we love the children of God, when we love God and do his commandments." What are they? (1) We love God; (2) we do his commandments. But, why should we need such a test? Is not one capable of love also able, of his own awareness, to know whether he actually loves the children of God? The answer, strangely enough, is: *He is not!* And, the reason, on reflection, becomes obvious. One may entertain affection for others from many considerations not related to religion at all, such as kinship, friendship, family, business relations, social contacts, etc.; but such does not involve the motivation under consideration by the apostle here. Love of the brethren, *because they are brethren,* and not necessarily because they are possessed of those characteristics which naturally evoke love, is that which prompts our love. We love the children of God because we love him, and because he taught us to love the brethren. The will of Christians has thus become the will of God in them.

"What did Peter mean when he exhorted elders to exercise 'oversight, not of constraint, but willingly, according to the will of God; nor yet for filthy lucre, but of a ready mind'? (1 Peter 5:2.)"

The words of the text, "exercising the oversight," are translated from the Greek participle *episkopountes,* derived from *episkopos,* the word rendered "bishops" in the American Standard Version and "overseers" in the King James' Version in Acts 20:28. The word means to exercise

154

superintendence, oversight, supervision; and, in doing this, elders or bishops are empowered by the Holy Spirit to direct the affairs of the congregations wherein such oversight is exercised. This they are to do "not of constraint," i.e., not in forced service and from a burdened sense of duty, but "willingly," freely, gladly, and in harmony with the will of God who requires it.

Such service is not to be done "for filthy lucre, but of a ready mind." The phrase "filthy lucre" is descriptive of gain which is base and dishonorable. In the apostolic age some elders were supported by the congregations they served; the apostle elsewhere taught that elders who rule well should be accorded "double honor," especially those who labor "in the word and teaching." (1 Timothy 5:17.) This practice should be followed much more often today than it is. So vast is the area of activity required of elders that the church will never fully realize its potential until it supports its elders full-time to meet the demands upon them.

So important is this work that, despite the troublous times which prevailed and the comparative poverty of the congregations when Peter wrote, some congregations, at least, did indeed support some elders financially; but, where money is involved there is always the danger of misuse and these words of warning were deemed necessary by the apostle lest some should be tempted to use their position for base ends and personal gain. Some teachers in that day turned religion into a trade, commercialized the gospel of Christ and treated "godliness as a way of gain." (1 Timothy 6:5.) Faithful and godly elders would, of course, avoid all suspicion of such practices, serving God with a "ready mind," eagerly, and with the sole desire to please the Father.

"How may elders lord it over the flock? (1 Peter 5:3.)"

Peter admonished the elders, one of whom he was, to serve with "a ready mind, neither as lording it over the charge allotted to" them, but "as ensamples to the flock." Verse 2, of this context, forbids elders to perform their duties from base and sordid motives of avarice and greed, and verse 3 warns them of unseemly ambition and abuse of powers. The words, "lording it over," translate a Greek word which means to rule highhandedly and autocratically and from an arrogant and domineering spirit. Men in positions of power are often tempted to do this, an example of which will be seen in 3 John 3. The "charge allotted' was the congregation where the elders served. Instead of exhibiting a spirit of arrogance in their work they were to be "ensamples" (patterns of conduct) for the rest, even as they seek to follow the pattern of Christ, the "chief Shepherd." (1 Peter 5:4.)

155

What is forbidden in the foregoing text is the *abuse* of authority, and not the proper *use* thereof. To cite this passage, as some today do, as proof that elders are without any authority in directing the affairs of the congregation is utterly to misapprehend the apostle's teaching. To deny to elders the proper exercise of oversight in the congregation is as much a perversion of New Testament teaching as it is for elders to abuse their rights and privileges through improper seizure of authority. (Hebrew 13:7,17.) There are tendencies in the church today toward both extremes each of which ought to be strictly curbed. Peter by no means forbade the oversight every congregation must have in order properly to discharge its responsibilities and the consequent exercise of authority such oversight entails; he sought to restrain the excesses and abuses which may, and often do result from such; and he directed attention to the fact that the power of a good example in the congregation is much more effective than the mere show of authority, and that to exhibit it in life is the best guarantee against abuses.

"Explain Exodus 4:24-26. Did God intend to kill Moses? Who is 'him' in verse 24? Who is 'his' in verse 25? Who is 'him' in verse 26?"

To Zipporah, Moses' wife, had been born Eliezer, their second son. In the covenant of circumcision which God had made with Abraham, male children were required to be circumcised on the eighth day following birth. Zipporah, of heathen origin, regarded the act with distaste and felt no compulsion to have the child circumcised and Moses appears to have been influenced by his wife to acquiesce in the disregard of the duty. On the night of the eighth day, while Moses slept, a sudden and severe illness fell upon him and he recognized, as did Zipporah, that this was an exhibition of the divine disapproval. God met Moses, intending to kill him, and Zipporah, because Moses was likely too ill to perform the rite on their son, did it herself, indignantly referring to Moses as a "bloody husband." In compliance with the will of God in the matter Moses' life was saved. Some expositors, including Adam Clarke, think that the threat was not to Moses, but to his son, but this interpretation is open to numerous objections. Yes, God intended to kill Moses for his disobedience, and refrained from doing so only when his edict was respected.

"In Isaiah 6:5, it is said that the prophet had 'seen the king, the Lord of hosts.' The American Standard Version says that he had seen Jehovah. In John 1:8, it is said, 'No man hath seen God at any time.' Did Isaiah literally see God?"

The word "God" is the name of the divine nature and this nature, prior to the coming of our Lord into the world no man could see, i.e.,

156

fully comprehend. Jesus is *the Word,* the expression of deity to man and thus "declared," *interpreted,* the Father. (John 1:1,18.) He is also "the express image" (Hebrew 1:3), (literally, the *imprint*), of the Father. God at "sundry times and in divers manners" (Hebrew 1:1), spoke to men through the long reaches of inspiration and there were countless manifestations, theophanies, divine appearances and revelations of the person of deity, but all of these were far short of a full-orbed divine revelation of the being of God. Those thus blessed saw God in his works, but not nearly so vividly as he was seen in Christ, or as we shall ultimately see him when life's restless and often confusing experience is finally over.

"How do we reconcile 2 Kings 18:5 with 2 Kings 23:25?"

The author of the book of 2 Kings in the first of the passages above alluded to ascribes to Hezekiah a position superior to that of all the other kings of Judah: "He trusted in Jehovah, the God of Israel; so that after him was none like him among all the kings of Judah, nor among them that were before him." In view of this affirmation, it is surprising to find much the same statement of preeminence assigned to Josiah appearing in the second of the two passages inquired about as follows:

"And like unto him was there no king before him, that turned
to Jehovah with all his heart, and with all his soul, and with
all his might, according to all the law of Moses; neither after
him arose there any like him."

A close examination of the statements will lead to the conclusion that the problem is apparent—not real. Though both were said to enjoy preeminence above that of all other kings of the realm, it should be noted that the superiority attributed to each *was not in the same area.* Hezekiah excelled all the kings of Judah which preceded and followed him in unquestioning trust in Jehovah; his faith in the Lord never faltered as was often the case with other monarchs of the realm. In this respect he differed greatly from his father Ahaz who chose to put his trust in men (2 Kings 16:7-10), and whose conduct before Jehovah was often reprehensible (2 Kings 16:3). Hezekiah followed the only course possible to prompt God to come to his aid and to assure a prosperous and fruitful reign. (2 Kings 18:6-8.)

Josiah's eminence was in his emphasis on the observance of the law of Moses and the commandments thereof (2 Kings 23:25), when such was essential to the restoration of the religious order and the return of the people to the proper worship of Jehovah. Hezekiah and Josiah were equally great in the two spheres of influence the sacred writer ascribes to them.

157

"Does 2 Corinthians 6:14 teach that it is sinful for a Christian to be married to a non-Christian, or for a Christian to be associated in business relationships with those not Christians?"

No, not necessarily. Forbidden is an unequal yoking of believers and unbelievers but that this does not positively restrain a child of God from being in such a relationship is clear from plain and unmistakable affirmations of Paul in 1 Corinthians 7:12,13, regarding the marriage of believers and unbelievers, and in 1 Corinthians 5:9,10, touching business associations with those of the world. In these passages the apostle teaches that these relationships, *when peaceable and not corrupting of character,* are permissible; it follows, therefore, that any interpretation of 2 Corinthians 6:14, which forbids that which is allowed in them is erroneous. It is not a valid objection to say that 1 Corinthians 7:12,13 involves a situation entered into before obedience to the gospel; if 2 Corinthians 6:14 prohibits all inter-marriage with those of the world, every child of God thus married is *commanded* by the apostle to extricate himself or herself from it: "Wherefore come ye out from among them, and be ye separate. . . ." (2 Corinthians 6:17.) But, in such a case, the apostle would be forbidding here what he allows in 1 Corinthians 7, and thus the interpretation is wrong.

The words, "be ye not unequally yoked," are the translation of a Greek phrase, *mee ginesthe heterozugountes,* literally, "Stop being unequally yoked. . . ." The verb is a present imperative, not aorist subjunctive, and the state, as well as the entrance upon it, is enjoined. Any relationship, whether in marriage or in business, which interferes with one's duty to God is condemned here and from such all children of God are to remove themselves. It is incorrect exegesis, however, to interpret Paul as forbidding the relationship, *per se.* Because of *risks* involved it is often the part of wisdom to avoid such relationships but matters of expediency must be distinguished from those of faith. It is high-handed presumption to make laws where God did not. (1 Timothy 4:1ff.) It is not a sin to be married to, or in business with, a non-Christian.

"Is Zipporah, Moses' wife, the same woman Moses married as recorded in Numbers 12:1-16?"

Yes.

(1) The woman of Numbers 12:1-16, was of the "land of Cush," the area to which Moses fled from Egypt and where Jethro, Zipporah's father, lived. (2) No mention is made either here, or elsewhere in the sacred writings, of another marriage of Moses. (3) To Moses and Zipporah were born Gershom and Eliezer, the only offspring attributed to Moses in the Bible. (Exodus 18:1-4.) (4) His pedigree is clear and de-

tailed and the members of his family specifically named. He descended from Levi through Kohath and he was the son of Amram by his wife Jochebed. (Genesis 46:11; Numbers 3:19.) He had one brother and one sister, both of whom are named. (Exodus 15:20.) (5) It appears certain, in the light of these facts, that the marriage to Zipporah, recorded in Exodus 3:16-22, is the only one contracted by Moses.

I think there is another and even more compelling reason why the conclusion above drawn follows. Moses, the great lawgiver of the old order, was himself a part of the system which reflected in type and in shadow the Christian age which followed. He is indeed the only Old Testament character to whom our Lord compared himself (John 3:14); and Moses identified himself in this likeness: "Jehovah thy God will raise up unto thee a prophet from the midst of thee, of thy brethren, *like unto me;* unto him ye shall hearken." (Deuteronomy 18.15.) Peter cited this prophecy and applied it to Christ. (Acts 3:22-26.) Thus, Christ was like Moses as a *prophet,* as a *lawgiver,* and as representative *of* his people. (See, also, Hebrews 12:24-29.) Christ has *but one bride, the church,* as Moses had but one wife, Zipporah. Would it not seem wholly inconsistent if Moses, who typified Christ, in these areas, had more than one wife? And, is there not great evidential value in this, in view of the fact that the culture of the day tolerated plural marriages? Would not Moses have been *very unlike* Christ in a vital sense with more than one wife?

"Was Judas, who betrayed the Lord, the son of Simon Peter, or the son of Simon Zelotes?"

Neither. He was the son of Simon Iscariot. (John 6:71.) Simon Zelotes was one of the apostles and he is identified in the lists of apostles in Luke 6:15 and Acts 1:13, as Simon Zelotes, in order to distinguish him from Simon Peter, another apostle. The lists of Matthew (10:4), and Mark (3:18), identify him as "the *Cananaean,*" by some believed to designate his place of origin, and by others to denote his earlier membership in the sect of *Zealots,* from the fact that a transliteration of the Hebrew word for zeal (*kanawn*) bears some resemblance to the word "Canaan." I believe the first supposition to be the more likely one.

"Who are the men in Luke 6:38?"

The word "men" does not occur in the passage as it appears in the American Standard Version:

"... give, and it shall be given unto you; good measure, pressed down, shaken together, running over, shall they give

159

into your bosom. For with what measure ye mete it shall be measured to you again."

The clause here rendered, "shall they give into your bosom," appears in the King James Version as, "shall men give into your bosom." The meaning is the same in both versions and means that those who give liberally will be able to receive a liberal measure in return, as is affirmed in the final clause, "With what measure ye mete it shall be measured to you again." The reference to "men" (KJV), and "they" (ASV) is indefinite and designed to include any to whom we "give" good measure.

"I am very confused about how, when and where a woman should teach. Would it be right for a young teen-aged girl to teach during the bus ride? Is this public teaching? There are men present and in some instances young baptized boys."

First Timothy 2:11,12 provides a simple solution to this problem and to all comparable ones. Forbidden by the apostle is such teaching and dominion as is "over the man"—*over the man* being a prepositional phrase governing both the teaching and having dominion. There is a vast difference between teaching *in the presence* of men and teaching *over* men, though this distinction is seldom recognized. It is the ultimate of absurdity to take the position—as some today do—that in every instance when women teach in the presence of men they are in violation of the divine ban to teach "over" men. Were such so, elders could never step into a classroom where a woman is teaching to determine the truth of her effort; a father could not be present when an older daughter instructed younger children! The rule is not whether the teaching is public or private, but whether it is "over" the man; and, inasmuch as teaching is done only when learning, its essential corollary, is present, it is not correct to say that any teaching *of children* though done in the presence of knowledgeable brethren is wrong. Woman must not teach over the man—they must not arrogate to themselves the right to engage in such teaching, for the reasons assigned in 1 Timothy 2:13,14.

Here, too, is the answer to the question of at what point women must cease teaching boys. Remarkable reasoning it is to assume that because a ten-year-old boy is baptized he suddenly becomes an adult. Priscilla assisted in the instruction of Apollos, a young gospel preacher, needed (Acts 18:24-28) but it was done in such fashion as not to be "over the man." This is the divine rule; we must be careful that we do not formulate human ones. First Timothy 2:8 forbids women to pray audibly *in the presence* of men in religious assemblies; 1 Timothy 2:11,12 does not allow women to teach "over men."

"What is the meaning of the statement, 'All things are lawful; but not all things are expedient. All things are lawful; but not all things edify'? (1 Corinthians 10:23)"

This statement is very similar to one occurring earlier in the epistle. (1 Corinthians 6:12.) There, it is applied to the eating of meats which, within itself was not wrong; but, under the circumstances was not expedient, wise, advantageous. The situation, prompting the statement, was this: In heathen temples of that day, animal sacrifices were offered. Following the sacrifice, the meat was carried to the market-place and put on sale. It was not physically contaminated; it was wholesome food; and there was, therefore, no inherent reason to avoid it. However, some brethren felt that the eating of this meat which had been used in idolatrous worship was wrong; and thus the apostle, desirous of helping the brethren to avoid offense to any brother, wrote:

> But food will not commend us to God: neither, if we eat not, are we the worse; nor, if we eat, are we the better. But take heed lest by any means this liberty of yours become a stumblingblock to the weak. For if a man see thee who hast knowledge sitting at meat in an idol's temple, will not his conscience, if he is weak, be emboldened to eat things sacrificed to idols? For through thy knowledge he that is weak perisheth, the brother for whose sake Christ died. And thus, sinning against the brethren, and wounding their conscience when it is weak, ye sin against Christ. (1 Corinthians 8:8-12.)

Here is a clear and simple statement of the operation of the law of expediency. It was not wrong, in and of itself, to eat such meat. However, weak brethren would be disposed to stumble and do wrong themselves, when they saw their stronger brethren engaging in that which they honestly and sincerely thought to be sinful. Paul taught that in such instances we must be willing to forego matters indifferent (things neither right nor wrong) for the sake of weak brethren. "Wherefore, if meat causeth my brother to stumble, I will eat no flesh for evermore, that I cause not my brother to stumble." (1 Corinthians 8:13.)

Obviously, there are limitations to the principle affirmed by him. If that to which a brother objects is, within itself, a duty we owe to God, we must perform it, regardless of his objection. Moreover, the objection must be based on an honest and sincere conviction. Wilful, self-centered and dogmatic individuals are not to be allowed to foist their opinions on the brethren. It was "lawful" for Paul to eat meat; but, under the circumstances which he outlines, it was not *expedient* because (a) it did not serve to edify, and (b) it might cause a weak brother to stumble.

Meat, *as food,* might properly be eaten when not attended by circumstances which would lead another astray. No moral principle, insofar *as eating meat,* is involved, and the question is to be settled in the realm of expediency. Suppose, however, a brother insists on drinking alcoholic liquors on the foregoing grounds? Such indulgence, unlike that of eating meat, is *wrong* within itself, violating other teaching of the Scriptures. Suppose another brother objects to our meeting on the first day of the week to break bread? (Acts 2:7.) This is a matter of faith, and not expediency, and we cannot yield.

Foregoing meat, under the circumstances hereinbefore outlined, is an example of waiving one's own liberty for the sake of another's conscience—*waived,* however, not *surrendered!* This is made clear in 1 Corinthians 10:30: "If I partake with thankfulness, why am I evil spoken of for that for which I give thanks?" Moreover, the weak conscience of another does not make it sinful for me to do that which I am not only allowed to do by my own conscience, but which I may do in a spirit of gratitude and thankfulness. Neither has one the right to speak evil of me for doing that for which I may properly thank God *in* doing. (1 Timothy 4:3.) The concession is made on the ground of Christian charity. The mere fact that another *thinks* I am wrong does not mean that I am in fact wrong; God, alone, determines this. In relinquishing the eating of meat Paul deferred to a *weak* brother, *because* he was weak, to keep him from stumbling, lest through seeing Paul do that which the weak brother regards as wrong, the weak brother might be tempted to violate his conscience in this or in some other matter which might well involve the violation of moral conduct, and lead to apostasy.

"Upon whom were the 'Ten Plagues' of the book of Exodus visited? Were they upon the Egyptians exclusively, or were some of them visited upon the Israelites? If upon the Israelites, why? If some, why not all?"

The first three plagues, of *water turned into blood,* of *frogs,* and of *lice* appear to have fallen upon all of the territory of Egypt, and thus to have included the enslaved Israelites. From the fourth, the *flies,* through the tenth, *murrain, boils, hail, locusts, darkness* and *death of the first born,* the land of Goshen, where the Israelites had their houses, was granted immunity from the afflictions which fell upon the people of Egypt because of the perversity and hardness of heart characteristic of their emperor Pharaoh.

This seems clearly to follow from the affirmation of Moses regarding a severance which Jehovah made between the land of Goshen and the rest of the realm of Egypt: "And I will set apart in that day the land of Goshen, in which my people dwell, that no swarms of flies shall be

162

there; to the end thou mayest know that I am Jehovah in the midst of the earth. And I will put a division between my people and thy people: by tomorrow shall this sign be." (Exodus 8:22,23.) (1) Why were the Israelites made to suffer through the first three plagues, the primary design of which was to punish Pharaoh and the people of Egypt? (2) Why were the Israelites given relief from the fourth through the tenth plagues?

The discipline and purifying effect of these burdensome and trying experiences were needed. Despite the clear and unmistakable evidence of God's participation and deliverance, they were given to discontent, to murmuring and to rebellion. The miraculous character of these occurrences, the obvious intrusion of Jehovah into their problems must have produced a profound effect upon them and there was no further need for them to be beset by the plagues which continued to oppress the Egyptians. Moreover, the division between the people of Israel and those of Egypt gave further evidence of Jehovah's hand in the matter. Indeed, the fact of severance must have had a profound effect upon Pharaoh and his people. Through the third plague, Israel had suffered as much as the Egyptians. The king must have drawn the conclusion that their God was of limited powers, since his people were also victims of the terrible plagues. Or, if not this, that somewhere, sometime, the plagues would be lifted, if for not other reason than to save his own people. But, with the division between Goshen and the rest of the land, these considerations vanished, and Pharaoh was face to face with the realization that God was not limited in power and that he did care for his own.

No less must have been the effect upon the people of Egypt. Thus far, few, if any, of the people were really aware of the cause of the affliction which they were suffering. And, had the Israelites continued to share in the bitter experiences the plagues brought, the heathen people of Egypt would have attributed the action to idolatrous deities which made no distinction between Israel and Egypt. But, when it became apparent to them that the Israelites were free of the plagues which Egypt suffered, it became clear to them that the God of Israel *intended* such distinction. This, too, must have led them to further inquiry as to the cause of the plagues and thus to the realization that they came as a direct result of Pharaoh's refusal to allow the people of Israel to leave the land of Egypt.

Taught with great emphasis in this historic incident is the fact that God does indeed make a difference between *his* people and those of the world. Though the righteous often suffer the same afflictions in this world as the wicked, eventually there comes the time when God makes a "division" as he did in the case of Israel and Egypt and blesses his own while punishing their oppressors. The lessons of history are at this point especially clear; God does not deal with all nations on the same basis; his favors fall upon those peoples who obey him and corruption and destruction await those who treat with contempt his precepts.

"Please explain 1 Corinthians 5:9-11."

These verses contain a clarification by Paul of a matter about which the Corinthians were confused. He had written to them an earlier epistle than *our* First Corinthians, not now in existence, in which he evidently warned them of association with evil people. (1 Corinthians 5:9.) They had interpreted this to mean *all* evil people and they wondered if by this the apostle meant that they were to withdraw themselves from all association with the world thus rendering business and commercial transactions impossible.

In the verses inquired about, Paul makes clear that he had reference to association with evil people *in the church:* "I wrote unto you not to keep company, if any man *that is named a brother* be a fornicator, or covetous, or an idolater, or a reviler, or a drunkard, or an extortioner; with such a one no, not to eat." The only way association with ungodly men of the world could be avoided would be to assume a manner of living contrary to that which should be characteristic of Christians—a hermetic and monastic existence—since sin is everywhere prevalent.

He had warned of such association in the church, on the ground that this would be interpreted by those about them as an endorsement of sin, and an inducement to sin by other members of the church. Hence, the faithful were to have no communion whatsoever with members of the church who had lapsed into sin—with them they were to have no fellowship, whatsoever—not even *to eat* with them. Eating here has reference to common meals, since it is obvious that no one under heaven has the right to determine who, among those who have obeyed the gospel, may, or may not, eat there. It is the *Lord's* supper, *not man's,* and thus man is not empowered with the privilege of deciding who may, or may not, eat at *that* table.

In further clarification of his earlier message to the Corinthians, Paul makes plain to them the fact that he had no reference to the outside world, by writing them: "For what have I to do with judging them that are without? Do not ye judge them that are within? But them that are without God judgeth." (1 Corinthians 5:12.) It was no part of Paul's plan to pass judgment upon the heathen world; this, God would do in the day of final account. Christians have no jurisdiction over those of the world; and, while they may deplore its excesses, they have no proper way of restraining it. But, those "within," i.e., *in the church,* they are in position to judge. Moreover, they must exercise disciplinary measures upon those who fall into sin and who resist all other efforts to restore them. Such was the situation in Corinth involving the incestuous man prompting Paul to say, "Put away the wicked man from among yourselves." (1 Corinthians 5:13.)

Thus, the duty of children of God to exercise discipline in the church is clearly taught. The apostle had occasion often to refer to this sad, though necessary, action: "Now we command you, brethren, in the name of our Lord Jesus Christ, that ye withdraw yourselves from every brother that walketh disorderly, and not after the tradition which they received of us." (2 Thessalonians 3:6.) "Now I beseech you, brethren, mark them that are causing the divisions and occasions of stumbling, contrary to the doctrine which ye learned; and turn away from them." (Romans 16:17.)

There are numerous reasons why this obligation is an important one and ought to be faithfully followed in New Testament churches today: (1) It is enjoined upon us by inspiration; (2) it is for the good of the offender who, through it, may be brought to repentance; (3) it protects the church from the contaminating influences of wicked and corrupt people; (4) it is a notice to the world that the church does not tolerate ungodliness in its midst.

"What did the apostle John mean when he said, 'This is he that came by water and blood, even Jesus Christ; not with water only, but with the water and with the blood. . . . For there are three who bear witness, the Spirit, and the water, and the blood: and the three agree in one.'? (1 John 5:6,8.)"

A simple analysis of the affirmation of the apostle will enable us to know what is affirmed here: (1) One came; (2) he who came was Jesus Christ; (3) Jesus Christ came by water and blood; (4) he did not come by water only, but *with* water and *with* blood; (5) there are three who bear witness—the Spirit, the water and the blood; and (6) these three agree in one.

Clear and correct answers to the following questions are essential to the proper understanding of the passage: (1) What coming of the Lord is referred to here? (2) What is meant by his coming "with" water and "with" blood? (3) What "water" and what "blood" are designated in the passage? (4) what "witness" is borne by the three? (5) How do the three agree in one?

Beyond doubt, the "coming" of Christ alluded to was his first advent into the world. He is said to have come with "water" and with "blood," and from 1 John 5:8, we learn that it was for the purpose of establishing witnesses to the fact of his coming, these witnesses being "the Spirit," "the water," and "the blood." He came with water at his *baptism* and the reference to "blood" is an allusion to his *death*. The Spirit (the third person of the Godhead) bore witness to the facts, and thus became the first of three witnesses to his coming. The Spirit was manifested at his baptism (Matthew 3:13-17); the Spirit recorded and bore witness to both his baptism and his death. Some expositors have seen in the "water" and the "blood" of the passage a reference to the blood and water which flowed from the "riven side" of the Saviour on the cross. (John 19:34.) There, however, the order is (1) blood; (2) water; here, it is (1) water; (2) blood. Moreover, it was evidently the design of the writer to point out historical facts in the life of the Lord, established by the testimony of the Spirit as evidence of his coming into the world. It seems highly improbable that the sacred writer, in offering such proof, would limit the matters mentioned to events occurring almost at the moment of death. It seems reasonable to conclude that the water refers to his baptism and the blood to his death—the first witness being at the *beginning* of his ministry, the *second* at its close.

The witnesses—the Holy Spirit, the water and the blood—bore testimony to the deity of Jesus, the lordship of him who was *baptized* in Jordan, with the approval of the Father, and from whose side, on the *cross,* the blood flowed. These three agree "in one" by which it is meant that their testimony is completely harmonious, each testifying to the same end. As there are three divine persons in one God, so there are three witnesses on earth testifying to the deity of Jesus. The evidence which they offer is constant and continuous; the Spirit's revelation, in the Scriptures, speaks to all generations; the act of baptism, portraying the burial and resurrection of Christ, is to be preached and practiced to the end of the age (Matthew 28:18-20), and the blood, which makes redemption possible, is ever available to those who appropriate it through the divine means. Moreover, where ever the people of God assemble on the Lord's day there is, in the supper of the Lord which they observe, a memorial of the blood which was shed and which, like that of Abel, offers unceasing testimony, evidence of the highest order, and a demonstration of the dedication of faithful saints in the observance of the blessed event which the supper memorializes.

"The Lord said, 'Lay not up for yourselves treasures upon earth, where moth and rust doth corrupt, and where thieves break through and steal: but lay up for yourselves treasures in heaven, where neither moth nor rust doth corrupt, and where thieves do not break through nor steal.' Does this not teach that it is wrong to accumulate wealth of any kind here on earth?" (Matthew 6:19,20.)

No.

Often, in the sacred writings, contrasts are drawn by offsetting an affirmation with a negation. In this construction, the adverb "not" is made to deny a proposition and the conjunction "but" precedes an affirmation put in immediate contrast with the proposition denied, for emphasis. Many such instances will at once come to mind to the observant student.

> "Whose adorning, let it *not* be that outward adorning of plaiting the hair, and of wearing of gold, or of putting on ofapparel; *but* let it be the hidden man of the heart, in that which is not corruptible, even the ornament of a meek and quiet spirit, which is in the sight of God of great price." (1 Peter 3:3,4.)

> "Christ sent me *not* to baptize, *but* to preach the gospel." (1 Corinthians 1:17.)

> "I suffer *not* a woman to teach, nor to usurp authority over the man, *but* to be in silence." (1 Timothy 2:12.)

It will be seen from these examples of this type of verbal construction that the first proposition is denied in order that the second may be emphasized. A contrast is drawn in which one thing is negated in order that the proposition following may be particularly emphasized. One is *denied* that the other may be *affirmed*. Thus, the contrast is verbal, not absolute.

For example, Jesus said, "Labor *not* for the meat which perisheth, *but* for that meat which endureth unto everlasting life." (John 6:27.) The words "the meat which perisheth," has reference to that which nourishes the body; "the meat that endureth unto everlasting life," that which feeds the soul. Because that which has to do with soul nourishment is infinitely more important than food for the fleshly body, the Lord instructs us to regard as more important and to labor for the former "meat" rather than the latter. This is, however, very far from saying that we were absolutely forbidden to work for the bread which sustains our bodies. On the contrary, we are expressly instructed so to do. (Genesis 3:19; Ephesians 4:28.)

A familiar passage of Paul reads,

> "And be *not* conformed to this world; *but* be ye transformed by the renewing of your mind, that ye may prove what is that good, and acceptable, and perfect will of God." (Romans 12:2.)

Are we thence to conclude that it is wrong to be in conformity with *any* practice of worldly people; if they travel in automobiles, we are to ride in horse-drawn vehicles; if they light their homes with electricity, we must use kerosene lamps; if they wear light-colored clothing, we must wear dark? There are those who draw such conclusions, absurd though they are. Such is wholly to misconstrue this frequent oriental figure of speech.

Obviously, when Jesus said, "Lay *not* up for yourselves treasures upon earth, where moth and rust doth corrupt, and where thieves break through and steal: *but* lay up for yourselves treasures in heaven, where neither moth nor rust doth corrupt, and where thieves do not break through nor steal" (Matthew 6:19,20), he is not absolutely prohibiting his faithful followers to exercise that prudence which he elsewhere taught; a dip into sacred history will reveal that some of the greatest and most devout men who ever lived, such as Abraham, Isaac, and David were men of wealth and were possessed of vast earthly possessions; there is indeed the recognition on the part of Paul of such men in the church, and to whom special instruction is given. (See especially 1 Timothy 6:17-19.) Jesus promised a sufficiency of this world's goods to those who serve him faithfully here, when he said they would have "an hundredfold in this time, houses, and brethren, and sisters, and mothers, and children, and lands, with persecutions; and in the world to come eternal life." (Mark 10:30.) In keeping with the principle embodied in all of these statements is the Lord's command to give priority to his affairs. "But seek ye *first* the kingdom of God, and his righteousness; and all these things shall be added unto you." (Matthew 6:33.) Is not the implication clear that when this is done, we may *then* busy ourselves in the proper pursuit of those matters which the Lord will, through our industry, "add" unto us? Indeed, is not this precisely the way the Lord *adds* "all these other things" to us?

"What did Peter mean when he said, 'And we have the word of prophecy made more sure; whereunto ye do well that ye take heed . . .' (2 Peter 1:19)? More sure than what?"

The "word of prophecy," literally, in the Greek text, "the prophetic word," is the body of doctrine received and recorded by Old Testament prophets. These were the men to whom the apostle primarily refers when he says that they "spake from God, being moved by the Holy Spirit," i.e., by inspiration. (2 Peter 1:21.) He included himself among those whom he affirmed have the word of prophecy "made more sure." Immediately preceding this statement, the apostle had recounted his remarkable experience in the "holy mount" of Transfiguration (Matthew 17:1ff), and some expositors have concluded that the comparison which Peter drew is between that scene and the prophetic word, thus making him to say that the prophecies were more convincing and provided better evidence of the deity of the Lord than the amazing and impressive events of the conference Jesus had with Moses and Elijah, which the three disciples, Peter, James and John, were privileged to see on a mountain in Palestine.

168

This was the view of the King James translators, hence their rendering, "We have a more sure word of prophecy," that is, something more certain on which to rely than the scenes witnessed in the mount. Had the apostle not been present on that occasion and had he received the report of the events there occurring from others, it is barely possible that he might have intended to convey such an idea; but, inasmuch as he includes himself by the pronoun *we* among those who have the prophetic word "more sure," such a conclusion, to this writer, is inconceivable. I am wholly unable to believe that Peter would have regarded any evidence as more convincing than that which he received when he saw Moses and Elijah and heard them discussing with Jesus the Lord's "decease" at Jerusalem. He saw the radiant light above the brightness of the noon day sun flash about the glorified Saviour. He looked upon the transfigured face of the Lord with his own eyes. He witnessed the appearance of Moses, the great lawgiver of the old dispensation, and Elijah, one of its greatest prophets, and he was so enraptured with the occasion that he wanted to erect three tabernacles, one for Moses, one for Elijah, and one for Christ and thus continue the glorious experience as long as possible. He heard the Voice from heaven identify Jesus as deity. Surely, no word of Isaiah, Jeremiah, Daniel, or other Old Testament prophet, could have supplied more irrefutable and convincing evidence than this.

A more reasonable and satisfactory view—that which the American Standard translators adopted—is that the word of prophecy was made more sure and further confirmed by that which he had witnessed, and which he was passing on to his readers. Being additional evidence, it would serve to strengthen, to corroborate, and to make more sure, the faith already existing which, in the last analysis, was based on the testimony of Old Testament prophets. The transfiguration scene confirmed the testimony of these prophets and holy men of God concerning the deity of Jesus, and established more clearly the relationship obtaining between God and his Son. The testimony of these prophets who had written long before was thus made more sure by that which Peter, James and John witnessed in the mountain experience. To these matters Peter's readers would do "well" to take heed, "as unto a lamp shining in a dark place, until the day dawn, and the day-start arise" in their hearts. Into a world of darkness the lamp of prophecy sheds its light bringing hope and cheer to all who keep within its lovely beams. To such a lamp all who would follow Christ and please his Father are to look. As darkness flees before the light, so the gloom of a sinful world fades as the "day-star"—Christ Jesus our Lord—lightens up our hearts. As the appearance of the sun announces the approach of day, so the reception of the prophecies—confirmed and supported by the Transfiguration—lights up the gloom of the world and brings happiness, contentment and eventual salvation in heaven to those who allow themselves to be bathed in its refulgent beams.

"When do children of God receive eternal life?"

At the moment of justification from past, or alien sins, so some among us are today saying, thus demonstrating that a sizable segment of our people are being influenced far, far more by denominational theology than by the New Testament or by the writers of restoration literature.

Those who defend the doctrine of the impossibility of apostasy have always urged that eternal life is a present possession and is enjoyed from the moment of salvation and since the life possessed is eternal—never ending—it cannot be forfeited or lost. The conclusion is indeed a consistent one if the premise is true. Obviously, life-unending, never ends! If, as an ever-increasing number among us contend, eternal life is co-equal with salvation from alien sins, we are logically obligated to concede the Calvinistic doctrine of eternal security—a child of God once saved, is never lost, since the life which he possesses never ends.

When debates were common such views were seldom entertained by members of the churches of Christ since in those encounters the truth, regarding eternal life, was clearly taught and emphasized. When such passages as 1 John 5:11,13, John 3:16, and other verses were cited in an attempt to show that eternal life is a blessing available to, and actually possessed by children of God today, it was pointed out that truth is always consistent with itself; the scriptures are never contradictory and must always be harmonized; there are two classes of scripture touching the theme of eternal life, one asserting that it is *promised* the other that it is *possessed* and each must be considered in the light of, and in harmony with the other. Titus 1:2 and 1 John 2:25 are examples of the former; 1 John 5:11 and 13, are examples of the latter. The first class informs us that we "hope" for eternal life and that it is "promised;" that which is promised is not yet realized; that for which we "hope" is yet to be received. ". . . hope that is seen is not hope: for who hopeth for that which he seeth?" (Romans 8:24.) Thus, we do not hope for that which we already have; we hope for eternal life (Titus 1:2); therefore, we do not actually possess it. We are promised eternal life (1 John 2:25); the promise of a blessing precedes receipt of the blessing itself; hence, we are not in *present* possession of eternal life.

How, then, may we properly harmonize the two classes of passages?

Not by urging that eternal life is *actually* possessed here, since this conclusion negates Titus 1:2 and 1 John 2:25. Any view which changes the "hope" of Titus to *realization,* and the promise of John to *present* possession conflicts with the plain affirmation of the text. It was the apostle John who penned the words, "And this is the *promise* which he

170

promised us, even the life eternal" (1 John 2:25), and it was the same apostle who also wrote, "These things have I written unto you, that ye may know that ye have eternal life, even unto you that believe on the name of the Son of God" (1 John 5:13). This latter affirmation cannot be properly interpreted to mean that we have *in actual possession* eternal life here, since this conflicts with the apostle's own statement that we possess it in promise. It must mean then that we have eternal life *in prospect* to be realized at the end of the age when, in triumph, we are forevermore beyond the possibility of apostasy. Until that glorious day, our approach to life is through the Son who has it:

"And the witness is this, that God gave unto us eternal life, *and this life is in his Son*. He that hath the Son hath the life; he that hath not the Son of God hath not the life." (1 John 5:11,12.)

The blessed assurance of eventual realization is based on the fact that God, who cannot lie, promised it "long ages ago," that is, before the Levitical period, and it is thus not dependent on the Jewish law. It is significant that "eternal life" includes both quality and duration. Obviously the quality of life which we possess here, while in the flesh and limited by its imperfections, is not analogous to the life awaiting us beyond. Neither the quality nor duration is comparable to that which shall ultimately be ours if faithfully we make our way to the heavenly city.

"Who are the women in 1 Timothy 3:11, referred to in the following statement, 'Women in like manner must be grave, not slanderers, temperate, faithful in all things'?"

It will be observed that preceding this verse are instructions by Paul to the young evangelist Timothy touching the qualifications and appointment of deacons and following it these instructions are continued. Why does the apostle, in the midst of detailed instruction regarding deacons, abruptly turn aside to list certain qualifications for women? The ASV text reads, "*Women* in like manner. . . ." The KJV has it, "Even so must their *wives* . . ." it evidently being intended, by these translators, to convey the notion that the *wives* of the deacons are alluded to in the passage before us.

It is far from certain that such was the apostle's purpose. (1) The word translated "women," in the ASV, and "wives" in the KJV (*gunaikos*), simply means *women* who may indeed be wives, but the married state does not necessarily inhere in the word; and the KJV rendering is an interpretation, not a literal translation. (2) Where wives of the deacons have been intended, it is likely that the apostle would have followed usual New Testament practice of referring to them as "your wives." (Cf. 1 Corinthians 14:34,35.) (3) If the inspired writer's design had been to set out requirements for deacons' wives, it seems certain he would have listed domestic or household duties, none of which is included among those given. (4) And, it is indeed remarkable that the apostle would list qualifications for wives of deacons and not have done so for wives of elders. No such list occurs nor is reference specifically made to individual characteristics thereof.

In view of the foregoing facts, it is not surprising that many students of the Word have concluded that these "women" constituted a class in the early church to whom special duties were assigned and that Paul, in this passage, designated some qualifications of those thus named for the work. It is significant that Phoebe is called "a servant of the church in Cenchreae," literally, a *deaconess* of the church in that city, the word servant being the translation of the feminine form of the word for deacon (*diakonos*). (Romans 16:1.) This does not mean that she held some *official* position in the church; the designation is functional and denotes the work she did, and not an office she held. In 1 Timothy 5:9-16, Paul provided for an enrollment of certain women with qualifications designated by him who were, according to the Greek Lexicographer Thayer, to "care for widows and orphans at public expense," i.e., from the church treasury. It is therefore quite likely that it was the design of the apostle to designate this class of women when, amid the qualification of *male* servants of the church, he listed certain requirements for *female* servants.

There is no sanction here, nor elsewhere in the sacred writings, for the denominational practice of having official deaconesses in the church. But, many congregations have faithful sisters especially qualified to whom the elders often turn for Christian duties when needs arise which neither they nor the deacons are suited to do. It is certainly not out of order to refer to these women as *deaconesses,* since it is a scriptural term and denotes a scriptural work. In a day when many among us do not shrink from having "ministers of education," "ministers of youth," "ministers of music," etc. etc., none of which terms is to be found in the New Testament, *either in Greek or in English,* we ought not to oppose the proper use of a term dictated by the Holy Spirit!

The qualifications of this class of women, gathered from 1 Timothy 3:11 and 5:9-16, are, (1) "grave" (serious-minded); (2) "not slanderers" (avoiding gossip); (3) "temperate" (calm in spirit); (4) "faithful in all things"; (5) at least 60 years old; (6) having been married but once; (7) having had children; (8) hospitable; (9) having demonstrated the ability to engage in humble, sacrificial work.

"The New Testament writers wrote primarily to churches and individuals regarding specific and local problems. Did these writers know that their writings would be accepted as final and authoritative?"

There are those who say they did *not*, and who are attempting to influence all they can to accept the view that the New Testament books were simply letters of local and limited significance and were never intended to become a body of truth to be regarded as inerrant and all-authoritative. Incredibly, those of this school are saying that Peter and Paul and John and other New Testament writers would be greatly surprised to know that their missives are considered to be infallible documents in this, the twentieth century.

This unworthy estimate of those writings can have but one effect and that is to prompt people to regard them as out-dated, obsolete, of little or no significance two thousand years removed from their origin. Those of this school admit that there is truth in them, but only such truth as would be found in the writings of pious people of any age and of value to us only when viewed in "proper perspective."

That such concepts are possible evidences how far, how very, very far, some among us have moved from the motto of those who went before us and called upon all to "speak where the Bible speaks to be silent where the Bible is silent, to call Bible things by Bible names, and to do Bible things in Bible ways." This plea is no longer valid to many; on the contrary, this liberal school regards the New Testament as simply a collection of ancient wisdom, a reflection of the views of the day in which it was produced, not always true, and in any instance to be adapted to the norms and standards of this day! This concept is unbelief of the most dangerous type—more threatening than outright infidelity, because it affects acceptance of the word while diluting it to the point of impotency.

Of course the sacred writers *knew* they were directed by the Holy Spirit and were therefore penning infallible truth: (1) The biographies of Christ were written that men might believe (John 20:30,31.) (2) Things not possible otherwise to know were revealed *by the Spirit* to New Testament writers. (1 Corinthians 11:9,10.) (3) Those who wrested these writings did so to their own destruction. (2 Peter 3:16.) Such was affirmed by Peter of "all the other scriptures" as well. Of what man unaided by inspiration may it properly be said that to alter in any sense his writings brings upon all who thus do their destruction? (4) Paul asserted that the gospel was made known to him *by revelation*—matters not known in earlier ages, as now revealed "unto his holy apostles and prophets *by* the Spirit." (Ephesians 3:3-11.) By the Spirit they came into possession of this knowledge! Moreover, they were edified by their *own* writings (Galatians 1:12), possible only of *inspired* men, since men unaided by inspiration are able to write intelligibly only of matters already learned. New Testament writers not only were aware of the reception of hitherto unknown truth, they regarded it as inerrant and they solemnly warned against any modification thereof. (Galatians 1:7-12; Revelation 22:18,19.) What other writers of the ages, however eminent, sought to guard their productions in this fashion? It is sheer madness to deny to the writers of the New Covenant (or to the Old), infallibility, and the time is long past when the faithful churches among us should purge themselves of the dangerous disbelief now characteristic of some among us.

"How was Christ made 'righteousness' for us? (1 Corinthians 1:30.)"

The verse, alluded to in this query, 1 Corinthians 1:30, reads in full as follows: "But of him are ye in Christ Jesus, who was made unto us wisdom from God, and righteousness and sanctification, and redemption." He is the *means* of righteousness, that is, it is *through* him we are enabled to receive the blessings of righteousness—the blessings which come to us through a life of righteousness. It is in this sense that we receive "the gift of righteousness," not righteousness itself, but that which righteousness bestows. *Righteousness* is right-doing—the keeping of God's commandments. (Psalm 119:172.) Neither here, nor elsewhere, in the sacred writings, is the denominational doctrine (lately espoused by some brethren) of imputed (transferred) righteousness taught. One might as well argue, from 1 Corinthians 1:30, that the *wisdom* of Christ is transmitted to the sinner in conversion, as to argue for a transference of righteousness. (Romans 5:17.) The "gift of righteousness" is salvation.

The blessings of righteousness are received through faithful compliance with the will of the Lord and through obedience to his commandments, and not through some mysterious bestowal of merit which the Lord possesses. We must remember that justification does not obliterate the history of sin in life; it simply releases the sinner from the guilt thereof. Paul, ever mindful of the great grace he had experienced, was never without the consciousness that he had persecuted the church of God and wasted it. (1 Timothy 1:12-17.) Pardoned, saved, justified, acquitted, no longer under the guilt of sin, it remained for him, through faithful adherence to the Lord's will, to exhibit personal righteousness, *right-standing,* with God. So it is with us. The blessing of salvation is through Christ. He is the *means* of righteousness (1 Corinthians 1:30), through him we receive "the gift of righteousness" (Romans 5:17), we are accepted by him when we work "righteousness" (Acts 10:34,35)

174

through unswerving allegiance to his will as set out in the New Testament. We must distinguish between a righteousness imputed (credited) to us because we are in a right relationship with God through obedience to his will, and a righteousness which Christ (through *his* submission to the will of the Father), is alleged to have transferred to us. The former, the New Testament clearly teaches; the latter is Calvinism.

There is a vast difference between not imputing *guilt* and in conferring *merit*. A pardoned criminal is no longer regarded as guilty of the crimes which led to his arrest and conviction, but he is thence by no means a valuable citizen simply because he has been pardoned! Righteousness is right-doing. To be righteous, one must do right. We do right when we keep the commandments of the Lord.

"I think I shall never realize fully my indebtedness to the GOS-PEL ADVOCATE. I have read it rather consistently for over 60 years. Sometime, when you have time, write a paragraph on Galatians 3:20 where Paul wrote: 'Now a mediator is not a mediator of one; but God is one.' The statement within itself is not difficult, but I seem unable to grasp its significance in the context."

Paul's purpose in Galatians 3 and 4 is to show (1) the temporal and limited design of the law of Moses and (2) the permanent and superior nature of the promise which God made to Abraham. The former he does by showing (a) miraculous manifestations of the Spirit came, not by the law, but through the message of faith (Galatians 3:2, margin); (b) the law was powerless to justify, it could only condemn, not save (vv. 11,12,14); (c) it was a temporary expedient, to last only until fulfilled and removed by Christ (Galatians 3:16,19); (d) it was provided through the ministry of angels (v. 19), and (e) it was appropriated by a *human* mediator. (Moses, v. 19. See Exodus 20:19; Deuteronomy 5:5.)

The promise, however (wherein is the gospel), was designed to be (a) the medium through which salvation would be made available to all men (Galatians 3:13,14); (b) it was intended to be a *valid* medium of salvation throughout the age (Galatians 3:15); (c) it came directly from God, and was not delivered by angelic intervention (v. 20).

"But," the apostle reasons, "suppose some unbelieving Jew
contends that the presence of a mediator, in the case of the
law, and its absence, in the case of the promise, demonstrates
the superiority of the law to the gospel?"

Quite the contrary; the fact of mediation in a situation supposes and requires the presence of two parties—not one. Such was characteristic of the law which issued from Sinai. It was a contract between God and the people of Israel, and its validity depended on *both* parties' faithful-

175

ness in the performance of its conditions. The promise (which embodied the gospel, through which salvation is possible for all men), did not derive its validity as a true and valid offer of salvation on any one but God—its offer is absolute, and not contingent. We must, of course, keep in mind that under consideration here is *not* whether the *blessings* of promise (the gospel of Christ, Genesis 12:1-3), are conditional—they are, indeed; the conditions are obedience to the gospel (2 Thessalonians 1:7-9), but whether the promise (the gospel), could ever be annulled, as was the law through the failure of one party (Jeremiah 31:31; Hebrews 8:6-13). There is no other party but God; and he will not violate his word. While we may fall to appropriate the blessings of the gospel, the gospel is not dependent on us; it results from an irrevocable decree of deity and it will continue to be available to men to the end of the age, *whether obeyed or not.*

But, did not Paul say that the law was "added" to the promise "because of transgressions"? Does not this show the imperfect character of the promise until the law was added? The Greek word translated "added" is *prostitheemi,* literally, something *placed beside,* not added to complete, but given independently and additionally. It was the apostle's purpose to show in Galatians 3:19, that the law came long after the promise and was added, not to embellish the promise, but to give man a greater awareness of sin. (Cf. Romans 7:13.) The law, far from nullifying the promise (the gospel), was intended to cause the Jews to recognize their need of it and, in the beginning of the Christian era, multitudes of them did acquire such a recognition. That many others did not do so was not due to any defect in the function of the law, or because the gospel was not valid, but because of unbelief—unbelief in the very scriptures the Jews affected to reverence so much! (Matthew 13:14,15; Acts 13:44-47.)

When then, is Christ declared to be the mediator between God and man, and of the new covenant? (1 Timothy 2:5; Hebrews 8:6ff.) We should keep in mind that the contrast drawn by the apostle was designed to show that the law, being the result of agreement between two parties—God and Israel—is inferior to the promise God made to Abraham because it failed through the unfaithfulness of the Israelites (Jeremiah 31:31), whereas the promise, being an unconditional decree of God, can never fail.

The mediation of Christ involves reception of the *blessings* of the promise—not whether the promise itself is to continue.

"What is 'The Rapture'?"

It is the fevered figment which once issued from the labored imagination of a future kingdom advocate, an airy will of the wisp of current

Premillennialism, of which there is not only not the faintest hint in the Scriptures but which is therein easily shown to be utterly, completely and forevermore false!

The theory alleges that there are *two* comings of the Lord, at the end of this age, the first of which has him appearing in the clouds, but not to the earth itself, and that at his appearance the saints will be caught up to meet him and to remain with him during "the tribulation," which is envisioned as a time of great trouble here on earth.

The "tribulation" according to this view will last for seven years, following which the Lord will come "with" his saints (the first coming, they say, was "for" them), and the thousand years' reign of Christ begins! This "coming is to be to the earth itself," the "tribulation" having ended. First Thessalonians 4:14-17 is the passage relied on by them to sustain their view of the first coming, and they cite Matthew 24:21 in support of their "tribulation" theory.

Matthew 24:21 reads: ". . . for then shall be great tribulation, such as hath not been from the beginning of the world until now, no, nor ever shall be." Because a period of "great tribulation" is here predicted to come upon the earth. Premillennialists, with absolute disregard of the context, imagine that this is the *tribulation* of their theory. Even the most casual reading of the chapter shows the utter and complete falsity of their position. (1) In Matthew 24:16 the faithful are told to "flee unto the mountains" during this time of trial for their protection, thus clearly evidencing the fact that they were not in heaven to which they had been raptured as the theory we are reviewing vainly supposes. (2) Verse 20 of Matthew 24 informs us that the disciples were told to petition the Father that their flight from the besieged city "be not in the winter, neither on a sabbath," the weather in the first instance, the locked gates of the city in the second, being a hindrance to their effort to flee to the mountains while "the tribulation" was on. The obvious truth is, Matthew 24 through verse 34 is a detailed discussion of the events attending the destruction of Jerusalem, and thus has no reference to the end of the Christian age. Josephus, the Jewish historian, relates that the Christians did indeed escape from the siege and not one perished in the terrible tribulation which fell upon the Jewish city and state, and the prophecy of our Lord in Matthew 24 through verse 34 finds fulfillment in those events.

Not only does 1 Thessalonians 4:14-17 provide no support for the "rapture" theory, it proves it to be positively false. It tells us that "the Lord himself shall descend from heaven, with a shout, with the voice of the archangel, and with the trump of God: and the dead in Christ shall rise first; then we that are alive, that are left, shall together with them be caught up in the clouds, to meet the Lord in the air: and so shall we ever be with the Lord." Before *any* are caught up, faithful

177

saints will arise, and all together will go forth to meet the Lord "in the air," and thus evermore to be with him. Note, carefully, that Paul explains we shall *ever* be with him—not for seven years only, as Premillennialists urge. Moreover, contemporary with these events, the earth will perish in a mighty conflagration. (2 Peter 3:9,10.) These significant facts settle the question: (1) The kingdom of Christ was set up in the apostolic age—on the first Pentecost following his resurrection. (Mark 9:1; Acts 2:1-4.) (2) The Lord will return on the clouds, but not to the earth itself, and the faithful will be caught up to be with him *forever*. (3) There will be no earth here for any reign following this age, because *this* earth is to suffer destruction. (4) The future abode of the saints, in the new heaven and earth, is in that place our Lord went to prepare—heaven. (John 14:2.)

"Please harmonize the following scriptures: Matthew 6:13 and James 1:13?"

Matthew 6:13 reads: "And bring us not into temptation, but deliver us from the evil one." The more familiar King James version has it, "And lead us not into temptation, but deliver us from evil." There is little, if any, difference between the American Standard rendering and the King James inasmuch as evil originates with "the evil one," anyway, and to "bring us not into temptation" means much the same as "lead us not into temptation."

We have here an excellent example of Hebrew poetry which, unlike English versification of meter and rhyme, obtains its rhythmic cadence in repetition of thought and parallel lines. A glance into the poetic books of the Old Testament will provide hundreds of instances. "He will have pity on the poor and needy, and the souls of the needy he will save." (Psalm 72:13.) "The evil bow down before the good; and the wicked, at the gates of the righteous." (Proverbs 14:19.) "Now my days are swifter than a post: they flee away, they see no good." (Job 9:25.) It will be observed that the second clause repeats and is explanatory of the first and the movement is like the steady swing of a pendulum, or the unvarying tramp of soldiers marching in step. It is this which gives it exquisite beauty and intriguing loveliness. The depth of feeling, and the rich spiritual tone of David's songs are without parallel in literature. Thus, Jehovah "leads us not into temptation," by delivering us from "the evil one," and this he does by providing us with a "way of escape" from temptation. (Matthew 4:1-13; 1 Corinthians 10:13.)

James 1:13 reads: "Let no man say when he is tempted, I am tempted of God; for God cannot be tempted with evil, and he himself tempteth no man." Affirmed here is the fact that God does not put temptation in the way of his people; when they are tempted, they must not attribute

178

such to God, for just as he cannot be tempted himself, neither does he tempt others. Here, the word *tempt* means to solicit to do evil. However, occasionally, the word is used in the Scriptures in the sense of testing or proving as, for example, in Genesis 22:1, where it is said, "God did tempt Abraham." (King James Version.) The American Standard Version has the better rendering here, "God did *prove* Abraham." Hence, in any instance, when God is said to tempt men, it is to test their faith, loyalty, devotion, to him, as in the case of Abraham; when it is said that God tempts no man, it is meant that he never encourages evil, or provides inducement to sin in the way of men.

"This question was raised recently during a class discussion, 'Do angels have wings?' This question concerns me since I have taught children's Bible classes where felt board figures portrayed angels with wings."

People often begin the study of biblical themes with an erroneous assumption and consequent confusion attends their effort throughout. It is easy to assign to scriptural terms a far too limited significance or to assume that what must be the meaning of a word or phrase in one instance is its significance in every other. Often overlooked is that in the description of heavenly beings and their actions anthropomorphic language is used which attributes to angelic or heavenly beings the shapes, qualities, characteristics and actions of men.

The word "angel" is the translation of the Greek *anggelos* and the Hebrew *malawk,* terms simply signifying a *messenger.* Thus, basically, the word does not denote the nature of the being at all, but rather the function which the being exercises, primarily in his relationship to deity. It is for this reason that the term appears in such a great variety of circumstances in the sacred writings. Not infrequently it is applied to human beings. Haggai is called the "messenger of the Lord" (literally, the *angel*), and Malachi thus designated John the Baptist the forerunner of the Christ. Priests are similarly identified in Malachi 2:7 and in Isaiah 42:19. Israel, the nation, is portrayed as God's messenger (angel). That prophet also spoke of "the angel of the presence," and Moses wrote of the angel who went before Israel—very evident allusions to our Lord Jesus Christ. Created beings, good and bad, are called angels (Hebrew 1:14; Jude 6) and heavenly beings, never possessed of flesh and blood, who neither marry nor are given in marriage, are mentioned and identified as angels, and the Hebrew writer tells us that it is the function of angels to serve those who are heirs of salvation (Matthew 22:30; Hebrews 1:13,14; Isaiah 63:9; Exodus 23:21).

From this very brief induction of the word "angel," or its equivalent, it will be seen that the term is of varied usage in the Scriptures. Angels

179

are both earthly and heavenly; possessed of flesh and blood, thus men; not of flesh and blood, and hence heavenly beings, and *not* men. Angels of the latter classification are spirits, incorporeal beings, and thus without the characteristics of men in the flesh though it appears from many references thereto, and they had the power of *assuming* the actions and functions of men.

1. They were capable of making themselves both visible and invisible (Numbers 22:31), and to appear under circumstances obviously miraculous in nature (Exodus 3:2). They could and often did assume the appearance of men as illustrated in the experience of Abraham in the plains of Mamre (Genesis 18:1,2), and the wife of Manoah when the birth of Samson was announced (Judges 13:6-13).

2. The ability to cover vast distances immediately is attributed to them (Exodus 12:29,30); Gabriel came from the very presence of God to Daniel while that faithful saint was engaged in prayer (see also Revelations 14:6). Because they are often said to *fly,* in the Bible, artists' imagination gives them *wings,* but all such references must be regarded as figurative and are used to convey to us the idea of motion far, far more rapid than man is capable of achieving by any means other than flying, as they did.

3. They were able to exercise vast powers; Sennacherib's army was crushed by the Lord through an angel (2 Chronicles 32:21,22); Peter was released from his chains and enabled to walk through an iron door which "opened of its own accord" (Acts 12:10).

Heavenly angels, not being corporeal, and capable of vast changes in appearance, cannot be visualized, with fleshly concepts, and we ought not to attempt to do so.

"What is the biblical distinction between the words, 'clergy' and 'laity'?"

In current usage, the "clergy" is that class of men in denominational churches who have been set apart by ordination for official religious duties and the "laity" are the rest of the members not thus ordained. These are not biblical distinctions, however; and the usage provides another illustration of how far afield from New Testament teaching the religious world about us has gone.

The word "clergy" derives from the Greek *kleros,* one form of which is translated "charge alloted." (1 Peter 5:3.) Here, the apostle admonished elders not to act as "lording it over the charge allotted to them, but to make themselves "ensamples to the flock." The "charge allotted," the clergy, over which they were to rule was the congregation in which they were appointed to serve. Peter taught here that the elders, far from exhibiting a spirit of arrogance and autocracy in the oversight to which they were set, were to serve as "ensamples" to the clergy, the flock, the church. Hence, in biblical usage, the entire congregation constitutes the clergy, and the word "laity" does not occur in the Bible. The denominational concept is thus wholly foreign to New Testament phraseology, and it conveys a notion in conflict with it. Here, again, is emphasized the importance of using biblical words to convey biblical notions, i.e., to call Bible things by Bible names and to avoid any use of Bible words in a context contrary to their sacred usage.

The denominational distinction of "clergy" and "laity" not only involves the improper use of the word, it sets up a distinction *in work,* between people, not recognized in the New Testament. The preachers of whom we read therein were thus designated *because they preached*—their work was and is functional, not official. All disciples had a hand in the spread of the gospel and the evangelization of the ancient world (Acts 8:4), and the Lord will expect no less of us today. The only proper distinction between those who publicly preach the word and all others in the church is that the former, by being supported in their work by the church, are enabled to spend more time, and thus to do more work; but, all members of the church, insofar as they have opportunity, and within the limitations which the Holy Spirit himself enjoined (1 Timothy 2:11,12), are to busy themselves in telling others the glad story of salvation.

"Paul commanded the Roman saints to greet 'one another with a holy kiss' (Romans 16:16), and Peter instructed those to whom he wrote to 'salute one another with a kiss of love' (1 Peter 5:14). Why is this practice no longer observed in churches of Christ?"

We must be careful not to attempt to draw from these verses that which is not in them. Neither here, nor elsewhere in the sacred writings, is the kiss, as a mode of greeting, enjoined. Throughout the biblical period, from Adam to John on Patmos, and in eastern lands to this day, greeting, by means of the kiss, has been and is practiced. Because it was a custom common to the day and the lands in which they lived, early Christians observed it. There are numerous allusions thereto in the writings of the "church fathers," as well as in the New Testament. The custom is mentioned by Justin Martyr, Tertullian, Chrysostom, Augustine and various other ancient writers, and it is referred to, in addition to the instances mentioned in the foregoing question, in 1 Corinthians 16:20; 2 Corinthians 13:12; and 1 Thessalonians 5:26.

It should be observed that Paul, in Romans 16:16, taught the disciples to greet each other with a *holy* kiss, and that Peter, in the reference he makes to the matter (1 Peter 5:14), admonished that it be a kiss *of love.* Thus, neither originated the mode, but both sanctified it, by urging

that it be observed in keeping with the morality and purity characteristic of the high calling they had espoused. Historians of the early
church inform us that the saints were careful to avoid the abuses to
which this custom might have led by separation of the sexes when the
church met for worship—a practice which had long been observed in
the synagogue. The so-called Constitution of the Holy Apostles, written
sometime between A.D. 300 and A.D. 400, has the following injunction:
"Then let the men give the men, and the women give the women, our
Lord's kiss. But let no one do it with deceit, as Judas betrayed the Lord
with a kiss." Kissing, as a mode of greeting, was no more sanctioned
than handshaking is today, both methods being customs of the times.
Inasmuch as Christianity requires sincerity in this mode of greeting
today, so it enjoined it in the kiss of greeting in that day. It was to be
"holy," hence, not impure; the "kiss of love," prompted by love, and in
exhibition of it.

"What is the meaning of the apostle Peter's words, 'Be subject to every ordinance of man . . .'?"

An "ordinance" is a thing commanded, a duty required by an authoritative source. Here, the obligation is clearly that of the civil government, as will be seen from an examination of the context: "Be subject
to every ordinance of man for the Lord's sake; whether to the king, as
supreme; or unto governors, as sent by him for vengeance on evil-doers
and for praise to them that do well." (1 Peter 2:13,14.) The king was
the emperor; the governors were lesser officials, including the procon-
suls, the magistrates, and other subordinate officials such as the
"Asiarchs," the "town clerks," etc. (Acts 19:31,35,38.)

It is the duty of children of God to submit to the laws of the land in
which they live, even though the government itself is corrupt, and the
officials which administer it are depraved. This is clearly taught here
and in Romans 13:1ff. And, neither here, nor elsewhere in the sacred
writings, did any inspired man designate any special form of government to which Christians are to submit, nor is there any instruction to
them to attempt to formulate any special type of civil government
under which to live. They knew full well that seldom would Christians
have any choice in determining the type or kind of government which
would operate where they lived, and they thus concerned themselves
solely with the conduct which should characterize Christians, regardless of the form of government to which they would owe allegiance.

It is noteworthy that the type of government which obtained when
Peter penned these words—the Roman monarchy—was dictatorial,
totalitarian and tyrannical; and the men who were empowered to direct
it were corrupt, depraved and dissolute. Early Christians were not told

to reform it (which they could not have done), but to obey it (which they could and did).

But that the Christian's allegiance thereto *is not unconditional,* however, follows from the fact that the apostle who penned these words, "Be subject to every ordinance of man . . ." *disregarded* the edicts of civil authority when forbidden to preach in the name of Jesus. "But Peter and John answered and said unto them, Whether it is right in the sight of God to hearken unto you rather than unto God, judge ye: for we cannot but speak the things which we saw and heard." (Acts 4:1-22.) When the law of God and the edicts of civil authority are not in conflict, Christians are required to obey both. When they oppose each other, Christians must disregard the secular for the divine. The overriding principle is stated by the apostle, "We must obey God rather than men." The test is easy and simple: Is the edict Christians are told to obey in harmony with the law of God? If yes, it must be obeyed, whatever the nature of the government which issues it is, and notwithstanding the depravity of the officials who enforce it; if no, it must be resisted, however worthy the government and benevolent its rulers may be in other respects. The principle admits of no exceptions, and cannot be disregarded with impunity. Our duty to God is supreme.

"Are deacons required to have children to serve?"

There is but little specifically said in the New Testament regarding deacons or their qualifications. First Timothy 3:8-13 is the only detailed passage dealing with the subject; and when to this is added such information as we are able to obtain from the etymology of the Greek word *diakonos,* and its usage, we have exhausted our sources insofar as inspired affirmation is concerned. No doubt obtains, however, regarding the nature of the work of deacons, since the original term so translated clearly designates a servant. Deacons are thus servants of the church.

The only reference to family relationships of deacons appears in 1 Timothy 3:12: "Let the deacons be husbands of one wife, ruling their children and their own houses well." The word "Let," when used by an apostle has all the force of a command, and means, "The deacons must be husbands of one wife, ruling their children and their own houses well," thus making it obligatory upon the deacon to be both married and to have children. It has often been argued that such was to characterize deacons *if* they had families. The saintly Lipscomb expressed this view of the matter: "We do not think that language intended to require they should be married and have children; but as that was the common state of man, directions were given as to what kind of wives and children they should have." Such is, of course, possible; however, it is my view that it is safer to take the words in their common and ordinary import and to conclude that a deacon (a) must be a married man and (b) have a family, although it is not affirmed of their children they are to be believers as is the case of children of elders. This enables men to serve as deacons who are younger than men qualified to be elders. (Titus 1:6.) The diaconate is a proving ground for the eldership. (1 Timothy 3:13.)

"What was the 'mystery of Christ' to which Paul often alluded in Ephesians 3?"

This was a matter revealed to the apostles and to the New Testament prophets by the Holy Spirit (v. 5); Paul was among those to whom this information came (v. 3); the details thereof were not known "in other generations" (v. 5); the "mystery" was that the Gentiles were fellow-heirs and fellow-partakers of the promise of Christ through the gospel (v. 6). These blessing obedient Gentiles were to share with those Jews who obeyed the gospel. (Ephesians 3:1-5.)

Our English word *mystery* has the meaning of something above or beyond comprehension or normal understanding, but such is not the significance of the Greek word *musteerion* translated "mystery" in the passage before us. It simply denotes that which is thus far unrevealed—a thing which may be, and often is, as clear and uncomplicated as any other plain and easily understood matter. The "mystery" alluded to by Paul was that it was God's intention to include the Gentiles in the scheme of human redemption and to make them fellow-participants in all the blessings attending it.

Details of this universal offer of salvation had not been known to earlier generations. (Ephesians 3:5.) True it was that it was early declared that "all the families of the earth" were to be privileged to share in the blessings which Abraham's seed would make available (Genesis 12:1-3; Galatians 3:8); nonetheless, the manner in which this scheme would be revealed, the channels through which it would be received, and the extent of Gentile involvement were matters not made known to Abraham, Moses or the Old Testament prophets.

Jews did indeed believe that all nations would be blessed by the coming of Messiah, but only if they espoused the decrees of Moses and the traditions of the fathers. It never occurred to them that the law of Moses was to be abolished and that Jew and Gentile would stand on the same footing before God as "fellow-heirs" in "the one body," the church. This was the *mystery of Christ* of which Paul so feelingly wrote.

"Why were Adam and Eve unashamed in their nakedness before their fall?"

Because they were unaware of their nakedness there was neither sin nor shame in it. This awareness was a part of the knowledge which the Tempter offered them: "And the serpent said unto the woman, Ye shall not surely die: for God doth know that in the day ye eat thereof, then your eyes shall be opened, and ye shall be as God, knowing good and evil." (Genesis 3:4,5.) When they yielded to the seductions of Satan on that fateful occasion, "the eyes of them both were opened, and they knew that they were naked; and they sewed fig-leaves together, and made themselves aprons." (Genesis 3:6,7.) Thus, the first effect of the sin was to make them painfully cognizant of their shameful state and the additional knowledge which Satan offered and which they had covered was not being experienced which, to their sorrow, they found to be far short of what they had expected.

Here before there was innocence there was now a deep sense of shame, and the desire to hide their nakedness from themselves and from God. Before they were as little children, now their guilty minds were turned on each other, and their sin was ever before them. With them now was no sense of joy, no note of satisfaction; with shame they regarded each other, and they dreaded the approach of God. (Genesis 3:8.) In an attempt to cover themselves, they fabricated aprons of leaves which they arranged in the form of girdles about their bodies, an arrangement unsatisfactory as evidence in the fact that God made provision for a different and better one. (Genesis 3:21.)

When at length they stood before their Creator, they were filled with fear and trepidation:

"And Jehovah God called unto the man, and said unto him, Where art thou? And he said, I heard thy voice in the garden, and I was afraid, because I was naked; and I hid myself." (Genesis 3:9,10.)

This is Jehovah's first query to *sinful* man and it was asked, not for the purpose of ascertaining their whereabouts, but to enable the man to *find himself!* It was an impressive call to the guilty pair to make confession and it details the first instance of fear in the Scriptures. And, sadly, it also records the first instance of falsehood in man's history since it detailed neither the truth nor the reason which prompted the fear:

"And he said, I heard thy voice in the garden, and I was afraid, because I was naked; and I hid myself." (Genesis 3:10.)

The truth is, Adam did not hide himself because he was naked; he was created in this manner, and lived innocently and happily in this state until he sinned. And, neither was he naked at the time God called to him because he had already devised the covering of leaves. *He hid himself because he sinned.* His consciousness of wrong-doing led him to fear the presence of Jehovah. Such continues to be true of Adam's posterity. Men are comfortable in the divine presence only as they enjoy assurance of acceptance by him. Those conscious of wrong-doing, like their ancient forebears, flee in fear from before him.

"In Acts 6:1, there is an allusion to Grecian Jews and also a reference to Hebrews. Were not all of them Hebrews? Why the difference?"

Both groups alluded to in the foregoing passage were descended from Abraham, ancestral father of the Hebrews, but they are distinguished as to place of birth and culture. A "Hebrew," when spoken of in contradistinction to the "Grecian Jews," was a Jew born *in* Palestine, who spoke the Hebrew tongue, or the dialect of it known as Aramaic, and who read the Scriptures in the original language, ancient Hebrew. A "Grecian Jew," sometimes called a Hellenist, from the Greek word *hellenes,* which means Greek, was a Jew born *out* of Palestine, who had been educated under Greek influence, who spoke the Greek language, and who had adopted, in large measure, the customs and modes of living characteristic of the Greeks.

"I've felt for a long time something needs to be said concerning the modern practice of public confessions. This week I received a bulletin which says of the local preacher, 'Brother _____ asked for the forgiveness of the congregation Lord's day morning because he felt that he had failed in pleading and encouraging many to repent.' Other bulletins list great numbers of responses and include 'all the elders.' Others are preaching, 'If one has had an evil thought since making a public confession he needs to make a public confession.' One says, 'I make a public confession three times a year.' "

I, too, am well aware of this situation, and I deplore it. Such evidences on the part of those who make, and who encourage others to make such confessions utter ignorance of what the New Testament teaches on this matter; and they need carefully to re-examine both the Scriptures and their own motives.

All, even the best of us, fall far short of our potential; and, were we to make confession following every conscious failure and weakness, we would be engaged in confession virtually every moment of our waking hours! And, if "all the elders" of the congregation need to make public confession of sin, this raises the question whether they ought to continue to serve in the capacity of "examples to the flock." What difference is there between making confession "three times a year," as does the brother above mentioned, and the Catholics who do so each week?

James 5:16 and 1 John 5:16, properly construed, teach that the publicity which attends the confession of sin should be exactly the same as the sin confessed—sins known only to God, confessed only to God; sins known only to a few, confessed to the few; a public sin, confessed before the church. First John 1:7,8, teaches us that sins involving frailties, weaknesses, unintentional lapses are continuously cleansed as we "walk in the light" of God's truth. Such failures ought to be taken to the throne of God in private prayer and not in the public assembly. The deplorable practice of establishing, in religious meetings, a "confessional" in which the purest, the best and the most faithful members of the church are prompted by contrived and emotional devices to respond to a public invitation to confess sin because of the shortcomings common to all of us, is a travesty of God's plan and a prostitution of the teaching of the New Testament touching the proper procedure in such matters.

"Is sanctification an action of man, of God, of both, or of neither?"

The noun "sanctification" is related in origin to the words "holy" and "holiness," the basic meaning being *separation* from that which is material and sinful. The prominent idea in sanctification is separation for a sacred purpose. The holiness of God, for example, results from his total separation from all evil; accordingly, man is sanctified or holy if the life is dedicated to God rather than to the world and worldly things.

The view of various "Pentecostal" groups that sanctification is a state of total sinlessness is wholly unsupported in the Scriptures, old and new. The Hebrew *kawdash*, the equivalent of the Greek *hangiasmos* (a setting apart), often rendered "sanctify" in the Old Testament, is used of *times, places,* and *things,* as well as of people, examples of which may be seen in Exodus 40:10-13; Leviticus 22:16-22; 20:7,8, and often elsewhere. Obviously, sinlessness cannot be affirmed of buildings, utensils, gold and other material matters. (See, specially, Matthew 23:16.) All such are sanctified when consecrated, set apart, to the service of Jehovah.

The rite of purification, observed under the law of Moses (Numbers 6:11; Leviticus 22:16-32; cf. Hebrews 9:13), cleansed only in a ritualistic or ceremonial sense; it did not purify the moral or spiritual nature of those participating. Such, indeed, characterized the entire Jewish system, serving only to keep the people reminded of the necessity of forgiveness by Jehovah to be actually realized in the death of Christ on the cross. (Hebrews 10:1-4.) David's petitions, "Purge me with hyssop, and I shall be clean: wash me, and I shall be whiter than snow" (Psalm 51:7), must be understood in the light of these facts.

Sanctification is attributed both to God and to men in the Bible. It is an action of deity in that the system, whereby men may be delivered from the world and its evil influences, originated with God; and it is also said to be an action of men who must appropriate the blessing through faith and obedience. Sanctification is said to be effected by the Father (1 Thessalonians 5:23), by Christ (1 Corinthians 1:2), by the Holy Spirit (2 Thessalonians 2:13), by the truth (John 17:17), by obedience to the gospel (1 Thessalonians 2:13,14). Moreover, God is said to "will" our sanctification, thus evidencing the fact that it involves man's response to God and not simply or solely an action wrought by him upon us.

Perfection in the flesh is unattainable (1 John 1:8,10), and the acceptable relation we are able to enjoy with the Father, the Son and the Holy Spirit results from the appropriation of the plan which they have provided to *keep* us justified. *If we keep on* walking in the light, the blood of Jesus Christ *keeps on* cleansing us from sin. (1 John 1:7.) This is a state of grace—not of human perfection—and we should be evermore thankful that in spite of our imperfections we may through grace enjoy his approval. Sanctification is thus a matter of degree and it develops as we become more and more consecrated to his service, and yield ourselves more fully to his will as expressed in his commandments. So long as we are in the flesh, we must "grow in grace, and in the knowledge of our Lord and Saviour Jesus Christ" (2 Peter 3:18), and "give the more diligence" to make our "calling and election sure" (2 Peter 1:10). To this end Paul prayed for the Colossians that they might "be filled with the knowledge of his will in all spiritual wisdom and understanding, to walk worthily of the Lord unto all pleasing, bearing fruit in every good work, and increasing in the knowledge of God." (Col. 1:9,10.)

"What is the righteousness of God?"

James, brother of our Lord, wrote, "The wrath of man worketh not the righteousness of God." (James 1:20.) Obviously, the genitive is objective, signifying the righteousness which God requires of others— not that which is characteristic of him. *Righteousness,* "denotes the state acceptable to God which becomes a sinner's possession through that faith by which he embraces the grace of God offered him in the expiatory death of Jesus Christ," and the "faith" by which this blessing is appropriated is "a conviction, full of joyful trust, that Jesus is the Messiah—the divinely appointed author of eternal salvation in the kingdom of God, *conjoined with obedience to Christ.*" (Thayer.) Arndt and Gingrich correctly assert that "since righteousness constitutes the specific virtue of Christians, the word becomes almost equivalent to *Christianity.*" And, to quote Thayer again, righteousness, "in the broad sense," is the state of one "who is such as he ought to be . . . the condition acceptable to God." It is, then, simply put, a state of justification available to man on the basis of Christ's sacrifice, and man's acceptance through the conditions required.

These lexical definitions are fully confirmed by affirmations of the inspired writers.

> "Then Peter opened his mouth, and said, Of a truth I perceive that God is no respecter of persons: but in every nation he that feareth him, *and worketh righteousness,* is accepted with him." (Acts 10:34, 35.)

Righteousness is thus that state or condition wherein one is in a *right relationship* with God. Our English word, "righteousness," derives from the word "right," which, in turn, literally suggests that which is straight (as for example, a straight line), and so designates a relationship with God which he approves. A righteous man is therefore one who is straight, *lined up properly with God!* (Psalm 119:172; 1 John 2:29.)

A simple and brief definition of righteousness is, therefore *right-doing;* to be righteous, one must do right. "He that doeth righteousness is righteous, even as he is righteous." (1 John 3:7.) Of a certain type of character it is affirmed that he is righteous. Who is he? He that *doeth righteousness.* No other is. He who does righteousness is right; but he who is righteous is one who does right; therefore, he who does right possesses righteousness. Conversely, an unrighteous person is a perverse one; a perverse one is an individual in a twisted (as opposed to a straight) relationship with God. It is hence clear that righteousness is that state or condition wherein one is approved of God, but God approves of those only who do right (keep his commandments); therefore, to possess the approval of God and the righteousness which he requires, one must *do* right, *by* keeping his commandments.

Here is clear and positive proof of the utter falsity of the denominational doctrine of *transferred* righteousness. It is by some alleged that in the process of salvation Christ transfers to the sinner the righteousness which he possesses and that thenceforth the sinner is clothed in the righteousness *which Christ himself exhibits!* It is a matter of grief to this writer that this view is rapidly finding its way into commentaries *being written by our brethren* who have been drinking too long and too well from human cisterns polluted by false teachers. One can only sadly wonder what the future holds for succeeding generations who will be influenced by these men as they follow the leading of denomi-

189

national theologians in the adoption of the view of an imputation of righteousness that is repugnant both to reason and to Scripture.

It is absurd to assume that one person is good *because* another is. True, because Christ died in our stead, our guilt is cancelled, and through obedience to his will we are privileged to go free; but, this is far from saying that we *thereupon* become positively good, in the absence of good works. There is the difference between the poles in (a) *not* imputing guilt (this, the Lord does for us); and (b) conferring merit (this, the Lord does not do), in the process of salvation. Salvation (pardon), denotes a change in position and relation to God and not, on that basis alone, a life of personal purity. A pardoned criminal is no longer regarded as guilty of the crimes which led to his arrest, trial, and conviction; but, he is thence by no means a valuable citizen, in the absence of active participation in civic affairs. Righteousness is rightdoing. To be righteous, *one must do right.* (1 John 2:29.)

Was not Abraham's faith reckoned (imputed, counted) to him for righteousness? Yes. In the absence of further duties, *at the moment,* God accepted Abraham's faith as an *act* of obedience—hence, righteousness—itself. (James 2:20-22.) Did not David speak of "the blessedness of the man, unto whom God imputeth righteousness without works?" (Romans 4:6.) The "works" here, were works of the law. The man to whom the Lord imputes righteousness is the one whose "iniquities are forgiven, and whose sins are covered." (Psalm 32:1,2; Romans 4:8.) Such a one actively complies with God's plan for his forgiveness, and is thus declared righteous (justified). *We must be careful to distinguish between a righteousness imputed to (credited to) man because he has a right relationship with God through obedience to his will, and a righteousness which Christ (through his own submission to the will of the Father) is alleged to transfer to the sinner. The former the New Testament teaches; the latter is Calvinism.*

Was not Christ made "righteousness" for us? (1 Corinthians 1:30.) The Lord became the *means* of righteousness for us in that it is through him we are privileged to receive "the gift of righteousness" (Romans 5:17); but this is accomplished through compliance with his will, and in obedience to his commandments, and not through some mysterious bestowal of merit. We should ever remember that justification does not eliminate the fact of sin; it simply releases the sinner from the guilt thereof. The history of the act must forevermore remain. Paul, fully mindful of the great grace which he had experienced, was never without the consciousness of the fact that he had persecuted the church of God and wasted it. Pardoned, saved, justified, acquitted, no longer under guilt, it now remained for him, through faithful adherence to the Lord's will, to exhibit personal righteousness (right-standing) with God. And so with us all. The marvelous blessing of salvation is available through

Christ. He is the means of righteousness; through him we receive the gift of righteousness—righteousness which God makes available to us through faithful allegiance to his will. The doctrine of *transferred* righteousness (the allegation that Christ's own personal righteousness is transferred to, and thenceforth belongs to the sinner), has no support in Scripture and is exceedingly dangerous because it encouraged people lightly to consider the commandments of the Lord. Were this monstrous theory true; if it could be shown that those who believe have transferred to them the personal righteousness of Christ, it would follow that all those in this category are as pure as Christ is; and that thenceforth their claim on heaven is not of grace but of merit. On this hypothesis, God could no more deny them entrance into the Heavenly City than he could his own Son! The doctrine is positively and palpably false.

"Why do we often hear someone serving at the Lord's table refer to the communion as 'a communion of the death, burial and resurrection of Christ'? Introducing the happy thought of the resurrection at the very time the worshipper is to be humbly concentrating his thoughts on the factors involved in the dreadful price paid for his salvation, I think has an inhibiting effect on the proper attitude needed by the worshipper as he partakes of the loaf representing Christ's broken body and the cup representing Christ's shed blood."

I think so, too. The scriptures do not support the view that the burial and resurrection of Christ are symbolized in the elements of the supper. Our Lord's burial is pictured in the baptismal act, and the resurrection is commemorated in Lord's day observance. On this day he arose. (Romans 6:1-11; Matthew 28:1; Acts 20:7;1 Corinthians 16:1,2.) These vividly portray and keep evermore alive in the minds of true worshippers the burial of our Lord in the borrowed tomb and his glorious resurrection early on the Lord's day—the first day of the week. The bread is indeed representative of his body, and the fruit of the vine pictures for us the blood he shed in our behalf as he made atonement for our sins and for the sins of the whole world.

But, it should not be supposed, as this queriest implies, that the representation of the bread is the *broken* body of Christ. The view persists that we *break* (literally, *pinch off*), the bread to represent the *breaking* of the body of the Lord, and intricate and detailed theories as to the proper method of breaking bread have evolved through the years to the disruption of the peace and harmony of the saints. The pale loaf pictures the body itself—not the breaking of it and the best texts omit any reference to a broken body. Compare the King James' rendering of

1 Corinthians 11:24 with the American Standard translation here, and see John 19:31-37.

"Is it wrong to use light wine on the Lord's table?"

As indicated elsewhere in the letter, this querist means by "light" wine, wine of lower than average alcoholic content. Our Lord, in the institution of the Lord's supper said to his disciples, "Take this, and divide it among yourselves: for I say unto you, I shall not drink from henceforth *of the fruit of the vine,* until the kingdom of God shall come." (Luke 22:17.) Grape juice, when fermented, is wine. It is, nevertheless, "the fruit of the vine." Grape juice, unfermented, is also "the fruit of the vine." It follows therefore, that *either* the fermented, or the unfermented juice of the grape, meets the requirements of the phrase which the Lord used.

Since either wine (of alcoholic content), or the fresh juice of the grape may be used, it becomes a matter of expediency in determining which is preferable. I much prefer the unfermented juice of the grape for many reasons: (1) It is vastly more pleasing to my taste than the alcoholic variety. (2) It may be obtained where groceries are sold, thus not requiring one to go into areas where hard liquor is dispensed. Christians have no business being seen at counters where whiskey and other intoxicating beverages are sold. (3) There are instances on record where people who were once alcoholics but have broken the habit have returned to it from the taste of wine at the Lord's table. These and other similar considerations have been regarded by our brethren as sufficiently weighty and convincing to prompt them to use only the unfermented juice of the grape on the Lord's table, with the rarest of exceptions. I am continuously engaged in meetings throughout the year, I have done this type of work for more than a quarter of a century, and in such association with hundreds of congregations throughout the land, I can at the moment recall but *four* congregations where I have conducted such meetings which used wine rather than unfermented grape juice.

"Is there merit in the argument that Jesus justified violation of God's law in the case of necessity or hardship as advocates of situation ethics allege in the instance of his disciples plucking grain on the sabbath day?"

There is not only no merit in the "argument" in the effort; it is a blasphemous attack on the integrity of him who is the very embodiment of obedience and whose most dominant aim was to do the will of the

Father who sent him. (Hebrews 5:8,9; 10:7.) The allegation rests on a gross misapprehension of the event as recorded in Mark 2:23-28.

Jesus and his disciples were walking along a public road which passed alongside a field of grain, likely wheat or barley. The disciples stripped off some of the grain, vigorously rubbed it between their hands to separate the chaff from the kernel and ate it. The law of Moses made provision for such action, provided no sickle or other gathering instrument was used. (Deuteronomy 23:25.) It was on the sabbath day when this occurred and the Pharisees, ever around and desirous of finding something with which to accuse the Saviour, regarded the action of the disciples as an infraction of the law of the sabbath. We should take careful note of the fact that this violated the Pharisaic *interpretation of the law*—not the law itself. The Pharisees reached this conclusion with their usual dubious and circuitous reasoning: plucking is a form of reaping, and the rubbing of the grain a kind of threshing; and, since reaping and threshing were forbidden on the sabbath, the Pharisees concluded that the Lord's disciples had violated the law of the sabbath.

The Lord answered the charge by an appeal to a familiar Old Testament incident: "Did you never read what David did?" he asked. There was more than a little irony in his statement. He said, in effect, "You claim to be conversant with all the law and the whole of the Old Testament scriptures. Is it possible that you have never read that David, whose conduct *you* approve, went into the tabernacle when Abiathar was high priest, ate the shewbread, which was intended for the priests alone, and gave some of it to those with him? With this historic event you are undoubtedly familiar. Why then, do you find fault with my disciples?"

In the days of Abiathar, the high priest, David came to the tabernacle at Nob and demanded the shewbread which was placed on the table in the sanctuary fresh each sabbath day. (1 Samuel 21:1-6; Exodus 25:23-30; 39:36.) Lawfully, it could be eaten only by the priests, and by them only on the sabbath day. Thus, David, their favorite saint had openly violated the law of the sabbath, and this with the sanction and participation of the high priest!

Are we then to conclude that Jesus conceded violation of the sabbath day by his disciples, as David did? Some, among us, have so concluded, and have sought to justify any such violation, on the ground of love or necessity, today.

But, does it seem likely that he who refused to turn stones into bread to terminate the torture of 40 days' fasting could countenance such action? If one may violate the law of God, when its observance involves hardship or suffering, may we not properly conclude that there is no such thing as suffering for the name of Christ or engaging in any sort of self-denial? Why then, did Jesus refer to David's case?

The Pharisees regarded David's actions as entirely excusable; otherwise, they would have replied to the Lord as follows: "Your own argument effectively condemns you. You identify the action of your disciples with that of David: David sinned; and, therefore, so did your disciples!" The Lord knew that the Jewish teachers who opposed him could not pursue this mode of reasoning because they justified David's procedure. Thus, the Saviour's argument followed this order: "David, when hungry, ate the shewbread, an admittedly unlawful act; yet, *you* justify him. My disciples plucked grain and ate it which the law allows; but, *you* condemn them. You stand convicted on the basis of your own logic!" This *ad hominem* argument utterly silenced them.

Having thus effectively squelched the Pharisees on their own ground, Jesus added, "The sabbath was made for man, and not man for the sabbath: so that the Son of man is lord even of the sabbath." (Mark 2:24-28.) That the sabbath was made for man, and not man for the sabbath implies that when the welfare of man conflicted with the observance of the sabbath, the former took precedence over the latter. *But, of this man was not himself to judge, since he could not do so with detachment and impartiality.* Jesus could, because he was lord of the sabbath; and, being its master, his conduct regarding it was above criticism. This took the matter outside the range of logic and placed it in the realm of authority. The Saviour again, as on so many other occasions, showed the errors of his opposers and justified his own authority, in one tremendous affirmation. The disciples of Jesus did not violate the law of God in the grain field; they ran aground of Jewish tradition which often nullified the law of God. (Matthew 15:1-9.) Neither here, nor elsewhere, in the Scriptures, is there any support for the dangerous and false deductions of those among us today who are parrotting Fletcher's *situation ethics* errors.

"Who was the 'She that is in Babylon,' referred to by Peter? (1 Peter 5:13.)"

The marginal reading of the American Standard translation is, "That is, the church, or the sister," and the King James translation has, instead of "*She* that is in Babylon," the "church that is in Babylon." The inclusion of the word *church* is an interpretation—not translation—inasmuch as there is no noun, corresponding to the word "church" in the Greek text.

The passage reads, "She that is in Babylon, elect together with you, saluteth you . . ." the words, "elect together with you," being from *suneklekte,* feminine form of *sunekiklektos,* elect with others, actually, the "co-elect woman." What woman?

194

Some students of the text conclude that the reference to a person is a metaphorical one and hence designates the church in Babylon. In support of this view, 2 John 1 is cited. There, however, the phrase, "elect lady," does not refer to a church but to an individual; and, in view of the fact that Mark is joined with the "co-elect woman" of the passage (1 Peter 5:13), it is most unlikely that a *figure of speech* and an *individual* would be joined in such fashion and the most reasonable supposition is that Peter alluded to a sister in the church in Babylon. What sister?

These facts appear concerning her: (1) She was *then* in Babylon; (2) she had visited the saints in Asia Minor; (3) she was well-known to the people to whom Peter wrote; and, the apostle was closely associated with her as reflected in the fact that he conveyed her feelings. What sister so well met these conditions *as Peter's wife?* She was "a sister-wife" (*adelphe gune,* a wife, who was also a sister in Christ), and she occasionally accompanied Peter in his travels. (1 Corinthians 9:5.) There was a special appropriateness in sending greetings from her to saints with whom she had formerly been associated and whom she well knew in an epistle that deals specifically with the duties and responsibilities of women. (1 Peter 3:1-7.)

"What is meant by the name 'Babylon' in 1 Peter 5:13?"

Because Rome is evidently designated as "Babylon" in Revelation (Revelation 14:8; 17:6; 18:2,10), all Catholic theologians and many Protestant expositors maintain that the reference is to be regarded as mystical and metaphorical and that Peter meant by it the city of seven hills on the famed Tiber river.

Opposed to this, and decisive in my view, are the following especially weighty considerations: (1) There is strong internal evidence in the epistle that it was penned *before* the destruction of Jerusalem in A.D. 70-73. (2) Eminent Talmudic authorities have written that the Jews did not begin to designate Rome as Babylon until *after* that event. (3) In the references cited in the Revelation where Rome is called Babylon, the allusion is never to Babylon alone, but always, "Babylon, the great," "Babylon, the strong city," etc. (4) The fact that the word "Babylon" is used thus mystically in the highly symbolic and figurative book of Revelation does not argue that reference thereto is the same in a book of decidedly different character such as First Peter. (5) Other geographical references in the book are admittedly literal. Why, then, should it be concluded that "Babylon" is the sole exception to this rule? (6) Peter wrote long before John penned the Revelation and thus could not have been alluding to John's use. (7) The name "Babylon," when figuratively used, is the symbol of confusion, corruption and apostasy. What possible reason could be assigned why the apostle would use the term in this sense in an epistle designed to protect those whom he wrote from just such a manner of life as that which the term, in Revelation, typifies?

Thus a candid consideration of all the facts leads to the conclusion that the word "Babylon" is to be taken in its ordinary geographical sense, and that Peter was in the well-known city by that name on the Euphrates when he wrote the epistle which bears his name.

"Can a Christian participate in body development contests such as Mr. Universe or weight lifting contests, where his body is placed on display?"

In view of what the Scriptures teach regarding modesty, avoiding the appearance of evil, and decency, it is indeed difficult to see how a Christian can engage in that which requires virtual nakedness in order to do so. Those inured to nudity—and such is characteristic of most people today—will scoff at the suggestion that children of God ought not to exhibit their bodies in such fashion, but those who love the Lord and who are responsive to his will will surely refrain from any practice which might reflect on the cause they have espoused.

Is not the reversion to nakedness a retreat to savagery? Generally speaking, the less civilized a nation is, the more disposed its people are to go undressed. If to this the objection is offered that Adam and Eve, the first man and woman, were created naked and lived for a time in the garden of Eden without clothes, it must be remembered that in the state of innocency which characterized them, they were without recognition of shame, but that when they sinned and their awareness of right and wrong developed, they felt the need of covering their bodies. Jehovah acquiesced in this and made for the fallen pair "coats of skins and *clothed* them." (Genesis 3:21.) We may from this truly conclude that it is the will of God that those possessed of the sense of right and wrong ought to be clothed. Moreover, we are informed that one possessed of demons "wore no clothes," but that when the demons were cast out, the delivered man was "clothed and in his right mind." (Luke 8:27-35.) May we not properly and reasonably conclude from this that people in their *right* minds choose to be clothed?

Many years ago, David Lipscomb, in an excellent article on what constitutes indecency, penned these words:

> Anything is indecent that suggests and creates improper thoughts and desires. Seeing a woman half naked suggests improper thoughts and creates lustful desires in man, hence it is indecent for a woman to appear half naked before men. The same is true of half naked men before women. It is indecent for either sex to appear half naked before the other.

196

It is also true that for those of either sex to appear half naked before others of their own sex destroys their sense of shame and modesty and educates them to have no shame or to be indecent before the other sex.

With the saintly Lispcomb's view on this I am in full agreement. That many people in the church today are no longer shocked by the nudity which parades itself unashamedly evidences the fact that many of us have lost all sense of shame in its presence and that our sensitivity of what is right and what is wrong is sorely impaired. Undoubtedly, the gradual acceptance of this situation had paved the way for the current toleration and eventual acceptance of the unspeakably dark and depraved practices of Sodom which now hover like a black and ominous cloud on the horizon. Must we go the way of Sodom before the people of this land, once famous for the dedication to the principles of morality and religion taught in the Bible, are brought to their senses?

"Please explain 2 Peter 2:20."

"For if, after they have escaped the defilements of the world through the knowledge of the Lord and Saviour Jesus Christ, they are again entangled therein and overcome, the last state is become worse with them than the first." These are those who were deceived by the false teachers of whom Peter warned throughout the epistle. Those duped were "entangled" (literally *entrapped,* as fishes in a net) by teachers who offered them license to engage in fleshly sins, but, instead of finding liberty, they became involved in the most abject bondage of sin. Their last state was worse than the first because (1) apostates are usually more abandoned in sin than those who have never known righteousness; (2) their guilt, and consequently, their punishment, would be greater because of their opportunities; and (3) those once enlightened, but who turn back to the world, are often more difficult to influence for good than alien sinners.

"What is the meaning of 1 Corinthians 7:14? Particularly, what is meant by the unbelieving companion being sanctified by the Christian spouse or husband?"

First Corinthians 7 contains a detailed discussion of marriage. In the context of the passage inquired about the question involved is, What is the situation and duty of a Christian married to an unbeliever? Paul's answer is clear and unequivocal: "If any brother hath an unbelieving wife, and she is content to dwell with him, let him not leave her." And, conversely, "The woman that hath an unbelieving husband, and he is content to dwell with her, let her not leave her husband." (1 Corinthians

197

7:12,13.) By apostolic edict, the matter is determined once for all: the relationship is not itself sinful, and is not to be dissolved so long as peace obtains. Moreover, should such dissolution of the marriage *relationship* occur and an unbelieving husband departs, but two courses are open to the believer if "fornication" is not involved: "But should she depart, let her remain unmarried, or else be reconciled to her husband." (Matthew 19:9; 1 Corinthians 7:10,11.) She must (1) either remain unmarried; or, (2) be reconciled to her *husband. Husband,* evidencing that the marriage *bond* continues.

Another weighty reason is assigned why the marriage relationship between a Christian and an unbeliever is legitimate: "For the unbelieving husband is sanctified in the wife, and the unbelieving wife is sanctified in the brother: else were your children unclean; but now are they holy." (v. 14.) The word "sanctified" means set apart, dedicated. An unbeliever, in a scriptural union with a believing wife, is in a relationship which God approves and in this relationship he is privileged to remain. Though not himself a Christian he is not in an adulterous or unclean union. Children, born to this union are not illegitimate; they, too, are sanctified because they are in a "holy" (approved) relationship, being sanctified by it. Were the Christian companion to insist on a separation solely on the ground of being married to an unbeliever, the inference would be that the children which issued from that relationship are illegitimate. This conclusion the apostle advanced in support of his affirmation that the union of a believer and an unbeliever is not of itself prohibited. The children from such a marriage are "holy" (in a proper relationship), and thus are not illegitimate. They are *holy* because they are the fruit of a holy union.

"In Matthew 5:31, Jesus said, 'It hath been said, Whosoever shall put away his wife, let him give her a writing of divorcement.' Then in verse 32 he says, 'But I say unto you, That whosoever shall put away his wife, saving for the cause of fornication, causeth her to commit adultery.' Why would a man be guilty of causing his wife to commit adultery if he puts her away for incompatibility?"

The Lord's words, "it hath been said," are an allusion to the law of Moses which had a statute recognizing "a bill of divorcement." (Deuteronomy 14:1.) It should be carefully observed that this liberty was "suffered," because of the hardness of heart then characteristic of the people of Israel. Neither God nor Moses sanctioned divorce, nor originated the decree: the affirmation of the existence of the "bill" was made, and the provision for it for the reason assigned, noted, Such was not part of God's plan "from the beginning" (Matthew 19:1-9), and was clearly a temporary device for the protection of women. It was by our Lord repealed.

A man is "guilty of causing his wife to commit adultery if he puts her away for incompatibility," because, (1) it is not a ground for putting a wife away and (2) in unjustly doing so he forces her into a situation where she will be tempted to contract another marriage which she has no right to do.

"Does the eldership of a local church possess the character of a self-perpetuating board? More specifically, does such an eldership have the exclusive power to select other men to be considered as elders, and to determine the validity of any scriptural objections raised by any member of the congregation?"

There are actually two questions involved here: (1) Is the eldership a self-perpetuating board? (2) When additional elders are being appointed does the eldership have the right to "determine the validity" of the objections offered to the men being considered? The answer to the first question is an unqualified "No!" The second question must be answered with a qualified "Yes."

While there is very definite and clear evidence of the appointment of elders in the apostolic church, details of procedure are not given. Paul and Barnabas "ordained" elders in the communities of Lystra, Iconium and Antioch (Acts 14:21-23), and Titus was instructed to remain in Crete to ordain elders in all the cities of the island (Titus 1:5), but there is no prescribed rule for the accomplishment of this end in the instances given. It is far from correct to say, however, that we are without divine direction in this matter; on the contrary, there is clear and positive information touching the Spirit's will in this important aspect of church work. Once we learn what was the Lord's will in the matter of selecting any man, or group of men, in the performance of church functions, we may properly conclude that such is his will in other comparable areas, though no specific rule is provided.

Luke, historian of the early church, gives us a detailed description of the *selection* and *appointment* of deacons in the Jerusalem congregation. We direct special attention to the fact that there were two actions—not one—involved: the selection by the people preceded, and differed from, the appointment by the apostles. "In those days, when the number of the disciples was multiplied, there arose a murmuring of the Grecians against the Hebrews, because their widows were neglected in the daily ministration. Then the twelve called the multitude of the disciples unto them, and said, It is not reason that we should leave the word of God, and serve tables. Wherefore, brethren, look *ye* out among you seven men of honest report, . . . whom *we* may appoint over this business." (Acts 6:1-3.) If ever a situation existed where it appeared proper for apostles arbitrarily to choose the men and appoint them, it would seem to be so here; the apostles were all present; their authority was unquestioned and their selection would have been infallible. Notwithstanding, the multitude of disciples made the selection, and this by divine decree. This, then, is the apostolic mode and must not be dispensed with. *May we not thence conclude that the right of those to be overseen to select the men whom they believe to possess the necessary qualifications to be elders is inherent and that if the apostles were precluded from such, that an existing eldership would have reserved to it no such powers?*

To the question, May an existing eldership determine the validity of any objections offered to additional men proposed for the eldership? the answer is a qualified "Yes." Because the elders watch for the souls of the saints (Hebrews 13:7,17), and are over them in the Lord, it is quite obviously their responsibility to the congregation to examine with closest scrutiny those suggested. But, this responsibility is neither exclusive nor is it limited to the eldership; it is the responsibility of all knowledgeable members of the church, *as individuals,* thus including the elders as such, to determine the fitness of those proposed to serve as overseers of the flock, such fitness to be ascertained on the basis of the qualifications set out in detail in 1 Timothy 3 and Titus 1.

"Please explain Romans 8:7,8."

". . . because the mind of the flesh is enmity against God; for it is not subject to the law of God, neither indeed can it be: and they that are in the flesh cannot please God." Earlier in the context in which these words appear, Paul wrote, "For they that are after the flesh mind the things of the flesh; but they that are after the Spirit the things of the Spirit." (v. 5.) By this he meant that those who are fleshly in heart are those who seek the things of the flesh; who find satisfaction in gratifying the desires of the flesh, but that those who are spiritual are those who give their attention to, and find delight in, the things of the Spirit— the duties and activities of the Christian life.

The former manner of life—living after the flesh—leads eventually to the second death: "For the mind of the flesh is death," i.e., those whose minds are fixed upon the things of the flesh will ultimately suffer eternal death. To set one's desires on the life of the flesh results in separation from God and all that is good; whereas, to fix one's love on the things of the Spirit—the manner of life which the Spirit dictates—produces the life everlasting. To this end, the same apostle admonished the Colossians to set their "mind on the things that are above, not on the things that are upon the earth." (Colossians 3:2.)

The truth is, the disposition which prompts one to fix the affections on the things of the flesh is, in reality, a state of rebellion against God as the verses inquired of affirm. Such an attitude is described as a state of enmity toward God because it produces a state of antagonism between the individual thus influenced, and God. Affections of this character are clearly not governed by the law of God, indeed, cannot be, because they are in obvious opposition to God. So long as one entertains the evil affections under consideration it is impossible to be subject to the law of God as expressed in his word. The law of God and these evil desires are wholly irreconcilable. To follow the one, the other must be repudiated. Hence, those who are "in the flesh" (influenced by fleshly desires) "cannot please God."

It is obvious the apostle uses the word "flesh" in these verses in a figurative fashion to denote evil desires which grow out of the life of flesh characterizing people in fleshly bodies; and that it does not directly denote the tissues which constitute the bodies, or the bodies themselves. This is made clear from the observation that follows in verse 9 of the context: "But ye are not in the flesh but in the Spirit, if so be that the Spirit of God dwelleth in you." That is, those who are influenced by the Spirit of God which dwells in the Christian are not "in the flesh"—influenced by fleshly dispositions and actions—but "in the Spirit"—directed and led into the life which the Spirit requires—because the Spirit of God dwells in them.

Here, as also in Romans 8:11, it is said that the Spirit of God dwells in Christians. It is the *fact* of such dwelling which is asserted and not the *manner* in which it is received nor the *mode* of such "indwelling." Clearly taught in the context is that the Spirit which dwells in us teaches us to live a life which is "not after the flesh," i.e., it directs to a godly life in keeping with the will of God. We may, therefore, properly inquire, From what source do we receive such instruction? Does the New Testament contain the whole of such information; or, do we receive guidance and information touching our duties and responsibilities independently of it? The answer is, obviously, The New Testament contains the whole of our duty today, making us complete and completely furnishing us unto every good work. (2 Timothy 3:16,17.) It must then follow that the Spirit dwells in us as we are influenced by him through his instrument—the Word of Truth—and in no other sense. This is the test of divine ownership: "But if any man hath not the Spirit of Christ, he is none of his." (Romans 8:9.)

"What did John, the apostle, mean when he said, 'Love not the world, neither the things that are in the world'?"

Obviously, the "world" which children of God are not to "love" is not the material universe in which we live and from which we draw our

201

life's support—God's original creation (Romans 1:20), nor the people who inhabit it. By the word "world" John did not intend to include the sunshine and the rain, the mountains and the seas, the sunset and the stars, the loveliness of the night, the sparkling freshness of the early morning, the sweet song of birds or the fragrance of flowers. He did not mean the dust of which our bodies are composed, the earth which supplies us with our food, and in whose gentle embrace we must at last rest.

Neither does the word "love" in the foregoing passage denote that tenderness of affection and warmth of heart which characterize both God and man toward those whose attributes and characteristics encourage and evoke such feeling. The "world" of the passage inquired about is a sphere or cosmos (*kosmos*) of evil, an order opposed to God and to all that is good, to whose pursuit all who abandon the Lord have dedicated themselves.

The "love" which the passage forbids is evil desire—affection for that which is wrong. The "world" which embraces such we are not to love, "neither the things that are in the world." There is thus a difference between the "world" contemplated by the apostle, and the "things" of it. It was the purpose of the apostle to forbid affection for *any* part of it, an injunction as needful now as when originally penned. Men may indeed, and often do, repudiate much of the world, and yet, like the young ruler, cling to a portion of it with such tenacity they lose their souls. There may be but "one thing" as in his case but this held on to is sufficient to lose one's soul. John further observed that, "If any man love the world, the love of the Father is not in him." Love for the world and love for the Father are wholly incompatible dispositions; they cannot exist in the heart at the same time.

> "No man can serve two masters; for either he will hate the one, and love the other; or else he will hold to one, and despise the other. Ye cannot serve God and mammon." (Matthew 6:24.)

"If the spirit is conscious after death, why is death often referred to as 'sleep' in the Scriptures?"

For at least two reasons: (1) Because faithful saints in death are at rest; there is rest in sleep; hence, the saints are said to be asleep in death. (2) The position of the body in death is that of one asleep and thus the term is applied to those in death. The rest from labor that death involves, the peaceful aspect of those in respose in death, and the position of the body all symbolize death. Indeed, our English word "cemetery" derives from *koimeterion,* a sleeping place. But, the spirit does not enter into unconsciousness, nor suffer annihilation in death.

On the contrary, all the characteristics of the spirit in life—memory, awareness, intelligence, etc.—are retained in the spirit world. (Revelation 6:6-9; Luke 16:19-31.) Paul declared that he had a great desire to depart "and to be with Christ," a state which he said was "far better" than any earthly sojourn. It is impossible to imagine the great apostle as affirming that it would be better for him to pass into a state of unconsciousness than to continue his work for the Lord on earth! The Psalmist wrote, "Precious in the sight of Jehovah is the death of his saints." Must we conclude that God wants his faithful followers to fall into unconscious inactivity and to become as if they had never been? (Phillipians 1:23; Psalm 116:15.) The idea is both opposed to common sense and to the plain teaching of the Scriptures.

"What are we to understand by the phrase, 'new heavens and a new earth' in 2 Peter 3:13? Some teach that it is a reference to the earth on which we now live and thus conclude that this earth is the future abode of the righteous."

So some do, but they are grossly in error in so doing. Peter plainly asserts in the context in which the words "new heavens and a new earth" appear that the present earth will disappear in the mighty conflagration which will engulf it at the last great day: "But the day of the Lord will come as a thief; in the which the heavens shall pass away with a great noise, and the elements shall be dissolved with fervent heat, and the earth and the works that are therein shall be burned up." (2 Peter 3:10.)

The "day of the Lord" to which the apostle alludes is the day when our Saviour will appear in the clouds in his second coming when he shall raise the dead and institute the judgment. (John 5:28,29.) Its coming is compared to that of a thief because of the unexpectedness with which it will break upon us. The "heavens" which are to pass away, along with the earth, in the universal fires of that unparalleled day, include that portion of the universe immediately above our heads where the birds fly. Associated with the destruction depicted by Peter will be the crash of dissolving worlds and the mighty roar of flames as they consume the earth and all that is in it. All material things are to melt from the heat of fires everywhere raging and the earth and the works that are therein are to perish. All that man has created of a material nature, houses, cities, memorials—anything—will end in that all-engulfing fire.

Notwithstanding the destruction of the present earth, Christians are privileged to look for "a new heavens and a new earth wherein dwelleth righteousness." There are two Greek words translated *new*; one denotes that which is young as opposed to that which is old; the other points to that which is fresh in contrast to that which is frayed and worn. It is the latter which is used in the text before us. The heavens and the earth, to which the apostle refers in this passage, will be fresh and new, not worn and old, as are the heavens and the earth visibly known to us. In this fresh, new abode righteousness will dwell. Righteousness exists wherever righteous people live. Thus, *the heavens and earth* here contemplated is to be the abode of righteous and saved people throughout eternity. Why is it thus styled and where is it?

Man is a creature of two worlds—the heavens about him, and the earth below him. His future abode is where Jesus now is and where he is preparing a place for us. Jesus is in heaven. Thus, the material heavens and earth are made by Peter to serve as the type of this future abode from which Jesus is to return in order to take us back there. (John 14:2.) The phrase, "a new heaven and a new earth," can mean only to embrace the place now being fitted out for the faithful. There, in the many mansions of our Father's house, our Lord is preparing a place for us, from which he will ultimately come, and then carry us to it. That "new heaven and new earth" is simply the antitype of our current abode. It is hence the typical description of heaven—the New Jerusalem.

These considerations clearly follow from the premises appearing in the apostle's description of these matters: (a) The new heaven and the new earth will follow the coming destruction of the present heavens and earth. (b) The earth which will *then* be is not *this* one. It is *this* earth on which future kingdom advocates erroneously expect to live. (c) Christ's present reign is from heaven (Acts 2:30), and this he will terminate on the occasion of his return for his saints (1 Corinthians 15:23ff). In view of the vital significance of these events to us, all we should take to heart the apostle's admonition:

"Wherefore, beloved, seeing that ye look for these things,
give diligence that ye may be found in peace, without spot
and blameless in his sight." (2 Peter 3:14.)

"Does Paul's statement in Romans 6:7, 'For he that is dead is freed from sin,' mean that 'he' under contemplation here is pardoned, forgiven, saved?"

No.

Such a conclusion results from (a) disregard of the context; (b) a misapprehension of what is meant by the word "dead," and (c) assigning a meaning to the word "freed" not intended by the apostle.

A view has surfaced in the brotherhood in some areas that (1) it is not correct to say that repentance kills the active life of sin; (2) that the individual who has separated himself from such a manner of life is thereby dead, but not forgiven; and that (3) the phrase "is freed from sin," does not mean that the person involved has simply terminated the old life of sin and is dead to it because of having been separated from it, but is actually saved, redeemed, forgiven.

This position is so obviously in conflict with plain affirmations of Paul in Romans 6:1-11, it is remarkable that it is seriously entertained by some among us today. A look at Paul's argument in this context should remove any doubt on the part of the discerning person as to the significance of the word "dead" in the foregoing passage.

Some among the apostle's opposers alleged with slanderous intent that Paul's position touching the end of the law encouraged people to sin. This charge he answered with an emphatic denial—God forbid—and then proceeded to show, with irresistible logic, that the conclusion by no means followed. "We who died to sin, how shall we any longer live therein?" The word *death* in its various forms, when figuratively used in the scriptures, as is the case here, simply signifies *separation* and the assertion above declares plainly that Paul and all he converted had *died to sin*—they were in a state of separation from such activity—and thus were not properly chargeable with *living* in it. This occurred when they repented; repentance is a change of will resulting in a reformation of life; the gospel which the apostle preached, far from constituting an encouragement to sin as his enemies alleged, actually destroyed it, as an active principle in life, by separating the one repenting from it. To "die to sin," is a metaphorical expression meaning to be released from the power and influence of sin, as a slave is by death released from the dominion and control of his master. Repentance is thus the means by which one terminates the influence and power of sin over the life.

Dead people, *not live ones,* are to be buried; and the sinner, having ended his active life of sin in repentance is now a subject of burial. Paul, continuing the figure, wrote:

"Therefore we are buried with him by baptism unto death:
that like as Christ was raised up from the dead by the glory
of the Father, even so we also should walk in newness of
life." (Romans 6:4.)

Thus the sinner, having repented, is dead—freed from his former manner of conduct—and is then a subject of burial in the waters of baptism whence he rises to "walk in newness of life," which *begins* on rising from "the watery grave."

The words, "For he that is dead is freed from sin," occasion no difficulty when considered in the light of the context in which they appear. The word "freed" is translated from the Greek word *dedikaiotai,* a term which does not mean acquittal or pardon, but rather *emancipation,* freedom from an *active* life of sin. It does not embrace the idea of

205

forgiveness *as here used*. The meaning, simply expressed, is that the person who has died to sin and is freed from it has ceased, terminated, brought to an end, the habitual life of sin formerly characterizing him, and must now be buried (being dead) in water, to rise to "newness of life" which follows the baptismal act.

It should be observed that the apostle does not affirm that those who are dead to the sins of their former life henceforth live *above* sin. Contemplated in Romans 6, is the means by which we receive absolution from the guilt of *alien* sins committed before baptism. "Knowing this," he wrote, "that our old man is crucified with him, that the body of sin might be destroyed, that henceforth we should not serve sin." (Romans 6:6.) The "old man" thus figuratively alluded to here is the former sinful manner of life. Such was "crucified with Christ," i.e., put to death with him so that the child of God is no longer enslaved in sin. So long as we are in the flesh, the weaknesses which it can never fully eliminate in life will lead to occasional lapses because of ignorance, inadvertence, stupidity, etc., but for all of those "who walk in the light" of truth, there is an advocate provided, and a method extended by which all such lapses may be overcome. (1 John 1:7-9; 2:1.)

"Explain the words, 'We must through much tribulation enter into the kingdom of God.' (Acts 14:22.)"

The church in Antioch, a Syrian city located approximately three hundred miles north of Jerusalem, early sprang into notice as the base of activity for the preaching of the gospel to the Gentile world. Here Paul and Barnabas were "separated" to this work by the Holy Spirit (Acts 13:1-5), and from the historic city each of the assaults against heathen citadels by Paul and his associates were launched.

The effort was immediately successful. "A great multitude both of Jews and Greeks believed," "many disciples" were made and whole cities breathlessly waited for the next Sabbath day to hear Paul preach. Unbelieving Jews, observing with envious eyes the widespread acceptance of the gospel, and fearful of its effect on current Judaism, leaped into action and caused to begin a series of persecutions which eventually drove Paul and Barnabas from city to city, culminating in the savage stoning of the apostle in Lystra, and the dragging of his body beyond the city's walls where he was left for dead.

Miraculously he was raised to life again; and, instead of fleeing like a craven coward, he returned to the scenes of his persecution where with courage and persistence he accomplished his work. As he journeyed through the cities of Asia Minor, so lately the scenes of his suffering, he confirmed the souls of the saints, exhorted them to continue in the faith, and reminded them that it is through many tribulations "we must enter into the kingdom of God." (Acts 14:22.)

The reference to the "kingdom of God" is to "the everlasting kingdom" into which the faithful are to enter at the last day. Into that kingdom no one will pass without "much tribulation." The word "tribulation" is derived from the Latin *tribulum*, the thrashing instrument or roller with which the Roman farmer separated the grain from the worthless husks. Metaphorically used here, it denotes the hardships, difficulties, persecutions, and all adversities, the appointed means for the separating in men of their chaff from their wheat, of whatever is worthless, trivial, useless, from that which is useful and real. These experiences are tribulations, thrashings of the inner man, without which there could be no preparation of any of us for the Heavenly Garner. James, in recognition of this fact, wrote: "Count it all joy, my brethren, when ye fall into divers temptations (margin, "trials") knowing that the proving of your faith worketh patience . . . Blessed is the man that endureth temptation ("trial") for when he hath been approved he shall receive the crown of life . . ." (James 1:2-12.)

The Lord walked along that lonely path, and it is to be expected that the disciple will "be as his master, and the servant as his lord." (Matthew 10:24,25.) From the earliest days of the Cause we love, the path of the sincere sufferer has been moistened by the tears of saints and sanctified by the shedding of martyrs' blood. Without it who knows but that the allurements of the world and the attractions of the current scene would turn us aside from our goal and make us to forget that we have "no continuing city here." There is much compensation in the fact that these trials create in us deep longings for rest and for a home "where the wicked cease from troubling and the weary are at rest."

Yes, *much* tribulation. But, let us thank God that we pass *through* it, and by such passage we are fitted to enter the gate of life eternal.

"Does Hebrews 6:4-6 teach that if one falls away from the grace of God it is not possible to be restored?"

"For as touching those who were once enlightened and tasted of the heavenly gift, and were made partakers of the Holy Spirit, and tasted the good word of God, and the powers of the age to come, and then fell away, it is impossible to renew them again unto repentance; seeing they crucify to themselves the Son of God afresh, and put him to an open shame."

The Hebrews to whom Paul wrote were Christian Jews, among whom false teachers had appeared who were telling them that Jesus was not the true Messiah but an imposter. They were told that Messiah was yet to come by whom and through whom they would be saved. To accept such teaching was to turn away from the only Saviour who could deliver them and thus their case became hopeless. They had shared in all the blessings of the gospel; they had been enlightened, they had tasted of the heavenly gift, they were partakers of the blessings made available to them through the Holy Spirit's revelation and they had experienced a foretaste of the joys awaiting the faithful in the world to come. To turn aside from him who made such possible and to seek to be saved on the basis of some other was to renounce the only way of salvation, and to place themselves in a situation wherein was no deliverance. This is not a description of the sort of apostasy which results from temptation and sin; this is an intellectual rejection and repudiation of the Lord himself and his Cause through which alone there is salvation. Those who so did would crucify afresh the Son of God, by alleging that Messiah had not yet died, and that there would yet be a sacrifice of sins made. To renounce the Christ and to seek salvation through some other is effectively to cut oneself off from all hope. Man may fall through weakness and ignorance and in penitence return; but, those who renounce the Saviour and seek salvation in some other fashion sin helplessly, sin irretrievably.

"In what sense was Paul 'alive without the law' as referred to in Romans 7:9? What is the commandment of which mention is made in verses 8-12 of Romans 7?"

The context in which these verses appear must be carefully considered in order properly to understand the apostle's teaching here. Under discussion is the law of Moses. It had just been shown that this law was no longer in force. (Romans 7:6.) The Jews, formerly answerable to it, were released from its restrictions. Was the law sinful and removed for this reason? By no means. (v. 7.) Were it not for the law there would not have been any knowledge of sin; the Jews would not have known, for example, that lust is sinful, because it was the law which said "Thou shalt not covet." Where there is no law, there is no transgression (4:15.) It is the function of law to provide a knowledge of sin, i.e., to create in people the realization of what sin is. When the law condemns an act this enables men to know that the act is sinful. It follows therefore that since the law condemns sin, it is not sinful. But it is said that the law leads to death. How?

It is a characteristic of sinful flesh to rebel against law; the existence of law prompts the wicked to rebellion. This stubborn and wilful disposition leads to spiritual death. But, it may be asked, Does that which is good produce death? The apostle answers: "No. It is sin that produces death. The law merely shows what is sinful." The law should not be blamed since it only makes "sin exceedingly sinful," (Romans 7:13), by revealing its nature and showing its consequences. The law was helpless to justify; therefore, it was removed so that a "better covenant," one established on "better promises" might take its place. The law accomplished its purpose in pointing men to Christ (Galatians 3:23-29), but it was removed in order that a new and better way might take its place. (Hebrews 8:1-13.) "The commandment" was the law of Moses; synecdoche for all the commandments it contains.

"May children of God use any form of alcohol for beverage purposes acceptably?"

The use of narcotics, a hurtful and ultimately fatal addiction, does not remotely pose the threat to the well being of our land that alcohol does. Drugs are illegal; those who traffic in them, or resort to their use, break the law and often suffer the consequences properly meted out to criminals; the liquor traffic operates with the sanction of law, parades its alleged appeals in the most respectable fashion, reaching out its frowsy arms like a giant octopus to embrace every man, woman and child in the United States. There is thus the ever present possibility that such adroit and seductive saturation appeals, its legalized operation and the widespread participation will deceive the minds and becloud the reasoning of multitudes of people who formerly shrank from its use.

Preachers, teachers, writers—all who have the responsibility of warning people regarding false and deceitful claims—should ever be mindful of the obligations that is theirs, and keep constantly before those with whom they have to do the deadly dangers of this iniquitous industry. It is an unmitigated evil, a vicious, subsidized syndicate of sin, ever allied with that which is most destructive and damaging to the community.

With tongue in cheek, its advocates prate of taxes they pay which go for the aged, the fatherless and the destitute. Of course they know that such tax money is not a tithe of the costs which result from the use of liquor itself. In painful and often fatal accidents, in crime, in unemployment, in grief and heartbreak—concomitants resulting from its use—is the real cost to be computed.

They tell us of the jobs which the alcohol industry provides; they boast of the contributions which they make to the communities in which they operate, the rise of rental values and increase in purchasing power from their payrolls. But, such diversion of funds through their hands is just that much money drawn off from honorable and worthy businesses, and it can be documented that where the liquor traffic is most active there suffering and broken homes exist in the highest ratio.

209

In a report which this writer took from a newspaper published in a small southwestern community it was pointed out that "of nine fatal accidents in the district" during one month six of them involved alcohol; in two of the wrecks it was not known whether or the subjects had been drinking and in only one instance was there a driver or pedestrian who definitely had not been drinking! Let it be noted that this was a matter-of-fact report in a daily newspaper without either religious or moral overtones.

Whether one intends it or not a vote to maintain legalization of liquor automatically makes one an accessory before the fact in every tragedy which issues from it.

The law of Moses provided that when a dead body was discovered under circumstances which indicated homicide, or death resulting from foul play, the distance from where the body was found to the nearest community was determined, and the elders of that city were required to show, in a judicial proceeding, that the death resulted through no fault of theirs. Inherent in this is the principle that we sustain, in God's sight, responsibility for the welfare of those about us. If I, by my vote, sanction the use of this deadly evil, I cannot escape the responsibility for the injury which results from it. We are indeed "our brother's keeper," and we must eventually answer for the harm which accrues to him through our actions.

As great as the harm is to adults who use intoxicating liquors, children are the really pitiful and helpless victims of this curse. Today, tens of thousands of frowsy, befuddled and stupid men and women lounge in taverns, saloons and bars while their children huddle helplessly in barren, unheated rooms and without sufficient food for their little bodies. We may be sure that each time a bar opens for business there are children who will suffer want and privation because of it. And, when those same children began to imbibe the deadly potion, the evil increases sevenfold. Whatever legislative bodies may say and do about it, the use of intoxicating liquors is a crime against humanity, and for our sakes and that of those about us, Christians ought to do their utmost to rid the race of this evil thing. We are certain that with no less than this on our part will God be pleased.

"Comment on the statement sometimes made, 'You can prove anything by the Bible.' "

The observation, "You can prove anything by the Bible," is often, with mindless abandon, asserted by those who reveal by such a statement that their respect for the authority and validity of its teaching approaches zero. What is clearly proved by such an affirmation is that (a) those who so affirm are ignorant of, or have disregarded the Book's own claims of inerrancy; (b) they are aware that the Source they minimize does not support their views of matters religious, and so (c) they would impeach the Book itself by questioning its integrity and reliability! (Isaiah 5:20; Proverbs 17:15.)

We do not think that those who so assert would be pleased were the accusation levelled against them, "Anything can be proved by you!" The implication of such a statement, universally known to be characteristic only of liars, deceivers and hypocrites, would be bitterly resented and rejected; yet these people do not hesitate to imply that God, Christ, the Holy Spirit and the scriptures are really unworthy of our respect and belief because they testify on all sides of all propositions! This sinful and perverse imputation is positively and palpably false and will be immediately repudiated by all thoughtful and discerning people. In defending the sacred writings against such a wicked charge, we are simply supporting the scriptures' own claims of trustworthiness, reliability and credibility. (Psalm 118:89; 2 Timothy 3:17,18).

Equally objectionable is the thoughtless and oft-repeated statement, "People just don't understand the Bible alike!" In this fashion do some seek to justify the endless conflicts and contradictions today shamefully existing in the religious world. The truth is, there is only one way to UNDERSTAND anything—the right way. People may misunderstand the teaching of the scriptures a hundred ways; there is really no end to perversions and misapprehension of scripture; but, all who understand the Bible at all, understand it correctly; any other view is not another "understanding," but a MISUNDERSTANDING of it.

It is axiomatic that a proposition cannot be both true and false at the same time; all truth is harmonious and is never in conflict with itself. It follows, therefore, the Bible being true, only one conclusion may be properly and logically deduced from any affirmation on any given subject, and the opposite conclusion is necessarily false regardless of who holds it, or how long it may have been held. Moreover, no true friend of the Bible will want to assign a "meaning" to any word or statement therein which conflicts with the plain and obvious teaching of the Book elsewhere.

Many matters are clearly and unmistakably taught in the holy scriptures. Among the most important of these is that while man, in his unregenerate state is lost, Jesus died for him and thus made salvation available through his vicarious suffering and death on the cross. To appropriate this salvation, man must comply with the conditions the Redeemer himself announced (Mark 16:15,16; Acts 2:38), and live a godly, consecrated, Christian life until the Lord calls him home to his ultimate and eternal rest. (2 Peter 1:5-11; Revelation 22:14.)

"How oft shall I forgive?"

"Then came Peter and said unto him, Lord, how oft shall my brother sin against me, and I forgive him? until seven times? Jesus saith unto him, I say not unto thee, Until seven times; but, Until seventy times seven." (Matthew 18:21,22.) The Rabbis—the Jewish teachers of the day—taught that to forgive a brother *three* times fulfilled all responsibility to him; and that though he should repent a fourth time and ask for forgiveness, the obligation was at an end. This Rabbinical rule resulted from an improper deduction from such passages as Job 33:29 and Amos 1:3, the last of which reads: "Thus saith Jehovah: For three transgressions of Damascus, yea, for four, I will not turn away the punishment thereof." The fisherman disciple, dimly aware that the limit imposed by tradition was too narrow, sought to broaden it to what he must have regarded as an especially liberal view, by taking the Jewish number prescribed—*three*—multiplying it by two, and adding one for good measure! "Until *seven* times?" he asked. Jesus taught him that his error, in principle, was as great as that of the Rabbis inasmuch as his number (seven times), still fixed a *limit* to responsibility. Our Lord' words, "Until seventy times," are not to be understood as seventy times seven, but to infinity. So long, and so often as a brother genuinely repents of his wrongs toward us, it is our solemn obligation to forgive him.

We can, indeed, do no less and claim forgiveness for our sins against the Lord.

"Put on therefore, as God's elect, holy and beloved, a heart
of compassion, kindness, lowliness, meekness, longsuffering;
forbearing one another, *and forgiving each other,* if any man
have a complaint against any; *even as the Lord forgave you,
so also do ye.*" (Colossians 3:12,13.)

Because the Lord forgives us, we are to forgive others; and to refuse to do so, is to dry up the springs of forgiveness in our own behalf. We are taught to pray: "Forgive us our debts, as we also have forgiven our debtors." (Matthew 6:12.) The *tenses* of this translation (American Standard Version), are faithful to the original text, and quite significant. "Forgive . . . as we have forgiven." This is a condition precedent to our own forgiveness.

"For if ye forgive men their trespasses, your heavenly Father
will also forgive you. But if ye forgive not men their trespasses, neither will your Father forgive your trespasses."
(Matthew 6:14,15.)

Our Lord, in the shadows of Gethsemane, prayed for himself (Luke 23:39), and on the cross for his enemies (Luke 23:34). In that sad and tragic hour he said, "Father, forgive them; for they know not what they

212

do." This plea, in behalf of his persecutors, was far from being a formal petition uttered once for the record; the verb is an imperfect, literally, *he kept on saying*, "Father, forgive them; they know not what they do." At each indignity, at every scornful word, the Lord repeated his prayer in their behalf! He repeatedly prayed for his tormentors.

We have seen that Paul enjoined two things of the Colossians: (1) forbearance; (2) forgiveness. To *forbear* is to endure, suffer, tolerate; *put up with*! Prominent among the obligations of all children of God is to "bear one another's burdens." (Galatians 6:2.) It is often easier to *bear* the burdens (share the loads) of others than it is to *endure* their weaknesses, peculiarities and eccentricities. It is, however, our duty both to bear and to forbear. It is enjoined upon us by precept and example. Paul taught it, and Christ practiced it; and he left us an example that we should follow in his steps. (1 Peter 2:21.) If we are by others irritated, we must remember that we often irritate others; and that the patience we are enabled to develop through the exercise of forbearance will heighten our spiritual stature here, and increase our joy hereafter. It is indeed, not possible for one to be happy *in this life* who has not acquired the virture of forbearance; miserable always is he who harbors in his heart resentment for fancied or even real wrongs.

Thus, to refuse to forgive others is to compound our own unhappiness in this life and to close the door of heaven against us in the next life. Malice, an unforgiving spirit, a heart saturated with resentment, are wholly incompatible with a tranquil life here and are dispositions certain to force the forfeiture of a blissful life to come.

The Greek of the phrase, "forgiving each other" (Colossians 3:13), is, literally, *to show favor to yourselves*. Being in the body of Christ—the church—(Ephesians 1:19-22), we are members one of another (1 Corinthians 12:27); and, inasmuch as the brother we forgive is a member of the same body to which we belong, we contribute to our own well-being, in restoring him to a proper relationship in the body.

"Will you please explain 1 Corinthians 11:34 which says: 'If any man hunger, let him eat at home'?"

Among the many departures which characterized the Corinthian church when Paul penned this epistle was the improper observance of the Lord's Supper. Its original design had largely been lost sight of; the emblems no longer signified in full what the Lord intended; and to the bread (representative of his body), and the fruit of the vine (which portrayed his shed blood) they had added other items of food and had turned the Memorial Supper into a common and ordinary meal. Such disorder had robbed the table of its meaning, and evidenced the fact that those who were thus participating were without spiritual discernment. (vv. 20-34.)

Paul sought to correct this unseemly abuse of the divine service by (a) directing attention to the excesses which were theirs (vv. 20, 21) by (b) reminding them that the usual and common place to eat food is at home and not in the assembly (v. 22), and by (c) showing that their actions resulted from a gross misunderstanding of the purpose of the Supper itself (vv. 25,26). And, there was another aspect of the matter which required the apostle's attention. The church in Corinth was composed of both rich and poor; some were able to bring more food than others in consequence of which those who were well supplied greedily ate theirs, refusing to "tarry" for the less fortunate, leaving some full and others empty. Their sins were many; they had corrupted the Lord's Supper; a state of gross disunity prevailed; covetousness and greediness were manifest; spiritual stupor possessed them and some of them were so far gone into this wordly, materialistic state that they were "asleep," and thus immune to spiritual impulses.

The querist adds, "We have a room in the back of our auditorium which is used for a Sunday School room; also a stove and refrigerator in it and serve meals at times. I don't think we should serve meals in the church building."

It is a misuse of Paul's statement in 1 Corinthians 11:34, to apply it to meals in the church *building*. (1) We have seen that it was penned to correct an abuse of the Lord's Supper—the mingling of a common meal with the Supper itself. It is improper exegesis to lift a statement from its context and apply it in a sense not intended by the sacred writer. (a) To oppose the eating of a meal in the building with this statement is to give it an unwarranted extension which would make it wrong to eat in a restaurant, on a picnic table in the park, or in somebody else's house! In none of these instances would one be eating "at home." It must be obvious that such was not the intent of the Spirit in 1 Corinthians 11:34. (b) The saints of the apostolic age, and this included the apostle who penned these words, often worshiped in the *houses* of members where meals were served and of which Paul doubtless partook. (Romans 16:5; 1 Corinthians 16:19.) Obviously, his teaching and practice in this matter are not in conflict. (2) There is no indication in the New Testament that any church of the first century ever owned a church *building*! Poverty, persecution, frequent expulsion from the land made such inadvisable if not impossible. A church building is an *expedient;* we may not properly apply to the building the divine rules governing the church (assembly).

Few people who are today living have preached the gospel longer or in more places than I; it has often been my privilege and pleasure to eat with the saints in church buildings throughout the land; from such practice I have never observed any departure; on the contrary, it is my observation that those congregations which engage in these "love feasts" (Jude 12, ASV), often exhibit a warmer, closer bond of fellowship for each other. It is right and it ought to be more often practiced.

"A couple here has served the Lord's Supper to a child which is now four years old for over a year. This has caused considerable controversy. They finally ceased to meet with us after making public statements as follows: 'A child is safe not being accountable for his sin thus he is in the church or kingdom. There is nothing wrong in serving a child, even all children of our town. We cannot hold closed communion, therefore, anyone should be encouraged to partake. Our child fully understands the significance of the Supper and needs to partake.' "

The couple is in grave error. Their statement and the conclusions they have drawn evidence a total lack of perception regarding the status of children, their relationship to the church or kingdom, the purpose of the Lord's Supper and the conditions precedent to its observance.

Only those who have been born *again* are in the kingdom. (John 3:3-5.) Children of the age of that contemplated in the question have *not* been born again; they possess the divine nature in their innocence and thus need no birth from above; therefore, they are not in the kingdom. The Lord's Supper is in the kingdom (Luke 22:29,30); infants are *not* in the kingdom; thus infants may not properly partake of the Lord's Supper, which is available only to those in the kingdom. The Corinthians were in the church (1 Corinthians 1:1,2); by divine edict, they observed the Supper in the church (1 Corinthians 11:23-30); only those who are added to the church by our Lord are in the church; but, only those who are *saved* by the Lord are by him and in the same process added to the church; children, three or four years old, being wholly pure, are without the need of salvation and are thus not members of the church (Acts 2:41,47). Therefore, children may not properly observe the Supper.

Christ suffered for "our sins" and his blood was shed to atone for them. (1 Peter 3:18.) In the Supper we "proclaim" this fact—an act impossible for one without sin. Moreover, there must be discernment, literally, *discrimination*, i.e., a recognition of the purpose and design of the body symbolized by the bread—obviously, an action wholly beyond the powers of a child of the age designated. (1 Corinthians 11:28.)

To say that a child three or four years old "fully understands the significance of the supper," is beyond belief.

"What is 'The Rapture'?"

A theological delusion, a figment of the imagination, a spin-off of the illusory and vain theories of Premillennialism. It, along with the larger body of doctrine from which it derives, is false in all of its parts. It is based on the allegation that the return of Christ will usher in a millennial reign in which Christ will occupy an earthly throne in Jerusalem and that immediately prior to these events he will secretly take out of the world his saints for a period of seven years (during which time a great Tribulation will fall upon the ungodly who are left behind), and following which he will return to the earth, establish his kingdom and rule in regal splendor over a material and earthly kingdom.

No essential element of the "Rapture" theory is true. (1) It seeks support for the "catching away" of the saints in 1 Thessalonians 4:15-18, but this passage deals with the final return of Christ, when the saints will indeed be "caught away" from the earth but *forevermore*, and not for only seven years. (2) Neither here, nor elsewhere in the sacred writings, is there the faintest suggestion of a secret or public rapture of seven years. (3) The Thessalonian scriptures conclusively prove that the Lord will never actually *put his foot on this earth again;* his appearing will be on the clouds from which he will call the saints away from the earth. (4) There will be no earth here from the time of catching away of the saints since this earth following that event will perish in the fires of the Last Great Day. (5) The "new heaven and earth" to which the saints will be carried is identified in John 14:2 as that place where our Lord now is preparing "a place" for us and to which he will take us at the end of the age. (6) Far from *beginning* his reign and establishing an earthly kingdom at his return, he will *end* his reign and "deliver up" the kingdom to his Father when he returns on the clouds.

The sharp contrast which obtains between the Premillennial theory and the clear, decisive teaching of the scriptures is easily seen in parallelling the two positions.

The Premillennial view:	The Scriptures:
1. Christ is *not* now reigning	1. Christ is now reigning (1 Corinthians 15:25.)
2. Christ will *begin* his reign at his return.	2. Christ will *end* his reign at his return (1 Corinthians 15:28.)

216

3. Christ will establish a kingdom at his return.	3. Christ's kingdom will terminate at his return (1 Corinthians 15:24.)

Events of the last day and their order are:
1. The dead, both righteous and wicked, will be raised. (John 5:28, 29.)
2. The judgment will follow. (Revelation 20:12-15.)
3. The saints will be carried to heaven, the wicked sent to hell. (Matthew 25:41-46.)
4. Christ will give his kingdom to God. (1 Corinthians 15:24.)
5. The earth will disappear in the all consuming fires of the judgment of God upon the wicked world. (2 Peter 3:10.)

"How may it be shown that John the apostle was 'that disciple whom Jesus loved'? (John 13:21-30; 21:20-24.)"

There were but three disciples—Peter, James and John—nearest the heart of Jesus and of whom such might have been affirmed. (1) It was not Peter because it was he who asked "that disciple," reclining next to our Lord at the Last Supper to inquire of the Saviour who the betrayer was (John 13:21-30); (2) it was not James—that disciple was martyred soon after the church was established (Acts 12:1ff), and thus could not have been the "disciple" who penned the biography of Jesus (and identified as the one "Jesus loved") near the close of the first century. Of no other could the statement have been penned saved John the apostle.

"Does the expression, 'Heaven and earth shall pass away . . .' Matthew 24:35, have reference to the cosmos and this literal earth, or does it have reference to the Jewish age or state?"

Here, as always in the study of the sacred writings, the context must be taken into account in order to determine the meaning. Under consideration is the fall and annihilation of the Jewish state. The certainty of it, the signs which would attend it and the deliverance of the faithful from its agonies are clearly and emphatically affirmed. And then, to establish the strongest possible grounds for accepting his prophecy he said, "Heaven and earth shall pass away, but my words shall not pass away." (Matthew 24:35.) The point of the illustration is, As ageless and eternal as this material world appears to be it will sooner pass in your day than my words shall fail! By no other could such language be properly used. Far from asserting that the heavens and earth were representative of the Jewish age soon to pass their permanence is made to represent the certainty of that which he affirmed. They will end only when the age of probation is no more and the saints are carried to *the*

217

place where our Lord now is and where he is making ready the future abode of his people. (2 Peter 3:1-10, John 14:2.)

"What is 'the end' spoken of in Matthew 24:6 and Matthew 24:13,14?"

Destruction of the temple, the fall of Jerusalem and the termination of the Jewish civil state. This occurred in A.D. 70.

"Explain the new heaven and earth of which Peter writes in 2 Peter 3:10-13."

The word "heaven" is used in the scriptures in three senses: (1) where birds fly (Matthew 8:20); (2) where the stars are (Hebrews 11:12); (3) where God dwells and Jesus reigns (Psalm 11:4; Hebrews 1:3). Man is a creature of two worlds—not one. He lives *on* the earth (from which he derives his food), and *in* the heavens (from which he obtains the air he breathes) in the first of the three senses in which the word "heaven" is used. He is unable to live long in either environment exclusive of the other. The astronauts, in their journeys to outer space, must take along their earth environment in order to survive. Man is neither a rodent nor a bird. Inasmuch as he is a creature of the heavens about him, and the earth below him, the terms *heaven* and *earth*, literally used to describe his material abode, are figuratively used here to denote his future abode.

Thus, the present heavens and earth serve as a figure of the heavens and earth to follow. Inasmuch as these words in their primary significance describe our present abode only this limitation must be recognized in the antitype, and so the phrase "new heavens and earth" must also be regarded as a metaphorical designation of the *future* abiding place of the righteous. (1) Jesus left the earth in order to *go* and prepare "a place" for his disciples. (John 14:2.) He will return from the "place" where he went at the end of this age, to claim his faithful followers and to take them to the "place" which he went to prepare. (2) He ascended to heaven and to his "Father's house" when he left the earth. (Acts 2:32-34; Psalm 11:4; John 14:2.) Therefore, the place which he went to "prepare" and to which he will carry his own at the end of the world is not on earth but in heaven. The phrase, *new heavens and earth,* thus figuratively designates the blissful abode of the saints now in preparation in heaven and from which place the Lord will return for them at the last day.

"Does Acts 15:29 forbid the eating of blood and the flesh of animals that have been strangled today?"

Yes.

Remarkably, there have been those who have thought that the prohibition to abstain "from blood" simply meant to avoid murder and that the command to abstain "from things strangled" has reference only to those animals which were offered to idols. This is undoubtedly to limit the application of the passage far too much. It seems clear from many affirmations of the scriptures that it was the intention of the Holy Spirit to forbid the eating of blood in any form and to require avoidance of any flesh which still contained blood. (1 Samuel 14:33; Deuteronomy 12:16; 15:23; Leviticus 3:17; 7:26; 17:10-14; 19:26; Genesis 9:4; Acts 15:29.) It will be observed that these references cover the whole range of the dispensations—Patriarchal, Mosaic and Christian.

Some forms of idolatrous worship involved the catching of the blood of sacrificed animals which was then consumed for food and this practice the Spirit banned for the reasons set out in Leviticus 17:13,14 and Deuteronomy 12:16,23. This practice was condemned, not simply or solely because it was associated with the worship of idols but because it is inherently wrong—and has been from the beginning of revelation—to eat blood. This is why "things strangled" are included among the forbidden items. "Strangled" derives from the Greek word *pniktos* which refers to flesh from which blood has not been drained. To consume such flesh was in the nature of the case to eat blood and so to violate the injunction against it. Those desirous of doing the will of God will exercise great care that they do not disobey the divine will in such matters.

"What is the 'Unpardonable Sin'?"

There is really no such thing. Neither the phrase nor the idea which it connotes appears in the sacred writings. The implication in it is that it is possible for one to so sin as to find it impossible to obtain forgiveness. There is no such situation. Taught repeatedly and with the greatest emphasis throughout the New Testament is the glorious fact that when (a) one genuinely repents of all wrong-doing, (b) *ceases the practice thereof* and (c) complies with the conditions applicable, pardon full and complete is by our Lord gladly and graciously bestowed. This, indeed has been the divine assurance through the ages. In the long ago Isaiah penned these comforting words,

"Seek ye Jehovah while he may be found; call ye upon him while he is near: let the wicked forsake his way, and the unrighteous man his thoughts; and let him return unto Jehovah, and he will have mercy upon him; and to our God, for he will abundantly pardon." (Isaiah 55:6,7.)

And, God promised through the new covenant, "And their sins and their iniquities will I remember no more." (Hebrews 9:17.) With such comforting assurances the scriptures abound.

The passage usually, but erroneously, designated as teaching the doctrine of "unpardonable sin," is 1 John 5:16, where reference is made to the "sin unto death." But, this is simply a sin which a brother will *not* confess—a fact which the larger context clearly shows. The Lord will forgive *every* sin a brother confesses (1 John 1:9); but, there is a sin which the Lord will not forgive (1 John 5:16); therefore, the sin which the Lord will not forgive is simply a sin which a brother will not confess. The context corroborates this view and the premises lead logically to this conclusion. If I witness sin on the part of an erring brother or sister and such may be brought to penitence and confession, I not only may, it is my duty, to pray for such with the assurance that the Lord will hear and answer the petition made. (James 5:16.) But, if the brother or sister persists in such rebellion it is a vain and useless exercise to pray for the forgiveness of impenitent persons, and the Lord will not hear and answer such a prayer for the brother or sister involved.

The "sin against the Holy Spirit" (Matthew 12:31,32), is, in principle, the rejection of the revelation which the Spirit, the third person of the godhead, made, first through our Lord, and then through his representatives. It is the denial of the Spirit's message initially by direct inspiration, and then through the Book, the practical effects of which is the rejection of the deity of our Lord, the repudiation of his sacrificial death, the annulment of the atonement and the implication that a sacrifice will yet be made. Those who thus do would crucify Christ "afresh" from the allegation that he who died on the cross was an imposter and that the Suffering Saviour must yet appear, and suffer. Salvation is denied those of this category, not because it is not offered to them, but because they have permanently rejected it. (Hebrews 6:1ff; 10:25-28.) The ever-flowing waters of the Well of Life are always available to those who desire to come and to quench their thirst. How we should rejoice that

"There is a fountain filled with blood,
Drawn from Immanuel's veins;
And sinners plunged beneath that flood,
Lose all their guilty stains."

"I have heard it said that a hot dog bun is just as scriptural as unleavened bread in the Lord's Supper. Would you please comment."

The statement is so foreign in spirit to that which characterized the institution of the Supper and is so opposed to the symbolism which that

Memorial Feast was designed to reflect that it is difficult to imagine such a viewpoint being seriously advanced. No informed person questions the fact that unleavened bread was used in the institution of the Lord's Supper but occasionally the view is presented that this was merely incidental in the fact that no other bread was available, save that remaining from the Passover observance when our Lord instituted it in the upper room.

Taught too by some today is the view that the intended significance of its use in that connection lies in the basic function of bread to produce and sustain life and that it is therefore immaterial whether the bread used is leavened or unleavened. But, this is to inject a concept nowhere alluded to by the sacred writers and it is to ignore the one which they emphasize. Jesus said, "This is my body" (Luke 22:19), by which he meant that the pale loaf portrays and vividly pictures the body of his flesh he was to give up for the sins of the world. Similarly, Paul pointed to this same concept when he wrote, quoting the very words of the Lord, "This is my body which is for you: this do in remembrance of me." (1 Corinthians 11:24.)

It is not a valid objection to say that at the feast of Pentecost on which day, following the Lord's resurrection, the church was established, leavened bread was specifically commanded (Leviticus 23:15-17), because the events of that day, described by the historian Luke, were not the actions of people observing a Jewish feast day but the carrying out of the Lord's will as reflected in earlier instruction touching the observance of the Lord's Supper.

Let it be carefully noted that it was *the bread of the passover feast* the Lord would not *again* eat with the disciples until it was fulfilled in the kingdom of God—the church. (Matthew 26:26-29.) That which they would eat *again* in the kingdom of God was that which they had formerly eaten in the paschal feast—unleavened bread. Prominent among the ideas associated with leaven in the scriptures where symbolism is used is the representation of corruption which leaven itself has undergone. It was to this characteristic of leaven our Lord pointed when he warned the disciples of "the leaven of the Pharisees," i.e., false doctrines of the Pharisees. This alone, would forbid its use in the Lord's Supper.

"If your answer to the first question is 'No,' would it not follow that if unleavened bread is bound, then we must use fermented wine?"

No. In each instance where reference is made to the "bread" of the Lord's Supper it is pointedly shown that it was the specific bread of the passover feast—unleavened. But, in every reference to the liquid of the Supper the phraseology is "the fruit of the vine," a generic phrase which can include either fermented wine or unfermented juice of the grape. Since either is included expediency will determine which of the two is to be used.

"Further, if your answer to question 1 is 'No,' would it not follow that to partake of the Lord's Supper scripturally, the Supper must be observed in an upper room?"

No. The "bread" of the Supper vividly pictures the body we are to remember and the "fruit of the vine" strikingly portrays the pouring out of his blood in our behalf. These elements are integral parts of the memorial feast. The upper room was merely incident to the occasion and sustains no essential relationship to the Supper itself, since the ordinance must be observed in *some* place. The Lord's *day* is an essential element in its observance being established to this day by divine edict. (Acts 2:42; 20:7.)

"Please explain 1 Peter 4:6."

"For unto this end was the gospel preached even to the dead, that they might be judged indeed according to men in the flesh, but live according to God in the spirit."—The words "for unto this end" indicate the purpose or object for which the gospel was preached to the dead, viz., that they might be judged according to men in the flesh, but live according to God in the spirit. That which was preached was the "gospel," God's power to save (Romans 1:16); and the preaching was to "the dead," dead and in the spirit land *when Peter wrote,* but alive and in the world when the gospel was preached to them. As a result of having heard this preaching, they observed the gospel and became Christians; but they had since died, and were thus dead when the epistle was written. While they lived they too were subjected to the evil speaking which Peter's readers were then suffering; and they, although judged and condemned by "men in the flesh" because of their faithfulness and fidelity to the cause, lived according to God in the spirit, i.e., in the higher, nobler life of the spirit. Such we conceive to be the meaning of what is doubtless one of the more difficult passages in the Bible. That these to whom the gospel was preached were not the same as those contemplated in 1 Peter 3:19,20, follows from the fact that those who were the objects of Noah's preaching rejected that patriarch's warnings and perished in disobedience in the flood; whereas, these who were the objects of the preaching to which Peter refers had accepted the gospel, and, though dead, had the approbation of God in the spirit realm.

"Were the seven chosen to look after the needs of the Grecian widows deacons?"

Yes. Though not specifically designated as such in the English text, the work which they did was to "serve tables" (Greek, *diakonein trapedzais*), and the word "diakonein" is a form of the word "diakonos" whence we derive the term *deacon*. The noun form of the word simply means a servant, and often appears in the sacred writings in this sense. It is occasionally translated "minister" in the New Testament. It is a functional, not an official, designation. Men who serve are servants; those who diakonize are deacons! Those who preach are preachers; those who teach are teachers whether so named or not. In a few instances, the word is used of those who serve the church. (Philippians 1:1; 1 Timothy 3:8-13.) Since the men who first performed such duties engaged in administering to the physical needs of people, it seems proper to conclude that this type of work is included in the duties and responsibilities of those who serve in addition to those implied and suggested in the qualifications given for deacons.

"When the need no longer existed did the work of the seven end?"

Yes. We must again emphasize that the work of all servants of the Lord is functional—never official—in nature and this includes elders, deacons and preachers. Men who no longer exercise oversight of the church are not elders; those who do not serve in the *diakonate* are not deacons; those who no longer preach are not preachers. Men selected to be elders and deacons are appointed to a *work* and not to an official position! When they no longer perform they no longer scripturally bear the designations formerly theirs. In the case of the seven, the dispersion of the Jerusalem church put a quick end to their work (Acts 8:1-4), and they resumed other useful and vital activities. Among those was Stephen soon thereafter to become the first martyr because of his teaching. (Acts 7:1ff.) It does not follow that there is no place for deacons in the work of the church today because the work of the seven ended. On the contrary, we may deduce from that case that the need for deacons will continue so long as the work they do remains and since it is a continuing matter in continuing congregations the work of deacons is contemporaneous with the existence of the congregation.

"Is it wrong for Christians to engage in the selling of beer in a retail establishment; or otherwise?"

It deeply grieves me, as I know it must every devoted disciple of our Lord, that such a question needs be raised and that it does evidences the extent to which worldliness, indifference, secularism and greed have permeated the church and influenced the thinking of many of its members; and, that there are preachers, elders and other active and influential members of the church who sanction and support such activity indicates how very much the world has invaded the church in many places these days.

Of course it is wrong!

It is wrong because it is positively forbidden in the sacred writings. Are not those who thus do aware of the divine denunciation of the God of heaven against those who give their neighbors "drink" and "also" start them down the road to drunkenness? (Habakkuk 2:15.) Do they have no fear of that certain and sure retribution which shall come upon all those who "call evil good" (Isaiah 5:20), who corrupt the morals of others (1 Corinthians 15:33), and whose "end" (ultimate destiny) is destruction (Philippians 3:19)?

It is wrong because it corrupts the community, lowers the level of the morals of the people who participate and provides the occasion which often leads to drunkenness and eventual premature death from acute alcoholism.

It is wrong because it destroys the influence of those who thus do, it weakens the influence of the church in the community; and it produces alienation, heartache and division in the body of Christ. Those who truly love the Lord will not inflict such great injury on his spiritual body—the church—nor follow a course certain to lead to the loss of their most precious possession, their immortal souls. Let us all follow the leading of the matchless apostle in all such matters who wrote, "It is good not to eat flesh, nor to drink wine, nor to do *anything* whereby thy brother stumbleth." (Romans 14:21.)

"Is it wrong for church members to allow their children to play on a ball team sponsored by a beer distributorship, where the children clearly wear clothing marked with the brand names of the beer?"

It is, indeed, and for all the reasons set out in answer to the previous question, and more. That innocent children should become pawns of a corrupt industry in advertising their baleful products demonstrates the adroitness with which this nation is being beset by the liquor industry and that parents would allow their children to be thus used shocks and dismays. The design is obvious; the results inevitable. These youngsters, the recipients of "favors" from these companies will look with favor on the products they sponsor and, in so doing, lose all inhibitions they may have held, ultimately becoming "customers" themselves. I shall evermore be thankful that I was privileged to grow up in a home where a can of beer or bottle of whiskey would have been tolerated with about the same degree of favor as a rattlesnake and for the same reasons! Parents who protect their children from the world's allurements when these children lack the wisdom and maturity to do so themselves will live to earn the gratitude of faithful and worthy offspring and spare themselves the grief and anguish which today often become the lot of other who have suffered their children to follow the primrose path.

"Was Paul the greatest of the apostles?"

A good brother takes exception to a statement that Paul was "the greatest of all the apostles." In his letter to me, he freely concedes that the apostle to the Gentiles had many great and wonderful qualities, but he feels that it is not proper, or in keeping with revealed truth to assert that he was superior to all the other apostles of the Lord.

Frankly, never before have I heard this conclusion questioned. In every area of activity we are privileged to examine, he stood head and shoulders above all others with whom he was associated; and, with the sole exception of the Saviour, he was truly the greatest man who ever lived on the earth.

(1) His capacity to toil and suffer and sacrifice for the Lord was simply without parallel. He himself said, "I labored more abundantly than they all. . . ." (1 Corinthians 15:10.) His was a larger field, and the success which attended his labors was vastly greater than that of any other—apostle or otherwise. Acts of Apostles records but few of his extensive labors and travels and reveals, by no means, all of the activities which abounded in his life. Never, in the world's history, was there a man—a mere man—so dedicated to the cause he unremittingly followed. His sufferings were *beyond measure,* to use his own words (2 Corinthians 11:23); and the catalog of suffering which he relates was by him declared without equal: "In labors more abundantly, in prisons more abundantly, in stripes above measure, in deaths oft. Of the Jews five times received I forty stripes save one. Thrice was I beaten with rods, once was I stoned, thrice I suffered shipwreck, a night and a day have I been in the deep; in journeyings often, in perils of rivers, in perils of robbers, in perils from my countrymen, in perils from the Gentiles, in perils in the city, in perils in the wilderness, in perils in the sea, in perils among false brethren; in labor and travail, in watchings often, in hunger and thirst, in fastings often, in cold and nakedness. Besides these things that are without, there is that which presseth upon me daily, anxiety for all the churches." (2 Corinthians 11:23-28.) With Farrar we are inclined to say that this narrative of suffering is "the most marvelous record ever written of any biography; a fragment

beside which the most imperiled lives of the most suffering sink into insignificance. . . ."

(2) His influence far, far exceeds that of any other New Testament character with the exception, of course, of him whom Paul served so faithfully and so devotedly—the Lord himself. Paul, more than any other, again with the exception of the Saviour, was responsible for the spread of the gospel throughout the Roman and Grecian worlds, and consequently, in our age and day also. It was the faithfulness and fidelity of the apostle which largely enabled Christianity, in less than three decades following its inauspicious and unpromising beginning, to bring the Roman empire to its knees and to introduce Christ into the highest councils.

(3) His writings, bearing the message of the Holy Spirit, are more numerous, more profound, and have more powerfully directed the course of human thought and action than any others. The depth of thought, the logical reasoning, and the profound comprehension of the epistle to the Romans is without parallel in writings either sacred or profane. Luther described it as "the chief part of the New Testament." Mayer said "it is the grandest, most complete composition of the apostle," and Coleridge called it "the most profound work in existence."

(4) Peter, grand man that he was, exhibited a very common human weakness when he "dissembled" at Antioch (Galatians 2:11-14), and "walked not uprightly according to the truth of the gospel," but, when did *any man,* apostle or otherwise, "withstand" Paul to the face "because he was to be blamed"? (Galatians 2:11.)

"Please give an exposition of Genesis 1:1."

"In the beginning God created the heavens and the earth," is not, as atheists, agnostics and infidels affirm, a fictitious, unhistorical and mythical story but a simple, sublime and satisfactory report of the creation by an inspired man. An analysis of it reveals that the *time* was in the beginning, the activating *force* was God, the *action* was creative in character and the *identity* of that created was the heavens and the earth. Each of these affirmations is of the most significant and far-reaching character and deserves our serious study and consideration.

In the phrase, "in the beginning," there is no article in the Hebrew text. It is simply and literally, "in beginning." It was designed to designate, not an order of things, but the period in which the things mentioned are declared to have been done. The original word signifies the head part, the first. Thus, what is contemplated here antedates time and denotes when God began the world through creative action. Inasmuch as he was there anterior to the beginning, he is before time and eternal in nature. John, in opening statements in his biography of the Christ, affirmed the same thing of the Word, the second person of the godhead and identified later in the text as the One who *dwelt* (literally, *tented*) among men. (John 1:1,14.) The eternity, the pre-existence of the Christ and his joint action with the Father (John 1:3), are unmistakably established by the sacred writer. These indisputable facts are articles of belief to all who regard the New Testament as a divine document. The alternative is unbelief.

Thus, the phrase, "In the beginning," designates the time when the events chronicled by Moses began. It actually designates the point at which the clock of time began in the timeless vastness of eternity. *Genesis* (a word denoting the coming into being of anything) is often styled the book of beginnings because it relates the beginning of time, of matter, of man, of sin, of death and the first promise of redemption. It was God who functioned "in the beginning." The word "God" is from the Hebrew *Elohim,* plural of *El.* Hebrew nouns derive from verbs which, in the third person singular is the radix or root. It is not always possible to determine the root of Hebrew words, and Hebraists differ over the significance of this word descriptive of deity. Adam Clarke, regarded in his day as the ripest Hebrew scholar in Great Britain, thought that the word derived from a verb meaning *to adore* and that the essential meaning of the term is one worthy to be adored or wor-shipped; however, most scholars believe that it comes from a term meaning lasting, powerful and enduring and that it is a reference to the limitless, all-powerful and eternal Creator of the universe. The word occurs 57 times in the singular, and about 3000 times in the plural in the Old Testament.

Our English word *God* means deity and is the translation of the Greek *theos.* It is used, through the New Testament, to denote the divine nature or essence possessed by the godhead, the Father, the Son and the Holy Spirit. In numerous instances, it is used under the figure of the *synecdoche,* where a part is put for the whole, or the whole for a part. In such instances *one* of the members of the godhead is called God. The three persons of the godhead are thus designated in the following instances: (1) The Father: "And Simon Peter answered and said, Thou art the Christ, the Son of the living *God.*" (Matthew 16:18.) (2) The Son: "In the beginning was the Word and the Word was with God and the Word was *God.*" (John 1:1.) (3) The Holy Spirit: "But Peter said, "Ananias, why hath Satan filled thine heart to lie to the Holy Spirit, and to keep back part of the price of the land? . . . Thou hast not lied unto men, but unto *God.*" (Acts 5:3,4.) There is but one divine nature or essence; but, there are three distinct persons or personalities pos-sessing this nature and there is but one God yet three persons in the godhead. It is, hence, entirely correct to refer to the personalities of the godhead as God the Father, God the Son and God the Holy Spirit.

The appearance of the plural form of God in Genesis 1:1, *Elohim,* and the use of plural pronouns in reference to God (Genesis 1:1; 1:26), has long been regarded by conservative scholars as an indirect allusion to the three persons comprising the godhead. Advocates of modernistic and liberal views touching creation deny this, alleging that the plural form is a relic of polytheism, or a form of majesty, or a reference to the manifold attributes of deity, or association with angels. There is no evidence that the "we" of majesty existed in Moses' day and other efforts at explanation are the products of unbelief. Man is possessed of numerous attributes but does not designate himself as is alleged of God and to attribute the usage to the inclusion of angels is to give them a hand in creation! Why should there be any difficulty whatsoever in accepting the plural form as an allusion to that which is so clearly and often taught in subsequent scripture?

"What is repentance? To what extent does it involve restitution?"

"Repentance" is from the Greek word *metanoia,* which means a change of mind. Those who repent change their minds regarding the course they have been pursuing and the attitudes and dispositions formerly characterizing them. It does not involve sorrow for sin (Acts 2:37,38), though it is *produced* by it, and it does not include reformation of life, though it *leads* to it. Sorrow for sin causes a person to repent, and repentance prompts to reformation of life; sorrow for sin is the cause; reformation of life, the effect. This distinction is an important one, though often beclouded and obscured in the minds of many today. The parable of the two sons provides an excellent demonstration of this analysis of repentance. (Matt. 21:28-30.)

"Restitution" is an act of justice wherein we restore to another that which we have unjustly deprived him of. (Cf. Exodus 22:1; Luke 19:8, Leviticus 6:2-5.) If the deprivation consists of *things,* these, or their value, must be restored, where possible; where such cannot be done, reasonable satisfaction must be made. Where the loss we have caused is intangible, and restitution cannot be made in kind, we must make every effort possible to remove the effects of our wrong. Our Lord, using an illustration from the Jewish law, taught us that acceptable worship is not possible when we have injured a brother and have not corrected it. If we have wronged him materially, we must correct it before offering our gifts to God; if we have slandered, besmirched and blackened the reputation of another, we must first be reconciled to him, by repentance and restitution, before God will accept us, and our service to him. (Matthew 5:23,24.) Often taught, and with great emphasis, in the Scriptures is the fact that we must make every possible effort to be right with our fellows, if we expect to be in fellowship with God. (Isaiah 1:11-20.)

"Who is the anti-Christ?"

John, the beloved apostle, in the first of his epistles, gives us the following remarkable description of one whom he styles *anti-christ:* "Little children, it is the last hour: and as ye heard that anti-christ cometh, even now have there arisen many anti-christs; whereby we know that it is the last hour. . . . Who is the liar but he that denieth that Jesus is the Christ? This is the anti-christ, even he that denieth the Father and the Son . . . and every spirit that confesseth not Jesus is not of God: and this is the spirit of the anti-christ, whereof ye have heard that it cometh; and now is in the world already." (1 John 2:18, 22; 4:3.) From this we learn that (1) when the anti-christ comes, the "last hour" will have arrived; (2) many anti-christs had already arisen and thus the last hour was upon the world when John wrote. Two questions arise; (1) What is the significance of the words, "the last hour"? (2) Who is the anti-christ described by John?

(1) The word "hour" in the passage before us, translates the Greek term *hora,* which signifies a fixed date or period. Obviously of figurative usage here, it designates a period of time determined in the divine mind and, as modified by the word "last," the final period in the events predetermined by the Father. What is described here is simply the last of the great ages or dispensations, arranged by the Father—the Christian age which began on the first Pentecost following our Lord's resurrection.

(2) The word "anti-christ" is made up of the preposition *anti,* meaning, in composition, *over against, opposed to;* and the word *Christ;* hence, one opposed to Christ. The word appears only in the writings of John, in the New Testament, and from other references made thereto by him we learn that anti-christ is (1) a liar; (2) a deceiver; and (3) a denier that Jesus is the Christ or that he has come into the world in the flesh. Such were the identifying marks of the "anti-christ" provided by John. Many others possessed the *spirit* of anti-christ.

Paul, though not using the name *anti-christ,* tells us of the appearance of "the man of sin," and "the son of perdition," and warns of impending apostasy because of his activities. (2 Thessalonians 2:3,4.) Among the characteristics of the *man of sin* set out by Paul were these: (1) he does not hesitate to oppose his will to the will of God; (2) he exalts himself against God; (3) he sits in the temple of God; and (4) he sets himself forth as God. Moreover, (a) he is the personification of sin; (b) the son of perdition; and (c) a participant in deceptive signs and lying wonders, and his intent is to deceive, if possible, the people of God. A careful examination of the description given by these inspired writers leads to the conclusion that the *anti-christ* and the *man of sin* are identical; the latter is very obviously the vicar of Rome, and so must the former also be.

If to this the objection is offered that John wrote, "Even now have there arisen many anti-christs; whereby we know that it is the last hour," long before the appearance of the apostasy and the first pope of which Paul writes, the answer is, While the great *anti-christ* predicted by John and described by Paul had not yet appeared, many were evidencing and exhibiting the same spirit which would be his when he did come, and these could properly be styled anti-christs. Religious literature abounds with reference to popish persons who exhibit the spirit of the papacy (though not active members of the church of Rome), and with equal propriety those of John's day who preceded the popes, but who possessed their spirit, might likewise be similarly designated. All who oppose the truth are of the spirit of anti-christ.

It may be said, "The pope does not today oppose the Christ nor deny him." But, he does precisely this! By arrogantly assuming to be the vicar of Christ, he claims to be the Lord's representative, empowered to act in his stead, presumptuously asserting his right to forgive sins from "the seat of Christ," in "the temple of God." He is a parody of the Christ, a counterfeit Christ and, though he imitates some of the characteristics of the Christ, this is exactly what would be expected of one who seeks to deceive. Not overlooked in this connection should be the words of our Lord,

> "For many shall come in my name, saying, I am the Christ and shall lead many astray. . . . For there shall arise false Christs, and false prophets, and shall show great signs and wonders; so as to lead astray, if possible, even the elect." (Matthew 24:5,24.)

All of these are of the disposition of anti-christ, imitators of his work.

"What is the soul?"

In an earlier effort we have examined the methods of materialists touching their doctrines of annihilation and no future retribution; and, we shall, in this paper, present their views regarding the soul. Here, again, it will be easily observable that they resort to arbitrary definition and utilize steretyped phraseology to establish their theological system of nonexistence in death and that their conclusions can be reached only by abandoning the proper principles of biblical exegesis.

Does man *possess* a soul? "No," materialists answer. "Man *is* a soul." How do they arrive at this conclusion? They cite Genesis 2:7, "And the Lord God formed man of the dust of the ground, and breathed into his nostrils the breath of life; and man became a living soul," assume that *man* and *soul* are properly interchangeable in Moses' affirmation, and thence conclude that man *is a soul!* They thereupon point to Ezekiel's text, "The soul that sinneth, it shall die," (Ezekiel 18:20); and triumphantly declare that they have established the utter and complete mortality of man.

Their premises are untrue, and their conclusion by no means follows: (1) It is not true that man and soul are convertible terms. "John became an American." Shall we thence conclude that John did *not exist* until he acquired American citizenship? Hardly. That it was not Moses' intention, in this passage so often cited by materialists, to designate, in detail, the constitution *of man,* is evidenced in the fact that the word *soul* from the Hebrew *nephesh* occurs, for the first time in the sacred writings, at Genesis 1:20, where it is assigned to fish, birds and creeping things! (See, also, another similar usage in Genesis 1:30.) As thus used, it is clear that the soul in these passages does not refer to anything peculiar to the constitution of man. It signifies, as its usage denotes, and the lexicons affirm, *any creature that breathes,* in all of these early occurrences in the book of Genesis.

(2) Nor is it correct to conclude that the phrase *breath of life* in the aforementioned statement of Moses ("And the Lord God formed man of the dust of the ground, and breathed into his nostrils the breath of life; and man became a living soul") sums up, or was designed to denote the *whole* constitution of man. The word "life," here is, in the Hebrew text, plural, literally *breath of lives (nish-math khay-yim.)* It occurs; in similar form, in three other instances in the early chapters of Genesis (6:17; 7:15; 7:22.) In the first of these the phrase is *ruach khay-yim;* in the second the same; in the third, *nishmatch-ruach khay-yim,* and out of the four instances where the phrase, the *breath of lives,* occurs in our translation *the last three are applied to the beasts, birds and creeping things!* It follows, therefore, that the phrase "breath of life," does not designate anything peculiar to man. And, in view of the fact that the word "soul," from the Hebrew *nephesh,* is similarly extended to include the animal world, birds and creeping things, it may not be properly limited to man, in the passage under consideration. Such passages as, "the soul that sinneth, it shall die" (Ezekiel 18:20), and "he made a path for his anger; *he spared not their soul from death,* but gave their life over to the pestilence" (Psalm 78:50), mean no more than the loss of physical existence; inasmuch as the word translated soul designates, in these instances, *a creature that breathes,* the death that is described is cessation of physical life.

The New Testament equivalent of *nephesh* is *psuchee,* the Greek term translated soul in the Christian scriptures. Of its 103 occurrences in the New Testament, it is translated *life* 41 times, *soul* 57 times, three

times by the word *mind,* once by *heart,* once *heartily.* It is most significant that it is never rendered by the word *spirit.* Being a generic term,
it is used, in the scriptures, to denote (1) life, which men, and beasts,
lose at death; (2) the entire person (a living being), Acts 2:41; (3) the
seat of feeling, hence, the heart; (4) the immortal nature of man which
may, as Thayer declares, "by the right use of aids," secure for itself
eternal blessedness. In this sense alone is it properly regarded as designating that part of man which never dies. When thus used, it describes that part of the human constitution which is also denominated
spirit, but it by no means follows that soul and spirit are convertible or
interchangeable terms. And, where the word soul refers to the immortal nature (as Revelation 6:6-9), the usage must be regarded as figurative inasmuch as the spirit is not dependent on breath for life! The
life which the soul designates is figuratively regarded as extending
beyond mere physical existence. This part of the nature of man is
usually called the *spirit.*

The word *pneuma* occurs about 385 times in the Greek Testament
and in all of its occurrences but one, is translated *spirit.* (This sole
variation is in Revelation 13:15.) It is not subject to death. Death,
mortality, corruptibility, decay, destruction are never affirmed of the
spirit. It is, in the nature of the case, impossible for a spirit to die. The
scriptures affirm deathlessness of the angels; and the angels do not die
because they are angels, but because they are spirits! In all of those
remarkable instances, where death is particularly described, and the
spirit, or *ghost* (old English for *guest*—one who abides, and thus a
fitting designation of the spirit, which, during life, abides or sojourns
in the body), is yielded up, it is never the word soul (*psuchee*) but always
spirit (*pneuma*) to which reference is made. Note such expressions as
"Father, into thy hands I commend my spirit" (Luke 23:46); "Lord
Jesus, receive my spirit," (Acts 7:59), where the word is always *pneuma*
(spirit), never *psuchee* (soul). Lexically, logically, and actually these
terms differ and must not be confused. If the Word of God operates to
"the dividing of soul and spirit" (Hebrews 4:12), it is not proper for
materialists to confuse them. Until such time as they can produce an
instance where mortality is affirmed of the spirit of man, (and they
could as easily prove that God will some day die), they shall continue
to fail in their endeavor.

What is the soul? Literally, it is *life,* sometimes regarded on various
levels beginning with that which is common of beasts, birds, creeping
things; then, life as it obtains on an intellectual plane (mind, heart,
affections, etc.), and, by an extension of idea, life, on a spiritual plane.
Essentially, and in unfigurative usage, it is the "vital force which
animates the body and shows itself in breathing" (Thayer), and is
always to be distinguished from the spirit, when so used. Thus distin-

guished, its characteristics may not be properly affirmed of the spirit—the undying nature. In those instances, when the term is used generically to embrace the spirit life, (as, for example, when we sing, "The soul never dies,") it is used figuratively and by extension of meaning for the *spirit*.

Our Lord is said to have given his life (*psuchee*, soul) for a ransom (Matthew 20:28), but he gave his *pneuma*, spirit to God. (Luke 23:46.) Christ allowed his life (soul, *psuchee*) to be taken, but his crucifiers were not able to seize or restrain his spirit. There is therefore neither reason nor revelation to support the materialistic practice of confusing these terms. What the Holy Spirit divides asunder we should not confuse. (Hebrews 4:12.) Adventists, "Jehovah's Witnesses," Christadelphians, indeed, all materialists, select *one* of the meanings of the word *soul*, and assign this significance to *every* occurrence of the term in defiance of the most elemental rules of lexicography. Their error here, as well as often elsewhere evidences in their attempts to defend their absurd positions, is obvious.

"I have a question: According to Exodus 24:9-11 man has seen God. Exodus 33:11 says, 'Thus the Lord used to speak to Moses face to face, just as a man speaks to his friend. . . .' Then, Exodus 33:20 says, 'You cannot see my face, for no man can see me and live.' Please harmonize."

There is no disharmony. What appears to be results from a misapprehension of the phrase, *face to face,* usually but erroneously understood to mean each in full view of the other. The reference is to the *manner* in which the revelation was made and not to the *position* of the parties by whom made. The revelation was "face to face," that is, direct, full and free, and not by medium or intermediary, as was so often characteristic of revelations in that day. The communication was not by messenger, by visions nor by dreams but with the directness, familiarity and openness with which one friend speaks to another. It is not possible for fallen man to gaze upon the divine nature. (1 John 4:12.) To "see" God is not necessarily to observe some visible form or representation corporeally of the divine nature; he is to be seen in his work, in his agents and in the influence upon others he wields. That this conclusion is the correct one is clear from Deuteronomy 4:12: "Ye heard the voice of the words, but saw no similitude. . . ."

"Is it in keeping with the scriptures for the church to withdraw fellowship from unfaithful members who no longer attend the services?"

Yes. "Now we command you, brethren, in the name of our Lord Jesus Christ, that ye withdraw yourselves from every brother that walketh

233

disorderly, and not after the tradition which he received of us." (2 Thessalonians 3:6.) The disorderly person contemplated by Paul in this passage was one "out of step," *having broken rank* with the rest. Such is truly characteristic of those who have abandoned the public meetings of the church. Thayer defines the word translated "disorderly" in the foregoing passage (*atakos*) as "disorderly, out of the ranks (often so of soldiers), irregular," and "deviating from the prescribed order or rule." The view that withdrawal may be done only from those in attendance results from a gross misunderstanding of what fellowship is and to what it extends. It is a seven days a week and 24 hours a day relationship—not simply or only from 11 to 12 o'clock on Sunday morning!

"Must the main ingredient of unleavened bread which God commanded the Israelites to observe as the passover feast be wheat? This is beginning to be a disturbing question in the mission field especially in Thailand where the main flours are rice, tapioca and maize." (From the Far East.)

There is no direct reference in the scriptures to the substance of the bread used by our Lord in the institution of the Supper; but, inasmuch as it was clearly that which had been used in the observance of the passover feast and designated as "unleavened bread," any study of the matter must relate to the bread of that feast. But, neither is there any statement in the Old Testament indicative of the kind of flour to be used to the exclusion of all others. This would lead to the conclusion that the kind of flour from which the bread was to be made is not significant. Allusions to the feast and to its elements abound in Jewish Talmudic writings and they mention that the flour might be wheat, spelt, barley, oats or rye though, quite strangely, they rule out rice or millet! This exclusion by them must be regarded as based upon traditional considerations and thus not valid to us. Some scholars have conjectured that the original unleavened bread of that historic Jewish feast was made from barley flour from the fact that its observance was associated with the commencement of the barley harvest but of this we cannot be sure. It is certain that in that day and place bread was baked from various kinds of flour.

In the days of our Lord on earth the poorer classes were often unable to afford the more costly wheat flour for their tables and so subsisted on bread baked from barley or other cheaper flours. Wheat flour is usually less expensive in our country than other flours and is universally used for making the unleavened bread used on the Lord's Table. But in lands where wheat flour is not available it would appear that such bread made from flour ground of any of the grains which are available is acceptable.

"There is a brother preaching that the blood of Christ was only efficacious from the cross to this date."

It would be difficult to imagine a doctrine more false, more easily refuted and more in conflict with the major thesis of the sacred writings than that of which the querist writes. From the offering of Abel until the cross, the rivers of blood which flowed from animals offered in sacrifice prefigured, anticipated and were validated by the offering which our Lord made at Calvary.

The blood of bulls and of goats was powerless to take away sin; the offerings of the old order foreshadowed the supreme sacrifice without which all such efforts through the centuries would have been in vain. Indeed, it is specifically affirmed that the efficacy of his atonement was retroactive in nature and extended to those of the first covenant: "And for this cause he is the mediator of the new testament, that by means of death, for the redemption of the transgressions that were under the first testament, that they which are called might receive the promise of eternal inheritance." (Hebrews 9:15.) Thus it was (a) "by means of death" (his death on the cross) that (b) "redemption" (his blood being the purchase price, 1 Peter 1:18,19) (c) the "transgressions" under "the first testament" (covenant) were ultimately blotted out.

If the thesis of which the brother inquires were true the uncounted multitudes of people who lived before the cross died without hope since it was not possible for the blood of bulls and of goats to take away sin (Hebrews 10:1-4), notwithstanding their compliance with the requirements imposed through the law and the prophets, and the assurances to them by inspiration supplied. (Hebrews 11:5,8-10,13-16,32-40.)

Of particular significance, in this connection, is the affirmation of the Hebrew writer regarding the hope which was theirs; a hope realized, not through the blood of animals, but by the precious blood of Jesus Christ:

"These all died in faith, not having received the promises, but having seen them afar off, and were persuaded of them, and embraced them, and confessed that they were strangers and pilgrims on the earth. For they that say such things declare plainly that they seek a country. And truly, if they had been mindful of that country from whence they came out, they might have had opportunity to have returned. But now they desire a better country, that is, an heavenly: wherefore God is not ashamed to be called their God: for he hath prepared for them a city." (Hebrews 11:13-16.)

235

This hope was grounded in the cross of Christ and not in that which merely prefigured it.

The sacrifice which our Lord offered was infinitely *better* than that which prefigured it and to this fact Paul pointed when he contrasted the offerings of the old order with that which was made on Calvary:

"For Christ is not entered into the holy places made with hands, *which are the figures of the true:* but into heaven itself, now to appear in the presence of God for us: nor yet that he should offer himself often, as the high priest entereth into the holy place every year with the blood of others; for them must he often have suffered since the foundation of the world: but now once in the end of the world hath he appeared to put away sin by the sacrifice of himself." (Hebrews 9:24-27.)

Were he not superior to the priests of the Jewish system and were his sacrifice not vastly better than theirs, his atonement would have required repeated offering of himself in order to achieve that which he accomplished when "once in the end of the world" (the Jewish age) he appeared for the purpose of putting away sin by one sacrifice, a sacrifice the benefits of which extended backward to Eden and forward to the end of the Christian age.

Zechariah wrote of a "fountain opened to the house of David and to the inhabitants of Jerusalem for sin and uncleanness," streams flowing from it to the "former" and the "hinder sea,"—one forward, one backward. (Zechariah 13:1; 14:8.) The *fountain* represents the pouring out of our Lord's blood on the cross; the stream *backward* portrays the provision made for the saints who died in the triumphs of faith under former dispensations; the stream *forward* those who thus die in this the Christian age.

"What is truth?"

"Pilate therefore said unto him, Art thou a king then? Jesus answered, Thou sayest that I am a king. To this end have I been born, and to this end am I come into the world, that I should bear witness unto the truth. Every one that is of the truth heareth my voice. Pilate said unto him, What is truth?" (John 18:37,38.)

Bible students are not in agreement as to the motive which prompted Pilate to raise the question with which he terminated his interview with our Lord. Some see in it the earnest longing of an honest heart which had thusfar been unable to discover truth and had long since given up the search; others, more properly, regard it as an exhibition of worldly skepticism which thinks there is no such thing as truth; or, if there is, that it is of little importance to the world. In either event,

Pilate felt no interest in the Lord's reply; notwithstanding his query, he did not remain for the answer!

The disposition, to regard truth as unattainable and its pursuit a useless and unnecessary exercise, has long been an acceptable view in denominational circles and those possessed of this concept have not hesitated to justify their departures from sacred writ on the ground that "it is not possible for everybody to understand the Bible alike." Others, not willing to cut the Gordian knot by such blatant denial of the word, have nonetheless reached much the same conclusion by the allegation that it is not possible to *know* the will of the Lord from the study of his word, and that those who claim to do so are arrogant in disposition, sectarian in spirit, and dogmatic in doctrine! It is now being taught that divisions arise because some among us claim to be *right*, to be identified with the *loyal* church and that such efforts to avoid denominationalism turn us into bigoted sectarians!

There are those who say we may be wrong on some of the basic matters in our distinctive plea and there ought never to have been any alienation and division over such issues as instrumental music in worship, premillennialism, marriage and divorce, and similar matters. Had the saintly David Lipscomb, the courageous J. C. McQuiddy and the eloquent N. B. Hardeman, the fearless Foy Wallace, Jr., the scholarly B. C. Goodpasture and other giants of the faith been theological weaklings and religious cowards, division over these issues would have been avoided but at a cost too awesome to contemplate—the loss of the souls of tens of thousands of people who now adhere to a pure faith and a scriptural practice but who otherwise would have long since been enmeshed in denominational error. How thankful we who are the recipients of that priceless heritage ought to be that these men and thousands of others who have so valiantly defended the faith through the years did not believe that *we may be wrong* on these matters!

If there is such a thing as truth; if it is accessible to us; if it is within the mental reach of those for whom it is intended, why should we not seek it and, having found it, claim it as our own? To urge that it is wrong to want to be right and, having achieved conformity to the Lord's will as set out in his Word to assert the fact, makes one a bigoted sectarian is in effect to say that there is really no such thing as truth; or, if there is, that is neither desirable nor necessary to separate it from error and to insist upon it for its own sake. Surely, it must be admitted that sometime, somewhere, *some* of the Lord's people have been *right* and are members of the loyal church! If so, may not those who are thus circumstanced *say so* without being liable to the charge that they are bigoted sectarians? For some years there has been a form of breast-beating among us which sees little that is good in the churches of Christ and little that is bad in the denominational world and we are by them

237

repeatedly urged to give up our "traditions" for the sake of unity in the religious world.

What *traditions*? We are never told; it is simply alleged that we are wedded to traditions which constitute a continuing barrier to union with our denominational friends. No one is so naive as to think that those peculiarities of ours which have developed through the years are a formidable obstacle to unity; we are not rejected by the denominational world because of our hours of meeting, the order of our services or the architecture of our buildings. Their repudiation of us results from basic difference over the name, the doctrine and the practice of the New Testament church. More specifically, whether men may properly honor Christ by wearing human names (Acts 11:26), whether salvation is by faith only (James 2:24), whether one may apostatize and fall away from grace finally to be lost (Galatians 5:4), whether baptism in water, is for (unto) the remission of sins (Acts 2:38), whether the Lord's Supper must be observed every first day of the week (Acts 20:7), whether God's praises may be sung to the accompaniment of mechanical instruments of music (Ephesians 5:19), and much, much more. These are distinctive characteristics of the Lord's church which separate us. Which of these features are traditions we may relinquish in order to attain acceptance with people of the denominational world? To say that the New Testament church is without distinctive features is sheerest nonsense. It differs in essential detail in every area from the institutions of men; each vital difference accentuates this distinctiveness as the two are compared with what the New Testament teaches regarding it.

If we *may be wrong* on some of these matters then, to the same extent, the denominational world *may be right* about them—a conclusion which logically follows, thus leading to a deterioration of conviction and consequent weakening of opposition to denominational doctrine and practice. Inevitably, this leds to questioning regarding our basic plea, hesitancy to insist upon it, and criticism of those who do. Those who reach this point no longer preach with conviction and power and their preaching produces converts equally weak and without conviction. "For if the trumpet give an uncertain voice, who shall prepare himself for war?" (1 Corinthians 14:8.) The apostles and those who followed their direction were best with no uncertainty regarding the matters presented. Timothy "fully" knew the doctrine of Paul (2 Timothy 3:10), and the faith in him was "unfeigned" because of the robust convictions of his mother, Eunice, and his grandmother, Lois. (2 Timothy 1:5,6.) Men believed and knew the truth in the apostolic age (1 Timothy 4:3), and were "filled with the knowledge of his will," in "all spiritual wisdom and understanding." (Colossians 1:9.) So ought it to be with us all today.

"What is the doctrine of the Perpetual Virginity of Mary?"

It is the allegation that Mary was the mother of Jesus and of no others. One theory alleges that these men—James, Joseph, Simon and Judas—were cousins of Jesus, children of a woman named Mary, who was a sister of Mary the mother of Christ! On this assumption, James, "the son of Alphaeus," (Matt. 10:3), is to be regarded as the same as James, "the son of Clopas," Alphaeus and Clopas being names derived from the same source, and thus the view is advanced that the James thus mentioned was one of the apostles. In answer to the objection that the brothers of Christ, in the flesh, did not believe on him during his public ministry and were not apostles, it is contended that the word "brethren" by which "James and Joseph and Simon and Judas" are identified in Matt. 13:55, does not necessarily describe the relationship which we ascribe to the term *brothers* today; and, that in reality they were simply cousins of Jesus—children of a sister of our Lord's mother, named Mary!

The objections which may be levelled at this theory are numerous and weighty indeed. (a) If it is conceded that the names Clopas and Alphaeus derive from the same source, these are distinct appelations and there is no reason to assume that in this, or in any other instance, they refer to the same individual. (b) The theory necessitates the conclusion that in John 19:25, when it is said that "There stood by the cross of Jesus his mother, and his mother's sister, Mary the wife of Clopas, and Mary Magdalene," there are but three women mentioned, and that "his mother's sister" is identified in this text as Mary "the wife of Clopas." It appears certain that there were four women mentioned in this passage, and arranged in two pairs: (1) the mother of Jesus and his mother's sister; (2) Mary the wife of Clopas, and Mary Magdalene. (c) The theory requires one to believe that *two* sisters were *both* named Mary by the same parents, and were both called *by this name!* Names are assigned for the purpose of distinguishing one individual from another; such a conclusion as the theory necessitates is impossible and absurd. (d) The contention that the word *adelphos* (brother) means cousin is without lexical support, or New Testament example. Moreover, there is a word for cousin (*anepsios*) occurring in the Greek text of Col. 4:10. (e) In none of the lists of apostles is there any suggestions that two or more of the brothers of the Lord were apostles; indeed, in Acts 1:13,14, and 1 Cor. 9:5, they are expressly differentiated. (f) The most weighty objection to this theory of all, however, is to be seen in the affirmation of John 7:5: "For neither did his brethren believe on him." It is evident that the fleshly brothers of Jesus did not accept his claim to deity during his public ministry; and that they became his disciples only after his death and resurrection.

Yet, if the theory be true, two of his brothers (James and Jude) were among the apostles.

But, did not Paul say, "Then after three years I went up to Jerusalem to see Peter, and abode with him fifteen days. But other of the apostles saw I none, save James the Lord's brother"? (Gal. 1:18.) Does this not identify James, "the Lord's brother," *as an apostle?* It should be remembered that, following the early days of Christianity, and long before the end of the apostolic age, the word *apostle* was applied to numerous individuals not of the original twelve, e.g., Barnabas (Acts 14:14); Andronicus, Junias and others (Rom. 16:7). (b) The marginal reading of Gal. 1:19, in the American Standard Version has the phrase, "but only" thus making the passage to mean, "I saw none of the apostles; I saw only James, the Lord's brother."

"Is it correct to say that no translation is inspired?"

It is being said with ever-increasing frequency that *inspiration* is characteristic of the original autographs only and that it does not extend to the translations of the scriptures in use among us today.

"No translation is inspired," we are told.

The conclusion which follows from this premise is quite obvious.

Most people are without an inspired Bible today.

If the truth of the premise be granted this conclusion irresistibly follows. Fewer than one per cent of the people in this country today have access to, or could read if they did, the original texts. The logic is unassailable. Only those who read the Bible in the original languages have access to an inspired text. More than 99 per cent of the population today cannot read the Bible in the original languages. Therefore, more than 99 per cent of the people are without an inspired Bible.

This conclusion we unhesitatingly reject. We reject it because the major premise on which it rests is wholly, totally and utterly false.

It is not true that most people are without access to an inspired Bible today. Moreover, it is grossly incorrect to assert that "No translation is inspired."

What is true, and what may properly be asserted is that *we have no inspired translators today.* This is far—very far indeed—from saying that we are without inspired *translations* today.

The popular notion, "no translation is inspired" results from a mistaken concept of (a) what inspiration *is,* (b) to what inspiration *extends* and (c) how inspiration was *achieved.*

"Inspiration," noun form of the verb "inspire," (*in* + *spirare,* to breathe into), denotes the result of the Spirit's infusion into the words of sacred writ. Thus Paul affirmed, "All scripture is given by inspiration of God. . . ." (2 Timothy 3:16.) Similarly, he wrote to the Corinthians:

240

"Which things also we speak, not in the words which man's wisdom teacheth, but which the Holy Ghost teacheth. . . ." (1 Corinthians 2:13.)

From the foregoing it will appear to the observant reader that the "inbreathing" was *into the text of scripture* rather than into the men who penned the scripture, though they were, of course, under divine guidance in what they wrote, a fact we learn from 1 Peter 1:11,12, and often elsewhere in the Bible. Inspiration thus consisted of the "inbreathing" of truth *into the word* selected to bear the message. Inspiration actually resulted from the injection of truth into the words they were prompted to write. Words, signs of ideas, thus became the vehicles to bear the ideas presented. Why were these words inspired? Because they were the vessels of the revelation of the Spirit, because they reflected exactly the "mind of the Spirit." This they did perfectly since the words were selected by the Spirit for precisely this purpose. They may properly be said to be "inbreathed" (inspired) because they achieved the design of the Spirit in reflecting the Spirit's message. This is *verbal* inspiration.

What difference would it make whether the words embodying the Spirit's message were English, German, French, or some other modern language if, in any given instance, the word expressed as fully and as clearly the idea involved as did the original Greek word, since the inspiration consists in the full embodiment of the idea and not in the nationality of the word?

The following graphic and visual representation of the matter will indicate the principle involved:

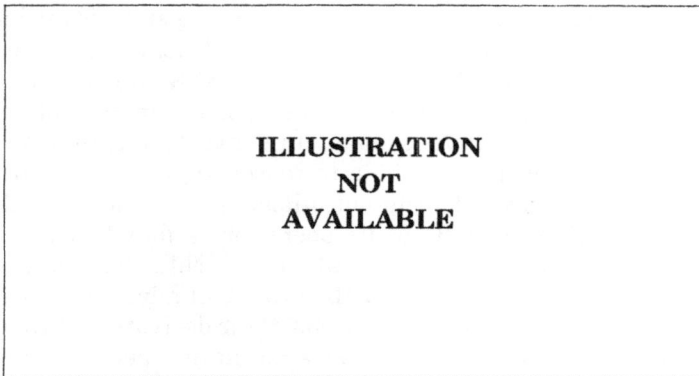

ILLUSTRATION NOT AVAILABLE

If the word, in the second instance, reflects as accurately and as fully the meaning of the Spirit why is not it as much inspired (inbreathed) as the former? It does, indeed; and there should be an end to the loose and thoughtless and obviously incorrect declaration so often heard these days that we are without inspired scriptures today except as they exist in original manuscripts. This conclusion will not bear the test of either reason or revelation. Paul often quoted from the Septuagint (a *translation* of the Old Testament into Greek) and designated it as scripture because the passages cited exactly represented the truth of the original text though a translation of that text. Do those who so freely assert that *no* translation is inspired seriously believe that the Bible which Paul read from, and often quoted, along with Christ and other apostles, was *uninspired*?

The test of any translation is, does it reflect *fully* and accurately the mind of the Spirit as revealed through those chosen by the Lord to make known his will to man? If yes, the words, whatever the language, embody the meaning of the spirit and are as inspired as the original presentation.

We may therefore find much comfort in the fact that the scriptures, taken from a dependable text and accurately translated, are infallible, inerrant, all-sufficient, the full and complete revelation of God to man. It is our view that the American Standard Version of 1901 is in this category and thus for more than a half century it has been exclusively used in our Uniform series of Bible School literature, published by the Gospel Advocate Company. Various modern speech "translations" and *all* paraphrases fall far short of this standard and cannot qualify as *inspired* scripture.

"Do you agree with the view that the 'Received Text' is superior to the Greek text used by the American Standard translators?"

No. Quite the contrary is true, as the following significant incident in the history of the Restoration movement will clearly indicate.

The postulate, that truth is always consistent with itself, is at once accepted by all thoughtful persons, and stands not in need of verification. Moreover, the principle is one of universal application, and by a judicious use thereof, it is possible to reason from the known to the unknown, and to arrive at facts not otherwise susceptible of demonstration. A striking example of its operation is found in Alexander Campbell's debate with the wily Presbyterian, N.L. Rice. In their discussion on the "mode" of baptism, Mr. Campbell advanced the theory that where words denote specific actions, their derivatives through all their various flexions and modifications retain the specific meaning of the root. That is to say, the primary meaning of the root must inhere in the word springing from it, however modified it may chance to become through later inflection. He then pointed out that *baptidzo*, (whence springs the English word, "baptize"), is a derivative of *bapto*, whose radical syllable *bap-* means, "to dip," and that any word ascending from this radical root can never exhibit a contrary meaning. He illustrated the principle thus: "Agriculturists, horticulturists, botanists, will fully comprehend me when I say that in all the dominions of vegetable nature, untouched by human art, as the root so is the stem, and so are all the branches. If the root be oak, the stem cannot be ash nor the branches cedar. What would you think, Mr. President, of the sanity or veracity of a backwoodsman who would affirm that he found in the state of nature a tree whose root was oak, whose stem was cherry, whose boughs were pear and whose leaves were chestnut?"

Declaring that no translator, ancient or modern, would have dared depart from this rule, he asserted that *bapto*, or any descendant of the family of words had never been rendered "to sprinkle" in any translation since the apostolic age. In reply, Mr. Rice advanced Revelation 19:13, which reads in the King James Version, "He was clothed with a vesture dipped in blood." The word "dipped" is, in the Greek, *bebammenon* a derivative of *bapto*. Adverting to the Syriac Version, a translation from Greek into Syriac believed to have been made as early as A.D. 150, and therefore the most ancient of all versions, he pointed out that this passage was therein rendered as to read in English, "He was clothed with a vesture sprinkled with blood." So also do the Vulgate and Ethiopic versions translate the passage. Triumphantly Rice shouted, "Although Mr. Campbell has said and published that no translator, ancient or modern, ever rendered any of this family of words 'to sprinkle,' I have proved that the translators of the venerable Syriac, the old Ethiopic and the Vulgate (all of whom, according to him, were immersionists) did so translate *bapto*." This, it must be confessed, was quite a strong case against Mr. Campbell's theory. But his studies in Philology had so thoroughly convinced him that the radical root *bap-* could mean only "to dip," he refused to surrender his position, and thereupon ventured the conjecture that in the manuscript which the translators of the Syriac, Vulgate and Ethiopic versions followed, a different reading appeared, and that the word "sprinkle" in that manuscript must be *errantismenon*, (whose root is *rant-*, "to sprinkle"), instead of *bebammenon*, (whose root is *bap-*, "to dip.") He insisted that Mr. Rice was logically bound to show that the word rendered "sprinkle" in these versions was a derivative of *bapto*, and not of *raino*, before his objection would be valid. This, of course, Mr. Rice could not do, seeing that there was no known copy of the manuscript in existence from which these versions were made. Mr. Rice made reply: "But he says, 'There must have been a different reading.' Where is the evidence? Is there any one copy of the New Testament in all the searching for the old manuscripts which presents a different reading? There is not one! Why then contend for a different reading? Simply because the claims of immersion demand it." And thus the matter stood at the close of the debate.

Nearly 20 years later Providence, in a most singular manner, verified Mr. Campbell's postulate and vindicated his claims regarding the meaning of the root *bap-*, establishing his contention that a different reading at Revelation 19:13 appeared in the manuscript from which the ancient Syriac, Vulgate and Ethiopic versions were made. On Feb. 4, 1859, in a convent on Mount Sinai, the learned German, Tischendorf, found the Codex Sinaiticus, one of the oldest and most authentic Greek manuscripts in the world, rivaling in accuracy the famous Codex Vaticanus, hitherto believed to be the most important uncial manuscript known. In this ancient document, Revelation 19:13 reads, "clothed with a vesture sprinkled over with blood." The words "sprinkled over" are from *perirerammenon*, a derivative of *raino*, "to sprinkle," and *peri*, signifying "over." Thus, Mr. Campbell's position that there was a different reading at this place was proved to be entirely correct. And what thus far had been only a conjecture on his part drawn from his knowledge of the laws of language, was demonstrated to be the truth, establishing beyond doubt that the translators had not deviated from the rule above given, and that *bapto*, or any of that family of words had never been rendered by the equivalent of "to sprinkle" in any language.

"Please give an exposition of the words, 'But sanctify in your hearts Christ as Lord: being ready always to give answer to every man that asketh you a reason concerning the hope that is in you, yet in meekness and fear.' (1 Peter 3:15.)"

To "sanctify" is to set apart, to hallow, to consecrate. To sanctify "Christ as Lord," is to regard him as worthy of the highest honors, and to assign to him the position of top priority in our hearts i.e., in that area which controls our spiritual life and being. The adversative "but" with which the admonition begins means "nay," "rather;" far from being terrified by the threatenings of wicked men of whom the apostle had earlier warned, Christ is to be enthroned in the heart and the only "fear" to be felt is of displeasing him.

Further, faithful disciples of the Lord are not to be hesitant in asserting the basis of their hope, or the grounds on which their faith rests, even in the face of any threat of persecution or of suffering. To "give answer" is, literally, to make defence; this, Christians are to be ever in readiness to do, whatever the consequences. It would appear from the context that it was the purpose of the apostle to encourage the suffering saints in the face of the "fiery trial" confronting them—not to seek refuge from pain and trial by lapsing into silence regarding their hope and him on whom it rested. (Acts 4:12.) They were to be ready to vindicate the cause they had espoused even as the author (Peter, the apostle) had earlier done. (Acts 4:1-22.)

It is inconceivable that one who has imbibed the blessings of the heavenly calling should be either ashamed or afraid to defend and vindicate it to the fullest extent of one's powers. With what profound sadness must the blessed Lord look upon one who from fear of personal harm or loss of material gain would compromise conviction and seek protection from persecution in silence in the hour of infamy such a course bespeaks.

The defence is to be offered, not defiantly or with threatenings designed to match those of the accusers, but "in meekness" toward those without, in order to allay as much antagonism as possible; and, this is to be done "in fear," lest the defence itself, by being improperly offered, might do harm to the Cause in whose interest it is being presented.

"What is the significance of the word 'sensual' in Jude's statement, 'These are they who make separations, sensual, having not the Spirit'? (Jude 19.)"

The word "sensual" in this passage is translated from the same Greek word as "natural," in 1 Corinthians 2:14: "The natural man receiveth not the things of the Spirit of God; for they are foolishness unto him and he cannot know them, because they are spiritually discerned." The root for the word "sensual" is the same as that translated "soul" in the New Testament—*psyche.*

These people of whom Jude wrote were, therefore, *soulish* characters. The word "soul" is a generic term; it is not possible to assign to it a specific meaning in each instance where it occurs—the context determines this. Here, in contrast with the higher nature of man it denotes that which pertains to a man as a man; and is, hence, the basis of a manner of life inferior and lower than that described as spiritual. The word sometimes refers to people as persons (1 Peter 3:20); sometimes, to the physical life man possesses in common with beasts (Psalm 78:50, Sept.); and occasionally, it is used to mean the same thing as the spirit of man. (Revelation 6:6-9.)

Thus, the soul stands midway between the body and the spirit. He who yields himself to the demands of the flesh becomes a fleshly person; he who by communion of his spirit with God's Spirit—through the teaching he has given— attains to a spiritual level in life. A "natural man," in the concept set out in 1 Corinthians 2:14, is a person who lives on the plane of the soul—a lower nature than that of the spirit—but higher than that of one who wholly yields to fleshly impulses and whose life is largely controlled by the flesh. Man is therefore a triune being— he is possessed of a body, a soul and a spirit. He is capable of living on either of these levels; and the manner of life he exhibits is an index to that which controls his being. Those who are "sensual" are influenced by a wisdom which is from below, rather than that which is from above, evidencing that they "have not the Spirit." Being without the guidance

245

of the Spirit through the word of truth, their lives are sensual, earthly, devilish. (James 3:15.)

"What is the meaning of the statement, 'And no one hath ascended into heaven, but he that descended out of heaven, even the Son of man, who is in heaven'? (John 3:13.)"

The Lord alone could speak of and teach about "the heavenly things," because he alone had been in heaven and had come to earth to reveal them, no man having gone from the earth to heaven to return with this information. He is called "the Son of man," and also the "Son of God," the former because of his birth of the Virgin into a fleshly existence, the latter because of his relationship to God. The words, "the Son of man, who is in heaven," have occasioned no little controversy among biblical expositors generally. Some assume that in view of his eternal nature it might be truly affirmed of him that he was also in heaven while here on earth, being omnipresent; but this we believe to be a begging of the question since it is certainly true that he was on earth, during his incarnation, in a sense he was not in heaven and that from the earth *he ascended to heaven*, indicative of the fact that he was then there in a sense he was not before he ascended. We do not believe that this is the true explanation. Others quickly cut the Gordian knot by denying this phrase a place in the text on the ground that some manuscripts omit it. It is, however, in many others and with sufficient textual evidence to justify its place in the Bible and we thus reject this effort to resolve the problem. We believe a more reasonable explanation and the correct one is that these words, "who is in heaven," are a comment from John (as were those in John 2:25), and that they were therefore penned near the end of the first century and long after the Lord returned to heaven.

"Explain John 15:22, 'If I had not come and spoken unto them, they had not had sin: but now they have no excuse for their sin.' "

The reference is to the unbelieving Jews whom the Lord long and earnestly attempted to teach but whose perversity and hardness of heart had prompted them to close their minds and to exclude from their hearts any semblance of his teaching. Patiently and at great length he tried to teach them that true faith in the Father leads logically to belief in the Son and that if they really loved the Father they would heed his teaching and obey him. Their obduracy he could not overcome and eventually ceased his efforts to turn them from their fatal course. Even now, in the presence of only his disciples, his mind turns again to their fate and to the reasons for it and led him to point out why they were utterly without justification for their unbelief. Those who are blind cannot see; but if the blindness is self-imposed they must bear the responsibility for not seeing though in blindness. If the Lord had not taught his opposers, they would not be guilty of sinning against the light they had never seen; but they had been privileged to walk in the light and this they deliberately refused to do and so their guilt consisted not only in not accepting the truth but also of repudiating it.

Here is clear and unmistakeable evidence of the fact that men are to be judged in proportion to the opportunities they enjoy. The greater the opportunity, the greater the guilt, and the greater the guilt the greater the punishment awaiting them. (Matthew 11:21-28; Hebrews 10:25-28.) Those who obey not the gospel are lost; lost for not obeying it; but, those who have heard it and deliberately rejected it have sinned not only against the truth but also against their own awareness of duty. A knowledge of the truth exhibits the sinfulness of sin (Romans 7:13), and enables one to see its enormity. Thus, one who rejects Christ, as did those Jews, will not only be lost because of sin but also for having deliberately rejected the Saviour. Jesus does not teach that those who have not heard the gospel are wholly without sin of any kind. His statement must be understood in the light of its context. He speaks particularly of their rejection of him; if he had not come into the world and have attempted to teach them they would not have been guilty of rejecting such teaching; inasmuch as he did come and they refused him they were without excuse.

"Our Lord said to Peter, the apostle, 'I will give unto thee the keys of the kingdom of heaven: and whatsoever thou shalt bind on earth shall be bound in heaven; and whatsoever thou shalt loose on earth shall be loosed in heaven.' (Matthew 16:19.) Is there significance in the fact that Christ used the plural form (keys), rather than the singular (key) here? Specifically, is there the suggestion that Peter used one key on the day of Pentecost to open the door to the Jews, and another at the house of Cornelius to admit the Gentiles? (Acts 10:1ff.)"

No. The word "keys," here and often elsewhere in the scriptures, is used figuratively and metaphorically to denote the means of access; to be given a key or keys is to be endowed with authority. It is said that when the Jews elected a man to be a doctor of the law there was placed in his hand keys to the temple library where the writings of the scholars were kept, indicating by this that he was now of that number and thus regarded as qualified to teach and instruct out of the law. The Lord simply suggested, by the use of a metaphor, that he was giving to Peter the power and privilege of announcing the conditions on which one

247

enters the kingdom. It should be noted that this authority was not limited to Peter (compare John 20:22,23), and it was exercised in a secondary sense only, since the final power was vested in the Lord. (Revelation 3:7.)

The assumption that Peter used one key at Pentecost and another at the house of Cornelius in Caesarea is obviously incorrect from the fact that the same terms of entrance into the kingdom were proclaimed in both instances. Peter, in discussing the bringing in of the Gentiles, said: "Ye know that how a good while ago God made choice among us, that the Gentiles by my mouth should hear the word of the gospel, and believe . . . and put no difference between us and them, purifying their hearts by faith." (Acts 15:7,9.)

It should never be forgotten that the "keys" Peter used (terms of entrance into the kingdom) have never been changed or replaced by others; the way into the kingdom is precisely the same today as it was two thousand years ago. (Mark 16:15,16; Acts 2:38; John 3:3-5.) That the Lord chose to give special attention to Peter as the recipient of the keys on this occasion does not mean that he occupied some apostolic office involving greater powers than the other apostles. In his infinite wisdom, the Lord saw in the fisherman disciple the characteristics he desired in the one who would be the first to preach the gospel in the Christian dispensation. That all the other apostles immediately began to engage in the same activity shows that Peter's position in the kingdom was not superior to theirs.

"Explain 1 Peter 5:3."

These words occur in a context in which Peter, the apostle, was discussing the duties and responsibilities of elders (shepherds) to the flock of God—the church.

The elders, of whom Peter was one (1 Peter 5:1), are admonished to feed the flock, exercise oversight thereof, (a duty involving all that is characteristic of the work of shepherds, such as directing, guiding, protecting and nourishing the charge alloted to their care), not by constraint (i.e. not reluctantly or unwillingly), not for "filthy lucre," (not disposed to seek the work simply to secure the material benefits issuing from it, vv. 2,3.) Though the adverb does not occur elsewhere in the Greek text, the adjectival form does in 1 Timothy 3:3,8 and Titus 1:7. This prohibition is interesting in that it evidences the fact that as early as this in the first century there was evidently sufficient wealth under the control of elders there was the temptation to some to use the position for personal and material gain.

Some elders in the church in that distant day devoted all of their time to the work and were accordingly regarded as "worthy of double honor," that is, of financial support, a stipend for special labors. (1 Timothy 5:17.) Human nature being what it is, there is the ever-present possibility that some men may use their religious influence for selfish purposes, examples of which are mentioned by our Lord in Matthew 23:14, and by Paul in 2 Timothy 3:6. In sharp contrast, the apostle noted the warm and enthusiastic readiness characteristic of faithful elders (of whom there are thousands in the church today who seek no favors at all except the approval of their Lord) serving sacrificially because of their dedication to the Cause for which the Saviour died.

The phrase, "neither as being lords of God's heritage," is better rendered "not lording it over the heritages," since there is no word in the Greek text for "God's," and the word *kleeros* (heritage) is plural in the passage. Those who would do the work of elders or bishops are warned not to be guilty of "lording over the heritages." The word "lording" forbids the exercise of authority wrongfully or oppressively. Some cite this statement of the apostle for the purpose of denying to elders any authority over "the heritages," but this is an improper deduction since the design of Peter was not to condemn the proper exercise of authority but its abuse. This passage must be understood in harmony with other affirmations of the scriptures touching such exercise. (1 Timothy 5:17.) Moreover, the words following, "being ensamples to the flock," show that it was the intent of Paul to point out that when elders seek to use their influence in this manner, i.e., by example, this is an effective guard against the abuse of power always possible in such situations.

"Heritages," in this passage, translates a plural noun signifying a "lot" or "portion." The idea is that each separate congregation is the *portion* or *lot* of the total body of Christ assigned to the elders overseeing the "lot" or "portion" committed to their oversight and care. They serve in this capacity subject to his will and under him as "the chief Shepherd," and their responsibilities extend over, but no farther than the "portion" or "lot" (congregation) they serve. (Cf. Acts 20:28; Philippians 1:1.)

Interestingly, all of the three ideas inherent in the proper function of those whom the Holy Spirit designated as directors of the church of the Lord are mentioned by Peter in this context: Elders, of whom the apostle was one (1 Peter 5:1); bishops (from *episcopos*—overseers, v. 2), shepherds (v. 2 cf. v. 4) where the "chief" shepherd (Christ) is put in contrast with the undershepherds, the elders of the church. Elders (presbyters), with respect of age and maturity, shepherds (pastors), feeders and tenders of the flock and bishops (overseers) indicate both the designations and the work required of those who thus serve.

"What is the 'Hermeneutical Principle' about which we are hearing these days?"

The word "hermeneutical" means of, or relating to hermeneutics. Hermeneutics is "the study of the methodological principles of interpretation (as of the Bible)." (*Webster's New Collegiate Dictionary.*) The word derives from the Greek infinitive *hermeneuein* "to interpret." Properly, it is the science of interpretation; but, the phrase is currently used in a frame of reference relating to the silence of the scriptures— specifically, whether it is permissible to do anything religiously which the scriptures do not positively and in so many words forbid, or if the will of God is expressly set out in his word thus allowing neither addition nor subtraction to what he has said.

It will be seen, therefore, that directly involved is the correct attitude one must exhibit toward the Word of God. Shall we regard it as no more than an ancient collection of general principles which we may, with impunity, mould, modify and merge with present-day concepts, or is it a full and complete expression of the will of God which we must accept without addition, without subtraction, without modification? No more vital question may be raised, because on its proper solution our salvation depends.

A simple induction from the scriptures themselves should forevermore settle the matter for those desirous of doing the will of God. Moses warned, "Ye shall not add unto the word which I command you, neither shall ye diminish from it, that ye may keep the commandments of Jehovah your God which I command you." (Deuteronomy 4:2.) Agur, the oracle said, "Add thou not unto his words, lest he reprove thee, and thou be found a liar." (Proverbs 30:6.) And, Paul added, "Every scripture inspired of God is also profitable for teaching, for reproof, for correction, for instruction which is in righteousness: that the man of God may be complete, furnished completely unto every good work." (2 Timothy 3:16,17.) Are these affirmations of inspired writers expressions of the divine will or are they meaningless platitudes we may with impunity reject?

The examples of the Old Testament, written for our admonition (Romans 15:4), are equally impressive. Cain and Abel, sons of Adam and Eve, were instructed to make an offering unto the Lord. (Genesis 4:3-16.) This offering was to be from their flocks. Cain, substituting human wisdom for the divine, and operating on the "hermeneutical principle" that one is at liberty to do in religion anything not specifically forbidden, and noting that Jehovah had nowhere declared that the fruits of his harvest would not be acceptable, chose to act on his own volition in the realm of the silence of the scriptures, with disastrous and ultimately fatal results. In contrast, faithful Abel did exactly as God di-

250

rected and is enshrined in Inspiration's Hall of Fame as one who took God at his word, veering neither to the right nor to the left in his response to it. (Hebrews 11:4.)

The antediluvian world, having plunged to incredible depths of depravity was, by the Lord, regarded as past redemption and he determined to destroy it with a worldwide flood. Noah was told to build an ark; to build it three hundred cubits long, fifty cubits wide and thirty cubits high; to include a window and a door; to pitch it within and without with pitch and to fashion it with first, second and third stories. (Genesis 6:13-16.) These instructions were detailed, specific and exact. Noah so regarded them, for of him the scriptures testify: "Thus did Noah; according to all that God commanded him, so did he." (Genesis 6:22.) That worthy patriarch did not dare deviate from the pattern given, and he ever lives as an example of the manner of life required to secure the heavenly favor.

Nadab and Abihu, sons of Aaron and priests of God, and obligated to offer sacrifices the Lord had designated and in the manner he had specified, "took each of them his censer, and put fire therein, and laid incense thereon, and offered strange fire before Jehovah, which he had not commanded them. And there came forth fire from before Jehovah, and devoured them, and they died before Jehovah." (Leviticus 10:1,2.) Here is an excellent example of the consequences of operating in the realm of the silence of the scriptures. True, the Lord had specified what fire to use—that which he had sent down from heaven—but he did not append thereto any list of types of fire not to be used! It is quite possible that these sons of Aaron reasoned as follows: "Our intentions are good and our motives are pure. The purpose of the fire is to consume and sacrifice; what difference does it make what kind of fire it is?" Their resort to the application of "sanctified common sense," and the "consensus of the wise" did not deliver them from the wrath of God their disobedience generated. Jehovah, in righteous judgment upon them, sent down fire from heaven which devoured them as a warning to all others disposed to ignore the divine principle of authority whether affirmatively, or in the area proscribed by the silence of the scriptures.

Those who seek to justify the use of mechanical instruments of music in Christian worship on the ground that the New Testament does not specifically prohibit them should ponder well these and numerous other Old Testament instances of those who presumed to speak and to act where the Lord has not spoken. No, the New Testament does not, in so many words, forbid the playing of a mechanical instrument in worship, but neither does it specifically forbid the counting of beads, the burning of candles and dancing in such devotions. But as Cain, Nadab and Abihu and countless others have painfully discovered, the command to perform an act by the Lord prohibits the performance of all other acts

251

as substitutes or additions. The command to sing (Ephesians 5:18,19; Colossians 3:16), is both authoritative and restrictive; authoritative in that it is an expression of the divine will in this form of praise in worship; restrictive in that it limits such activity to his expressed command.

God led Israel through the trackless wastes of the wilderness "in a pillar of cloud" by day, and a "pillar of fire" by night. The people were privileged to move, either night or day, only as God directed them. (Exodus 13:21,22.) Any resort to a euphemistic scheme—such as is being done today with the phrase "the hermeneutical principle" to justify actions not in the realm of divine authorization—would have been disastrous. The grand slogan of the Restoration, "Where the Bible speaks, we speak; where the Bible is silent, we are silent" is more than a catchy phrase, it is an apt expression of the basic principle couched in the solemn warning of the beloved apostle, "Whosoever goeth onward, and abideth not in the teaching of Christ, hath not God: he that abideth in the teaching, the same hath both the Father and the Son." (2 John 9,10.)

"Please give a simple grammatical analysis of Matthew 19:9, which reads: 'And I say unto you, Whosoever shall put away his wife, except it be for fornication, and shall marry another, committeth adultery: and whoso marrieth her which is put away doth commit adultery.' "

"Whosoever shall put away his wife except it be for fornication, and shall marry another," is the complex subject of the predicate, "committeth adultery." The subject, "whosoever shall put away his wife," is a partial, compound sentence; its simple subject is "whosoever," and its complex predicate is "shall put away his wife and shall marry another." The predicate of this clause is composed of two simple verbs, "shall put," and "shall marry." "Shall put," is modified by the adverb "away;" "his wife," is the direct object of the verb, and "except it be for fornication," is a casual, adverbial element. This sentence is a subordinate element in which "it" is the subject, and "be for fornication," the predicate. "For fornication," modifier of "shall put away," and "shall marry another," is a causal, adverbial element. "Shall marry," has, as its object, the word "another."

We have seen that the verb, "committeth adultery," is the simple predicate of "whosoever shall put away his wife except it be for fornication, and shall marry another." In the phrase, "committeth adultery," "adultery" is the object of the verb "committeth;" "whoso marrieth her which is put away doth commit adultery," is a complex sentence. This portion is a complex element joined to the principal clause by the

252

coordinating conjunction, "and." The complex subject is "Whoso marrieth her which is put away," of which the simple subject is "whoso." "Marrieth," is the predicate, modified by "her," a simple objective element. "Her" is modified by the clause, "which is put away," and the verb "doth commit," has as its object, "adultery."

It will be seen that two persons, capable of committing adultery, are involved in this passage. (1) "Whosoever shall put away his wife and shall marry another [except for fornication]" and (2) "whoso marrieth her which is put away [except for fornication]" Whether the "whosoever" of this passage commits adultery (enters into an adulterous relationship) depends on two circumstances: Is he the innocent party in the break-up of his marriage, and did he "put away the other party" for "fornication?" In the absence of these conditions, the divine alternative is clear: "Let [him] her" (a) "be reconciled," or (b) "remain unmarried." (1 Corinthians 7:11.) He who marries "another," [except it be fornication] not only is guilty of adultery, he also causes the one whom he marries to become equally guilty by entering into a union not divinely sanctioned. We have seen that the verbs "shall put," and "shall marry," are governed by the conditional clause, "except it be for fornication," and are joined by the coordinating conjunction, "and." One may not with impunity separate them, nor absolve the sin resulting from disregard of the prohibition involved.

The application is obvious: A marries B. B becomes unfaithful to the marriage vow by committing fornication. A divorces B "for fornication," and marries "another," C, an unmarried person. Neither A nor C is guilty of adultery.

D and E contract a scriptural marriage. D, on some legal pretext, not including "fornication," divorces E. Neither D nor E, in such a case, may scripturally remarry. Should either contract a second marriage, while the other remains single, the resulting union is an adulterous one. It should not be overlooked that the verbs "shall put," and "shall marry," are joined with their subject, "whosoever." He who marries the one not "put away" "for fornication," is guilty of adultery. Moreover, "Whoso marrieth her which is put away doth commit adultery." Not if "whoso" marry just any one, but the "one" specified in the text, "Her which is put away," in a case not "for fornication." (But see the answer to the next question.)

"A is scripturally married to B. B unscripturally divorces A and marries C. A, the innocent party, free because of the fornication of B to remarry, does not choose to do so. B eventually comes to realize the sinfulness of his relationship with C, and in genuine repentance, terminates his adulterous union with C. A

still loves B. A is convinced of B's penitence, and both A and B wish to remarry and reestablish the union originally approved by the Lord. May they scripturally do so?"

No, some are saying. I can only respond that, in my view, they are wrong—grievously wrong—at this point and that, on the contrary, such a union, which restores the original divinely approved relationship, is exactly what the Lord desires. A negative response to the foregoing question springs from over reaction—the laudable effort to deny to an adulterer a union disapproved of God, (a proper denial), is extended to the denial of a union God approves (an improper denial.) The extension is unwarranted. Those who so do, draw two erroneous conclusions. (1) They assume that the person who "puts away" his wife in Matthew 19:9 is included in the "Whoso" of the final clause; hence (2) to return to her and to the union God originally ordained is to thrust both parties—the one guilty of fornication and the innocent of the original arrangement—into an adulterous marriage!

The conclusion is not in the premises, and the argument is unsound for many reasons. He who puts away his wife and marries "another," is not by these words forbidden to return to his former companion, because the word "another" (*alleen*, another of a different kind) does not include the first wife. The English definition of "another" is, "different or distinct from the first considered." (*Webster's Collegiate Dictionary*.) It follows, therefore, that the "whosoever" of the first clause is not in the "whoso" of the final one, since this "he" is already married to "another." The prohibition in the words, "and whoso marrieth her which is put away doth commit adultery," is there because any marriage, not broken because of fornication to "another" (not the same one), is prohibited. Therefore, to extend this prohibition to embrace one not included in "another" is unwarranted.

There are numerous reasons why the position herein reviewed is wrong. (1) It strikes at the doctrine of restitution so often, and with such great emphasis, taught in the sacred writings. (2) Again and again the prophets picture apostate Israel as Jehovah's adulterous wife, consorting with her heathen lovers, and for which he "put her away." "And I saw, when for all the causes whereby backsliding Israel committed adultery I had put her away, and given her a bill of divorce . . .," (Jeremiah 3:8.) If the "argument" under examination has any significance by way of analogy, Israel once put away, could never return to God; yet, in this same context (Jeremiah 3:22), he said, "Return, ye backsliding children, and I will heal your backslidings." True to his word, he received her back with open arms when she repented of her adulteries. (See, also, Exodus 34:15; Deuteronomy 31:16; Judges 2:17; Ezekiel 16:17.)

(3) Hosea's marriage to Gomer, "a wife of whoredom" is used by the Holy Spirit to symbolize the desire of God to take back adulterous Israel. It cannot be certainly known whether the narrative is figurative or literal; Adam Clarke may be right: "Under the figure of a wife proving false to her marriage vows, and bearing children that would follow her example, the prophet represents the shameful idolatry of the ten tribes, which provoked God to cast them off." If literal, it cannot be proved from the text that Gomer was wicked when Hosea first married her. She was a "wife of whoredoms" because of her ancestry.

(4) The relationship of Christ to the church is that of a wife to her husband. (Ephesians 5:23-33.) Christians are said to be espoused unto one husband— Christ. (2 Corinthians 11:2; Revelation 21:10.)

The analogy is obvious; the application is clear. If the view herein reviewed has merit, Israel in apostasy, God's unfaithful wife, could never return to him; an apostate church could never be restored, an unfaithful follower, "put away" because of sin, is forevermore excluded from God's house. But, Jehovah did take back his penitent people; a church may repent and turn to God; the fallen may be restored and be a part of the bride of Christ. In the case supposed, A, on the basis of B's penitence and reformation of life may properly take B back into a marriage relationship approved of God. Deuteronomy 24:1-4 is not pertinent to this problem. Its edicts, as a part of special legislation by Moses, enacted in a period of great moral laxity, designed for the preservation of the marriage state, and for the protection of wives, was expressly annulled by the Lord in Matthew 19:1-9. That legislation of Moses forbade remarriage of the original parties even after the second husband had died! Romans 7:1,2 clearly teaches that in this, the Christian age, death terminates any marriage relationship.

"Josephus, the Jewish historian of the first century, has a brief reference to Jesus in his famous work, *Jewish Antiquities*. Some writers have questioned the genuineness and authenticity of this comment. What is the statement, and how dependable is it?"

Whiston's translation of the statement in question from Josephus follows:

> Now there was about this time Jesus, a wise man, if it be lawful to call him a man; for he was a doer of wonderful works, a teacher of such men as receive the truth with pleasure. He drew over to him both many of the Jews and many of the Gentiles. He was (the) Christ. And when Pilate, at the suggestion of the principal men amongst us, had condemned him to the cross, those that loved him at the first did not forsake him; for he appeared to them alive the third day; as

the divine prophets had foretold these and ten thousand other wonderful things concerning him. And the tribe of Christians, so named from him, are not extinct at this day. (*Jewish Antiquities*, Book 18, chapter 3, section 3.)

Opinions regarding the reliability of this remarkable passage have varied greatly, depending on the viewpoint of the writer about Jesus. Believers in his deity have seldom questioned it; unbelievers, in general, have repudiated it. Sifting through the great amount of material produced by writers on the subject reveals that views regarding it may be summed up under three heads: (1) The passage is spurious; it was not penned by Josephus; it is an interpolation added long after the original work was published. (2) Portions of the statement are genuine; other parts are spurious and interpolated. (3) The passage is genuine and authentic and may properly be accepted as unbiased testimony from a contemporary who was not a believer, and therefore all the more weighty for this fact.

Those holding the first view attempt to support it by pointing out that Josephus' reference to Jesus is not cited by any writer either in or out of the church in the first 200 years of Christianity; it is out of character for an unbelieving Jew to refer to Christ in such fashion; and the style of writing is not that generally followed by the famed writer.

It will be observed that these objections are all of a subjective nature, and they arise from preconceived notions regarding the person of Jesus. They are little more than afterthoughts dredged up to support a stance of unbelief in lieu of any reasonable and proper investigation of his identity. An argument from silence is proper and conclusive when determining the will of others; but the absence of an item in a series of events may be due to many factors none of which proves it did not exist. Baptism, as a condition precedent to salvation is obligatory only because it is specifically commanded; that it is *not* specifically said in the sacred writings that our Lord was six feet tall does not prove that he was *not*!

Justin Martyr, for example, did not cite the witness of Josephus to Christ, either because he had no copy of the work or, what is more probable, preferred to rely on Old Testament prophets to support the Lord's deity rather than an unbelieving Jew! Would a Christian writer of this century be faulted from failure to cite Ingersoll in some of his favorable references to Christ in writing in support of the divine origin of Christianity?

Equally weak is the allegation of inconsistency in a favorable reference to Christ by an unbelieving Jew. On this ground, the testimony of Nicodemus and Gamaliel—both unbelievers—would be rejected! Objections based on style are equally invalid; indeed, it can easily be shown that the passage in question reflects in arrangement and phraseology precisely that characteristic of the author in question. One example will suffice: Josephus, in the statement under study, mentions "ten thousand other wonderful things" said regarding Jesus, a hyperbole for a great number. This usage occurs in 14 other undisputed places in his writings! The allegation that reference to Jesus is partly true, partly false, is open to all the foregoing objections as to that thought to be false, and impeaches the veracity of the author regarding that believed to be true! Such a view collapses from its own weight.

We have seen that objections to the passage in Josephus are conjectural, unsupported by evidence whatsoever. But, what may be said in defense of it? Every manuscript and every version of Josephus' works known to man include this affirmation regarding Jesus. There is no fact in history more reliably supported by documentary evidence. If the inclusion of this famous passage in every manuscript, in every version, in every language and in every copy ever printed does not settle the question of genuineness, then all history may be mythical and we can be sure of nothing we do not discern through our senses. It is not without great significance that, for the most part, those who reject the authenticity of this passage, repudiate the biographical details regarding Jesus in the books of the gospel—Matthew, Mark, Luke and John.

"What is the significance of the phrase, 'in no wise,' often occurring in the New Testament?"

It translates the intensive double negative *ou mee*, usually joined with the conjunctive aorist but also occasionally with the conjunctive present and the indicative future. For examples see Matthew 5:18; Mark 14:31 and Luke 10:19. It declares that something shall not occur in the strongest possible fashion. A few instances, selected at random from the New Testament, will indicate the forcefulness of this common Greek particle, as well as to show us what great assurance we have in the promises of God.

(1) "He that cometh to me I will in no wise cast out." (John 6:37.) The meaning is, "he who comes to me I shall not, under any circumstances, cast him out." It is the rhetorical device *litotes*—where an affirmation is expressed by the negative of the opposite or contrary. There is no more emphatic way of asserting the negation. To come to the Lord in his appointed way, only to be rejected, is impossible and inconceivable. No, never shall one who so does be "cast out."

(2) "For I will be merciful to their iniquities, and their sins will I remember no more," literally, "in no wise again ever." (Hebrews 8:12.) It is the positive promise of Deity that sins forgiven in this, the Christian age, can never be again brought up against us. (cf. Isaiah 54:17; Romans 8:33.) That which the blood of bulls and goats could not do—

purge the worshiper of the guilt of sin permanently—Christ could and did do in his death on the cross, and we are thus assured that no charge can thenceforth be sustained against the elect of God.

(3) "There shall in no wise enter into it anything unclean, or he that maketh an abomination and a lie: but only they that are written in the Lamb's book of life." (Revelation 21:27.) Just as it is inconceivable that those who have been delivered from the power of sin and death by the sacrifice of the Saviour, and who serve him faithfully, should ever be shut out, it is equally impossible that the unwashed shall have entrance there when the gates of the city open for the redeemed at the last day. How very precious then, is this little Greek phrase, and how thankful we should be that its assurances are ours.

"Who are the 'spiritual hosts of wickedness' referred to in Ephesians 6:12, and what are the 'heavenly places' mentioned in the passage?"

The context in which these phrases appear reads: "Finally, be strong in the Lord, and in the strength of his might. Put on the whole armor of God, that ye may be able to stand against the wiles of the devil. For our wrestling is not against flesh and blood, but against the principalities, against the powers, against the world-rulers of this darkness, against the spiritual hosts of wickedness in the heavenly places." The figure with which the apostle began this discussion was of military conflict; for the moment, that metaphor is dropped and another figure, that of wrestling is used, perhaps to indicate the personal battle a Christian must wage against evil forces in addition to the team effort also involved.

Opponents in the struggle are not "flesh and blood," i.e., human beings, but principalities, powers, world-rulers of this darkness and the spiritual hosts of wickedness. The first of these terms denotes rulers, possibly evil angels; powers, another order of wicked spirits, and world-rulers still another. These are called "world-rulers" because of the extent of their evil influence. The sphere of their influence is darkness; they thrive only where the light of truth does not shine. Their rule is in the world of darkness, not literal darkness, or course, but the shadowy world of evil, wickedness, rebellion and depravity.

"Heavenly places" are the spheres where these corrupt and wicked spirits exist. It should be observed that in our Bibles the word for "places" is in italics, signifying that there is no corresponding word for it in the Greek Text. A better rendering of the text would be simply, "in the heavenlies." It designates exalted places, without necessarily indicating the character of them. These wicked spirits occupy an exalted position in their spheres of activity, and Christians are thus faced with formidable foes. These evil spiritual beings live and move in the realms of darkness, and are intangible, invisible and deadly. They are, however, powerless to defeat us if we put on the whole armor of God. That armor is described in Ephesians 6:13-18.

"Are biblical miracles fact or fiction?"

David Hume, born in Edinburgh, Scotland, in 1711, is, without doubt, the progenitor and parent of current agnosticism. Unbelief was, with him, a way of life; by the time he was 16 years old, he was freely expressing his skeptical views regarding the existence of God and all related religious matters.

He insisted that "the doctrine of an Absolute First Cause is unwarrantable in philosophy," and he vigorously rejected the assumption that the law of cause and effect is a proper and valid one.

His career in unbelief was launched when half in jest, and in a move to embarrass and confuse a Catholic priest who had related to him that a miracle had been wrought, asserted that a miraculous occurrence, in the nature of the case, is contrary to the experience and observation of most men, and cannot therefore be acknowledged as true, despite any evidence to the contrary.

On further reflection, he came to believe that there was indeed validity in his thesis first advanced in levity; he then refined and expanded it, and presented it in the following proposition:

For miracles we have the testimony of a few persons; against them we have universal experience; therefore, this stronger testimony nullifies the weaker and more questionable.

Hume, by this "argument," was quickly elevated to prominence in the world of unbelief and soon became the "high priest" of skepticism. Strauss, the German agnostic, became so enamored with Hume's proposition, in his work on miracles he declared that the "argument" devastated the doctrine of God and forevermore settled the question.

The Scotch skeptic's effort, despite the enthusiastic claims of his admirers and fellow unbelievers, is sophistical, false and easily refuted. It rests on the premise that since many people of the world never witnessed a miracle, the "non-experience" of this segment of humanity—called improperly "universal experience,"—is more weighty and dependable than the testimony "of the few" who claim to have seen miracles.

Two obvious fallacies appear on the surface of this effort. (1) The "experience" of many people, when that number is one or more less than *all* people does not reflect the "universal experience" of mankind; the observation of any number, however great, who have not been involved in an experience does not thereby prove that others have not been participants in such an experience. If the state charges that A, with malice aforethought, shot B with a gun, and B, in consequence of A's felonious act, dies, one million people could conceivably be summoned to appear in the trial of the case and say they did not see A shoot B; but, if C, a credible and competent witness, testifies that he saw A shoot B, the validity of the state's case against A is abundantly established. Whether a crime has occurred is determined, not by those who did not see it, but by those who did!

(2) Hume's "argument," seen in simplest fashion, is that an alleged event which most people did not see occur, therefore did not occur, and could never have occurred!

What did these skeptics mean by the phrase, "universal experience?" They define it as "the uniform and undeviating experience of all mankind in all ages of the world." With this definition Bible believers will not quarrel. But, a number of questions immediately arise. Who collected, and by what means, evidence of this alleged uniformity of belief in every place, in every age, and from every person involved? What were the qualifications of the person or persons conducting such a survey? Who has been the custodian of this information collected from every person, in every place in every age of the world? Could these unbelievers or their modern counterparts vouch for the credibility of all those involved in the survey? Were there neglect or failure in this effort in any age, in any place, involving any person, any conclusion resting on the premise advanced becomes invalid. Were there any person, in any place, in any age they did not interview, he may have had knowledge of a miracle and their proposition fails.

(3) Moreover, the experience of human beings have differed and do differ greatly, and in many areas of observation uniformity is not possible. Common to the temperate and arctic zones is snow—along the equator countless numbers of people have never seen the fluffy whiteness, and would regard any description of such as fanciful and false. If to this the objection is offered that these people live where snow never falls, so it is, and so also is it the case that many people have lived in areas where miracles have never occurred. And, as it is not the "universal experience" of man that snow never falls, though millions never saw it, so it is that the experience of people, however numerous, who never witnessed a miracle is not the universal experience of mankind, and is, therefore wholly irrelevant in determining what may have occurred elsewhere. The proof of miracles is to be sought and found among the peoples and in the places where they occurred—not where they were unknown. Remarkable reasoning it is that would attempt to rule out as evidence the testimony of the only people competent to testify, and to substitute those who freely confess to ignorance of the matter in issue.

260

It is of no little significance, and strongly corroborative of the scriptures which testify of the miracles of the first century, that both believers and unbelievers admitted to the fact of miraculous events in our Lord's ministry, though the latter class refused to accept the conclusions logically following from such premises. See, especially, John 11:42,47; Acts 4:1-30.

Finally, it should not be overlooked that the events both believers and unbelievers witnessed were a part of "the universal experience" of man and that they are the only qualified, credible and competent witnesses to testify in any proceeding the design of which is to determine the reliability of the miraculous element of the scriptures. The beginning of our Lord's miracles was at Cana in Galilee, in consequence of which "his disciples believed on him." (John 2:1-11.) These events were not rare and unusual in his ministry; they occurred often and in the presence of many people.

> Many other signs therefore did Jesus in the presence of the
> disciples, which are not written in this book: but these are
> written that ye may believe that Jesus is the Christ, the Son
> of God; and that believing ye may have life in his name.
> (John 20:30,31.)

Nicodemus, who came to Jesus by night, expressed the sentiment of reasonable and thoughtful people when he said, "Rabbi, we know that thou art a teacher come from God; for no one can do these signs that thou doest, except God be with him." (John 3:2.)

"Do the scriptures teach that the wicked are to experience endless suffering in hell?"

They do, indeed, and in the most direct and unmistakable fashion. An induction from a few passages—and the number might be greatly extended— leads the honest reader irresistably to this conclusion.

"For it is profitable for thee that one of thy members should perish, and not that thy whole body should be cast into hell." (Matthew 5:29.)

"Ye serpents, ye generation of vipers, how can ye escape the damnation of hell?" (Matthew 23:33.)

"These shall go away into everlasting punishment." (Matthew 25:46.)

"Fear him, which after he hath killed, hath power to cast into hell." (Luke 12:5.)

In other passages that fearful place is described as one of "outer darkness," of "weeping, wailing and gnashing of teeth," and "where the worm dieth not." (Matthew 8:12; Mark 9:44.)

It should be observed that these are the words of our loving Lord, and they were designed to describe in clearest detail, and in the most

261

vivid fashion, the ultimate destiny of the finally disobedient through endless ages.

If the Bible is a credible document—and of course it is—conscious suffering is to be the lot of the wicked in the world to come. The punishment the Righteous Judge will administer at that last great day is pain inflicted because of sin; it is inseparably associated with disobedience, and it is the action of the divine government for the violation of its laws. Some seek to soften the impact of the penalty by advancing the notion that the punishment threatened will be limited to remorse of conscience, unhappy memories of neglected opportunities, hopelessness and despair. These are doubtless to be some of the *consequences* of eternal punishment, but not the *penalty*. One convicted of murder does not, by deep remorse from his horrible crime, thereby cancel the penalty which has fallen upon him because of his felonious act. He must still expiate his crime. (Romans 6:23.)

Many men and women today languish in lonely cells deeply regretful of their unsocial behavior and who would give the world to go back in time and cancel the act or acts which brought them to their present painful state. But bitter regrets alone will not discharge the debt they owe.

A well-known warden of famous Sing-sing prison many years ago wrote of walking slowly down the corridors of that formidable fortress at the midnight hour and of hearing the sobbing of distraught men separated from their loved ones and friends in the free world, some of whom would never enter it again. "Death," the "wages of sin," particularly mentioned by the apostle, is not physical, but spiritual; it is not annihilation, as some allege, but eternal separation from God and all that is good. The death is forever, because the separation it entails is eternal; and its duration is marked out, in the sacred writings, by the same adjective which designates the duration of heaven's occupancy by the righteous. "These shall go away into everlasting (*aioonion*) punishment but the righteous into life eternal" (*aioonion*). (Matthew 25:46.) Our heavenly Father is described as "the everlasting God." (Romans 16:26.) Hell will be the habitation of the wicked so long as God himself exists.

Those who would palliate the punishment or seek to shorten its duration by pointing to the love, long-suffering and patience of God, ignore other attributes of deity, and disregard the fact that his goodness is evidenced just as much in his characteristics of justice and truth as in his love and long-suffering. As a matter of fact, love and long-suffering are valid only when the principles of justice and truth are also operative in the divine government. To promise punishment and then to unilaterally cancel it is impossible to One who is not only the God of love but also the God of truth! He will not do so because he

262

cannot do so, and maintain his character. God cannot impeach his own veracity, since "it is impossible for God to lie." (Hebrews 6:18.) Were he to cease to be just and truthful, he would cease to be good. The effort to emphasize some of the attributes of the great Jehovah to the neglect of others, or to array some against others, is to compromise the divine character.

He who holds the destiny of us all in his hand is a God of love (1 John 4:8), but he is also a God of wrath because of his aversion to sin—the transgression of his law—the penalty of which is conscious suffering in hell fire for ever and ever. The penalty is grounded in his goodness, his sense of justice and right; his law requires it, and the wicked deserve it! "Seeing it is a righteous thing with God to recompense tribulation to them that trouble you; and to you who are troubled rest with us, when the Lord Jesus shall be revealed from heaven with his mighty angels, in flaming fire taking vengeance on them that know not God, and that obey not the gospel of our Lord Jesus Christ: who shall be punished with everlasting destruction from the presence of the Lord, and from the glory of his power when he shall come to be glorified in his saints . . ." (2 Thessalonians 1:6-10.)

"How may the apparent difficulty involving dates given by Moses and Stephen regarding the age of Abraham when that patriarch left Haran for the land of Canaan be resolved?"

The "difficulty" alluded to is this: In Genesis 12:4 it is said that Abraham was 75 years old when he left Haran to go to Canaan; it is said in Genesis 11:32 that Terah died at the age of 205. Stephen, in Acts 7:4, asserts that Abraham did not leave Haran until after his father Terah's death; it is alleged that Genesis 11:26 asserts that Abraham was born when his father was 70. Hence, 70 (age of Terah when Abraham was born) plus 75 (age of Abraham when he left Haran) equals 145. Terah was 205 when he died. 145 subtracted from 205 leaves 60, the number of years Terah is alleged to have lived after Abraham left Haran, in which case he did not die in Haran, as Stephen claimed in Acts 7:4.

The "difficulty" is an imaginary one, and is based on a misapprehension of one of the statements made regarding Terah and his age on the occasion of the birth of his sons Abraham, Nahor and Haran. Genesis 11:26 reads, "Terah lived seventy years and begat Abraham, Nahor and Haran." Those who affect to see a difficulty in these matters assume that the statement designates the age of Terah at the birth of Abraham; but, it should be noted that two other sons are mentioned in the text and the conclusion that it was the design of the sacred writer to designate the age of Abraham—in contradistinction to the others mentioned—is an unwarranted one.

It was the purpose of the writer to list the sons of Terah and to indicate the age when the first one was born. Unless the three sons were born at the same time, the passage mentioned does not necessarily indicate the age of Terah when Abraham was born. It is clear that Abraham and Nahor were considerably younger than Haran from the fact that Nahor's wife was Haran's daughter. Haran was the first of the three sons to die which supports further the view that he was the oldest son of Terah. Usually, the oldest child is mentioned first in such lists, but in this case, since Abraham was, by far, the most prominent of the three, his name is placed first in the list. Haran was thus the oldest of the three sons, and the text was designed to indicate the age of Terah at the birth of his first son, Haran—not Abraham.

An interesting parallel is seen in the allusion of the same Old Testament writer to the age of Noah in Genesis 5:32: "Noah lived five hundred years: and Noah begat Shem, Ham and Japheth." It is easily seen by a glance at the ages of Noah and Shem that Noah was 502 years old when Shem was born. (Genesis 3:13; 11:10.) It seems clear therefore that it was the intent of Moses, who recorded these events, simply to designate the age of Terah on the occasion of the birth of his first son—Haran. Stephen's account is thus a correct one and here, as always, a reasonable approach to the study of the scriptures fully vindicates the biblical accounts. The "difficulty" alleged is not Stephen's but that of those whose methods of interpretation are defective.

"A religious group, the self-styled 'Jehovah's Witnesses,' teach that the Lord is a created being and that he was the first creature of the series in God's creation. They attempt to prove this by citing statements in Colossians 1:15-18 and Revelation 3:14 where Christ is called "the firstborn of all creation," "the beginning," "the firstborn from the dead," and "the beginning of the creation of God." What is the meaning of these statements?"

So clearly taught throughout the sacred writings is the deity of our Lord that any deduction from a passage or series of passages which denies this is positively and palpably false. "In the beginning was the Word, and the Word was with God, and the Word was God. The same was in the beginning with God. All things were made through him; and without him was not anything made that hath been made." (John 1:1-3.) He was with the Father when the creative process began. It follows, therefore, that since he was there when the beginning began, he did not begin with the beginning, thus antedating it, and his eternal nature is shown. He was, indeed, himself the creator of all things, rather than being himself created: "All things were made through him ('by him,' KJV); and without him was not anything made that hath been made." (John 1:3.) "He made the worlds," (Hebrews 1:2), He was "before all things," and in him "were all things created." (Colossians 1:16,17.) He is God, i.e., possessed of the divine nature (John 1:1), and it is inconceivable that deity (God) could be created.

Our Lord is "the beginning," not because he began, but because he caused all else of creation to begin! The article does not appear before "beginning" in the Greek text, and the word is a proper noun, designating Christ as Beginning, i.e., the Originator of all things. He is called "Beginning" simply because he began all things! It is a gross misapprehension of this passage to offer it in support of the theory that Christ is a created being.

He is the "firstborn of all creation," because he ranks above all creation—a position he would not hold were he merely a created being. The term is one of primogeniture, indicating the position of the first-born of the family as to rights and privileges enjoyed. In early Jewish literature, God, the Father, is called the first born of the world, by which, of course, it is not meant that the Father is a created being and came into existence at a certain time and place. Our Lord is the "first-born from (literally, out of) the dead," because he stands first in the position of those who have returned from the dead. This does not mean that he was the first one to rise from the dead; Lazarus antedated him in this act, but it does signify that of those who were raised, he was and is preeminent. He is above all others in this respect that he rose from the dead to die no more. Those terms used in reference to Christ, and considered in the question, were designed to indicate priority in time, and supremacy in position of our Lord over all creation.

"Is not the active participation of 'Christian' women in the business world today in violation of the scriptures regarding her proper place and work?"

Because Eve, the first woman, was deceived in the transgression, a woman is forbidden by the Lord to participate in some religious activities in the church. She is prohibited from being an elder (1 Timothy 3:2) and she is forbidden to usurp authority or to teach over men (1 Timothy 2:11,12.) But, to conclude from this that her role in life is limited to bearing children and to keeping house is unwarranted and certainly not in the premises of the passages cited.

The current feminist movement has triggered reaction because of its insistence of unrestrained activity, and has prompted some to assume that a woman's place in God's plan is largely one of drudgery and toil at home. This is a gross misapprehension and has led to justified resentment by many women toward those who so insist. It is quite true that women in the nomadic society which largely characterized the Old Testament period were, in the nature of the case, with limited occupational and economic privileges, but it is far from correct to say that even in that day the woman was not privileged to participate in any activities out of the house, as the instance of the "worthy woman" of Proverbs 31 clearly reveals; and in the New Testament there is ample evidence that Christian women did thus freely engage. Lydia, "a seller of purple," travelled far from her home on business trips and there is certainly no indication that she was required to terminate this activity when she obeyed the gospel. (Acts 16:14,15.)

Proverbs 31 is a vivid description of a woman's life in that distant day, both as to home and family relationships and also as to the world at large. The text clearly evidences the fact that she enjoyed freedom and responsibility in the business world (v. 13); her advice and counsel were received with respect and appreciation (v. 26); she had occasion to, and often did, make many business decisions affecting both her and her family (vv. 13,16,18,24); and her life was a busy one, including management of her own affairs and those of her employees (v. 15.) She enjoyed the esteem and love of her family, and the respect and admiration of the business community in which she moved (v. 31.) She was reliant, self-assured, confident and fully capable of meeting all the challenges of the day; she performed her duties with skill, wisdom and effectiveness. She thus had both a family and a career, and she managed both with precision and personal fulfillment. It is no wonder she was called a "worthy woman."

"If Jesus is the Son of God, why is he called 'Everlasting Father' in Isaiah 9:6?"

The prophet Isaiah, in one of his most famous passages regarding Messiah, wrote: "For unto us a child is born, unto us a son is given; and the government shall be upon his shoulder: and his name shall be called Wonderful, Counsellor, Mighty God, Everlasting Father, Prince of Peace." The Hebrew words translated "Everlasting Father" are literally "father of eternity." In Hebrew usage, the father is the originator; hence, the phrase, "father of eternity," applied to Christ, means that he is the author or the creator of all of that is embraced in eternity—timelessness in each direction! This does not mean that eternity had a beginning, or that it will ultimately end; it does evidence the fact that Christ is the originator of all that is in eternity's span. By him were all things made, so John affirmed (John 1:2,3), and in him all things consist, i.e., adhere. Moreover, he upholds all things by the word of his power (Hebrews 1:3) and directs the worlds from his throne in the skies.

266

The second Person of the godhead—not the first—was the actual creator of the world. (John 1:1,2).

"We learn from the book of Genesis that Adam, the first man, lived for 930 years, and his wife, Eve, must also have lived for centuries since it is affirmed that to Adam was born 'sons and daughters,' and there is no record that he married more than once. How do we account for such great life spans? Is it possible that a different method of computing time was used in those early days?"

Some have thought so, and the "explanations" have been quite ingenious. For example, it has been proposed that a year in the primal span of man's existence on earth was no more than a month, and that the ages given, when divided by 12, would be more realistic and in keeping with the actual length of the lives of the first patriarchs. This theory collapses from its own weight when it is seen that this would require some of those worthy characters to be begetting children when no more than five normal years old! Others have thought that perhaps the earth's orbit around the sun was more rapid than now and since a year is determined by the length of time the earth takes to travel this distance, the year was shorter. Of this there is no evidence whatsoever; such theories are imaginary and provide no solid grounds for such a conclusion. There is no reason to suppose that there has been any substantial change in the earth's operations, and therefore the people of the early ages did indeed live for hundreds of years.

Their environment was ideal, the bodies they occupied were largely free of disease, the food they ate was wholesome and uncontaminated, and the debilitating effects of sin had not wrought its fearful toll on them and their immediate families as it later did on their posterity. Following the world-wide flood these conditions changed, and life expectancy was sharply reduced. Few men lived beyond the "three score and ten" of man's alloted years of that period and those who did were beset by disability, illness and loss of zest for life. (Psalm 90:10.) In this, as in so many other ways, the effects of sin are easily seen.

"John wrote, 'Whosoever transgresseth, and abideth not in the doctrine of Christ, hath not God. He that abideth in the doctrine of Christ, he hath both the Father and the Son.' (2 John 9.) What is the meaning of the phrase, 'doctrine of Christ?' Some say that it means the doctrine (teaching) about Christ; others think it means the doctrine which Christ taught. Which view is the correct one?"

It is the doctrine which Christ personally, and through his disciples, taught—the message of salvation. It is most certainly not the genitive of the object, but of the subject, and signifies the doctrine which Christ originated and propagated through his chosen representatives. As the "doctrine of Balaam" was the doctrine which Balaam taught (Revelation 2:14), so the "doctrine of Christ" is the doctrine which Christ taught either personally or through agency. This is the uniform usage of the New Testament. See, for example, John 18:19; Luke 4:32; Mark 11:18 and Matthew 22:33. These allusions to "his doctrine," make clear the significance of the phrase, "the doctrine of Christ." Thus, the words, "doctrine of Christ," simply mean "the doctrine which is Christ's,"— that body of teaching for which Christ is responsible. Only those who want a wider fellowship than the teaching (doctrine) of Christ permits have ever argued otherwise. It is significant that the word "transgresseth" in this passage derives from a Greek word (*proago*) whence comes our English word progressive. Thus, literally, "Whosoever becomes progressive and abides not in the doctrine of Christ has not God." Some rejoice in their progressive stance in religion; but the real choice is between God and errorists. To fellowship those who teach false doctrine is to lose one's fellowship with God. Religionists often boast of their progressiveness in religion, and movements in and out of the church have risen based on the concept of progressiveness. Progress is proper only when it is in the direction of Christ; and in some matters it is infinitely better to be non-progressive, particularly in not going beyond what the Lord has said. John makes clear that any movement which is away from the teaching of Christ is progress in the wrong direction, and results in the loss of God himself. We must ever be on guard against any semblance of departure from "the doctrine of Christ,"—his teaching as set out in the New Testament.

"How far back into biblical history may writing, as a means of communication, be traced?"

By implication to the beginning of the race. Adam and Eve began life with a vocabulary; they enjoyed the ability to communicate with each other from the moment their relationship began; and it is reasonable to suppose that as their need for the transference of thought other than direct communication arose, the power to record their thoughts was theirs also.

It is quite well known that the Babylonians were prolific writers centuries before Abraham and his family migrated to Canaan from Ur of the Chaldees which was nearly 2000 years before our Lord came to the earth, and that illustrious patriarch's descendants found writing to be in common use by the people of the land into which they moved when they claimed the inheritance of their father. The first mention of books written by the Israelites following their bondage in Egypt is in

Exodus 17:14. Though these early writings are called "books," they were really "rolls"; the material on which the writing was done was either skins of animals or strips of papyrus—a very primitive type of paper made from the papyrus plant which grows in profusion to this day in the land of Egypt. From this is derived the word "volume," from the Latin *volumen,* meaning something rolled up.

Writings were also inscribed on soft clay which, when heated, hardened into permanence, or they were engraved on stone, a very fortunate practice which greatly extends our knowledge of the ancient world and its peoples.

There are numerous references in the Old Testament to writings of great antiquity—uninspired chronicles of ancient events. Because they weren't inspired, they were not made a part of the 66 books constituting the canon of scripture. Among these are the Book of the Wars of Jehovah and the Book of Jasher (Numbers 21:14; Joshua 10:13); History of Samuel the Seer and Nathan the Prophet, containing details of the reigns of David and Solomon (1 Chronicles 29:29; 2 Chronicles 9:29), and many others. It appears to have been customary in that day to record and preserve the official acts of the kings; and evidently many of these state records were in existence when the Chronicles were penned. Prominent events of the reigns of Solomon and Jeroboam were recorded in the Visions of Iddo the Seer (2 Chronicles 9:29; 12:15), and there are other references to files containing historical information in 2 Chronicles 13:22; 20:24; 26:22; 32:32; 33:18,19; 35:25. The Apocrapha, occasionally published between Malachi and Matthew, is an interesting record of many matters occurring in the 400 years' period between the Testaments. These uninspired writings were in existence while our Lord and his apostles were on the earth and were certainly known to them, but from none of these documents did they quote, though they often cited Old Testament scripture, clearly evidencing the fact that they did not regard these writings as canonical scripture.

"Brother Woods, some time ago you had an article in the GOSPEL ADVOCATE on 'The Incomparable Book'. Would you please reprint it in your second volume of Questions and Answers?"

The Bible is this earth's most precious possession. So immeasurably great is the contribution it makes to humanity's needs, were all other books ever written to suffer destruction and all worldly wisdom they contain to perish, the glorious, unfading light which its holy pages radiate would continue in undiminished fashion to illumine fully the way to heaven. Without it, though we were possessed of all the worldly wisdom of the ages and had at our fingertips all the knowledge of all the books in all of the great libraries of the world, the door of heaven would forevermore be closed to us.

It is unique, incomparable and utterly without comparison—preeminently, The Book, wherein divine mysteries are made plain, Deity is revealed to man, and man to himself. From its inexhaustible stores of heavenly wisdom there unceasingly flows an unquenchable spirit enabling all those who fully imbibe to resist every attack by the devil, to see by its power truth triumph over error, purity over corruption and righteousness over evil; by its examples, the motivation which springs from its remarkable influence it wrought in the lives of those great characters who espoused it the record of which remains for our edification and emulation. The indomitable will of a Galilean fisherman, an exile on lonely Patmos, the Lord in the court of Pilate and the martyrs who suffered sword or flame take us far, far beyond the powers of mortal mind to estimate the influence the events thus chronicled have exerted in the lives of those who follow. (Hebrews 11:32-40.)

To it, its faithful devotees turn again and again in hours of need and ever find in its sacred pages its thrilling and never-failing message of hope and comfort. No crisis, no trial, no trouble in life ever arose it cannot resolve. The young, when first realizing its power for good, the mature, in need of guidance in life's perplexing problems, and the old, in seeking the comfort which can come only through the realization of a better and more enduring home in the skies, all turn to it and find, in lavish abundance, the message for which their hearts sigh. In hours of sorrow, through long nights of weariness and pain, and in death's inevitable approach, it is always there to soothe, to sustain and to provide the peace which passes understanding.

In a world where all that is peculiar to it is mortal and corruptible only this incomparable book is immortal, incorruptible and eternal, being wholly unaffected by the flight of the centuries and the erosion of the ages which all material things must eventually suffer. The majesty of once great Babylonia, the glory of Greece, the power of Rome, their great cities, their powerful armies and their flourishing civilizations have long since perished and live only in memorials and books of ancient history; and if the Lord delays his coming, our own proud land and civilization will go the way of the peoples of past millenniums and suffer the destiny of those ancient kingdoms of which only faint traces yet remain. It may indeed be that in some distant age a curious student from some faraway land will dig into the mouldering ruins of one of our great cities, seek to translate some fading inscription on a crumbling memorial excavated from some mound covering artifacts of our day and age in an effort to learn something about the people of the 20th century. Should he by chance discover in his archaeological search a buried capsule containing a copy of God's holy Word, its message of

270

hope, of comfort and of salvation will be as potent and precious as it was when fresh from inspiration's pen it came. "For all flesh is as grass, and all the glory of man as the flower of the grass. The grass withereth, and the flower thereof falleth away: but the word of the Lord endureth forever." (1 Peter 1:24,25.)

"What is the difference in meaning, if any, in the words 'Hebrew,' 'Israelite' and 'Jew?' "

In spite of the fact that these words are often used interchangably, and preachers tend to disregard any distinction between them in the pulpit and in the press, they do not mean the same and ought not to be confused. The name "Hebrew" was originally assigned to Abraham on the occasion of his arrival in the land of Canaan by the original inhabitants of the land—the Canaanites. It derives from a Hebrew word signifying "to pass over," and is believed to have been given to Abraham and his family by these people from the fact that the ancient patriarch came from beyond the river Jordan or Euphrates over which he and his very large household had passed.

The word "Israelite" derives from the name "Israel" assigned to Jacob by the angel of Jehovah at Peniel. (Genesis 32:28.) All of Jacob's descendents thus became Israelites. Various terms are used in the Old Testament to describe them; they are often called children of Israel, house of Israel, people of Israel, etc. (1 Samuel 13:19; 2 Kings 6:23; Numbers 20:14; Isaiah 41:8.)

The word "Jew" comes from the name Judah, one of the two tribes which refused to go along with the rebellion led by Jeroboam following the death of King Solomon. Benjamin, the other tribe, was incorporated into Judah for civil and religious purposes, and the name Jew was given to the people of both Judah and Benjamin without distinction.

Thus, all Jews were Israelites, being descended from Jacob whose name was changed to Israel; but not all Israelites were Jews—only those Israelites who were of the tribes of Judah and Benjamin. All Jews and Israelites were Hebrews, being descended from Abraham, the first Hebrew, but not all Hebrews were Israelites or Jews; the Arab peoples, descendents of Abraham through Ishmael, are Hebrews, but they are very, very far from being Jews!

The apostasy of Israel was complete by 721 B.C., when the people had become so assimilated with the Assyrians among whom they lived, they lost their tribal identities and passed out of history as distinct peoples. Apparently, some of the people of the various tribes—Levites, for example, of whom we read in the New Testament, did not go along with the rebellion and attached themselves to either Judah or Benjamin, thus maintaining their individual identity. By the time of the

271

Babylonian captivity (587 B.C.), the name Jew came to be applied to all descendents of Jacob then living, and in the New Testament to designate, in large measure, those who rejected Jesus as Messiah. (John 6:41-52.)

There is a figurative use of the words "Jew" and "Israel" also therein to designate the chosen people of God under the New Covenant—Christians. (Romans 2:28,29; Galatians 6:16.) Paul sometimes identified himself by the name of his most illustrious ancestor, declaring that he was "a Hebrew of the Hebrews," that is, one of pure blood. He was of the tribe of Benjamin and thus properly a Jew, and consequently was able to say, "I am a man which am a Jew of Tarsus." (Acts 21:39.)

"Who were the Nicolaitans of whom we read in the book of Revelation?"

They were a short-lived sect, and their origin is hidden in antiquity, but we are able to learn something of their teaching and character from the brief allusions made to them in history both sacred and profane. They appear to have attained some prominence in the apostolic age and are mentioned on two occasions by our Lord in the letters he dictated to John, the apostle, to be sent to the churches at Ephesus and Pergamos. (Revelation 2:6,15.) That the influence of this sect was of such character and had reached such prominence that our Lord felt it necessary to warn the saints regarding it evidences its threat to the church of the first century.

The church in Ephesus was commended for having resisted the influence of this heretical group and for its courageous stand against it. In the epistle to the church in Pergamos, however, the Lord charged some in the church there of holding to the doctrine of the Nicolaitans which he compared to "the teaching of Balaam."

There is evidence that the devotees of this doctrine defended the eating of meats offered to idols, encouraged and engaged in idolatrous worship and participated in licentious and ungodly conduct. They were, beyond doubt, a paganistic and corrupt sect the church was to avoid. Their name, Nicolaitans, has led to the assumption that the sect was founded by Nicolaus who, in turn, has been identified as the proselyte of this name mentioned among the seven in Acts 6:5, but this is a fanciful supposition and devoid of any documentary evidence. It is most unlikely that one so honored and so talented as this early disciple would have espoused views and engaged in practices so foreign to that authorized by the Lord.

The Nicolaitans no longer exist, but there are those who carry on their aims and duplicate their practices. The disposition to compromise the truth, to mix it with worldly philosophy and to accept a standard of living far below that taught in the scriptures, has supporters in every age. Palatable though their offerings may be to those who love the world, the end thereof is the way of death. Of them Jude wrote: "But these rail at whatsoever things they know not: and what they understand naturally, like the creatures without reason, in these things are they destroyed. Woe unto them! for they went in the way of Cain, ran riotously in the error of Balaam for hire, and perished in the gainsaying of Korah." (Jude 10,11.)

"Why did the Lord say to his disciples, 'Because it is given unto you to know the mysteries of the kingdom of heaven, but to them it is not given. For whosoever hath, to him shall be given, and he shall have more abundance: but whosoever hath not, from him shall be taken away even that he hath. Therefore speak I to them in parables . . .' (Matthew 13:11-13.)?"

It should be observed, first of all, that the "mysteries" to which the Lord alludes were not difficult or incomprehensible matters, but simply things not hitherto revealed. They were often of obvious import when made known. Two classes of people are contemplated in the statement: those to whom the "mysteries" were revealed; those to whom they were not. It was not that one group was to be more favored than the other; the difference was not in some arbitrary choice in behalf of a favored few, but in the disposition of those to whom these matters were to be given. This, the Lord explains in these words: "They seeing see not, and hearing they hear not, neither do they understand." Lest the conclusion be drawn that this response was also the result of an arbitrary selection, the Saviour explained: "In them is fulfilled the prophecy of Esaias, which saith, By hearing, ye shall hear, and shall not understand; and see ye shall see, and shall not perceive; for this people's heart is waxed gross, and their ears are dull of hearing, and their eyes they have closed; lest at any time they should see with their eyes, and hear with their ears, and should understand with their heart, and should be converted, and I should heal them." Thus the gospel does not find its way into the hearts of some people, not because "Christ intended that his doctrine should be beneficial to only a few" (Calvin), but because multitudes of people simply do not want the gospel, will not allow it to enter their hearts and therefore never learn what its benefits and blessings are.

But why speak in "parables" to thus disposed? Though these people were uninterested in, and unwilling to accept the truth—as are millions of dying humanity about us today—the Lord, in mercy, put his lessons in parables (simple illustrations) with the hope that these seed thoughts would eventually germinate and spring forth to life in them.

Another reason, hinted at in the text, may be seen for his having so spoken. So blinded by the world were they, the lessons of the kingdom plainly put would have been of no interest whatsoever to the worldly multitudes; but by clothing the lessons in parabolic dress some curiosity was evidenced that may have led to beneficial results in the future. For the time being and, sadly for some, for all eternity, the spiritual sickness which possessed them made them immune to the appeals of the gospel, and the Lord, in justice, allowed the consequences of disobedience to fall upon them. It is of interest to note that the Greek word translated "closed" in the sentence, "And their eyes they have closed," is literally, "And their eyes they have sleepily closed," i.e., with utter drowsiness they disregarded the message, wholly unalert to its import and value. They deliberately gave themselves up to a manner of life which would effectively keep them from hearing and then contemplating the only message of life and salvation. Finally, the warning of the Saviour in verse 12 is of awesome import: "For whosoever hath, to him shall be given, and he shall have more abundance: but whosoever hath not from him shall be taken away even that he hath." We either use, or lose, our blessings; the law of atrophy is an inevitable one and knows no exceptions. An organ of the body unused, eventually becomes useless; opportunities not improved, ultimately are withdrawn. The lesson is a vital one and ought by us all to be duly considered.

"Why is it said in 1 John 5:6 that Jesus 'came by water and by blood'?"

The verse, in full, reads: "This is he that came by water and blood, even Jesus Christ; not with the water only, but with the water and with the blood." From it we learn that (a) one came; (b) the one who came was Jesus Christ, our Lord; (c) he came by water and blood; (d) he did not come by water only but "with" water and "with the blood." The "coming" alluded to is quite obviously that which he accomplished when he came into the human family on the occasion of his virgin birth. Witnesses to that fact are later declared to be "water" and "blood." (1 John 5:8.)

It seems, therefore, to be quite clear from the context, that the reference to the water was to his baptism, and to the blood to his death on the cross. On the banks of the Jordan following his immersion at the hands of John, he was declared to be the "only begotten" by the audible voice of the Father; it was from this point that he entered upon his public ministry to be terminated only by his death on the cross. (Matthew 3:15; John 19:34.) To these facts the Holy Spirit bore umistakable witness. Evidence, entirely convincing to reasonable people, and divine proofs, numerous and weighty, abound, evidencing the fact that he was sent forth from the Father, and by him. The Holy Spirit came in visible form at his baptism; the Spirit recorded and bore witness both to his baptism and to his death. Quite fittingly then, it may be said that our Lord "came by water and blood."

These two instances in his life, the first at the beginning of his public ministry, and the second at the end of his earthly life, were cited by the apostle for their evidential value in showing divine attestation of that ministry. At the Jordan, his work began; at the cross it was finished, and he so affirmed by the announcement then made: "It is finished." (John 19:30.) For 20 centuries baptism has borne testimony to the central fact of our redemption—the burial and resurrection of Christ (Hebrews 10:1-4; 1 John 5:10; Romans 6:1-6); and the Lord's Supper, for an equal period, similarly portrays the blood, the shedding of which made possible that redemption. (1 Corinthians 11:23-29.)

"What were the circumstances which led to the production of the 'King James' or 'Authorized' version of the Bible?"

This well-known and justly famous translation of the scriptures was begun at the behest of James I, an English monarch, in the early years of the 17th century, because of objections offered by the Puritans to the "Bishop's Bible." The Bishop's Bible, so designated because it was produced by more than 15 learned bishops of the church of England, prior to the appearance of the King James version, was the "authorized version" in that church for nearly a half century. The king proposed that a new version should be undertaken; it should be produced by the most scholarly men of the realm; it should be reviewed by the bishops of the church and ultimately examined by the king himself.

In consequence of this plan, 54 of the greatest scholars in England were chosen and designated as executors of this important task, but only 47 names appear in the final list of translators. It is of interest to note that seven of these translated the Apocrypha, and these writings were in earlier editions included.

Rigid rules were laid down to guide the translators in their work, a condensation of which follows: They should follow the format of the "Bishop's Bible" and depart from it only when the original text required it; "ecclesiastical terms," such as the word "church," were to be retained, as were proper names and titles; words of more than one meaning were to be assigned that meaning agreeable to the text and to former usage; chapter and verse divisions were to be maintained; no marginal notes were to be added, except brief explanations of Hebrew and Greek words; each scholar of each company was to translate the portion of scripture assigned, and the results examined by the entire panel until agreement was reached; in case of irreconcilable differences, the matter in issue was to be passed to, and determined by "the chief persons of each company," and finally by "three or four of the most and grave divines in either of the Universities, not employed in translating. . . ."

In consequence of these rules each portion of the sacred text passed under the special scrutiny of each translator in the panel assigned that portion of scripture. The renderings then were required to be adopted by the whole panel. When the particular book was finished on which the panel worked, it was sent on to the other companies to be examined, and it is thought that the manner in which this was done was for one to read the translation, the rest to hold in their hands some Bible, including the original text and others in French, Spanish, Italian, etc. If they discovered any fault, the reading was suspended and the difficulty removed; otherwise, the reader continued. In this way they took every possible precaution to insure that the translation was faithful to the text and accurately rendered. At least six different revisions were made by these learned men before the work was pronounced done. The work began in the spring of 1607; three years were devoted to the original effort, and more than nine months to revision. The first publication of this work, destined to influence the English-speaking world as no other book ever did, was in 1611. The original edition carried the following title: "The Holy Bible Conteyning the Old Testament, and the New: Newly translated out of the originall Tongues: And with the former translations diligently compared and reuised by his Maiesties speciall Commandement. Appointed to be read in Churches."

Its message of salvation, the unparalleled beauty of its sentiments and the stateliness of its style and content have made it the most beloved book ever written.

"Can a man or woman, just catch his or her mate gone, get non-Christian counsel, place restraints on the other partner and then move out, lock, stock and barrel, without the other knowing anything about it until he or she arrives home? Is there a difference between 'separation' and 'desertion'?"

The only grounds the New Testament sets out on which an innocent person may put away a wife or husband and marry another is fornication—unfaithfulness to the marriage vows. (Matthew 5:32; 19:9.) However, in 1 Corinthians 7:11, Paul deals with a case where a brother or sister is separated from his or her companion for reasons other than fornication, and his specific instruction to them is to be reconciled *or* remain single. As to the difference between separation and desertion, it is perhaps fanciful; any separation involves wrongdoing on the part of one of the parties and often on the part of both. I am inclined to think that there are really fewer "innocent" parties than we suppose; often one may not be guilty of fornication, but may fail to live up to what the Lord expects of married people in other ways.

"May a meeting house, paid for out of the church treasury, be used by Christians for purposes proper and right but not directly related to religious affairs?"

It is unfortunate that some people do not distinguish between the church and the church house; the Christians who meet for worship and the meeting house where they meet! (Romans 16:5.) The church is a body of baptized believers, called out from the world, over which Christ reigns as head, and which is directed by the Holy Spirit by means of the Word. When those thus constituted meet for religious activity, the church has assembled; the place or the circumstances associated with such a meeting is neither relevant nor material. The meeting might just as properly be in a boat out on the high seas, in a giant plane high above the earth or in a cave far below the surface of the ground. The church is composed of people—not brick and timber!

It follows, therefore, that it is the assembly of Christians convened for worship that is sacred (1 Peter 2:9), sanctified (1 Peter 1:2), holy (1 Peter 21:5) and dedicated to the service of the Lord. (Romans 12:1,2.) The place of assembly, the building in which the assembly occurs and the grounds on which the group gathers are not sacred, sanctified or holy. The effort to equate the meeting house with ancient sacred buildings of the Israelites and Jews—the tabernacle and the temple—is an improper and misguided one. Any analogy which exists is between those sacred edifices and the people of God who constitute the church—not the building or place where they meet. Paul reminded the Corinthians, "Know ye not that ye are the temple of God, and that the Spirit of God dwelleth in you? If any man defile the temple of God, him shall God destroy: for the temple of God is holy, which temple ye are." (1 Corinthians 3:16,17.) God's building is the church—not the building in which the church meets.

It should not be forgotten that no New Testament church of the first century owned any property at all; often the people were so poor they could not have financed such a structure; they were often subject to immediate expulsion from the countries where they sojourned; and the officials in those pagan lands would not have granted permits to build had the early Christians been able so to do.

The church building is not essential to the performance of any obligation required of the church in the New Testament. Every duty, every responsibility may be carried out by the church without a building. The meeting house is, indeed, a marvelous expedient; it would be a bit cold in winter and quite wet in the rainy season to assemble under a tree or in the fields; nonetheless, the church could thus do and still meet every divine requirement. This obvious fact makes any effort to legislate regarding the building in which the church meets irrelevant and absurd. Children of God may properly do in such buildings what would be proper for them to do as Christians in any other building in which they choose to assemble with others of like precious faith and practice, in the pursuance of matters in the public interest.

We should maintain the proper perspective in all such matters and not be guilty of making laws where God made none. (1 Timothy 4:1-10.) The church is not the meeting house; the Lord built the church; men build the church building. The church building is an expedient designed for the use and comfort of those who constitute the church, and it may therefore be properly used by Christians in any honorable and proper activity which Christians may do in assembled capacity.

"Why is it said that 'an evil spirit from the Lord' troubled king Saul? (1 Samuel 16:14,15.)"

In verse 14 of this context it is said that "the spirit of the Lord departed from Saul." The rebellious monarch, because of his awareness that the favor of God had been transferred from him to David, and that the judgment of Jehovah was soon to fall upon him, fell into a state of deep mental depression and appears to have become an insane man. The more he became involved, the deeper the depression became, thus greatly intensifying his mental malady and troubled, agitated heart. This "spirit" (disposition) is said to have come from God, because the Lord, being the controller of the universe, suffers, permits and tolerates whatever happens. He is often said to do what he merely allows. For example, it is said that the Egyptian Pharaoh hardened his heart by refusing to let God's people go, but it is also said that God hardened Pharaoh's heart; and he did it by making demands on the king to which Pharaoh was unwilling to accede. (Exodus 8:32; 10:1.) When men reject the gospel of Christ it is said that God sends them "a strong delusion," (2 Thessalonians 2:11,12), by which it is meant that he simply allows them to suffer the consequences of their own actions. Though the blame is theirs, God is said to do it because he sets in motion the events which lead to their rejection of him.

The Hebrew word translated "evil" in the passage under study means, among other things, distress, anxiety, grief and adversity. These all possessed the troubled king because he had rebelled against God and against the laws which God had ordained. This passage does not teach that the Lord, in some arbitrary fashion, determined that Saul should be afflicted by some demon or demoniac power, nor does it mean that

278

God created the ugly and mean disposition which characterized Saul in his last days. This unhappy and miserable situation resulted from his own wicked and perverse disposition. Saul was "troubled," (literally, terrified); this particular agitation was not a moral one, as seen in the fact that his disturbed mind was soothed by the music from David's harp. Apparently, Saul worried so much about his situation that it drove him into insanity. It is not surprising that this was seen as the natural and necessary consequence of his own wrongdoing. It seems, therefore, clear that the "evil spirit" was simply the wrought-up state of mental agitation and melancholy disposition which God suffered (allowed) Saul to have because of his wicked actions.

"What does the Holy Spirit do for the Christian today, and how does he do it?"

The Holy Spirit strengthens (Ephesians 3:16), sanctifies (2 Thessalonians 2:13), saves (Titus 3:5), justifies (1 Timothy 3:16), witnesses to us (Hebrews 10:15), prompts us to love God (Romans 5:5), leads us as God's sons (Romans 8:16), and will eventually raise us from the dead. (Romans 8:11.) He does this by means of the word of truth, his instrument: He strengthens us by providing the "whole armor of God," which includes the sword of the Spirit (Ephesians 6:10-17; 2 Timothy 2:1.) He sanctifies by the truth, which is God's word. (John 17:17.) He saves by supplying the "engrafted word," which is "able to save" our souls (James 1:21.) The Spirit justifies "by faith," which comes by hearing God's word. (Romans 5:1; 10:17.) He witnesses to us by the scriptures which testify of Christ. (John 5:39.) He causes us to love God by presenting God to us as a lovable being. (John 3:16.) He leads us by providing a lamp for our feet and a light for our path. (Psalm 119:105.) All that we know about how to live the Christian life is set out in the New Testament; by this instruction the Spirit leads and guides us in the right way. The reader will be unable to think of any directives the child of God needs which the word has not supplied. We are strengthened with might "by his Spirit in the inner man," (Ephesians 3:16) by being "rooted and builded up in him," and the word of God is fully "able" to accomplish this. (Colossians 2:7; Acts 20:32.) Hence, the Spirit strengthens by means of the word which he gave. And, similarly, in the resurrection, the Spirit will raise us up by means of the words of Christ when we SHALL HEAR HIS (Christ's) VOICE, and come forth from the tombs. (John 5:28,29.) Here, too, as always, the Spirit will act by means of the words of Christ!

"Is it permissible or scriptural for men who serve as trustees of church property to constitute themselves into a board of directors and claim the right to oversee the church (congregation) with elders?"

For reasons well known to lawyers and students of common and statutory law, churches cannot hold property in the name of the church organization. Real estate and other similar properties must be deeded to "trustees" who then hold such real estate in trust for the church. This is a legal and material matter, wholly unrelated to the church and its functions. It is an arrangement to meet state and legal demands and is permissible and necessary because Christians are required to be in subjection to the civil law, when this law is not in conflict with the law of God.

But such an organization has no spiritual significance, and must not be confused with the divine organization set out in the New Testament. No; it is neither scriptural nor permissible for such a group to assume control of the church. (1) It violates the divine arrangement set out in the New Testament (Hebrews 13:17; 1 Timothy 5:7); (2) it sets up, and empowers an unscriptural organization to operate in an unauthorized manner and without New Testament precedent (Acts 14:23); and those who claim to adhere to New Testament teaching must reject such an effort. The practice springs from a confusion of the church and the church property (see answer to the question regarding the relationship existing between the church and the church building elsewhere in this book), and will not be tolerated by those who believe that in order to please God we must adhere to his will as set out in the scriptures. (2 Timothy 3:16,17.)

"Shall we know each other in heaven?"

This is truly a question of more than merely curious interest. Every thoughtful person who has suffered the poignant pain of parting from those near and dear and has tenderly laid their physical forms to rest in the tomb is vitally and absorbingly interested in the implications which this question raises. He knows that he shall see them no more in the land of the living; they have passed beyond the door of death to return to this world no more. If there is no future recognition, the moment of parting at the grave, however forbidding the thought may be, becomes the hour of final separation. Soon we, too, shall divest ourselves of the mortal robe with which we are clothed here, and go to join the teeming millions of our race who have lived and loved and at last gone to take their places in the silent halls of death. On the morning of the resurrection day we shall rise to stand in judgment and to hear the pronouncement of our eternal destiny. If there is to be no recognition, we shall there be among total strangers; every memory we now possess will have been obliterated and every bond here severed, and as strangers we shall enter heaven and so live there forever and ever.

If a careful study of the sacred writings should lead us to such a conclusion, it will, it must be acknowledged, greatly alter our conceptions of heaven and the abode of the sainted dead. Whether fully aware of all the implications which attach to the matter or not, our hope of heaven and our expectation of future bliss have been conditioned on the understanding that some wondrous day we shall be privileged to gather up the sundered threads of this existence so rudely severed in death, and in the company of dear loved ones and valued friends gone on before enjoy the ineffable bliss of paradise forever and ever and ever.

Are we prepared for such a conclusion?

Our whole being instinctively and unhesitatingly shrinks away from such a supposition. We are, in the first place, *unwilling* to accept the conclusion that heaven will be peopled with those who are utter strangers to them here, that every vestige of memory will have been obliterated there, and that we shall never again be privileged to see and know those we have loved a while and lost here. And, secondly, we find ourselves *unable* to visualize a place of perfect happiness as heaven is alleged to be thus stripped of what is surely one of its sweetest joys and most fondly anticipated delights.

The view is opposed to reason, (a) because it ignores one of the most deep-seated and well-recognized desires of the heart: a glad reunion with the precious loved ones on the golden shores of the heavenly city. The separation which death inevitably brings is physical and outward and visible only; the ties of affection, regard and memory are as tangible and definite and real as any which subsist in life. Our loved ones are gone from us in bodily presence only; they live on in our hearts with immortal and imperishable vigor. The granite stones which we erect to their precious memory, the tears which fall from our weeping eyes on their graves, and the flowers which we place on their sacred mounds bear unmistakable testimony to the love and affection we feel for them and the memory which is enshrined in our hearts. "She was going unto the tomb to weep there," is the record of not only Mary, but of millions of others in every age and country and clime. The soul longs for assurance of a happy reunion beyond death, and diligently searches (and not in vain, we shall later show) for evidence in the scriptures that such a longing is not a delusion and fantasy.

(b) The wisest and greatest and best of all ages have confidently looked beyond the sombre curtains of death and thought that there is such a place as the scriptures reveal heaven to be. Among the heathen the most enlightened and elevated minds, though without the full light of truth, while groping in the feeble glimmer of reason and grasping for whatever truth they might thus imperfectly see, were able to visualize a place of pleasure where a communion with the departed dead would be possible. Socrates, one of the wisest and best of the Grecian philosophers, condemned to death by unjust judges, calmly submitted to his fate, and talked with his friends almost to the moment when he took the fatal hemlock. In his speech to his judges following his sentence of death, he said:

"If death is a removal to another place, and what is said to be true—that all the dead are there—what greater blessing can there be than this, my judges? Or if, on arriving at Hades, released from those who pretend to be judges, one shall find those that are true judges, and who are said to be there—Minos and Radamanthus, Aeacus, and Tripotolemus, and such others as were just during their own lives—would this be a sad removal? At what price would not any one estimate a conference with Musaeus, Hesoid, and Homer? I, indeed, should be willing to die often, if this be true. For me, the sojourn there would be admirable, when I should meet with Palamedes, and Ajax the Son of Telamon, and any other of the ancients who has died by an unjust sentence. The comparing my sufferings with theirs would, I think, be no unpleasing occupation. But the greatest pleasure would be to spend my time in questioning and examining the people there as I have done here, and discovering who among them is wise, and who fancies himself to be so and is not. At what price, my judges would not any one estimate the opportunity of questioning him who led that mighty army against Troy, or Ulysses, or Sisyphus, or ten thousand others whom one might mention, both men and women? with whom to converse and associate, and to question them, would be an inconceivable happiness."

Such would indeed be "an inconceivable happiness," and when to the opportunity afforded of interviewing the great and illustrious characters of all ages, we add the unspeakable privilege of talking with and seeing those nearest and dearest to our hearts, our innermost being thrills with joy at the anticipation of such, and heaven glows with undying lustre as we long for its joys and rich delights. Whose soul is it which does not go wild at the prospect of *seeing* and *knowing* illustrious prophets, priests and kings; of being associated with the great and wise and good of all ages; of sitting at the feet of Peter and Paul and the Lord? And when to this we add the wondrous prospect of seeing our dear loved ones in their immortal state, no longer weary and sad and worn and sick, no longer clothed in bodies weak with pain and ravaged by disease, but arrayed in the imperishable splendor which shall ever characterize the good, the pure and the blest, who can avoid the conclusion of the peerless apostle that it is "very far better" there?

No. The hope of a glad and happy reunion "just over there" is not a cruel delusion, a vain and empty fantasy. Those who silently weep in loneliness may take comfort in the fact that they sorrow not in vain, or as others who have no hope.

"Please give scriptural proof of future recognition."

In an answer preceding this, attention was directed to the philosophical and reasonable basis of the doctrine of future recognition in the heavenly sphere. While neither philosophy nor reason constitutes the *final,* or, for that matter, even an *authoritative,* word on any matter of divine providence, it will be admitted by thoughtful persons that when each approves and endorses the idea, such amounts to corroborative and presumptive evidence of the truth of the matter under consideration; and when to such presumptive proof is added the infallible testimony of sacred writers, faith and reason combine to establish the truth of the matter beyond reasonable question. Having, in this inquiry, listened to reason, we are now to hear revelation on the subject of future recognition.

In this field, the evidence is so abundant, the proof so varied and the references so numerous one wonders where to begin. By this it is not meant that the doctrine is taught in formal propositions or announced in direct statements. One will search in vain for any positive affirmation thereon by any biblical writer. On this subject, as on a great many matters of equal importance, we are dependent on incidental allusion, logical deduction and necessary inference for the proof with which we hope to sustain our proposition. Such evidence, as every one skilled in evaluating it knows, is no less credible or relevant because undesigned. And, it is, in the nature of the case, all the more abundant, for this reason.

1. There is, for example, the incidental allusions to impending joy which Paul expected to experience in the life to come because of the faithfulness and devotion of those to whom he had preached and among whom he had labored. They were his "joy and crown" (Philippians 4:1), those whom he fondly and confidently expected to afford him with the occasion for "rejoicing . . . in the day of the Lord Jesus." (2 Corinthians 1:14). "For what is our hope, or joy, or crown of rejoicing?" he asked, and then answered his question thus: "Are not even ye in the presence of our Lord Jesus Christ at his coming?" (1 Thessalonians 2:19.) But what would be the manner of his realization of such rejoicing? Again

he answers. "He which raised up the Lord Jesus shall raise up us also by Jesus, and shall present us with you." (2 Corinthians 4:14.) Who among us can believe that these who were to be raised would be total and utter strangers to Paul, and he to them, with no memory of any former association, with the recollection of their great obligation to him completely blotted out, not even knowing that it was he who led them out of darkness into light and from the power of Satan unto God? Truly, the words, "shall present us with you," must signify more than the mere gathering of unfamiliar personalities, the assembly of strangers.

2. The comforting assurances of holy writ, penned by inspired men for the purpose of soothing sorrowful hearts and comforting the sad and grief-stricken, imply a reunion of consequent resumption of association in a better land: "But we would not have you ignorant, brethren, concerning them that fall asleep; that ye sorrow not, even as the rest, who have no hope. For if we believe that Jesus died and rose again, even so them also that are fallen asleep in Jesus will God bring with him . . . Wherefore comfort one another with these words." (1 Thessalonians 4:13,14,18.) Two classes of the dead are here contemplated: (1) Those who died in Christ; (2) those who died out of Christ. Loved ones of the former class are not, as those of the latter, without hope; on the contrary, their loved ones will reappear with the Lord when the sign of the Son of man is seen in the clouds, and be privileged again to be associated with those whom, in death, they left behind. In consequence, we are admonished and encouraged (a) to entertain hope and (b) to find comfort in this fact. But, on the assumption that the personality of those we have loved and lost is obliterated, their memories of us and ours of them forevermore gone and with no tangible marks of identity remaining, how is *hope* possible and where is there occasion for comfort in such a circumstance? Before such a prospect, the mind quails, hope fades into despair, words calculated to comfort become empty mockery, and the passage is without significance.

3. The doctrine of rewards and punishments, taught so clearly and at such great length in the scriptures, implies and necessitates the conclusion that future recognition is an assured fact. In the field of criminal jurisprudence, for example, a man is regarded as worthy of punishment for unsocial acts committed, only when it appears that he is mentally capable of recognizing the nature of his deed. However violent the act and vicious the deed, when it is shown that the one having committed it is mentally incompetent, penal processes are immediately suspended, and the man is committed to an institution for the insane. Are we, in the light of this humane and reasonable consideration of law—a law which affects itself to be founded on the law of God—to assume that a benign Father will, nevertheless, disregard the

competency of the culprit, and administer punishment *for acts of which the person being punished has no recollection whatsoever?* We shrink from the very suggestion of such an imputation.

Moreover, the scriptures clearly establish the fact that in judgment men will be possessed of the memory of deeds done here, and will allege such in extenuation of, and in protest to, the decision there to be handed down: "Many will say to me in that day, Lord, Lord, did we not prophesy by thy name, and by thy name cast out demons, and by thy name do many mighty works?" (Matthew 7:22.) Further, in numerous instances, individuals, now in the disembodied state, are declared to be possessed of a distinct and vivid recollection of events occurring on earth prior to their passing: "I saw under the altar the souls of them that were slain for the word of God, and for the testimony which they held: and they cried with a loud voice, saying, How long, O Lord, holy and true, dost thou not judge and avenge our blood on them that dwell on the earth?" (Revelation 6:9,10.) These were personalities in the spirit realm; they had an awareness of their surroundings; they knew why they were there—they had been murdered; they inquired when judgment would be exercised on those guilty of their murder. If there is not here a clear and convincing demonstration of consciousness following death; if this passage does not establish a definite and mental connection between this life and the next; if it is not shown that there is a positive and certain retention of memory with reference to events occurring here, then there is an end to all reasonable exegesis, and we may as well be done with any effort to ascertain the meaning and significance of any passage in the scriptures by the usual and ordinary rules of interpretation.

4. The case of the rich man and Lazarus (Luke 16:19-31), whether a parable or not, supplies us with a glimpse of the state of the dead, lifts the curtain of the future and enables us to look for a moment on the scenes of the yet-to-be. The consciousness which each of the leading characters possessed, their awareness of their surroundings, and the memory which they retained of the world from which they had but lately left all point irresistibly to the conclusion which we have reached. And, couched in the two words, "Son, remember," is a necessary inference for all for which, in these articles, we contend.

5. Paul, in a chapter designed to deal at length with the resurrection state, represents the risen saint as standing on the verge of his empty grave and shouting the song of trimph: "O death, where is thy victory? O death, where is thy sting?" (1 Corinthians 15:55.) This consciousness of triumph is possible only on the supposition that memory is able to carry across the chasm of death the recollection of the destiny with which all men, until the Lord comes, are faced.

6. A phrase of peculiar significance, and especially relevant to our present study, occurs in connection with the record of Abraham's death.

In a passage poignantly pathetic, one which simply touches the heart with its simplicity and pathos, and picturing the passing of the venerable patriarch, his demise is recorded thus: "And Abraham gave up the ghost, and died in a good old age, an old man, and full of years; and was gathered to his people." (Genesis 25:8.) The phrase, *"And was gathered to his people,"* occurs with slight variation in the chronicle of Ishmael's death (Genesis 25:17), the death of Isaac (Genesis 35:29), Jacob (Genesis 49:29,33), Moses and Aaron (Deuteronomy 32:50). This phrase cannot properly be understood as referring to the burial of their bodies, for Moses, as an example, was buried in a secret place "in the valley in the land of Moab," far from the sepulchres of his fathers. The reference must, therefore, be to his spirit, and to its reunion with the spirits of his ancestors gone on before. Jacob was "gathered unto his people," while in the land of Egypt, and thus long before he was borne to Canaan and entombed in the soil of his homeland. (Genesis 49:33-50:1-3.) It seems certain, in the light of these facts, that the phrase, "gathered unto his people," refers, not to the fact of death, nor to the place thereof, but to the journey of the spirit to the unseen world.

The grief-stricken David, with the body of his dead child yet unburied, said, "Can I bring him back again? *I shall go to him, but he shall not return to me."* (2 Samuel 12:23.) The question which the humbled king raised is rhetorical, the answer obvious. He could not bring the child back. He was aware that the spirit of the child was not there, though the body yet remained. The comfort which he derived was conditioned on journeying to the place where the child was. Are we to conclude that the monarch believed that, on the occasion of such a reunion, this child would be to him no more than any other child, that he would, indeed, be unable to know whether it was his own child or not? We cannot believe it.

Jesus, in a discourse dealing with the wickedness of his contemporaries, affirmed that the men of Nineveh, who repented at the preaching of the fiery prophet Jonah, would rise up in judgment and condemn those of his generation. In order to do what is here affirmed of them, it will be necessary for the men of Nineveh to be in judgment; to be in judgment in their own characters and clothed with the personalities which they possessed here; to retain the detailed and minute memory of events then occurring, and particularly, of the waywardness, rebellion and perverseness characteristic of those about whom the saviour spoke. (Matthew 12:38-41.) Only on the supposition that the memory of men in the next world extends to this is such a circumstance as these verses relate possible.

Time and space require that we desist, though only a small portion of the available evidence has been presented. Sufficient has been offered, it is believed, to enable the candid mind to feel complete confidence in the validity of the doctrine, and to find comfort and consolation therein.

"Discuss some of the objections to the doctrine of future recognition which are sometimes offered."

Future recognition is *not* repugnant to reason and it *is* supported by scripture. These two handmaids thus join hands to commend to us a doctrine which has brought comfort and blessed assurance to countless millions through long ages of suffering, sickness and eventual death. Despite the abundance of evidence which obtains and the consolation which the doctrine brings, objections have been raised and arguments against it offered. That such arguments are offered and objections raised does not establish a presumption that the doctrine is false, or that the evidence by which it is sustained is insufficient or weak. Objections have been, and are being, offered against every cardinal doctrine of the Christian religion. When the mind is disposed to cavil, human perverseness is such that it finds at hand unbelief on which to feed and ground which to itself is sufficient to oppose that against which it arrays itself.

The objections which are filed against the doctrine of future recognition have their origin in a defective concept of the nature of the next life or in projecting the limitations of this life into the next, or both.

1. It is, for example, alleged that we will have lost, in the next world, the physical characteristics and recognizable distinctions which we possess in this; and that with these gone and with ourselves nothing but "spirit beings" there will be nothing with which to identify us with this existence. By "spirit beings" is usually meant ghost-like wraiths of the same nature as a child imagines fairies to possess. How may such intangible and immaterial beings be recognized, it is asked.

In reply it should be said that such concepts as the foregoing grow out of a gross misapprehension of the teaching of the scriptures with reference to the nature and characteristics of the resurrected saint. The resurrection of the body—this body changed from a mortal to an immortal one—is taught in the fullest, most explicit and most satisfactory manner. "It is sown in corruption, it is raised in incorruption." (1 Corinthians 15:42.) What is the antecedent of the "its" of this entire passage? "For this corruptible must put on incorruption, and this mortal must put on immortality." (1 Corinthians 15:53.) What corruptible, what mortal? Corruptibility and mortality are affirmed of some part of us. Of what part? Not the spirit, certainly; for it is neither mortal nor corruptible. Reference is, therefore, to the body. But the affirmation of the text is that "this" mortal shall put on immortality. What mortal? The one we now possess. What is it about us that we now possess that is mortal? *This* body. The "manner of the body" which it pleases God to give us is that which undergoes the change thus indicated. (1 Corinthians 15:35-38.)

Job said, "For I know that my Redeemer liveth, and that he shall stand at the latter day upon the earth: and though after my skin worms destroy this body, yet in my flesh shall I see God: whom I shall see for myself, and mine eyes shall behold, and not another." (Job 19:25-27.) Here, in the most positive fashion possible, the resurrection of the body, the preservation of the personality, and the identity of the individual are taught. Job believed that *he* (as Job) would see God; that he would see God in the flesh (with the change implied through which bodies must pass in the resurrection), and that it would be Job who experienced this with his own eyes, and not another.

But to set the matter at rest once for all, we have only to examine the references respecting the resurrection of the Lord's body. He was "the firstfruits of them that are asleep," the pledge and token of the resurrection of all the rest. (1 Corinthians 15:20.) When he shall appear, "we shall be like him." (1 John 3:3.) But the body in which Jesus came forth possessed the same distinctive features as those which were buried. The disciples looked with transfigured gaze upon his lovely form; they thrilled with rapture to his familiar voice; with wonder and reverent joy they touched him with their hands and examined the cruel spear-thrust in his side. So full and satisfactory was the evidence thus afforded them that ever thereafter they had the fullest assurance of his identity and from this conviction they never wavered. If, then, his resurrection is indeed a demonstration of the certainty of ours and if we are truly to be as he was, does it not follow that those who know us as well as the disciples were acquainted with him before his death will see in us the same recognizable characteristics?

2. Others base an objection to the doctrine of future recognition on the Lord's reply to the Sadducean cavil that "in the resurrection they neither marry, nor are given in marriage, but are as angels in heaven." (Matthew 22:30.) But this, far from sustaining the objection, establishes its opposite; for it asserts that the risen saints will be as "angels in heaven," who surely must possess the faculty of memory and who are undoubtedly acquainted with each other. This statement of our Lord was a reply to the Sadducees who, in objecting to the doctrine of the resurrection, presented a hypothetical case which was designed, if not to make the doctrine of the resurrection impossible, to make it look at least ridiculous. The statement was made to show that the marriage relation will not be maintained in the next life. It should be noted that this passage teaches that the relation of marriage is to be terminated; not that the recollection will be blotted out.

3. Some affect great difficulty in accepting future recognition on that ground that should we know each other there, and some of our loved

ones are not there, the consciousness of this fact would mar the bliss of heaven. But this supposition, instead of solving the difficulty, increases it; for, if we are unable to recognize *any* of our loved ones there, we must then be uncertain whether any of them are there, in which case we should worry about *all* of them! Much better, on this hypothesis, for some of them to be there, and know them, than for all of them to be there and not know one of them. The conclusion which those who offer this objection reach is grounded in an erroneous concept with reference to the attitude which shall characterize us in the next world. It assumes that we shall ignore the manner of life and characteristic of those who have failed to reach heaven and desire their presence in spite of the way in which they have lived. When the mists have cleared, and all imperfect conceptions are gone, we shall be able fully to acquiesce in the righteous judgments of God. We shall then be able to see clearly that those who are not in heaven do not deserve to be there; that they made no effort to reach that place; that, on the contrary, they resisted every effort to lead them there. Knowing this, we shall then be able to accept without question the wise decisions of the Judge of all the universe and recognize fully that he doeth all things well.

Objections raised to the doctrine of future recognition are not valid. It is grounded in hope, it is sustained by faith, and love longs for its realization. *It is the truth.* Let us derive great comfort and consolation from it.

"What is meant by the statement, 'We have an Advocate with the Father, Jesus Christ, the Righteous?' "

"My little children, these things write I unto you that ye may not sin. *And if any man sin, we have an Advocate with the Father,* Jesus Christ the righteous: and he is the propitiation for our sins; and not for ours only, but also for the whole world." (1 John 2:1,2.) No more comforting and consoling passage was ever penned. Affirmed here in unmistakable fashion is the availability of God's wondrous plan to justify, and to keep justified, every son and daughter of Adam's race who will conform to the arrangement provided. For those willing so to do, Christ becomes "an Advocate with the Father."

An "advocate" is a lawyer or an attorney. (*Parakletos,* in early Greek literature is one "called to one's aid in a judicial cause," hence, a pleader, intercessor.) Christ is, therefore, our lawyer or attorney representing us in heaven. We file our petition with the Father; and Christ, our local representative, pleads our case and argues in our behalf.

In his advocacy of our case, the usual defenses of those arraigned before the bar of justice are not available. (1) The accusation cannot be squashed on legal grounds. The indictment is entirely valid. It is set out in a document the validity of which is and must forevermore remain unimpeachable. (2) Nor is it possible for counsel to argue that his clients are innocent of the charges levelled against them. (a) The evidence of gult is conclusive; (b) defendants have pleaded guilty. "We before laid to the charge both of Jews and Greeks, that they are all under sin; as it is written . . . there is none that doeth good, no, not so much as one." (Romans 3:9,12.) "All we like sheep have gone astray; we have turned every one to his own way." (Isaiah 53:6.)

(3) A plea for a change in the charge to one involving lesser guilt on the ground of ignorance cannot be made because there are no mitigating circumstances. Defendants concede their guilt and confess to a knowledge of the law before which they stand accused. (4) A plea for suspension of sentence on the ground that defendants have learned their lesson and will not therefore be disposed to violate the law again is without merit; and, moreover, contrary to known facts. "Every one that committeth sin is the bondservant of sin." (John 8:45.) Those once in violation of the law become repeaters and thus habitual offenders.

(5) Equally invalid is the plea that the crime charged is really of no consequence and that the accused should be released because their acts are inconsequential. On the contrary, so serious is the sin, and so grave and far-reaching the consequences that no member of the human family escapes the effects thereof. "The wages of sin is death." (Romans 6:23.)

Our Advocate's clients are guilty, guilty as charged, guilty of the highest crimes with which human beings may be charged.

Is their case hopeless? Does their guilty plea make inevitable their conviction and ultimate punishment? By no means. For, it is in just such a plea, and through the advocacy of such an Advocate that escape is possible. But for such a plea, he would not have taken *our* case; and without his representation our conviction and punishment would have been certain. What are the grounds on which he defends us?

It will be observed that John declares that Christ is the *propitiation* for our sins. (1 John 2:2.) To propitiate is to *atone,* to make *expiation.* To expiate is to *pay the penalty for.* Because Christ first paid the penalty for us, he is able to serve effectively as our lawyer in heaven. He argues the case on his own merit, not ours. It is what he did for us that constitutes the ground of our hope. The penalty of the broken law was death. Christ simply took upon himself this penalty and allowed it to be executed in his own person so that we might go free. In his death he made *satisfaction* for us, so that he might live again to make *intercession* for us. He satisfied the demands of the law, and on this basis intercedes for us in heaven.

It is most difficult for us, at this distant date and so far removed from the terrible and tragic circumstances under which it occurred, to visualize fully the horror of death by crucifixion. No more diabolical method of death was ever designed even by the most depraved human ingenuity. The shame and sorrow of that blackest hour in all human history are beyond our comprehension. But it was in that event that the ground of our hope lies. By our Lord's willingness to endure this, we are privileged to go free.

There is an incident in ancient Greek history which illustrates the principle involved. Aeschylus, a citizen of Athens, was tried and condemned to death. As he was about to be led forth to the place of execution, his brother Amyntas, who had courageously fought in defense of Greece, losing one of his hands in the bitter struggle, appeared in the courtroom and, without a word, and in the sight of all, lifted the stump of his handless arm in a dramatic gesture. When the judges saw the evidence of his sacrifice in behalf of their country, they immediately moved to pardon Amyntas' condemned brother. Amnesty was provided, not because of the merit of the accused; he was without such; it was instead bestowed in consideration of him who had interceded. He who intercedes for us, in heaven's highest tribunal, suffered not *one, but five* bleeding wounds in our behalf, on Calvary's cruel tree. We are sure that God is not indifferent to such!

We must remember that the Lord will take our case, and argue in our behalf, only if we submit our cause wholly into his hands. May this we ever do wholly, humbly, unhesitatingly; assured that he will not fail us in our coming hours of need.

"What is an easy and convincing method of proving that Jesus is the Son of God and possesses the divine nature?"

The word *God* is one of the Spirit's designations for the divine nature. Under the figure of the synecdoche, where a part is made to stand for the whole, or the whole for a part, the word *God* is used to designate each of the divine Persons constituting deity; and, while there is but one God—one divine nature—the Scriptures clearly teach that there are three distinct personalities possessing this nature. The Father is called God (John 3:16), the Son is called God (John 1:1), the Holy Spirit is called God (Acts 5:3,4). In these instances, the word *God*, the name of the divine nature, is severally applied to each part, under the figure above designated, though there is but one divine nature; hence, but one God. (Deuteronomy 6:4.)

Thus, when reference is made to "the deity of Christ," it is meant that Christ possesses the divine nature; that he is a part of the godhead; and that he is, therefore, GOD. And, inasmuch as divine attributes are ascribed to each of the persons in the godhead, it is entirely correct and in order to refer to them as God the Father, God the Son, and God the Holy Spirit, the three constituting *the one God.*

The books of the Gospel were written, in large measure, to prove the deity of Jesus (John 20:30,31), and other scripture abounds with evidences to this end. Because of necessary limitations of space, we can do no more than suggest, in barest outline, the vast scope of this evidential material, any one division of which is sufficient to lead reasonable minds to accept, without doubt, his deity: (1) His pre-existence, by which it is meant that he existed before creation, and is thus eternal. (John 1:1.) (2) His possession of all of the divine attributes, which could never be exhibited by a mere creature. (Revelation 1:5; 1 Timothy 1:1.) (3) His acceptance of divine titles wholly improper for ordinary mortals. (John 10:35; Philippians 2:5-8.) (4) His absolutely perfect and sinless life among men; his fulfillment of all of the Messianic predictions of the Old Testament; his remarkable miracles, and his trimphant resurrection from the dead. (Romans 1:4.) Those who knew him best, on earth, bore similar testimony to his unique character; and, his enemies, unable to deny the reality of his supernatural acts, conceded they were superhuman, and attributed them to the devil!

Those who are disposed to *discount* the testimony of inspiration touching our Lord's nature, must *account,* in some fashion, for the historic proofs which everywhere abound. That such a man as our Lord lived no knowledgeable person today denies. The Roman writers Tacitus, Suetonius and Pliny all bear witness to this fact. That he was crucified on a cross by order of Pilate is likewise by all admitted. Thus secular history establishes the fact that Jesus of Nazareth both lived and died. To this point, there is agreement between believers and unbelievers. Deposited in a borrowed tomb in old Jerusalem was the body of a man whom all—enemies and friends alike—believed had disappeared forevermore from the earth. The disciples, dull of mind, and unable to comprehend the Lord's teaching, believed they would see his face no more, and his enemies rejoiced in this concept. Yet, a movement, destined to shake the earth in a few short years, came forth from the tomb.

"Why did Jesus refuse to answer the question submitted to him by the chief priests and elders as recorded in Matthew 21:23-27?"

> And when he was come into the temple, the chief priests and the elders of the people came unto him as he was teaching, and said, By what authority doest thou these things? and who gave thee this authority? And Jesus answered and said unto them, I also will ask you one thing, which if ye tell me, I in like wise will tell you by what authority I do these things.

The baptism of John, whence was it? from heaven, or of men? And they reasoned with themselves, saying, If we shall say, From heaven; he will say unto us, Why did you not then believe him? But if we shall say, Of men; we fear the people; for all hold John as a prophet. And they answered Jesus and said, We cannot tell. And he said unto them, Neither tell I you by what authority I do these things.

The "chief priests" were those officials among the Jews responsible for the temple worship. This involved a great variety of duties including the sacrifices, the lighting of the lamps of the sanctuary, the care and maintenance of the sacred buildings. Among them were various orders, and they were quite numerous. It is believed that approximately 24,000 priests were stationed in Jerusalem, and another 12,000 in Jericho. Many of these men, when our Lord was there, were ignorant, corrupt and self-serving, and were divided into warring sects. The Aaronic priesthood, originated by command of Jehovah through Moses (Exodus 29:1ff; Leviticus 8:1ff), was now largely without honor and had lost much of its influence of earlier years. So great was the deterioration of the order in New Testament times, it bore little resemblance to that ordained of God in the days of Moses and Aaron. "Elders," among the Jews in that dispensation, were civil, as well as religious, leaders of the people.

The action of Jesus in cleansing the temple and casting out those who had profaned it (Matthew 21:12; Mark 11:15-19; Luke 19:45-48; John 2:13-22), infuriated the Jewish authorities. The trading they had tolerated in the sacred precincts of the temple area was exceedingly lucrative; they certainly shared in the profits attending these transactions; and the expulsion of the traders from the area was not only costly to them, it was also regarded as a challenge to their authority and a contemptuous disregard of their official position. Normally, they would have regarded such action as of sufficient gravity to justify seizing and summarily punishing the perpetrator on the spot, but they were aware of his widespread influence with the common people and the authorities did not dare to risk the antagonism of the people at this point. They sought first of all to impair this influence by questioning his authority to act, as he had done, in such matters. Their query was presented in two forms: (1) By what authority do you do these things? (2) Who gave you this authority? They hoped to force him to deal specifically with this question, By what *kind* of authority, *civil* or *religious,* by man or from God, do you claim to act?

Had he replied, "From God," they would have charged him with blasphemy. Had he replied, "From Caesar," they would have accused him of treason, and immediately have taken him before Pilate, the Roman governor. Had he answered, "None," this would have put him in the position of being a law violator, and his influence would have been impaired with the people. Their purpose was thus one of entrapment.

Jesus answered, "I also will ask you one thing ... the baptism of John, whence was it? from heaven, or of men?" His response to them said, in effect, "We must first determine whether you are qualified to discuss authority. Do you know its ultimate source? To test your knowledge of this matter, tell me about the baptism of John. Was it divinely authorized, or was it a commandment of man?" This remarkable reply impaled those conniving Jews on the horns of the dilemma they intended for him! John the Baptist was widely regarded by the people to be a prophet sent from God; were they to answer that the baptism of John was "from men," they would have aroused bitter resentment among the people, and toward themselves antagonism, by questioning the right of a prophet to speak; had they answered that the baptism of John was from heaven, they would find themselves in the position, as religious leaders, of rejecting one whose actions they had just conceded to be from God!

Caught in their own trap, they said they could not tell. They thus found themselves to be in the embarrassing positions of not being able to answer a simple question, though they professed to be religious leaders of the people. By their evasive and dishonest tactics they demonstrated their unworthiness, and abdicated their right to be regarded as spiritual advisers of the people.

Here, as in every such instance, our Lord demonstrated consummate wisdom and great skill in dealing with errorists; his irresistible logic and his infinite grasp of truth enabled him always to triumph over error and to put to rout his adversaries. It is not surprising that the chapter in which these events are recorded concludes with the observation, "And no man was able to answer him a word, neither durst any man from that day forth ask him any more questions." (Matthew 22:46.)

"Please comment on David's statement, 'Thy word have I hid in mine heart that I might not sin against thee.' (Psalm 119:11.)"

The blessings and benefits of God's word are ours only if the teaching of this precious volume is stored up in our hearts and allowed to find expression in our lives. "Let the word of Christ dwell in you richly," (Colossians 3:16), is Paul's pointed admonition to this end. We are all possessed of a mental, moral, spiritual and physical nature; only when each of these elements of our being is trained and cultivated are we fully developed as God would have us to be. (Luke 2:52.)

Teaching and training of others, having as its goal fewer than all of these elements of our being is deficient and leaves the individual thus neglected deprived of the training so essential to his well-being, dwarfed in one or more of the areas of his nature which God gave him, and denied the potential in life every human deserves. It matters little how much one may learn of life from history and philosophy, the arts and sciences, and the myriad other sources of materialistic knowledge, one without training in the scriptures is an uneducated person. A knowledge of the Bible is, indeed, necessary for one properly to evaluate and put in proper perspective all other human wisdom. There is hardly any area into which the inquiring mind may probe but that the scriptures provide direction and guidance.

The translators of the King James Version of the scriptures in 1611, in their long preface (unfortunately omitted from most editions of that work printed today), wrote: "If we are ignorant, the scripture will instruct us; if out of the way, they will bring us home; if out of order, they will reform us; if in heaviness, they will comfort us; if dull, quicken us; if cold, inflame us."

Early interest in the scriptures, on the part of a child, and the commitment to memory of as much of the Bible as possible in the impressionable years, is the surest guarantee of later faithfulness and the best possible protection against materialism, worldliness and a life of sin in later years of maturity. The great English philosopher Locke wrote: "For true morality, I would direct a young man to none other book than the Bible, specially the New Testament scriptures. Let him study them, for therein are contained the words of eternal life." In contrast, the infidel Celsus (born near the middle of the second century, A.D.), in explaining why Christianity had spread so rapidly and widely, wrote: "They got hold of their children in their homes and taught them Christianity." The heathen Roman ruler Julian (A.D. 350) expelled every Christian teacher from the schools; less than 200 years later, another Roman emperor ordered that no Christian might teach in the public schools of the realm.

The Law of Moses, in sharp contrast with this effort to exclude the influence of the scriptures from public education, required parents to keep ever before the minds of their offspring the precious words of holy writ: "And these words, which I command thee this day, shall be in thine heart: and thou shalt teach them diligently to thy children, and shall talk of them when thou sittest in thine house, and when thou walkest by the way, and when thou liest down, and when thou risest up." (Deuteronomy 6:6,7.)

All of us should commit to memory as much of the sacred text as possible. It is an excellent form of mental exercise, and it will greatly strengthen our "mental muscles" as bodily exercise enhances our physical powers. More, it will fill the mind with noble thoughts, provide an ever-present source of rich material for meditation, and best of all, put into our minds and hearts the teaching of the Holy Spirit regarding the way of salvation and ultimate deliverance from the power and presence of sin.

A good and great gospel preacher more than 60 years ago wrote: "Let those teachers in the Sunday morning classes, as a supplement to the material provided in the lesson helps, assign a portion of the Bible to be memorized during the week and recited the following Sunday. Those who thus do will live in the hearts of those so influenced, along with the scriptures, by their influence enshrined there, and when the teachers have passed on from this world, they will still be influencing for good those they caused to commit portions of the sacred writings to memory." This writer believes this advice to be sound and practical and urges all who teach to pursue it.

"What is the biblical (not the philosophical or theological) difference between faith, knowledge and opinion?"

Biblical faith is the belief of divine testimony. (John 20:30,31.) Elementary knowledge is information in the mind derived by perception. An opinion results from inferences (though not necessary ones) resting on premises not possible to prove.

It will be seen that each of these terms denotes a particular mental state; some things we know; other things we believe; on some other matters we form opinions. Each differs from the other in the manner in which it is derived and, in this respect, is not interchangeable in meaning or usage with the others. We know that ice is cold, not because someone told us it is, but because we have experienced it through the senses; we believe there is a city named Moscow, on the basis of testimony we regard as reliable, though we have never seen it; it is our opinion that some day there will be a worldwide nuclear war, though we have neither witnessed such a conflict, nor has anyone on whose testimony we may infallibly rely told us there will be.

While knowledge, in its strictest sense, derives from the senses, there are some things we can be fully assured of, though they are not immediately perceived by the five senses. Some matters are presented to the mind in such fashion we regard them as intuitively true, and do not doubt them. For example, "Things equal to the same thing are equal to each other," is a postulate self-evident to the rational mind, requiring no further propositions or premises to establish. Many matters set out in the sacred writings are so sure and certain that it is said we "know" them, though they are neither seen, felt, tasted, smelled or heard. (2 Corinthians 5:1.) This is a derived meaning of the word "know," and applicable only to such matters as indicated. This distinction the Holy Spirit very carefully preserved in the Greek words *ginoosko* (I know from having learned in some fashion and I thus have the matter in my mind), and *oida,* a perfect verb, denoting that which comes to me from without, objective knowledge. It is for this reason that when the knowledge contemplated is the result of experience the word is *ginoosko.* (cf. Philippians 3:10; Ephesians 3:19.) Many things are beyond the realm of human apprehension in the usual way of receiving them into the mind, and they can be laid hold on only by faith when infallible testimony supports it, and by opinion when the premises lead to conclusions at best probable. Faith is therefore infinitely more dependable than human knowledge, being based on infallible testimony. My senses may deceive me; God never will. (Hebrews 6:18.)

Faith rests on testimony (John 20:30,31; Romans 10:17), and the strength of the faith is determined by the clarity of the testimony and one's willingness to accept it. Anything less falls into the realm of opinion. Biblical faith then, is the belief of divine testimony; knowledge, in its primary sense, is a conclusion grounded in personal experience; and opinion results when the conclusion drawn is not sufficiently supported to produce faith. I know that Nashville, Tenn., exists because I live there; I believe that Ronald Reagan lives in the White House in Washington, D.C., based on evidence I regard as reliable, though I have not been in the President's Mansion when he was there; and it is my opinion that in the latter part of the 21st century there will be interplanetary travel. These distinctions in faith, knowledge and opinion are vital to any proper understanding of the scriptures on these themes.

Faith then, depends on infallible testimony, opinions on probability. Some matters are probable, others are more probable, still others less so, and some are improbable. The degree of probability we determine for ourselves through the exercise of perception and judgment. All of us reach conclusions in this manner, but they are, and should evermore be recognized as opinions and nothing more—not matters of faith. Opinion, because it operates only in the realm of human judgment, can never resolve any issue regarding the weal or woe of man. If a proposition to us appears to be probably so, to another, equally wise and capable, it may be regarded as not probably so; and thus the matter passes into an area of non-resolution. Opinion is utterly without value in the determination of truth. Faith involves that which is beyond the senses; it cannot exist in the absence of testimony; testimony implies and necessitates credible witnesses, and the value of the testimony of the witnesses is determined by their competency and reliability in the matters of which they speak. The competency and veracity of the biblical writers is not an issue with those who truly love the Lord. (John 15:12; 1 John 2:4; 5:3.) This matter has long since been settled in heaven. (Psalm 119:89.)

Faith, of the three mental states herein considered, is infinitely more reliable, being based on divine affirmation. Knowledge is dependent on the senses which may, and sometimes do, deceive us; opinion, relying on varying degrees of probability, sometimes misleads. We must not from this conclude that faith is limited to direct statement; commands, in the Bible, are indeed expressions of the divine will, and must be obeyed, but they are not more binding than are the examples of those who were carrying out the expressed will of the Lord in areas of duty characteristic of all children of God. The early church observed the Lord's Supper every first day of the week (Acts 20:7); this, they did in carrying out the apostles' doctrine (Acts 2:42), and the duty devolves upon us—and is as much a matter of faith—no less certainly, though there is an absence of a specific commandment to us to this end.

In the area of faith, children of God are restricted to the teaching of the scriptures; in matters of opinion they have wide latitude so long as opinion is not suffered to invade those areas where faith motivates. Faith does not supplant opinion—each operates in different fields; opinion must never be allowed to displace faith. The current effort to deny that singing God's praises in the church (an obvious act of faith), is authorized, and to insist, at the same time, that the use of instrumental music which is now conceded to be no more than an opinion in justification thereof, is proper, evidences how dangerous is the confusion today prevailing regarding these matters. There is indeed a realm for opinion involving matters either obscurely taught, or not at all, in the scriptures, but this does not sanction or authorize the use of such matters to the disruption of peace, fellowship and unity in the Lord's body. The command to perform an act such as singing in worship to God (Ephesians 5:19), involves, by implication, everything necessary to its discharge—*and just as certainly excludes all else*! The command to sing does not authorize the addition of mechanical instruments of music, any more than the command to pray authorizes the worship of images.

Freedom to act, in matters of religion, is far from being unlimited, and the restrictions are the Lord's. Any effort to turn faith into opinion or opinion into faith in matters of religion, is to reject the will of the Lord, to substitute human judgment for the divine, to vitiate the cause the effort affects to serve, and to abandon all right to any proper and just claim of loyalty to the word of the Lord. It must never be forgotten that God's will is as clearly expressed in the silence of the scriptures as it is in their positive affirmations, and in any instance where God has not spoken we must assume that it was because he chose not to speak! To presume to speak for him in such instances is surely the ultimate in presumption, and will not go unnoticed by him at that Last Great Day. (Deuteronomy 4:2.)

298

"Did Solomon forbid drunkenness only in discussing the dangers of the 'wine cup,' or did he condemn the use wine itself as a beverage?"

"Who hath woe? who hath sorrow? who hath contentions? who hath complaining? who hath wounds without cause? who hath redness of eyes? They that tarry long at the wine; they that go to seek out mixed wine. Look not thou upon the wine when it is red, when it sparkleth in the cup, when it goeth down smoothly: at the last it biteth like a serpent, and stingeth like an adder." (Proverbs 23:29-32)

This is a finely dramatic passage, emphasizing in a most impressive manner the evils arising from the use of strong drink. The wise man sits musing upon various classes and types of humanity. In his vision an object in whom is concentrated every species of misery arises, and he asks, "To whom, to what men—to what class of men—belong this cry of lament, this load of sorrow," and the answer is at hand, "Those who sit long and late over the wine, who look upon it when it is red." This is truly a vivid description of a man enslaved by drink. He is full of *woe;* on his shoulders rest the troubles of the world. His griefs and sorrows are greatly multiplied; and he contends with all who will listen. He bears about in his body various wounds and bruises, caused by his brawling with others and his eyes are bloodshot and red from much tippling. And, however attractive the wine may be, however red and appealing in the cup, it will sting with all the venom of an adder when once it is taken into the body. This should be remembered when reading the alluring advertisement of liquor dealers.

This section teaches us that tipplers and lovers of strong drink are miserable, contentious in word and in deed, subject to marks of violence, betraying their habits by their disfigured faces.

The plea that Solomon here warns against drunkenness only, or the excessive use of intoxicating drink, is contrary to the terms and the spirit of the passage. Drinking, in the sense of intoxication, is not necessarily implied at all; and it is not intoxication, but *wine* that is described in verse 31; nor can intoxication be said to *bite at last.* It is manifestly the design of the wise man to point out the physical cause of all the misery he portrays, and this he finds in the *nature* of intoxicating liquor, and hence both reason and revelation constrain him to counsel abstinence. When men learn that alcoholic drink *abuses* them they will cease to talk the virtue of not *abusing* it.

There is never any excuse today for the use of intoxicating liquors in any degree. Formerly, it was urged by some that it had medicinal value, and many justified its use for this purpose. But in recent times the medical profession has outlawed the use of liquor for such purposes, and there is therefore no semblance of excuse for indulgence therein today. It is alarming at the apathy that obtains, even among many professed members of the church toward the multifold evils of strong drink. Not infrequently, members of the church actually defend legalized liquor and urge that it is better for the state to license the use thereof than to attempt to prohibit it altogether. Such individuals deserve no milder punishment than to feel the sickening crunch of broken bones and to hear the moans of their loved ones caused by some drunken driver. Claims that there is less drinking today than under prohibition are false; but even if this were true, the nation at least had not legalized and endorsed a vicious evil. Never let it be said that the Lord's people ever made it legal for some boy and girl to saturate themselves in the vile stuff. Our influence should always be against it in every form.

"What is situation ethics?

A brother writes, "I have a problem which has bothered me for some time . . . The following quotation from a current brotherhood publication states the problem very well:

Situations do arise in which more than one moral alternative must be considered. In such situations the exceptional moral principle may negate what would normally be considered "right" exchanging it for a situationally higher principle. For example, under normal conditions it is right to obey the speed limit. But when an exceptional moral principle is introduced to the situation (an injured person in the car) it becomes right to exceed the speed limit and possibly wrong not to do so.

Biblical examples of this point include Rahab, who lied to protect the men of Israel in her home (Joshua 2:1-7) and who was catalogued among the "Heroes of the Faith" (Hebrews 11:31) *for doing so.* Jesus said, "Give to the one who asks you, and do not turn away from the one who wants to borrow from you." (Matthew 5:42) But for a special situation in Thessalonica Paul ignored that teaching and gave this moral teaching. . . ." (2 Thessalonians 3:10-12.)

Jesus himself approved the action of David and his companions when, on a time of special need, they ate the bread which was lawful only for the priests to eat. (Leviticus 24:5-9; 1 Samuel 21:6; Mark 2:23-28.) Admittedly, the need to choose between ethical alternatives raises the possibility of moral license. The individual must determine in the light of God's word and with his help, whether he is exercising *agape* or selfish ambition.

Our querest adds, "My problem with the above statements is that I was brought up believing that one should stand fast for the great principles of Christ at all cost, even at the risk of death. I remember feeling that I would die rather to lie or steal, even when quite young.

Just in the last three or four years have I become aware of the above teaching. Just recently, our preacher preached almost the identical thing from the pulpit; I have read it in several magazine articles. . . . How can I reconcile the statement that God 'hates' a lying tongue with the article which states that Rahab was a hero of faith because she lied? How can I reconcile the statement that Jesus approved unlawful deeds to satisfy a person's hunger? If a person is hungry, does this mean that stealing is justified? That in order to avoid being killed, killing another is justified? Perhaps I had thought that such actions were sinful and contrary to God's nature, but fell within the realm of a judge's pardon; but that we cannot anticipate that pardon by willfully doing wrong. Our preacher explained it by saying that the above things were *wrong,* but it would be *a greater wrong* not to do them, and that no sin is charged when a person does a *lesser* wrong. Another question might be, did Jesus ever lie under *any* circumstances; steal under *any* circumstances; do unlawful deeds under *any* circumstances? If Jesus did lie under certain circumstances, then God could also lie under certain circumstances. How can we be sure what those circumstances are?"

The sentiment which our brother cites from "a current brotherhood publication," and from his local preacher is *situation ethics.* The view regards *love* as the highest, and in the case of conflict with others laws, *whether of God or man,* the *only* standard of right. Where love prevails, law, even in conflict with it, must give way—even the laws of God! One may, the writer avers, violate the laws of men and the law of God with impunity, provided love influences to a course believed to be the best for others. Thus love may supersede law—even the law of God. Man's judgment is made the criterion of what is proper for God to command and what is not; and, all law, whether of God or men, may, at will, be disregarded, when, in man's view, it conflicts with the "higher" principle of love!

This shocking conclusion is opposed both to reason and to revelation; the instances cited (e.g., Rahab, David and Paul), are grossly misapprehended and improperly applied, and the basic assumption is wrong because it seeks to make love *the rule of righteousness* when it is, in reality, *the incentive which leads to righteousness.* John said, "For this is the love of God, *that* we keep his commandments. . . ." (1 John 5:3.) Love does not determine what righteousness is; it recognizes it, because God commanded it, and does it for this reason. Further, John said, "His commandments are not grievous" (*barus*), "burdensome, difficult to fulfil" (Arndt & Gingrich). They are a blessing, and not a burden, to man.

"Is is ever 'right' to do 'wrong?' "

A writer, in a magazine designed to circulate among members of the churches of Christ wrote, "under normal conditions it is right to obey the speed limit. But when an exceptional moral principle is introduced to the situation (an injured person in the car) it becomes right to exceed the speed limit and possibly wrong not to." Waiving the legal aspects of the question (e.g., exceptions involving emergencies, emergency vehicles, when a vehicle becomes an emergency one, etc.), we shall examine the brother's argument as he presents it.

(1) The laws of the land, *including* speed laws, are ordained of God. (Romans 13:1ff.) Paul solemnly warned, "Whosoever therefore resisteth the power [civil authority], resisteth the ordinance of God: and they that resist shall receive to themselves damnation." (13:2.) God ordained civil power because it is absolutely essential to man's wellbeing. It is not possible for man to survive in a state of society without civil law. Anarchy is the alternative.

(2) These laws have taken shape over a long period of years; they were forged in the furnace of experience, and have been honed by use so that they represent the best and most practical regulations our legislative bodies are able to devise. Our speed laws, particularly, in school zones, and residential areas, where specifically designed for the safety and protection of all, whether drivers or pedestrians.

(3) To disregard these laws is to put in jeopardy other people. Our situational brother contends that it is an exhibition of the law of love, to violate the law of man (and, consequently, the law of God) in behalf of an injured person. Does the law of love justify the risk of grave injury or death *to others?* There are instances where injured people, being rushed to the hospital by intemperate driving, have experienced another accident and suffered further injuries. Does love prompt to such risks? Our brother's argument is invalid. *His illustration involves the violation of law and love!*

The brother further argues, "Biblical examples of this point include Rahab, who lied to protect the men of Israel in her home (Joshua 2:1-7) and who was catalogued among the 'Heroes of the Faith' (Hebrews 11:31) for doing so." This conclusion is grossly erroneous. Rahab was commended, and chronicled among the heroes of the faith, *not because she lied,* but because her faith in God's plan and purpose prompted her to take the grave risks which she did. She rightly regarded opposition to God as vastly more dangerous than possible discovery by her countrymen of the acts involved, and she thus exhibited great faith. This faith earned for a her a niche among the great people of the past—*not her falsehood.* There is no more reason to suppose that this aspect of the incident was approved of God than the *treachery* of Jael (Judges

4:17-24), or the *vow* of Jephthah (Judges 11:1-40) in keeping with a remarkable characteristic of scripture to report truth, whether favorable or unfavorable to those involved. The historian merely recorded the fact of Rahab's falsehood without evaluating it.

Matthew Henry very aptly says, "We are sure that God discriminated between what was good in her conduct and what was bad; rewarding the former, and pardoning the latter. Her views of the divine law must have been exceedingly dim and contracted. A similar falsehood, told by those who enjoy the light of revelation, however, laudable the motive, would of course deserve a much heavier censure." He who is the very embodiment of *truth;* who by the *truth* makes men free; and, whose mission in the world was to dissipate error with *truth,* cannot look with favor on an effort designed to disregard it. Moral law has, as its end, the welfare of the race; and, genuine happiness here, and hereafter, is dependent on man's adherence thereto. It is supreme folly for man presumptuously to say that it is in order to set aside these laws on the ground that his judgment is superior to God's will in specific situations. The claim, however sincere the motive, is rebellion against God at the highest level.

"Does love for man take precedence over the laws (commandments) of God? Is love "the highest moral principle," and to be exercised, though such involve disregard of the divine edicts? Is it true that what is "right" may indeed differ in any given situation, depending on what the "loving" response is? Is there an "intrinsic conflict between the way of law and the way of love through Christ?"

In an earlier answer we have examined, in detail, the writer's allegation that "situations do arise in which more than one moral alternative must be considered." Another such instance, we are informed, occurred when Paul "ignored" our Lord's teaching!

"Jesus said, 'Give to the one who asks you, and do not turn away from the one who wants to borrow from you.' (Matthew 5:42.) But for a special situation in Thessalonica Paul ignored that teaching and gave this moral instruction: 'For even when we were with you, we gave this rule: if a man will not work, he shall not eat. . . .' (2 Thessalonians 3:10-12.)"

This is hardly an instance of situation ethics. Were we to concede the conflict between Christ and Paul which the author alleges, this passage puts Paul in the position oif the defender of *law* against *love! Did not the apostle know that the welfare state, in which every person may do his own thing, without the annoying problem of making a living, is the highest realization of love? And, besides, the world owes "us" a living;*

and wealth and property ought to be re-distributed, anyway. To demand, as the apostle does, that a man must work before he can eat, is law, on its lowest level, not love! This is situation ethics.

Of course, we concede no such conflict between Paul and Christ. The effort does gross injustice to our Lord and the great apostle. Our Lord's edict, "Give to the one who asks you . . ." must be interpreted in the light of its context, and in harmony with his teaching elsewhere. "If ye shall ask anything in my name, I will do it." (John 14:14.) To ask in his name, is to ask by his authority and in keeping with his will. Since he gives in this manner, he does not require of us to act in any fashion contrary to his will. To give indiscriminately is not love. A gun to a would-be murderer, charity to a deceiver, and alcohol to a drunkard are not acts of love, but of injury. Further, Paul's injunctions to the Thessalonians, grounded as they were in the well-being of the people to whom he wrote, actually exhibited the principle which Jesus taught. Strange indeed that a writer affecting loyalty to the scriptures would attempt to array Paul against Christ. The effort borders on blasphemy.

We are informed in the article under review that Jesus himself approved the action of David and his companions when, on a time of special need, they ate the bread which was lawful only for the priests to eat. (Leviticus 24:5-9; 1 Samuel 21:6; Mark 2:23-28.)

The Pharisees charged the disciples with violating the law of Moses because they gathered a portion of grain on the sabbath day to allay hunger. The charge was false (Deuteronomy 23:25); it was the Talmud, not the law, which did this. Jesus replied by pointing out that on an occasion of special need David ate bread lawful only for the priests to eat. The Pharisees justified David's act; yet, they condemned an act identical in principle on the part of the disciples of Jesus. The allegation of the writer under review is that the disciples of Jesus violated the law, and that Jesus justified it by an appeal to the case of David.

The conclusion does not follow. Jesus cited the case of David, and the shew-bread, but he did not approve of David's action, either here, or elsewhere, in this instance. It is an argument *ad hominen,* an appeal to their own reasoning; and, it ran like this: David's action, in this matter was in violation of the law, yet you justify him in it; my disciples engaged in an act which the law permits, yet you condemn them. Jesus taught his disciples to observe all of the law, even its most minute portions, observing that not one "jot" or "tittle" should pass until all are fulfilled. He warned that "Whosoever shall break one of these least commandments, and teach men so, shall be called the least in the kingdom of heaven." (Matthew 5:17-20.) If we are at liberty to regard *love* as the only "universal and permanently binding ethical rule," as the writer under review alleges, taking precedence over all of the divine edits of scripture, every man becomes a law unto himself; reason, not faith, determines the proper course, and the New Morality becomes the order of the day.

"Much is said regarding the qualifications of elders. What are the qualifications of preachers set out in the Bible?"

(1) Rebuke false teachers sharply. (Titus 1:3.)
(2) Speak the things that become sound doctrine. (Titus 2:1)
(3) Teach aged men, young men, aged women, young women. (Titus 2:2-5.)
(4) In all things show oneself a pattern of good works. (Titus 2:7.)
(5) Use such speech that no evil thing can be said of one. (Titus 2:8.)
(6) Teach servants their duty to their masters. (Titus 2:9.)
(7) The foregoing things to speak, exhorting and rebuking with all authority, meanwhile allowing no one to despise him. (Titus 2:15.)
(8) Instruct people to be subject to civil authorities, speak evil of no man, but be gentle, showing meekness toward all.
(9) Avoid foolish questions, contentions and strivings about the law. (Titus 3:9.)
(10) Reject heretics after the first and second admonition. (Titus 3:10.)
(11) Rebuke not elders. (1 Timothy 5:1.) Treat elder women as mothers, young women as sisters.
(12) Against elders receive not accusations, except before two or three witnesses.
(13) Those that sin rebuke before all. (1 Timothy 5:20.)
(14) Observe these things without preferring one before another, doing nothing by partiality. (1 Timothy 5:21.)
(15) Lay hands suddenly on no man.
(16) No partaker of other men's sins.
(17) Keep oneself pure. (1 Timothy 5:22.)
(18) Follow righteousness, godliness, faith, love, patience and meekness. (Ibid.)
(19) Teach the rich their duty. (1 Timothy 6:17.)
(20) Keep that committed to one's trust. (1 Timothy 6:15.)
(21) Avoid profane and vain babblings. (1 Timothy 6:20.)

In addition are all the characteristics of Christians, since preachers are, first of all, expected to be Christians, and then proclaimers of the world.

"Explain Luke 6:29,30."

Jesus said, "To him that smiteth thee on the one cheek offer also the other; and from him that taketh away thy cloak withhold not thy coat

305

also. Give to every one that asketh thee; and of him that taketh away thy goods ask them not again." (Luke 6:29,30.) This unique and remarkable affirmation of our Lord to his disciples involves a philosophy of religion wholly foreign to that which characterized the law of Moses. The law which issued from Sinai did indeed require the people to love their neighbors (Leviticus 19:18); but, it did not specifically order them to love their enemies; and, inasmuch as the Jews believed their neighbors were no other than their own people, they drew the conclusion that they were not required to love their enemies. In the light of numerous Old Testament utterances the view was not wholly untenable, though Jewish teachers of our savior's day carried it far, far beyond what God ever intended.

For example on various occasions the Israelites were positively forbidden to make peace with their heathen neighbors; and, against the seven nations of Canaan they were instructed to wage a war of annihilation and extinction. (Exodus 34:11-16; Deuteronomy 7:2; 23:6.) The "imprecatory" Psalm delivered by David by inspiration (doubtless intended to be interpreted metaphorically, and not literally), certainly encouraged the disposition of antagonism toward foreigners which appears to have been wellnigh universal among the Jewish teachers of the New Testament period. (Psalms 137:7-9; 139:21,22.) We must keep the proper perspective in mind in dealing with these matters, and to remember that the heathen nations bordering Israel were a constant threat to her existence, and to the preservation of the doctrine of the one true God; and it is not surprising that feelings of bitterness were fierce and deep. Unfortunately, the Jews carried the matter to the point of despising *any* people not Jews, whether they were antagonistic toward them, or not.

Our Lord taught us that instead of hating others, we are to "do good to them that hate" us. This is not to say that we are to have exactly the same feeling toward those who evilly treat us as we would toward those who are kind and good to us, and who love us. Our Lord has special friends whom he chose to be with on occasion, rather than others (John 11:3; 13:33), and it would be far from correct to assert that he felt the same warmth of affection for Judas who betrayed him, as he did for the disciples who eventually died for him. We are to love our enemies, if such we have; we are to avoid all bitterness, malice andd unkindness toward them, and to do them good; but, this does not mean that we are expected to experience the same warm, emotional response from corrupt, evil and depraved persons which we do from those who are good, kind and loveable.

Love for enemies conveys a different notion, and is the translation of a different Greek word from that used to describe love for dear ones in the Bible. Jesus prayed for those who mistreated him, and we can do the same for those who oppose us, but this does not mean that Jesus acorded the blaspheming Jews who clamored for his death the same place in his heart which John, the beloved disciple, enjoyed!

If one smite us on one cheek, we are to "offer also the other." Matthew's fuller report of these words reads, "Resist not him that is evil: but whosoever smiteth thee on thy right cheek, turn to him the other also." (Matthew 5:39.) It is most unlikely that our Lord intended a literal interpretation of his words here. If the statement is to be literally construed, are we free to resort to retaliation, when the second cheek has been turned, and smitten? On the assumption that the statement was intended to be physically followed, when such has been done we will have complied fully with the obligation. Obviously, our duty goes far beyond any literal concept which thus follows. The example of our Lord himself confirms this exegesis. When an officer, in those last, dark hours before his death, viciously struck him, Jesus did not invite further indignity, but instead rebuked the man for his wicked and unjustified act (John 18:22); and, when Paul was struck in the face while on trial in Jerusalem, his sense of justice was outraged, and he spoke out sharply against the offender (Acts 23:1-3).

What *is* taught in Luke 6:29,30, is that instead of hating others, we are to do them good; we are not to return evil for evil; and we are not to retaliate, *in kind,* when we are mistreated. Physical assault on Christians today, is rare; but, mental, psychological and emotional attacks are common. In all such instances we are to return good for evil in imitation of our Lord who, when he was reviled, "reviled not again; when he suffered, threatened not; but committed himself to him that judgeth righteously." (1 Peter 2:22,23).

If one take our "cloak" we are not to withhold our "coat." The *cloak* was the long, outer garment worn by day and used as covering at night. The law of Moses forbade that it be taken as surety for a debt. (Exodus 22:26,27.) The coat was an inner garment. Here, also, as above, it is not likely that Jesus intended a literal interpretation of his words. What is taught is that, in order *to do right,* we must be willing to go beyond what is demanded. He does not put us at the mercy of every thug who comes along. And, when he said, "Give to every one that asketh," we must understand this in the light of the context, and the general teaching of the Bible. It means no more than that we are to minister to the *proper* needs of others. Paul ruled that those who will not work should not be given food (2 Thessalonians 3:10), and Jesus said, 'Give not that which is holy unto the dogs." (Matthew 7:6.) Obviously, he does not require us to give money to an alcoholic to purchase liquor or to an addict to buy drugs. The obligation of the instructions of our Lord are summed up in his magnificent affirmation, "As ye would that men should do to you, do ye also to them likewise" (Luke 6:31), and if we are thus motivated, we will not go wrong in determining what our duties are to others.

"Discuss the difference in the translation of 2 Timothy 3:17,18 in the King James and the American Standard Versions."

"Every scripture inspired of God is also profitable for teaching, for reproof, for correction, for instruction which is in righteousness: that the man of God may be complete, furnished completely unto every good work." (2 Timothy 3:16, 17.) Such is the rendering of this vital passage by the American Standard translators. The King James translators preferred the following rendering: "All scripture is given by inspiration of God, and is profitable for doctrine, for reproof, for correction, for instruction in righteousness: that the man of God may be perfect, throughly furnished unto all good works."

The two translations differ principally in that the former—the American Standard—asserts that "every scripture inspired of God is also profitable . . ." and the latter—the King James—declares that "all scripture is given by inspiration of God, and is profitable . . ."; the former affirms that "the man of God is furnished completely unto every good work"; the latter that "the man of God . . ." is "throughly furnished unto all good works."

Which of these renderings is the preferable one has been a subject of debate since the days of Origen—who lived not long after the close of the apostolic age. Thus, these differing renderings have had their defenders almost as long as the New Testament has been in existence. The question has been to determine whether it was the design of the apostle to say that *all the scripture there is,* is inspired of God; or, whether he intended to say that every scripture *which is inspired of God* is profitable. . . .To say, "Every scripture inspired of God . . ." *assumes* inspiration; to say, "All scripture is given by inspiration of God . . ." is to *assert* inspiration. The American Standard Version reflects the first view; the King James translation, the second opinion.

Neither rendering does violence to the passage; both renderings are grammatical; both of them make crystal clear that the sacred writings are *"God-breathed,"* the words "inspired of God," being from the Greek *theopneustos,* thus indicating that the breath of God enlivens them. The phrase, "Every scripture inspired of God," does not mean that some scripture is not inspired of God; the word "scripture" never appears in the Bible other than as inspired matter. The meaning is that every part of scripture, the whole of it, issues from God—there is no portion of it not inspired. Peter's familiar words indicate the manner in which this was accomplished: "Men spake from God, being moved by the Holy Spirit." (2 Peter 1:21.) With Clement of Rome (who wrote, not long after the apostolic age, a letter to the church in Corinth), we conclude that the scriptures are "the true utterances of the Holy Ghost, and an assertion of the full inspiration of the Bible."

While it is reasonable and proper to conclude that the apostle's affirmation is *primarily* an allusion to the Old Testament Scriptures, in view of the fact that it was extended to embrace "every scripture inspired of God," the New Testament is most certainly included also. The passage is therefore a declaration of the utility of *all* inspired scripture.

These writings are declared to be "profitable" (valuable, useful), for "teaching" (instruction in all matters essential to man's salvation here and hereafter); for "reproof" (conviction of error whether in doctrine or manner of life); for "correction" (restoration of the erring to the right way); for "instruction which is in righteousness" (literally, *training which is in righteousness,* to the end that the "man of God" may be proficient in the performance of all of the duties and the responsibilities of the Christian life).

The ultimate *object* of these inspired utterances is that the man of God may be "complete, furnished completely unto every good work." The "man of God" is the man whom God approves; and, he is approved of God because of his conformity to God's will as expressed in his Word. Such a one is "complete," mature, fully developed in the Christian life, because of his adoption of the precepts of God's will. The Greek word translated "complete" here, denotes a "harmonious combination" of all of those qualities and characteristics which constitute a faithful Christian. That which enables one to be "complete" (fully mature in the Christian life), is the scripture "inspired of God."

The extent to which the scriptures are capable of thus operating is neither partial nor insufficient; the person involved is not only *complete,* he is "completely furnished unto every good work." There is verbal repetition here, but not of meaning. The completeness, of which the apostle writes, is characteristic of the man of God *in person,* and *in work.* (1) The scriptures enable him to be fully mature *in life,* and (2) thoroughly equipped *in work.* He is both complete and completely furnished, the words, "furnished completely," being derived from the same Greek root as the word "complete." This sufficiency, provided by the sacred scriptures, extends "unto every good work." If the words are to be assigned their usual and ordinary import; if, in this instance, the Holy Spirit intended to convey, by the words, "every good work," their simple and obvious significance, it follows that there is no area involved not embraced in this phrase. Included, is every good work of the church, as an organized body, every good work of individuals, conceived of as Christians, every good work of men, women, old and young, wise and otherwise, rich and poor—all humanity, either good or bad. One might as well argue that the edict to preach the gospel to *every* creature, capable of believing the message (Mark 16:15,16), is limited in scope, as to contend for anything less than what is ordinarily embraced in the word "every" in 2 Timothy 3:16! *There are no other good works than those thus contemplated.*

The *all-sufficiency* affirmed of the scriptures here, embracing both character and work, will permit of no supplement or complement. The sufficiency thus achieved is not by the word *plus* a personal, direct work of the Spirit, apart from it upon the "man of God," as some among us today affirm. If there are influences wrought upon either the alien sinner, or the faithful child of God, in addition to, or apart from the scriptures, to the extent that such influences operate, the word is insufficient, incomplete, lacking in the ability to "furnish completely" unto "every good work." Its power, on this hypothesis, is partial, needing the additional influences alleged. In which case, the apostle's remark claims for the word more than it is able to accomplish. Are our brethren, who argue for a separate, direct work of the Spirit, willing to concede this conclusion? Whether they do, or not, it follows; and whether such is intended or not, such a conclusion is an impeachment of the sufficiency of the scriptures.

Do we then deny any influence of the Spirit, in conversion and sanctification? On the contrary, we affirm it. With N. B. Hardeman, we say, "The Spirit . . . influences through the gospel, which is God's power. The word is the medium through which the Spirit accomplishes his work." (Debate with Ben M. Bogard). The Holy Spirit strengthens (Ephesians 3:16); sanctifies (2 Thessalonians 2:13; saves (Titus 3:5); justifies (1 Timothy 3:16); witnesses to us (Hebrews 10:15); prompts us to love God (Romans 5:5); leads us as God's sons (Romans 8:16), and will eventually raise us up from the dead (Romans 8:11); but he does all this, and much, much more, by means of the word of truth, his instrument: he strengthens us by providing the whole armor of God, which includes the sword of the Spirit (Ephesians 6:10-17; 2 Timothy 2:1); he saves by supplying the "engrafted word" (John 17:17) which is able to "save" our souls (James 1:21); he justifies "by faith" which comes by hearing God's word (Romans 5:1; 10:13); he witnesses to us by the scriptures which testify of Christ (John 5:39); and he causes us to love God by presenting God to us, in the scriptures, as a loveable being (John 3:16). He leads us by his word (Psalm 119:105), and he will raise us up by means of the *words* of Christ, when we shall *hear the voice of the Son of God* and come forth from the graves (John 5:28,29).

The Holy Spirit, through inspiration of the writers, gave us the message of life and salvation set out in the New Testament. To follow the New Testament is to follow the leading of the Holy Spirit, who gave it; to reject the New Testament is to reject the Spirit—its author. Every blessed influence which the Spirit exercises—and there are many—

every wonderful fruit which the Spirit so lavishly bestows; every rich spiritual need we sustain from the moment the gospel is heard until we die, is supplied us by means of the word which the Spirit gave—not through an exercise of the Spirit apart from, and in addition to, it. With the great and good David Lipscomb we affirm: "The only spiritual instruction, guidance, or influence possible to man is to be gained through coming to the word of God and taking it into the heart as the seed of the kingdom, treasuring it there, and guiding our feelings, thoughts, purposes and lives by its sacred teaching." (*Salvation from Sin,* p. 93.) And, to quote brother Hardeman once more: "Every single step in the divine plan, from the time the sinner decides to become a child of God until he sweeps through the gates into the heavenly realm—every step is effected by God's word! There is no such thing as the Spirit of God operating away from or distinct from the written word." With this sentiment this writer is in full agreement!

"Do repentance and baptism sustain the same relationship to remission of sins in Acts 2:38?"

Some time ago an article appeared from this writer bearing title: "On the Force of the Preposition *Eis*" and treating of the passage, "Repent and be baptized every one of you in the name of Jesus Christ for (Greek *eis*) the remission of sins, and ye shall receive the gift of the Holy Spirit." (Acts 2:38.) Among other things it was said that "The verbs 'repent,' and 'be baptized,' are joined by the copulative conjunction 'and.' They are thus equally related to their object, 'the remission of sins.' Consequently, the relation which repentance bears to its object, baptism also bears, seeing that it has the same object and that its relation is expressed by the same preposition . . ." It must therefore follow that 'for' cannot mean 'because of' as to baptism, and 'in order to,' as to repentance, seeing that a word cannot have two meanings at the same time and in the same place. But since repentance is clearly 'in order to' the remission of sins in the passage, so also is baptism."

One wrote, "I notice your article entitled 'On the Force of the Preposition *Eis*.' I am sure you have done your best in trying to explain this so that you may carry out your doctrine of baptism being essential to salvation. So I will ask you to notice Acts 2:38, 'repent' and 'be baptized' are tied together by the conjunction. The word 'repent' is in the second person, plural number, therefore is a direct, unequivocal command, and the Greek for 'be baptized' is third person, singular number. You should know before you try to teach others that verbs must agree with the subject in number and person. Therefore, the two words, 'repent' and 'be baptized,' cannot be joined to the same predicate."

This objection to the very obvious significance of the passage is not original. Sectarian debators ignorant of the Greek New Testament, or possessing only a smattering knowledge at most, have turned frequently in desperation to this in a vain effort to escape the irresistible force of Peter's statement. No scholar worthy of the title would suffer his name to appear in connection with such a criticism; so doing betrays an utter unfamiliarity with the simplest rules of construction of a Greek sentence. Scholars everywhere hold with Hackett, an eminent Baptist of an earlier generation that " 'In order to the forgiveness of sins,' we connect naturally with both the preceding verbs (i.e. 'repent,' and 'be baptized'). This clause states the motive or object which should induce them to repent and be baptized. It enforces the entire exhortation, not one part of it to the exclusion of the other" (*Hackett's Commentary on Acts,* p. 54).

Put concisely, the objection runs thus: *metanoesate* (repent) is plural number, second person. *Baptistheto* (be baptized) is in the singular number, third person. A verb must agree with its subject in number and person, therefore *metanoesate* and *baptistheto* do not have the same subject. The subject of *metanoesate* is "ye," (plural number), and the subject of *baptistheto* is "every one of you" (singular number). Thus the sentence has two independent clauses, (1) "repent ye" and (2) 'be baptized every one of you in the name of Jesus Christ for the remission of sins." The subject of the first clause is "ye," the predicate "repent." The motive or object is not stated; the command to repent is given imperatively and without reason. The subject of the second clause is "one," modified by the adjective "every," and the prepositional phrase "of you." The verb "be baptized" is modified by the double prepositional phrases "in the name of Jesus Christ," and "for the remission of sins." The prepositional phrase "for the remission of sins" therefore modifies "be baptized" of the second clause, and has no connection with the verb "repent" of the first clause. Thereupon the conclusion is drawn that the verb "repent" cannot have the same object as "be baptized," because they do not agree in person and number. Consequently, since the object "remission" modifies "be baptized," and the preposition "for," signifies "because of," the sense of the passage runs thus: "Repent ye (reason for repenting not stated in the passage) and be baptized every one of you in the name of Jesus Christ for (because of) the remission of sins."

So far as we know it has never been contended that the verbs "repent," and "be baptized," have grammatically the same subject. On the contrary, in the Greek of Acts 2:38, the subjects of the verbs do not appear in the sentence at all; they adhere in, and must therefore be taken from, their verbs. Herein consists the first fallacy of the criticism under consideration. It is absurd to force a Greek sentence into conformity with the rules of English grammar. While it is true that the verbs differ in their substantives grammatically, it is our purpose to prove that they embrace and contemplate the same persons; and more, that the form in which they appear is even more emphastic in teaching the essentiality of baptism for remission of sins.

The context reveals the design of the apostle as expressed in the words of the passage under consideration. As a result of Peter's sermon the multitude were convinced of their guilt in the tragedy of the ages. The overwhelming consciousness that from their fingers dripped the innocent blood of the Son of God cut them to the heart, and crying out, they asked, "Men and brethren, what shall we do?" Do for what? Surely to escape the consequences of their guilt. At least Peter so understood it, for he proceeded to inform them of the means whereby they should receive remission of sins. Two things he commanded them to do: (1) repent and (2) be baptized; thereupon, they were promised "remission of sins." One can only stand aghast and marvel at the reckless ingenuity that would dare lay unholy hands on a passage involving matters of such transcendent moment to the human family. Far better is it to accept without question these words of life and be blessed thereby.

Our critic is grievously at fault in contending that verbs whose subjects differ in number and person cannot take the same object. They can and in many instances in the sacred writings do take the same object. The rule is as follows: Imperatives when connected by a conjunction, expressed or implied, have the same object, unless a different object is expressed or implied. *Metanoesate* is in the imperative mood, second person, plural number. *Baptisheto* is in the imperative mood, third person, singular number. They are connected by the conjunction "and." "Remission" is the only object expressed in the sentence, and no other is implied. Therefore, the rule is operative in this case. Thus the conclusion must follow that the verb "repent" sustains to "remission," the same relation that "be baptized" sustains. But since "repentance" is clearly "in order to" remission, so also is baptism.

Attention is directed to a sentence of similar construction in the New Testament. "Wherefore, brethren covet (Greek *zeloute,* literally 'be emulous') to prophesy, and forbid not (Greek *me kooluete*) to speak in tongues. Let all things be done decently and in order." (1 Corinthians 14:39,40.) The verb of verse 40 is *ginesthoo,* rendered "let be done." The verbs *zeloute* and *kooluete,* are second person, plural number, imperative mood. *Ginesthoo* is third person, singular number, imperative. Though differing in number and person, none can be heard to say that they do not embrace the same persons and therefore take the same object. Thus the rule above set forth is established and the contention of our critic falls to the ground. We have said above that the form in which the sentence appears is all the more emphatic in teaching the essentiality of baptism. Said Peter, "Repent ye (collectively) and be baptized (individually) every one of you in the name of Jesus Christ for the remission of sins." It is surely not difficult to see that "every one of you" is included in the "ye" who were commanded to repent. To illustrate: A contractor hires carpenters to build a house, and says to them, "All of you come, and let each man bring his tools." Certainly, "all" in the sentence is the same as "each man." Yet, "all" is plural, while "each man" is singular, and despite disagreement in number, they embrace and contemplate the same persons.

Critical analysis of Acts 2:38 is necessary only to expose the sophistry of those who wrest the scriptures to their own destruction. Those who are content to let the Bible speak for itself have no difficulty with the passage. It is as clear as a bell on a frosty morning. Faithful men who approach the Bible for no other purpose than to gather the meaning and mind of the Holy Spirit could never concoct such a monstrous criticism as that under consideration. In this connection let it be remembered that baptism is said to be "for" only one thing in all the Bible. While we learn by implication and necessary inference that it has other designs. It is significant and highly so, that it is declared to be "for" only one thing. Peter declares that it is "for" the remission of sins. Students of the New Testament have no other alternative than to accept this statement at face value. To do otherwise is to join the forces of infidelity. Here is the battleground, this is the essence that the Bible declares baptism to be "for" the remission of sins; that it puts "into Christ" (Romans 5:3), and "saves." (1 Peter 3:21.) Yet, sectarian preachers join in a mighty refrain in teaching the people that baptism "is not for" the remission of sins; that it "does not put onto into Christ," and that "it does not save." Then, let the issue be carefully drawn. It is not, What did Peter mean? for he surely meant what he said: It is rather, Did Peter tell the truth? This decision every accountable person must make.

"What are the claims of the Papacy?"

The structure of Catholicism has been built on the assumption that Peter was the first pope, that he was infallible, and that his successors are invested with the same infallibility. To establish this claim, the Catholic Church must prove the primacy of Peter. It is insisted the church was built on Peter, and the following passage is offered in support thereof: "Thou art Peter, and upon this rock I will build my church; and the gates of hell shall not prevail against it." (Matthew 16:18.) We are told that the word "Peter" means "rock," or "stone," (John 1:42.) and since the church is build on a "rock," the passage above is conclusive proof that the church was built on Peter. Hence, the passage should read, "Thou art a rock, and upon this rock I will build my church." That this view is untenable and at variance with the facts clearly appears on examination of the substantives of the sentence. The nouns, "Peter," and "rock" are not of the same gender in the Greek Testament, nor are the words of the same significance. "petros," translated "Peter," is masculine gender, and signifies "fragment," while "petra," rendered "rock" in the passage, is feminine gender, and means "bedrock," "a solid foundation." Paraphrasing, the passage runs thus: "Thou art Peter (petros, masculine gender, a small fragment), and upon this rock (petra, feminine gender, the solid bedrock that I am the Christ, the Son of the Living God), I will build my church, and the gates of hell shall not prevail against it."

The claim of infallibility for Peter is as easily refuted. Instead of being immune to the mistakes of men, the scriptures teach quite the contrary, and proof is not wanting that Peter, the impulsive, impetuous one, was especially susceptible to the manifold temptations to which the flesh is heir. Indeed, we are led to believe that his rashness rendered him the most unstable of the apostles, save Judas, and that despite the sobering and refining influence of the persecution and suffering which he endured for the Lord, outcroppings of this instability are in evidence throughout his life. Of this we are assured that Jesus rebuked him sharply on sundry occasions, and in later years when national pride and racial bigotry in his heart build against the "middle wall of partition," which Jesus had forevermore abolished, Paul "withstood him to the face, because he was to be blamed" (Galatians 2:11), administering a stinging rebuke for his dissimulation.

Finally, the assumption so boldly advanced by Catholics that Peter occupied the papal chair as bishop of Rome from A.D. 43 to A.D. 68, is without historical basis. It cannot be proved that Peter ever saw Rome, much less that he spent 25 years there. In the year A.D. 44 Peter was imprisoned by Herod. Josephus fixed this date as the year in which Herod died, and an account of his passing is recorded in the same chapter that tells of Peter's imprisonment. (Acts 12.) Thus Peter could not have been in Rome at that time. Moreover, the epistle to the Romans was written about A.D. 58. In the last chapter of this letter Paul sends greetings to 27 persons, yet did not mention Peter. Is this not singular if Peter was "vicar of Christ and prince of the apostles"? Imagine a devout Catholic addressing a letter to high ranking dignitaries of the church in Rome today and ignoring the "Holy Father." As the end drew near, Paul penned a farewell message to his son in the gospel, Timothy, and said, "Only Luke is with me." (2 Timothy 4:11). Be it remembered that this was uttered in the loneliness of prison in the city where Peter is supposed to have been bishop. Had the "prince of the apostles" abandoned Paul to his fate? Why was he not there offering spiritual guidance to the "doomed son of the church"? The second Epistle of Peter was written about this time, yet no mention is made therein of the tragic event, or the loss sustained by the untimely passing of the prominent disciple. The conclusion is irresistible that in this, as in every other distinctive doctrine, the church of Rome stands at variance with the teachings of the holy scriptures.

"Why do some people teach that repentance precedes faith in the plan of salvation?"

This position they take, not by choice, but of necessity. They teach that forgiveness of sins is at the point of faith, and without further acts of obedience, and according to this view repentance obviously cannot come after faith, for in that event the sinner would be saved from his sin before he repented. In order to clear away this difficulty, and to include repentance among the conditions of pardon, they have simply switched the items, thereby holding that repentance precedes faith in natural sequence.

This view is not only at variance with the plain import of the scriptures but it is contrary to sound reasoning. Repentance is a change of mind with reference to one's manner of life; and it is therefore absurd to expect one to be led to effect this change until he is convinced that some good reason exists for so doing. Faith in Christ supplies the motive and thus becomes the ground of repentance. Until this faith leads its possessor to repentance, it is vain to expect it. The penman of Hebrews said, "But without faith it is impossible to please him: for he that cometh to God must believe that he is, and that he is a rewarder of them that diligently seek him" (Hebrews 11:6). Any repentance which comes before faith is "without faith," and therefore not pleasing in the sight of God. If it were possible to repent before believing in Christ, it would still be "impossible to please God" in so doing. Nor is the objection valid that the faith therein mentioned is faith "in God," and not "faith in Christ"; for acceptably to believe in God, one must also believe that "He is a rewarder of all them that diligently seek him," and since God rewards only through Christ, to believe in God is to believe in Christ also. "Or despisest thou the riches of his goodness and forbearance and longsuffering; not knowing that the goodness of God leadeth thee to repentance?" (Romans 2:4.) The goodness of God furnishes motive for repentance. But since the goodness of God was manifested in giving his only begotten Son to die on the cross for our sins, it follows that before we can know that God is good we must believe that he has given his Son to die for us, and this cannot be believed without faith in the Son. It is therefore impossible for faith to come other than in its natural sequence.

"Explain the force of the preposition *"eis"* in Acts 2:38"

"Then Peter said unto them, Repent, and be baptized every one of you in the name of Jesus Christ for the remission of sins, and ye shall receive the gift of the Holy Spirit." (Acts 2:38.) This remarkable passage exhibits in one full view the inseparable connection which exists between repentance and baptism, whose consequent or object is the remission of sins. Were this the only passage in the sacred writings touching on the question, our assurance of the essentiality of baptism would not be lessened thereby, for to this point the passage speaks intentionally, clearly and decisively. Indeed, it is impossible for one candidly to approach the passage and gather any other meaning who is content to let the scriptures speak for themselves. An unbiased observer is led at once to see that remission is made to depend on baptism in precisely the same sense in which it is made to depend on repentance, and that the connection thus established is of a nature so permanent that remission of sins in all cases is dependent thereon, and may not therefore be enjoyed except in this manner.

To the foregoing, objection is made that baptism is "because of" remission of sins, and that such is the significance of the preposition "for" in the passage under consideration. The view thus taken with reference to baptism makes the passage to read . . . be baptized every one of you . . . "because of" the remission of sins. This is precisely what is contended by those who deny the essentiality of baptism. But a portion of the sentence is lacking. Inserting it, what follows? "Repent and be baptized . . . 'because of' the remission of sins." This is a singular situation, truly.

The bitterest opponents of baptism would scarcely be heard to say that repentance is because of remission of sin. Logically and grammatically, however, this conclusion must follow. The verbs "repent," and "be baptized," are joined by the copulative conjunction "and." They are thus equally related to their object, which in this sentence is "remission of sins." Consequently, the relation which repentance bears to its object, baptism also bears, seeing that it has the same object and that its relation is expressed by the same proposition. There is an inflexible rule of language touching on this very point. "The sense of a word cannot be diverse or multiform at the same time and in the same place." Again, "In no language can a word have more than one literal meaning in the same place" (Ernesti, pp. 9,11). In the sentence before us, the relation of the verbs "repent," and "be baptized," to their object, "remission," is expression by the preposition "for." It must therefore follow that "for" cannot mean "because of," as to baptism, and "in order to" as to repentance, seeing that a word cannot have two meanings at the same time and in the same place. But since repentance is clearly "in

317

order to" the remission of sins in the passage, so also is baptism. Dr. Hackett, a distinguished translator and author, and a member of the Baptist church, was led by these considerations to write: "*Eis aphesin hamartioon,* in order to the forgiveness of sins (Matthew 26:28; Luke 3:3); we cannot, naturally, with both the preceding verbs. This clause states the motive or object which should induce them to repent and be baptized. It enforces the entire exhortation, not one part of it to the exclusion of the other" (*Hackett's Commentary on Acts*).

The preposition *eis* translated "for" in the sentence, "Repent and be baptized . . . for (*eis*) the remission of sins," is of almost innumerable occurrence in the New Testament. Of its significance in hundreds of passages there is no dispute; it is always and everywhere permitted to have the meaning assigned to it by the lexicons; a meaning that is always prospective, which looks to an end or object yet to be gained. Mr. Henry Thayer, in his great *Lexicon on the New Testament,* defines the word thus; "*Eis,* a prep. governing the Accusative, and denoting entrance into, or direction and limit: 'into,' 'towards,' 'for,' 'among'." So Dr. Robinson: Eis, a prep. governing only the Accusative, with the primary idea of motion into any place or thing, and then also of motion or direction 'to', 'towards', 'upon', any place or object. The antithesis is expressed by *ek* out of" (*Robinson's Greek-English Lexicon of the New Testament*). Dr. W. E. Jelf, in his "Grammar of New Testament Greek", Vol. 2, p. 296, says of *"eis": "*It expresses the same relations as *en* (in), except that it has the notion of direction, whither, while *en* has the notion of rest, where. It is used to express the direction or motion of an action—into an object, or up to an object—into immediate contact with it, especially to express the reaching some definite point."

That "remission" is in the accusative case is not without is significance here. It is the function of a preposition governing the accusative to exhibit the object or design of the word of words which it governs, and in this instance the preposition *eis* is employed to demonstrate the relation which "remission" sustains to the rest of the sentence. Since "remission of sins" is the object or design indicated by the preposition, it follows that the words "repent and be baptized" find their object or design in "remission of sins." That this usage is uniform throughout the New Testament, may be seen from actual instances in passages gathered at random from the sacred writings: "I long to see you that I may impart unto you some spiritual gift, to the end that ye may be established" (Romans 1:11). The words, "to the end," are, in the Greek, the one word, *eis*. Shall we understand Paul to mean that he desired to impart some spiritual gift "because of" their establishment, or "in order to" their establishment? Clearly, the latter, and a literal rendering of the passage runs thus: "I long to see you that I may impart some spiritual gift in order that you may be established." "And they took counsel, and bought with them the potter's field, to (*eis*) bury strangers in." (Matthew 27:7.) Quite obviously, they did not purchase the field because it was already a place to bury strangers, but in order to make it such a place in the future; and so here, as in every other occurrence in the New Testament, the preposition indicates the purpose or aim of the thing done.

The clearest exposition of its usage, however, is in Matthew 26:28, where a similarly constructed sentence is found. 'For this is my blood of the New Testament, which is shed for many for the remission of sins." Let it be noted that the words "for the remission of sins" are the same as in Acts 2:38. Observe too, that the preposition "for" (*eis*) is performing its usual function of pointing out the object of the verb. In this instance, the verb is "is shed," and "remission of sins," is the object. Does this mean that Christ shed his blood "because of" remission? If the word "for" is to be given the meaning claimed for it in Acts 2:38, this conclusion is inevitable. Examine the following parallel:

Christ's blood was shed . . . . . "For the remission of sins" (*Eis aphesin hamartioon*).

Repent and be baptized . . . . . "for the remission of sins" (*Eis aphesin hamartioon*).

Unless it be granted that Christ died "because of" the forgiveness of our sins, it must follow, indisputably, that baptism with its proper antecedents is "in order to" remission of sins.

The reason which led the translators of the Revision to render *eis* in Acts 2:38 by the word "unto" instead of by "for" as in the King James Version, is highly interesting and especially significant in its bearing on the force of the preposition uner consideration. The preposition "for" is ambiguous, and in many instances its force can be ascertained only by an examination of the source from which it sprang, or the context in which it appears. To illustrate: Jesus said, "Take no thought for (Greek *dia*, because of) your life." (Matthew 6:25.) Consider now Matthew 26:28: "This is my blood . . . which is shed . . . for (Greek, *eis*, in order to) the remissions of sins." It is not difficult to see that the word "for" does not have the same significance in these two passages. In some instances in the Authorized, or King James Version, "for" is permitted to stand as the English equivalent of each of the following Greek prepositions: *dia*, "on the account of," *anti*, "instead of," *eis*, "in order to," *epi*, "upon," *huper*, "for the sake of," and *props*, "at." Only a word of considerable ambiguity could convey so many different meanings. We have seen that the force of *eis* is always prospective; that it looks to an end or design yet to be. To eliminate therefore, the uncertainty associated with the word "for", and to express to the English reader the thought of the passage with the same precision, that inhered in the text for the Greek reader, was the aim of the translators, and

319

the preposition "unto," literally "on-to," was selected as the word that of all others in our language most nearly conforms to the preposition *eis*. Obviously, "unto" can never have a retrospective, or backward meaning, and in the passage, "Repent and be baptized. . . . unto remission of sins," baptism looks not backward to sins already forgiven, but forward to the object "remission," which is its purpose and design.

Brother McGarvey dissented from this view, holding that the translators were in error in attributing "unto" to the Anglo-Saxon "onto," and that the prefix "un" has has its usual significance of "not," as in the words unnatural, uncommon, etc. If this be the true origin of the word, it does not adequately convey the meaning of the preposition for which it stands, and these considerations led brother McGarvey to strike "unto" out of the text in Acts 2:38, and to insert the "for" of the Authorized Version in its stead in his *New Commentary on Acts.* This, however, is a question which has to do with the meaning, of English words only, and does not affect the matter under consideration.

"Discuss the debates of Jesus."

Our Lord a debater?

Harsh though these words sound, and objectionable as the idea is to many weak and compromising elements in the church today, the truth is that our Lord was the greatest controversialist of all time. He often engaged in polemics with the leading authorities of his day, and with such success that not one of his opponents was ever able to answer his arguments, or find flaws in his reasoning. The *Pharisees,* a religious sect whose members advocated the strictest of views regarding any contact with non-religious people, found fault with Jesus because he associated with "publicans and sinners," ate with them (Mark 2:14-17; Matthew 9:9-13; Luke 5:27-32), exposed their hypocrisy and warned the people that their teachers were false guides and deceitful workers (Matthew 23:1ff).

The Jewish leaders, well aware that our Lord posed a serious threat to their positions of influence and leadership, demanded to know by whose authority he taught. (Matthew 21:23-25; Mark 11:27,28.) When he submitted a problem to them which they were wholly unable to answer, he taught a lengthy series of parables designed to show the wickedness and the eventual destruction of the Pharisaical sect. The parable of the marriage of the kings' son (Matthew 22:1-14), was delivered for the purpose of showing that the gospel is for all, and that when the Jews rejected it, they would be cast out and those in the "highways," that is, the Gentiles, whom the Jews despised, would be invited and accepted in their place.

The Jewish leaders were visibly angered by this obvious reference to them; and, unable to answer the Lord in honest and straightforward fashion, they resorted (as false teachers usually do) to artifice, stratagem and craftiness. They "took counsel how they might ensnare [trick] him in his talk." (Matthew 22:15.) Their purpose was to induce the Lord to say *something* with which they might later accuse him before the people, and thus impair his standing with them who thus far highly regarded him. The *Herodians* were members of another Jewish sect who also opposed Jesus and his teaching. (Mark 3:6; 12:13.) This party is believed to have been formed under Herod, the king, from whom it derived its name; and its chief tenet appears to have been the view that it was proper and right to pay homage to the king in order that the political situation in Palestine might improve to the advantage of the Jews. At this point they clashed with the *Pharisees,* who bitterly resented the presence of the Romans (who maintained an army of occupation in the land at the time), and ordinarily there was no association or fellowship between these Jewish sects. But, faced with a common enemy, Jesus Christ our Lord, they were willing to forget, for the time, their own differences, and they combined their forces in an effort to entrap the saviour.

Representatives of the *Pharisees* and the *Herodians* together confronted the Lord; and the attempt to ensnare him began with fulsome and hypocritical praise. They said to him, "Teacher, we know that thou art true, and teachest the way of God in truth, and carest not for any one; for thou regardest not the person of men." (Matthew 22:16.) This description of Jesus was true, of course; but these wicked men did not believe what they were saying: and the effort was designed to throw the Lord off guard by such effusive compliments, and thus, if possible, to blind him to their actual purpose. They then slyly said, "Tell us therefore, What thinkest thou? Is it lawful to give tribute unto Caesar, or not?" This question involved one of the most sensitive and delicate matters facing the Jewish people. The Jews were then in subjection to the Roman government and they were obligated to pay taxes assessed by, and used to maintain, that which was to those loyal Jews, an obnoxious and distasteful power. Caesar was the Roman emperor; to pay taxes to Caesar was to support the government; they regarded the occupation of Palestine by the Roman army as opposed to the will of God for his chosen people, and the tax was a symbol and token of this bitter and distasteful situation.

The question concocted was designed in such shrewd fashion, so its proponents believed, to involve Jesus in grave difficulty regardless of his answer. Should he say, "Yes, it is entirely in order to pay the tax," his opponents believed this would immediately alienate the people, most of whom entertained deep feelings of hate for their Roman oppressors; if he said, "No, it should not be paid," the *Herodians* would immediately report him to the Roman authorities as a seditious rebel and opposer of the government. In either event, they hoped, his influence would be destroyed. How could he possibly escape from such a dilemma? Their effort, though craftily fashioned, failed to take into account the divine wisdom which was his.

Jesus "perceived their wickedness"; their intent was evident to him from the beginning; and he told them so: "Why make ye trial of me, ye hypocrites?" Such was our Lord's method of "loving response" to these false teachers who were leading precious souls to perdition. (Matthew 22:18.) He asked for a piece of "tribute money," the coin by which the tax was paid, and asked, "Whose is this image and superscription?" Stamped on the Roman coin our Lord received was the image of Caesar, the Roman emperor. He knew, of course, as did they, whose image was on it, and his question was intended to focus attention on Caesar. He said to them, "Render therefore unto Caesar the things that are Caesar's; and unto God the things that are God's." Our Lord thus gave utterance to what has been described as "one of the wisest, deepest, and yet simplest maxims ever uttered in human language." It is a fundamental and basic truth that what belongs to one should be thus rendered; Jesus did not attempt to enter the political scene and settle the issues over which the *Pharisees* and *Herodians* argued; he simply announced that both God and Caesar are entitled to what is theirs! The money belonged to Rome; the Jews did not hesitate to use it in their businesses; it was right that they should pay for such use. This answer satisfied those who favored the tax, because it showed sound reasoning for such. That which belonged to God was his, and should be so regarded. From this conclusion neither party could retreat. Thus both parties were successfully met and routed on their grounds. They recognized their failure, "marvelled, and left him and went away." Truth triumphed in this historic debate.

"What is the shortest prayer recorded in the Bible?"

Among the shortest petitions addressed to God in the scriptures is that found in Psalms 12:1. David, facing formidable enemies, deeply troubled, uncertain what course was best to follow, and fully aware of his own ability to cope with his problems, earnestly cried out, "Help, Lord!" Surely every faithful disciple today can emphathize with the embattled Psalmist, and remember when he, too, turned to the Lord regarding his troubles with the realization he had no other to whom to turn. How wonderfully comforting it is to know that when all others fail us or are unable to help us, we can go to him with assurance, confident in the fact that he has promised all who faithfully serve him

322

that they will not be forgotten, and that he will aid, support and protect his own against dangers both seen and unseen. "Fear thou not; for I am with thee: be not dismayed; for I am thy God: I will strengthen thee; . . . yea, I will help thee, saith the Lord, and thy redeemer, the Holy One of Israel." (Isaiah 41: 10-14.)

The Bible abounds with these wonderful promises to the faithful. "All things work together for good to them who love God." "As thy day is, so shall thy strength be." "As one whom his mother comforteth, so will I comfort you." "My grace is sufficient for thee."

"When sin-stricken, burdened and weary,
From bondage I longed to be free,
There came to my heart the sweet message
'My grace is sufficient for thee.' "
"Though tempted and sadly discouraged,
My soul to this refuge will flee,
And rest in the blessed assurance:
'My grace is sufficient for thee.' "

"Why did Paul refer to the body as a 'tabernacle'?"

An eminent Jewish Talmudic scholar once said, "He who does not teach his son a trade teaches him to steal." Because this sentiment was widely current in Israel most Jews taught their children some manual trade even though the sons were professionally trained. We believe this practice, were it more widely followed in our day, would solve many current problems. Paul, though possessed of the finest education possible in this day, was nevertheless early taught to make tents and this manual skill served him in good stead when it was necessary to make his own living while preaching the gospel. (Acts 18:3).

The apostle, in his message to the Philippian church, wrote of conflicting desires: a desire to depart and to be with Christ and a desire to remain among the saints for their good: "For I am in a strait betwixt two, having a desire to depart, and to be with Christ; which is far better; nevertheless to abide in the flesh is more needful for you." (Philippians 1:23, 24.) To "depart" here is from *analusai*, aorist infinitive *analuoo*, a word once believed to signify the loosing of moorings preparatory to setting sail, but now thought more likely to mean the breaking up of an encampment; literally, to "take down one's tent, and be off." (See Lightfoot's comments on Philippians 1:23.)

A tent suggests a temporary sojourn only; Abraham, Isaac and Jacob dwelt in tents while in Canaan because they were only sojourners there; they were in search of "a better country, that is, a heavenly," where God had prepared for them a city. The tent, because it can be easily

323

and quickly dismantled, has become a symbol of the frailty of life. (Isaiah 38:12; 2 Corinthians 5:1-3.)

The Word (Jesus Christ our Lord) was made flesh "and dwelt among us." (John 1:14.) "Dwelt" here is not the usual word for living in a place; it is the translation of *eskenose,* third person singular of the aorist indicative of *skenoo,* a tent. The second Person of the godhead thus took up residence in a tent of flesh while on earth. From his royal court in the sky our blessed Saviour condescended to come down into a world of woe and to dwell in a tabernacle (tent) of flesh with us in order that some day we may settle down permanently with him in everlasting habitations in the highest heavens. With Paul we may indeed rejoice to say, "For we know that, if our earthly house of this tabernacle (tent) were dissolved, we have a building of God, a house not made with hands, eternal in the heavens." (2 Corinthians 5:1.)

"What is the answer to the charge that if baptism is essential to salvation a third party is injected between a sinner and his God?"

Those who contend for the doctrine of justification by faith only have been exceedingly resourceful in collecting fancied objections to the doctrine of baptism "for the remission of sins." (Acts 2:38.) Prominent among them is the claim that if baptism is essential to one's salvation, a third party is injected between the sinner and God thus making salvation dependent on the will and consent of another person. Instances are often brought forward wherein individuals, faced with death and without opportunity at the moment to be baptized, are alleged to have been saved simply by "trusting Christ."

It is significant that there are *no such cases* in the New Testament. The book of Acts is a case history of conversion. Sundry instances of people being saved are therein set forth and under a great variety of circumstances but there is no instance where any person was promised salvation or rejoiced from having received it without having been baptized.

Numerous reasons exist why such is so. It is of the very nature of God's plan to save that human agency must be utilized. It is a maxim of law that one intends the natural and logical consequences which necessarily follow from one's acts. Jesus sent out his apostles for the express purpose of evangelizing and or baptizing those thus evangelized. (Matthew 28:18-20.) In providing that the work was to be done in this manner he ordained human agency in the preaching of the gospel and the discipleship of all men. Let such instrumentality be eliminated and the work of salvation would cease. The relationship obtaining between God and his works is clearly shown in the Corinthian epistles. Christians are declared to be workers together "with him," in this noble enterprise. (1 Corinthians 3:9.) It is of course true that it is God "who makes the seed grow," but the seed must first be planted and it is in this area that human instrumentality is by our Lord authorized. "Without faith it is impossible to please him." (Hebrew 11:6); faith "cometh by hearing, and hearing by the word of God" (Romans 10:17), and it is not surprising in the light of these facts that the question should be rhetorically propounded. *"How shall they hear without a preacher?"* Those who seek to exclude baptism from God's plan concede that it is essential that the sinner have the gospel preached to him in order to hear of salvation and they are thus logically stopped from denying human intervention between God and the sinner in baptism while intruding it between the sinner and his belief. The design of the argument is, of course, to eliminate water baptism from God's plan, but, the effort fails since it was the Lord and not man *who put it there.* Jesus said, "He that believeth and is baptized shall be saved." (Mark 16:16). Peter told inquiring sinners "repent and be baptized . . . for the remission of sins." (Acts 2:38). All the adroitness and human ingenuity that can be brought to bear on these passages can never make them to say and to mean that *he that believeth and is not baptized shall be saved* or that *baptism is not for the remission of sins* as Peter so clearly affirmed.

"What is the place of preaching in God's plan?"

"For the preaching of the cross is to them that perish foolishness; but unto us who are saved it is the power of God. . . . For seeing that in the wisdom of God the world through its wisdom knew not God, it was God's good pleasure through the foolishness of the preaching to save them that believe." (1 Corinthians 1:18-21.) The most potent and powerful influence exercised on mankind through the centuries since our Lord returned to heaven has been the preaching of the primitively pure gospel. This, of course, will be denied by some, and scoffed at by others but it is nonetheless true that the gospel of Christ, faithfully proclaimed, has exerted a greater influence on the world than the combined armies of mankind. Imperial Rome, invincible and unconquerable by force of arms, yielded to the armies of the Lord and her proud legions fell one by one before the onslaughts of the soldiers of the cross. Bound "by the cords of the gospel" it had earlier sought to destroy, that mighty empire lives in history as an example of the futility of resisting those who take their orders from the Lord.

It has ever been so, and when faithful and brave defenders of the truth go marching forth to war against error and evil, lifting aloft the banner of the Lord in courageous array, victory is ultimately theirs.

Denominationalism in all its varied forms, though formidable and mighty, presents fewer difficulties to overcome than the idolatry and paganism prevailing throughout the world in the apostolic age. Actually, in many ways, our task is much easier than that confronting the apostles and first century preachers. Those ensnared in the bewildering mazes of denominationalism do profess to believe in one God, and to regard Jesus as his Son and the Saviour of the world. When we compare our efforts with those who blazed the trail for Christianity, our feeble attempts pale into insignificance. Why? Human nature remains the same. The gospel, God's power to save, is as potent as it was when first preached. (Romans 1:13-17.) People are as much in need of salvation now as then and sin is as fatal in its working as ever. What explains our comparative failures?

Can it be that we are not preaching the ancient gospel with the fervor and zeal which characterized the earliest defenders of the faith?

This conclusion the thoughtful observer finds easy to accept. The conviction obtains that in far too many instances today brethren are leaving the Word of God "to serve tables," thus reversing the order of the apostles. (Acts 6:2.) In such instances, the *study* has become an *office* and the preacher a religious bellboy. Should he be inclined to demur, knowing in his heart that such prostitutes his proper mission in life, he is informed that times have changed and he must adjust himself, *or else.* The "or else," too often becomes the deciding factor and another preacher graduates into an ever-increasing number of men no longer with the time or the disposition to give themselves "to the ministry of the Word," and prayer.

On occasion, elders in need of hiring a preacher have actually let it be known that the ability to preach is of secondary importance to a pleasing personality! It is to be assumed that if these brethren stood in need of a doctor because serious sickness has invaded their homes they would not really care whether he could practice medicine or not so long as he exhibited admirable social graces. Or, if they were desirous of employing a lawyer they could not care less whether he had real ability in the law, so long as he had a pleasing personality and could entertain the people in the courtroom! Such gross and utter disregard of the responsibilities of the eldership shocks and dismays us and points up how far afield we have moved from the apostolic order. Such concepts involve the total abandonment of the mission divinely originated for those who preach the Word.

The number of men engaged in the work of preaching is larger than it has been in modern times, and more preaching is being done today than at any time since the beginning of the Restoration plea. But, it will hardly be questioned, at least by those who have occasion to listen to a variety of preachers in widespread areas of the brotherhood that familiarity with God's Word has not kept apace. Many factors are doubtless responsible, but it is very true that there has been a noticeable shifting of emphasis from the careful and detailed exposition of the scriptures to matters of the moment. In an earlier day, brethren "opened the scriptures," and "expounded" them. They had no time for (and they would have spurned it if they had) the modern topical type of preaching consisting solely of meaningless platitudes and inanities pleasing to the ear but powerless to save. The hour is late. The midnight hour for us all is not far distant. It is high time for elderships, the Christian colleges, the religious periodicals and all who love the Lord to give greater emphasis to the mission and method of the apostolic age.

"Comment on what good books mean to you."

Were it not for history's priceless deposit—books in all their varied and wonderful forms—but little of man's glorious past would have been preserved for us and his marvelous achievements through the ages would be virtually unknown. The privilege of consorting with those who lived before us and of reliving their experiences is surely one of the noblest and grandest vouchsafed to man. In books one is privileged to enjoy the company of the world's wisest sages, ride along with the ages' most famed generals and drink deeply of the wisdom of the earth's most profound philosophers. Fortunate indeed is he who has made books his friends; they are ever available to cheer the heart, stir the soul and edify the intellect and, when, on occasion, they must be neglected, they feel no resentment, patiently waiting to flood our hearts and minds with their rich resources when we are ready to turn to them again.

Supreme in its position and incomparably greater than all others, the Bible is preeminently THE BOOK, containing the mind and the message of God to man, and the way of salvation. On it more scholarly effort has been expended than any other, and innumerable books are at hand to assist us in studying that book which alone can infallibly point out to us the way to heaven.

A good library is truly a fabulous fairyland, a place of genuine delight, affording a happy haven from the swirling currents of a restless world. In it we are in the intimate fellowship of the greatest intellectuals, the most profound thinkers and the greatest reasoners of all time. No barriers have been erected to exclude us; here is one of the few areas of human experience where the rich are at no advantage, rich and poor alike being privileged to drink at will from this ever-flowing fountain. Into what other select company of distinguished scholars may one appear at will and there converse to his heart's content? How else may one in life associate with the spirits of the sainted dead and share in the intellectual and mental labors of their lives on earth?

Were I, after a long and eventful life of intense activity as a gospel preacher asked to designate what, in my view, are the most vital aims which should characterize all who teach and preach the word, high on the list would be the accumulation of a useful library, the cultivation of an affection for good books and the formation of regular habits of study. No day should be permitted to pass which does not provide for communion with good books.

"It is said that the prophets 'searched diligently" and sought for themselves information concerning the things of which they wrote. What does this mean?"

The passage the querist alludes to reads "Concerning which salvation the prophets sought and searched diligently, who prophesied of the grace that should come unto you: searching what time or what manner of time the Spirit of Christ which was in them did point unto, when it testified beforehand the sufferings of Christ, and the glories that should follow them. To whom it was revealed, that not unto themselves, but unto you, did they minister these things, which now have been announced unto you through them that preached the gospel unto you by the Holy Spirit sent forth from heaven; which things angels desire to look unto." (1 Peter 1:10-12.)

To encourage the saints to bear patiently the trials through which they were passing (1 Peter 4:12, the apostle informed them that the salvation referred to was not only the subject of prophecy, but that the prophets themselves had engaged in minute and detailed inquiry to determine, if possible, the nature and the time of the events which they had predicted. There is no article before the word "prophets" in the Greek text, and the reference is, therefore, to prophets as a class. These men "sought" (*ekzeteo,* to seek out, to engage in minute study, to scrutinize closely), and "searched diligently" (*exereneo,* to trace out in detail, to explore, as one carefully sifts ore to find the precious metal) their own writings in an effort to learn the time and the nature of the tokens by which these events would be ushered into the world. By prayer, by close study, by meditation, by the exercise of all their mental faculties, they sought to learn the significance of the matters which had occasioned their prophecies.

Here is indisputable evidence of the verbal inspiration of the prophetical writings. These prophecies, far from being the productions of the prophets, unaided by inspiration, were so far above and beyond them, that they were dependent on others for instruction enabling them to grasp the significance of their own writings. A remarkable example of this will be seen in the instance of Daniel inquiring of the angel the meaning of the matters revealed to him. (Daniel 7:16; 9:2,3.) The Holy Spirit, by whose powers, and under whose influence they spoke, prompted them to give utterance to matters which were outside their apprehension, and which they sought, through patient scrutiny, to understand. They were not only *prophets,* they were *people,* and as such, had an absorbing interest in matters of such vital moment as that which occasioned their prophecies. Their primary purpose being consummated in the prophecies, they continued to pore over their predictions in an effort to learn what they signified.

They prophesied of the grace that should come, "who predicted the special grace intended for you alone." This does not mean that these disciples alone were the objects of the prophecy alluded to, or that the grace would not be shared by others, but that those of this dispensation, of which they were a part, were the recipients of the blessings predicted. The word "grace" means unmerited favor, and the reference is, therefore, to the blessings which have come to the world in this dispensation through the manifestation of grace to men. This is the "grace and truth which came by Jesus Christ." (John 1:17.) The word "grace" in this verse sums up the blessings of God vouchsafed to men under the present dispensation.

In verse 11, reference is made to the diligent and painstaking search the prophets instituted into their own writings, and the writings of other prophets to learn the significance of the matters predicted. The nature of their inquiry is said to have been with reference (a) to what time (*chronos*) and (b) what manner of time (*kairos*) "the Spirit of Christ which was in them did point unto." *Chronos,* time, is a simple term denoting duration, the lapse of moments; *kairos* describes the periods into which time is divided. Both of these words occur in our Lord's reply to the request of the disciples for information regarding the time of establishment of his kingdom, when he said, "It is not for you to know time (*chronos*) or seasons (*kairos*) which the Father has set within his own authority." (Acts 1:6-8.) The prophets are thus represented as searching for the time when the events mentioned were to occur; or, if failing in that, the dispensation or age in which they could be expected. Thus, the matters about which they appear to have been especially concerned were the date and circumstances of the Lord's advent, and the consummation of the scheme of redemption from the salvation of man. Daniel 9:25 was doubtless one of the passages particularly studied in an effort to determine the time of the Lord's appearance and the nature of the events described.

The prophets "testified" (bore witness) "beforehand of the sufferings of Christ, and the glory that should follow" by "the Spirit of Christ" which was "in them." The Spirit of Christ is the Holy Spirit, the third person of the Godhead. (Romans 8:9; Galations 4:6.) From this important truth several considerations follow: (1) the Holy Spirit dwelt in the prophets, directed their thoughts, and supplied the revelations which they delivered; (2) the same Spirit that influenced the apostles and inspired men of the New Testament period operated similarly in the Old Testament era (2 Peter 1:20,21); (3) the Spirit *of Christ* having been in the prophets, it follows that Christ existed during the times of the prophets, and this verse thus becomes an important text in support of the deity and pre-existence of the Lord Jesus.

The Holy Spirit, in the prophets, led them to testify with reference to "the sufferings of Christ and the glory that should follow," or, more correctly, "the sufferings *appointed* or *destined* for Christ and the glories after these." That the expected Messiah should suffer was a matter clearly revealed by the Old Testament writers. (Isaiah 53; Daniel 9:25-27.) Numerous references to such predictions occur in the New Testament. "But the things which God fore-showed by the mouth of all the prophets, that his Christ should suffer, he thus fulfilled." (Acts 3:18.) "Having therefore obtained the help that is from God, I stand unto this day testifying both to small and great, saying nothing but what the prophets and Moses did say should come: how that the Christ must suffer, and how that he first by the resurrection of the dead should proclaim light both to the people and to the Gentiles." (Acts 26:23.) The Lord himself, in his famous interview with the two disciples on the road to Emmaus, gave utterance to the same sentiment: "O foolish men and slow of heart to believe in all that the prophets have spoken! Behooved it not the Christ to suffer these things, and to enter into his glory? and beginning from Moses and from all the prophets, he interpreted to them in all the scriptures the things concerning himself." (Luke 24:25-27.) The apostles and other inspired men entered into great detail regarding these matters, and gave much emphasis to them in an effort to overcome the repugnance the Jews felt to the idea of a suffering Messiah. Such a view many of them regarded as inconsistent with other prophecies which represent him as a triumphant and reigning Messiah. Such views continue to constitute a stumbling block in the way of the Jews today. They disregard the fact that Christ was *both,* i.e., a suffeirng Saviour, and a reigning Monarch; in him both lines of prophecy merge and find fulfillment.

"Is Christ a created being?"

The implications of this question are surely shocking to all faithful Christians. There is in it the suggestion that some people concede the historicity of the Christ of the scriptures, but deny that he is uncreated and eternal, and co-existent with the Father. This view of the nature of Christ is that advocated by those who style themselves Jehovah's Witnesses. Since we are to examine it in detail, it is well for us to take a brief look into the background of those who subscribe thereto.

The movement had its origin in the efforts of Charles T. Russell, usually referred to as "Pastor Russell," born in the vicinity of Pittsburgh, Penn., and raised to believe the principles and precepts of historic Christianity but who, at the age of 20, repudiated the religion of his parents and became skeptical toward all religion. In this state he remained, until he began to read the writings of Mrs. Ellen G. White, founder of Adventism, from whom he adopted his views of the nature of man, future punishment, and other peculiar positions of that alleged prophetess; and, from this beginning, launched a mighty movement which spread rapidly throughout the world, and from which he acquired great wealth and much eminence. Headquarters of the movement were eventually established in Brooklyn, N.Y., with branches in many lands; and from there its missionaries and literature are sent out to more than one hundred countries, and its tenets are preached in approximately that many languages. Its devotees are most industrious in the propagation of its distinctive doctrines.

In 1950, the organization, known as "The Watch Tower Bible and Tract Society," issued its "New World Translation of the Christian Greek Scriptures," alleged to be a translation "the most accurate to date," (page 792), and is now in process of publishing a translation of the Old Testament Scriptures.

Following the death of the founder of the movement, "Judge" J. F. Rutherford assumed leadership of the organization, and through unusual ability as an organizer and writer greatly extended its sphere and influence. From his prolific pen flowed an unending stream of material which the society published.

The movement has been variously known as Russellism, Rutherfordism and Millennial Dawnism, designations which they reject; and it has been styled by its devotees as "International Bible Student," "Jehovah's Witnesses," and members of "the New World Society." Its teaching is an admixture of Adventism, Swedborgianism, Unitarianism; and, on the nature of Christ, *Arianism*.

A tract entitled, "What Do Jehovah's Witnesses Believe," issued by the Watchtower press, warns that reviewers of their doctrines often present a biased and unfriendly picture of their positions, and asks, "We would not expect to obtain from the scribes and Pharisees a correct picture of what Jesus believed, would we?" We think their caution is proper; and we shall, therefore, appeal *only to their official publications*, carefully documenting each statement thereform, in ascertaining what they really believe. On the same page of the leaflet (p. 2), where the

331

foregoing statement appears are these words, "Jehovah's first creation was his Son." Following this, they cite certain scriptures, which we shall hereafter examine in detail. For the moment our purpose is to determine, from their writings, what Jehovah's Witnesses believe and teach regarding the nature of Christ.

Their tract declares, "Jehovah's first creation was his Son." This statement, appearing in a leaflet, the design of which is to acquaint people with the tenets of the movement, is simple, unequivocal and without ambiguity. From it we learn that this religious society believes and teaches that (a) Christ is not eternal, but a creature of Jehovah; and (b) he was the first of all God's creatures to be made. It is proper to deduce from this that having been *created* by Jehovah; he was non-existent until this creative act occurred; and is, therefore not co-existent with the Father nor equal with him.

This view is often stated and affirmed in a variety of ways in their official publications: "He is not the author of the creation of God; but after God had created him as his first-born Son, then God used him as his working Partner in the creating of all the rest of creation" (*Let God Be True,* Page 33, Revised Edition).

"Who was the first son of God created? The very one who is 'the beginning of the creation of God' identifies himself to us. He is the same one that later was born as a man by the miracle of God and was called Jesus Christ" (*The New World,* page 16).

In their book, *Creation,* page 15, under the sub-heading, "Beginning of creation," they insist that "long before the creation of the earth, when there was no sea, when there were no springs and lakes, before there were any mountains or hills, yea, before the sun and the moon and the stars were made, God began his creation; and that beginning was his beloved One, known in the Bible as the Logos. The world Logos is one of the names or titles given to the beloved Son of God, and carries with it deep meaning."

"The term Logos is one of the titles applied to the first or beginning of God's creation." (*Deliverance,* page 12).

"Jehovah God had now set out on the purpose of endless creation. He now had beside him a 'master workman' endowed with wisdom. This had received life from God. This made him the Son of God. In begetting this Son or bringing him forth to life Jehovah was the only Producer or Creator, unassisted. His first living creature was therefore the 'only begotten Son of God'." (*The Truth Shall Make You Free,* page 43).

"The question now arises as to the other creatures that were produced after God's firstborn Son, the Word. Were these other creatures each a direct creation of God as his Son the Word was?" (*Ibid.,* page 48).

These quotations might be indefinitely extended, but these will suffice to show the clear and unmistakable position of those who call themselves Jehovah's Witnesses on the nature of Christ. They reveal the view that Christ *received life from God,* is a creature, was created in the beginning of God's creation, is not the author of the creation of God; and is, hence, not eternal.

What was the name of this "creature" which the writers of the Watchtower society seek to identify as Christ before he came to the world? Russell long ago sought to answer this question in these words: "Our Redeemer existed as a spirit being before he was made flesh and dwelt amongst men. At that time, as well as subsequently, he was properly known as 'a god'—a mighty one. As chief of the angels and next to the Father he was known as the Archangel (highest angel messenger), whose name Michael, signifies, 'Who is God,' or God's representative. As he was the highest of all Jehovah's creation, so also he was the first, the direct creation of God . . ." (*Studies in the Scriptures,* series 5, page 84). Other writers for the Watchtower organization have expressed the same view: "Being the only begotten Son of God and the 'first born of every creature,' the Word would be a prince among other creatures. In this office he bore another name in heaven, which name is 'Michael'" (*The Truth Shall Make You Free,* 1943, page 48).

These quotations, taken verbatim from the official publications of the Watchtower society, reveal with unmistakable clarity that "Jehovah's Witnesses" believe and teach (a) Christ is not eternal; (b) he was *created* by the Father long ages past; (c) he lived in heaven, a spirit being, from the time of his creation until he came to the earth and was endowed with flesh; and (d) during this interval he was *Michael,* the archangel.

We have indicated earlier that these people cite certain passages of scripture in an effort to sustain this shocking and incredible theory. It is our intention to examine *each passage* they offer which bears any remote relation at all to the subject, and scrutinize it minutely. The first scripture they usually offer, in their attempts to justify such a position is Revelation 3:14: "And to the angel of the church in Laodicea write: These things saith the Amen, the faithful and true witness, the beginning of the creation of God." The One identified here as "the Amen," and "the faithful and true witness," is, undoubtedly, Christ himself. This seems conclusively to follow; and we conclude it without hesitation. The One thus identified is declared to be "the beginning of the creation of God." Watchtower writers urge that the significance of this phrase is that Christ was created as the first, or beginning act, of God (*Let God Be True,* revised edition, page 32).

The meaning of this statement turns on the significance of the word *archee* translated *beginning* here and approximately 40 times elsewhere in the common version. It cannot be properly interpreted to mean that which is caused to begin, as "Jehovah's Witnesses" allege. On the contrary, it designates him who is the beginning of creation in the sense that he was there and caused creation to begin! As Lange well says: "The Logos was not merely existent, however, in the beginning, but was also the *efficient principle,* the beginning of the beginning . . . and when it is said that the Logos was in this beginning, his eternal existence is already expressed, and his eternal position in the godhead already indicated thereby." (Lange's Commentary on John 1:1). It follows, therefore, that Revelation 3:14 teaches that Christ is "the beginning of the creation of God," in the sense that he was "the efficient principle," the active agent in causing it to start! (Compare John 1:3).

Fortunately, we are not dependent on deductions in determining the significance of this passage with reference to what it teaches regarding the eternity of Christ. All truth is harmonious; and the scriptures never contradict themselves. Melchizedek, "king of Salem, priest of the Most High" is said to have been "without father, without mother, without genealogy, having neither beginning of days nor end of life, *but made like unto the Son of God,* abideth a priest continually" (Hebrews 7:1-3). The sense in which this ancient priest was "made like unto the Son of God" was that he had "neither beginning of days nor end of life." If this passage bears any significance at all, it teaches that Christ is *without beginning or end.* It is, therefore, a thorough refutation of the Watchtower theory.

Often cited by these writers in support of this theory is Colossians 1:15, which asserts that Christ "is the image of the invisible God, the first-born of all creation." Because he is described as "the firstborn of all creation," it is alleged that Christ was the first creature in the creation. They say, "Thus he is ranked with God's creation, being first among them . . ." (*Let God Be True,* Rev. ed., page 33). They assume that the word "firstborn" is used literally to indicate that Christ came into existence as the *first* of God's creatures. They err in the assumption that the word is to be assigned a literal significance in this passage. It is obvious that the term has a figurative usage here. A creative act is one thing; a birth is another. It is absurd to affirm that Christ was *born* of God, in the usual sense of the word, if he were *created.* Moreover, the passage itself proves that Christ possessed the same nature as the Father since he is "the image of the invisible God." Being of the same essence and nature as the Father, Christ is as eternal as He; and this passage may not be properly cited to show that our Lord is a created being. On the contrary, he is before all creation, being *author* of creation himself: "For in him were all things created . . . all things have been created through him, and unto him; and he is before all things, and in him all things consist" (Colossians 1:15-17). The translators of the Watchtower Version, well aware of the force of this statement, have deliberately tampered with the text here and inserted without any justification the word "other" to make the foregoing statement read: "By means of him all *other* things were created . . . all *other* things have been created through him and for him. Also he is before all *other* things by means of him all *other* things were made to exist" (Page 589, *New World Translations*). Theirs is a serious offense against the Word of God with reference to which warnings are often penned in the sacred writings (Cf. Deuteronomy 4:2; Proverbs 30:6; Revelations 22:13). Colossians 1:15 simply suggests that Christ is prior to all creation so that without him creation would not have occurred. As "the first born of all creation," he is anterior to all creation, and therefore *no part of creation.* The word "firstborn," is from the Greek *proototokos,* and means born before. Thus Christ is separated from, and declared to be anterior to, *creation.* In being before all creation, he was not himself created. *What is before all creation must be regarded as eternal.* Christ was before all creation; therefore, he is eternal!

Moreover, the passage reveals that not only was Christ (a) before all creation and (b) the author of it, he is the *end* or design of creation, for *all* things were created "for him." He is, therefore, not a created being. It teaches us that *Christ* created all things; and from the Hebrew writer we learn that "he that built all things is God" (Hebrews 3:4). It follows, therefore, that Christ is God (theos), i.e., possesses *deity.*

Though decisive against the theory, John 1:1, which they grossly mistranslate, is frequently cited by "Jehovah's Witnesses" in an effort to bolster their view that Christ is merely a creature and not an eternal part of the godhead. "In the beginning was the Word, and the Word was with God, and the Word was God," the passage reads in reliable versions; and these people concede that reference to Christ is made by the phrase, "the Word," or Logos, as it is in the Greek Testament. Regarding this passage they have said: "Hence he may be called 'the Word or Logos.' Being a mighty one and holding this high official capacity as Logos, and being before all other creatures, he was a God, but not the Almighty God, who is Jehovah . . . Happily, the New World Translation of the Christian Greek Scriptures (published 1950) renders John 1:1,2: 'Originally the Word was, and the Word was with God, and the Word was a god. This one was originally with God' " (*Let God Be True,* Rev. ed., pages 33, 34).

It will be observed that the phrase, "and the Word was God," of the American Standard Version (the King James Translation, and all other reliable ones) is made to read in the Watchtower Bible, "and the Word was a god." Specifically, the indefinite article "a" is inserted, and the word *God* is spelled with a lowercase "g" rather than capitalized, as in the usual versions of the scriptures. From this they deduce the view that Christ is merely "a god," a phrase which they thereupon interpret to mean *a created being.* Moreover, they take great liberty with the first phrase of the text, *en archee een ho logos,* "In the beginning was the Word," by the rendering, "Originally the Word was," to which they attach a footnote, reading, "Literally, 'In (At) a beginning,'" by which they insinuate their doctrine of Christ's *creation* in the indefinite article "a" of the footnote. This is an unwarranted handling of the Greek text in that it disregards the rules requiring the definite article in translation though not in the Greek text. Here, the beginning is sufficiently definite without the article, and is undoubtedly an allusion to the beginning of Genesis 1:1. In this beginning the Word *was, een,* existed, not *egento,* became, or came into being. The meaning is, Before creation, before anything was made, at the very beginning of creation, the Word already *was.* The *beginning* (archee) here, and also that of Genesis 1:1, was evidently the beginning of creation; and inasmuch as the Word (logos), Christ *was there,* he was before all creation, therefore, no part of it. He was indeed the agent of creation, "All things were made by him; and without him was not anything made that was made" (John 1:3). It would not be possible to affirm the eternity of Christ more positively than is done in this great prologue of the gospel of John.

The Word (*logos*), the Christ, was not only *in the beginning* and before creation, "the Word was *with* (pros) God." As Vincent well says, "with (*pros*) does not convey the full meaning," but "there is no single English word which will give it better. The preposition *pros,* which with the accusative case, denotes motion toward, or direction, is also often used in the New Testament in the sense of *with;* and that not merely as being *near* or *beside,* but as a living union and communion; implying the active notion of intercourse . . . Thus John's statement is that the divine Word not only abode with the Father from all eternity, but was in the living, active relation of communion with him" (Vincent's *Word Studies,* Vol. 2, pages 33, 34). This intimate union of Christ with the Father is described by the Lord himself in John 17:5 and John 1:18.

"And the Word was God!" God, from the Greek *theos* denotes *deity;* and by a common figure of speech (the *syncedoche*), where the whole is put for a part, the name of the divine nature is assigned to the second person of the godhead as, for example it is assigned to the first person in John 1:18 and to the third person—the Holy Spirit—in Acts 5:3,4.

The affection of scholarship in a lengthy article in the appendix of the so-called New World Translation of the "Jehovah's Witnesses" to justify their rendering of the clause, *kai theos een ho logos,* "and the Word was God," (ASV and KJV), as "and the Word was a god," does not obscure the fact that these translators have abandoned true scholarship and evolved their own rules in their determined effort to deny to our Lord eternity of being.

The order of the words in this clause is such as to give emphasis; *God* is a predicate noun in the clause, not the subject. It is obvious that the subject is "the Word." The inspired writer is revealing who the Word is, not who God is! The Watchtower writers make much of the fact that the article (*ho*) *the,* does not appear before *theos* (God) in the passage, hence their rendering, "and the Word was *a god.*" This rendering is untenable for various reasons: (1) It is a recognized principle of Greek grammar that the subject takes the article and the predicate omits it. "Hence arises the general rule that in the simple sentence the subject takes the article, the predicate omits it. The subject is definitely before the mind, the predicate generally denotes the class to which the subject is referred, or from which it is excluded, *but the notion of the class is intself intermeriate*" *(Handbook of the Greek Testament,* Green, page 193). (2) If the article appeared before the predicate noun here, it would be the equivalent of saying the Word (Christ) is the entire godhead, which would be untrue. He is one of three persons who constitute it. It should be observed that in the second clause of the sentence, *kai ho logos een pros ton theon,* "and the word was with God," the article appears before *theos;* for here God (as the first person) is specified absolutely. In the third affirmation, the article is omitted because it was John's design to denote the character or nature of the Word as *deity,* rather than to specify his person. Thus (a) our Lord *existed* in the beginning before *all creation;* (b) he was *with* the Father in intimate communion before anything was made; (c) he was, himself, the active agent in creation; (d) he was *God* (deity) in the beginning. There are three distinct propositions in this marvelous affirmation of the apostle: (1) In the beginning Christ already *was;* therefore, without beginning himself, and pre-existent. (2) He enjoyed the closest association and fellowship with the Father, being "with (pros) God." (3) Lest it be assumed that all of this might be, and yet the second person be an inferior being, John declares that Christ *is* God—is possessed of the nature of God.

The wondrous being who is anterior to all creation and therefore uncreated, timeless and eternal, is identified at verse 14 of John 1: "And the Word became flesh, and dwelt among us . . ." This was, of course, the Christ. No more important passage may be found in the scriptures respecting the nature of Christ. It declares (1) his eternity; (2) his close relationship to the Father; (3) his work in creation; (4) his *distinction* from the Father; and (5) his possession of the *nature* of God. These fundamental propositions inhere in John's great treatise, and cannot be obscured.

Writers for the Watchtower society often cite Proverbs 8:22-30, in an effort to sustain their theory of a *created* Christ. In this highly figurative portion of scripture Wisdom is personified by the sacred writer and declared to be before creation: "Jehovah possessed me in the beginning of his way, before his works of old. I was set up from everlasting, from the beginning, before the earth was . . . then I was by him as a master workman . . ." The word "possessed" has the marginal reading, *"formed."* It is alleged that Christ is alluded to under the figure of Wisdom in this passage and that it was he who Jehovah formed in the beginning. This passage, far from proving that Christ is a created angel, as Jehovah's Witnesses teach, demonstrates his eternity and timelessness! (1) The "Wisdom" of the passage was possessed "in the beginning;" (2) he was before "his works of old;" (3) he was "set up *from everlasting.*" If *Wisdom,* in this passage, refers to Christ, it affirms his eternity, instead of controverting it. Further, it establishes the deity of Christ: Wisdom is said to have been with the Father as "a master workman" (Verse 30). Christ is uniformly declared to have been the creator of the universe in the scriptures (Colossians 1:16; Hebrews 1:2,10; John 1:3). The creation is often appealed to, in the Bible, to prove that he who accomplished this is the true God rather than the idols (Isaiah 40:18-27; Jeremiah 10:13-16; Proverbs 3:19). But, it is impossible that a creature should be endowed with attributes which only deity can possess. Christ possessed all of the attributes of God, *theos,* deity. Therefore, Christ is God, possesses the divine nature, and was, in eternity, equal of the Father!

This, indeed, is affirmed by Paul, in the great declaration of Phillipians 2:5-8 which reads: "Having this mind in you, which was also in Christ Jesus: who, existing in the form of God, counted not the being on an equality with God a thing to be grasped, but emptied himself, taking the form of a servant, being made in the likeness of men. . . ." Christ was (1) originally in the *form* of God. The "form" of anything is the manner in which it reveals itself; and this, of course, is determined by the nature which it has. Christ was in the form of God—deity— therefore, he possessed the nature of deity. (2) He was *on an equality with God.* (3) He did not regard this equality with God as a "thing to be grasped," i.e., held on to as an improper assumption—he was entitled to it as the equal of God! (4) He voluntarily surrendered this position and came to the world to be endowed with flesh in order that he might serve as our High Priest. This passage, in the most positive fashion, demonstrates the eternity, deity, and position of Christ before he came to the world. Aware of the force of this passage on their doctrine, the Watchtower society in its "New World Translation" offers this pitiful paraphrase and ridiculous rendering: "Keep this mental attitude in you which was also in Christ Jesus, who, although he was existing in God's form, gave no consideration to a seizure, namely, that he should be equal to God. No, but he emptied himself. . . ." When men deal thus with the sacred scriptures, they forfeit their right to the respect of their readers, abandon any semblance of scholarship, and demonstrate their departure from the truth.

338

We have now examined the *principal* passages cited in various publications of the Watchtower society to support this organization's view that Christ is merely a created being, and not co-equal with the Father and eternal in nature, and have found that each of these, where they touch the issues at all, teach his eternity, deity and full equality with God the Father, instead of that which "Jehovah's Witnesses" allege.

"Are we not much too prone to forget the lives and labors of the great and good men who preceded us in the fight for primitive Christianity?"

It is a common characteristic of the people of this nation to pause occasionally, and recall with grateful remembrance those whose lives and labors were dedicated to those principles we hold dear. It is well that this is so; a nation will not easily relinquish those rights and liberties obtained at great sacrifice so long as it is able to keep vividly in mind the sacrifices by which they were secured. The word "remember" is of frequent mention in the Bible. Israel was often reminded of the past, the prophets often recalled for her the lessons the years held; and the memory of those years was ever a restraining influence about the people of Israel. They forsook Jehovah only when they had forgotten him, and they forgot him easily when they permitted the memory of his dealings with them to pass from their minds.

The thousands who read this and have obeyed from the heart that form of doctrine delivered to them have much to be thankful for. It is easily possible that we might be hopelessly enmeshed in bewildering mazes of Romanism or denominationalism had it not been for those who labored so successfully in the restoration of primitive Christianity. The mere contemplation of the things accomplished in this respect brings to this writer a glow of pride and a feeling of gratitude second only to that he feels to the Lord himself. In the face of the most intense opposition, under difficulties of which we know nothing, and confronted by obstacles seemingly insurmountable they struggled forward until the religion of Christ and his apostles, long buried under the accumulation of the ages emerged, and became a living, present reality.

In debates that made history, these men fought unceasingly for the pure faith and primitive practice of apostolic Christianity. Owen, the champion of infidelity, Rice, the wily Presbyterian, and Purcell, the cunning Catholic, were stopped in their tracks by the Sage of Bethany. A hundred others of eminence were unable to withstand his rapier-like thrusts of the sword of the Spirit in discussions that ranged across the pages of the Christian Baptist and the Millennial Harbinger for more than forty years. Associated with him in propagating the primitive plea were others of giant intellect and tremendous learning. Stone,

Scott, Lard—the list might be almost indefinitely extended—were without peers in the field of letters and literature. From the pulpits and by means of the printed page, they matched wits with the most brilliant men of the day; and no armor of human device could withstand the old Jerusalem blade they so ably wielded.

But it is not of these that we would call attention to just here. We have in mind those who moved on smaller fronts but who fought just as valiantly and effectively as those whose names are heralded far and wide as leaders in the Restoration Movement. Lacking even the essentials of an education, they nevertheless matched wits with the foremost defenders of denominationalism; and no weapon formed against them could prosper; the learning and talent brought to sustain false and unscriptural views were of little avail, who though destitute of the aids and adornments of learning were thoroughly familiar with the word of God, and with it annihilated the positions of those to the contrary. They were men of one book; and, like David who had only his sling and a few smooth stones from the brook, they put to flight the ponderous Goliaths clad in the vulnerable armor of tradition and the doctrines and commandments of men. Unsung and unheralded, their very names for the most part unfamiliar to the thousands who have entered into the fruits of their labors, they nevertheless move grandly and majestically across the pages of the past, and sleep in peace, their labors done, until the day of final accounts.

Among them was Jonas Hartzel, a farmer, with little learning who, possessed of strong determination and having a wide acquaintance with the sacred Scriptures, did not hesitate to cross swords with the most eminent of denominational preachers. The following incident in the life of brother Hartzel admirably illustrates the advantage the truth gives in a discussion though opposed by all the aids and appliances of learning when these aids are on the side of error. Mrs. Julia King, wife of a judge in Warren, Ohio, a prominent member of the Congregational Church, heard brother Hartzel preach, learned the truth, and obeyed the gospel. Her social position and former standing in the church of which she had been a member required much moral courage to relinquish; and her change caused much comment and excitement in the community. Chagrined at the turn of affairs, her former pastor, Mr. Waldo, a man of much learning, and extensive educational attainments, sought an interview with her for the avowed purpose of convincing her of her error, and of inducing her to return to the fold. The interview was readily granted, and brother Hartzel was invited to be present.

Much to Mr. Waldo's astonishment, the lady was well prepared to defend the step she had taken; and brother Hartzel, seeing that she needed no assistance from him to sustain the cause of primitive Christianity, remained silent. Irritated at being completely foiled by the sister, Mr. Waldo indicated his willingness to debate the issues involved with brother Hartzel. His challenge was accepted, the debate continuing two days. Not satisfied with his efforts, Mr. Waldo, the Congregational minister, sought another discussion. This, too, was accepted; but before the discussion was scheduled to end, unable to meet the avalanche of Scriptural proof about him, Mr. Waldo finally conceded that he had nothing more to offer. Thus greatly humiliated and completely routed he retreated from the field, wholly unable with all of his learning to successfully meet the truth in the hands of a plain farmer.

Occasionally the discussions would become ludicrous in the extreme, but even in a battle of wits, these brethren were well able to take care of themselves. In a discussion touching the "mode" of baptism, it was insisted that the "certain water" of Acts 8 where the eunuch was baptized must have been very limited in extent and deficient in quantity, and the advocate of sprinkling and pouring concluded by asserting that, in his opinion, the "certain water" was nothing more than a "crawfish hole." Those who are familiar with the habitat of the crawfish know that the hole is no larger than one's finger, and that the water is often some distance below the surface, frequently entirely out of reach. When our brother came to reply to the "crawfish argument," he said, "If the supposition of the gentlemen be correct, it will make good sense to insert the term he has chosen in the place of 'water' in the text." Proceeding with all gravity, he began to read: "And as they went on their way, they came to a certain crawfish hole, and the eunuch said, 'See, here is a crawfish hole, what doth hinder me to be baptized?' " At this, a ripple of amusement ran through the audience. The brother continued: "And he commanded the chariot to stand still, and they went down into the crawfish hole, both Philip and the eunuch" (here the audience began to laugh) "and he baptized him; and when they were come up out of the crawfish hole"—this proved too much, and the audience burst into long-continued laughter. When quiet was finally restored, the brother turned to his opponent, now wholly discomfited, and said, "Were we not discussing a serious and important matter, I should feel inclined to say that my friend here was 'crawfishing.' " This reference to the habit of the animal's advancing backwards was too much; and the audience again exploded. Nothing more was heard of the "crawfish argument."

On another occasion, one of our brethren was called to meet a representative of one of the denominations on the plan of salvation. So effectively was the sword of the Spirit wielded that at the close of the first day his opponent declared that "his back ached, his head hurt and his mind would not work," and abruptly closed the debate.

Time would fail to tell of the glorious labors of these heroes of the faith who toiled without money and without price for the restoration of primitive Christianity. Unknown, their names forgotten by men, yet having turned "many to righteousness," they shall shine "as the stars forever and ever," in heaven's jeweled crown. We have received from them a glorious heritage. May we ever be true to the Cause in which they labored so successfully.

"When you find time in the Query department, write an article harmonizing Matthew 22:32 (God is not the God of the Dead) and Romans 14:9 (that he—Christ— might be Lord both of the dead and the living). How can it be that deity is not the 'God of the dead' and yet be Lord of 'both of the dead and the living'?"

Here, as often elsewhere in the sacred writings, it is of the greatest importance to consider carefully the context in determining the meaning of the terms used. The word "dead" appears in both of these pages, but as the context shows, of vastly different significance in each verse. Matthew 22:23-33 records, in detail, a controversy our Lord had with various Jewish sects, all of whom were antagonistic, and each of whom failed in the effort to answer his invincible arguments and respond effectively to his irresistible logic. First, the Pharisees and Herodians were routed, and the Sadducees then sought to embarrass him with an argument they had come to believe to be unanswerable. This Jewish sect was perhaps the most intellectual of all the Jewish parties. Its members were materialists; they rejected the doctrine of angels and spirits and consequently, any future life involving a resurrection. They regarded the doctrine of the resurrection as embodying a vain and delusive hope. If there were no spirits, obviously there would be no resurrection of the body, since there would be no spirit to occupy it in the next world!

The Sadducees presented a case designed to render the Lord's teaching regarding the resurrection of the body, if not impossible, at least ridiculous. They assumed a case where a woman married a man who preceded her in death, leaving no children. The Law of Moses provided that in such an instance, "her husband's brother shall go in unto her, and take her to him to wife, and perform the duty of an husband's brother unto her." (Deuteronomy 25:5.) In the case offered, this brother also predeceased the woman, and they imagined the extreme, though not impossible, situation that, in all, seven different brothers were married to her. They then triumphantly asked, "In the resurrection whose wife shall she be of the seven? for they all had her." It was their intent to show that the doctrine of the resurrection could not be true, because it presented difficulties impossible of solution. They could not see how it would be possible to determine which of the brothers would be her heavenly husband, so they proceeded to cut the Gordian knot by affirming that there would be no future life and, consequently, no bodily resurrection.

The Lord quickly and easily disposed of their objection based on the dilemma they offered, by asserting that "in the resurrection they neither marry nor are given to marriage, but are as the angels," by which he simply meant that fleshly relationships will not there exist, and there would be no occasion for marriage. Thus, the conclusion the Sadducees drew was not due to any difficulty associated with the doctrine the Lord taught, but resulted from their own ignorance of the scriptures. Death would be no more; there would then, be no necessity for the perpetuation of the marriage relationship in order to perpetuate the race. This is very far from meaning that there will be an end to the love and devotion resulting from such relationships in this life; quite the contrary, eternity will provide limitless occasions for the cultivation and enhancement of these begun here and not fully realized until eternity.

Having effectively disposed of the objection to the doctrine of a future life by the Sadducees, Jesus proceeded to show that the scriptures, which all of the Jewish sects affected to receive, taught the doctrine of life beyond death in the most irresistible fashion. "But as touching the resurrection of the dead," he said, "have ye not read that which was spoken unto you by God, saying, I am the God of Abraham, and the God of Isaac, and the God of Jacob? God is not the God of the dead, but of the living." It must not be overlooked that this argument was directed wholly toward the Sadducees and that it developed from the objection they had offered to an existence beyond the grave. He used the word "dead" in precisely the sense they did in the argument they presented. They taught that a dead person had simply ceased to be; such a person was *non est*—without any existence. Were God the God of such a person he would indeed be the God of the dead, and since the dead were, in the eyes of the Sadducees, non-existent, and a non-existent thing is nothing, God would be God of nothing! Hundreds of years after the patriarchs Abraham, Isaac and Jacob died, Moses wrote that God is their God (Exodus 3:6.) He is not the God of the dead; therefore, Exodus 3:6 teaches that Abraham, Isaac and Jacob are yet alive! Obviously not alive in the flesh, because they were buried centuries before Moses penned these words. But one conclusion is possible: they are alive in spirit. God is their God, and since God is not the God of the *non-existent,* they live on in the spirit world.

Here is irrefutable proof that death does not terminate our existence, and that the spirits of men survive the dissolution of their bodies and live on when their earthly life ends. The doctrine of "soul-sleeping" is

343

thus proved to be positively and palpably false. Of this fact, biblical evidence abounds. Neither time nor space permits the presentation of proof which may be drawn to this end from the appearance of Moses and Elijah on the Mount of Transfiguration (Matthew 17:3), the desire and expectation of Paul as expressed in his Philippian letter (Philippians 1:23) and the solid and well-grounded hope of the faithful, as evidence in 2 Corinthians 5:8-10, and many other wonderful declarations touching the future life in the holy writings.

Hence, God is not the God of the non-existent. (Matthew 22:32.) God—in the person of Christ—is the God of all whether in the spirit world, or yet on earth in the flesh. (Romans 14:9.)

"Please explain John 9:1-3. What is meant by the statement, 'Neither did this man sin, nor his parents: but that the works of God should be manifest in him'? Does this mean that God created him blind to demonstrate his power?"

It is most likely that the blind man was a well-known figure in Jerusalem; many were acquainted with him and were well aware of his disability. (John 9:8.) Of the six miracles associated with blindness mentioned in the books of the gospel, this is the only one in which blindness had existed from birth. This, in the eyes of the blind man, made the miracle all the more notable: "Since the world began it was never heard that any one opened the eyes of a man born blind." (John 9:32.) Though many marvelous techniques today exist in treating eye disorders, modern medical science has no cure for those congenitally blind. Blindness was more common in that day than in ours and minor eye disorders easily corrected today were then without remedy.

The appelative *Rabbi* means "teacher." Quite often the disciples thus addressed the Savior. (John 1:38,49; 3:31; 5:25.) The disposition they exhibit is in sharp contrast with that of the unbelieving Jews in chapter 8. The disciples were willing to be, and were about to be taught by the Lord and they indicated such by this mode of address.

Their question, "Who sinned, this man, or his parents, that he should be born blind," resulted from the view that all difficulties, troubles, misfortunes, illnesses, and the like, are the result of some special sin. This view the disciples held; yet, they were unable to see how such could be so in this case. Blindness began before this man was born; how could his own sin have occasioned it? If it were not because of his own sin, was it because of the sin of his parents? They seemed not to have considered that neither conclusion was true and that there was an alternative they had not contemplated. The view they expressed is a persistent one and is held by many today even though the book of Job

344

is a clear refutation of it and Jesus also taught that it rested on a false premise. (Luke 13:1-5.)

Some have affected to see here some indication that the disciples may have held to the doctrine of "transmigration of souls" (the view that the man may have lived and sinned in some former age) but there is nothing in the text to support this nor can it be shown that the Jews of that day ever advanced such an idea. The doctrine, that sickness and physical disabilities are the result of specific sins and are *penalties* administered for this reason, is false; it is true that people often suffer the *consequences* of the sins of their ancestors in weakened bodies and premature deaths; and parents may, by improper physical habits, pass on to their children impaired constitutions, but these are consequences and not penalties for punishment for sins, and ought not so to be classified. The doctrine of Original Sin, subscribed to by many today, partakes of this error. Ezekiel, referring to a similar view prevalent in his day, refuted it in this remarkable statement: "The word of Jehovah came unto me again, saying, What mean ye, that ye use this proverb concerning the land of Israel, saying, The fathers have eaten sour grapes, and the children's teeth are set on edge? As I live, saith the Lord Jesus, ye shall not have occasion any more to use this proverb in Israel. Behold, all souls are mine; as the soul of the father so also the soul of the son is mine: the soul that sinneth, it shall die." (Ezek. 18:1-4.) Penalties are administered for personal sins only. "Sin is the transgression of the law." (1 John 3:4.)

Thus, the reasoning which prompted the query of the disciples appears to have been this: Physical disability is the result of somebody's special sin. In the case of the blind man it was either his, or his parents'. It seemed hardly possible to attribute it to the blind man since this affliction had existed from birth. Was it then the sin of his parents which produced it? Their major premise was false, as the Lord proceeded to show, and thus neither conclusion followed.

"Jesus answered, Neither did this man sin, or his parents: but that the works of God should be manifest in him. This statement is not an unqualified one. The Saviour did not mean that neither the man nor his parents were *sinners*. The query was restricted and the answer must be viewed in the same restricted sense. Neither did this man sin, nor his parents *that he should be born blind,* is the import of the passage. The answer, while rejecting both hypotheses advanced by the disciples, dealt with the *results* which were to attend it, leaving unanswered the central question: Why was this man born blind? Jesus taught them that instead of wrestling with the age-old problem of the relationship of sin and suffering they should see in this case the marvelous blessing which the love and grace of God would produce. The blindness of the man would thus afford an opportunity for God to bring to him, and to all who witnessed the results of the miracle, the privilege and blessing of salvation. They would be enabled to realize that he who could give physical light to the blind could also provide spiritual light to those groping in the darkness of sin and death. There is nothing here nor elsewhere in the scriptures to support the view, often advanced, that God occasions evil in order to demonstrate his powers by removing it or that people are sometimes made to suffer affliction by arbitrary divine decrees.

Finally, it is important to note that the conjunction "that" in the passage under study does not denote *cause* but *effect,*—the man was not born blind so that God might be glorified, but God was glorified as the effect of his blindness. A comparable statement will be found in John 9:39, "For judgment I am come into this world, that they which see not might see; and that they which see might be made blind." Quite obviously, our Lord, who is himself the "light of the world," did not come to make men blind who before could see; but, his coming was a judgment upon those who refused to accept him, thus leaving them blind spiritually. This was an *effect* (in consequence) the offence might abound; actually, the law was given to restrain sin. Other instances of this usage of the conjunction are in Matthew 23:34,35 John 12:40 and 1 Corinthians 11:19.

"Is the objection that is sometimes offered to older English versions of the Bible that the same Greek word is often rendered by several different English words and phrases a valid one?"

No.

One of the most common misconceptions of the usage, idiom and syntactical characteristics of languages is the assumption that in translation—the transference of thought from one language to another—it is simply a matter of finding words exactly corresponding in meaning, and thenceforth in each instance where the word appears to render it by the same word in the language in which it being translated.

The truth is that no two words in the same language are of exactly the same significance, much less of other languages, and words may be synonymous in meaning and interchangeable in usage, yet not be precisely of the same meaning. Words survive because they carry a meaning belonging to them and to no others, and any correct use of them must be in harmony with, and in appreciation of this fact. Not only is this true, the same word may convey in other contexts a different meaning because of its relationship to other words in the sentence. It cannot be overemphasized that words derive their meaning both contextually, and by use and the assumption that uniformity in translation—always using the same English to translate the same foreign

346

word—would lead inevitably to glaring errors in translation and in meaning.

A casual look into a Greek lexicon by a discerning reader will readily confirm this. The word "suffer," in the King James Version, is the rendering of two different Greek words; and, in many other instances from combinations of the same roots. To "provoke" appears about a dozen times and is translated from eight different Greek words. *Krino*, to judge, is rendered 15 different ways in the English text. These are not arbitrary or capricious variations; they are necessary to exhibit in our language the varied shades of meaning characteristic of the words and phrases being translated. A practice, unfortunately quite commonly engaged in by superficial students in seeking the meaning of a Greek word is to open a lexicon, note its root meaning, arbitrarily select one of many meanings given and thenceforth assume that this is its significance wherever appearing.

This "school-boy" approach to the study of the New Testament Greek is certain to lead to gross error. The word *theatron* means a theater and this significance is assigned to the word as its primary meaning by Arndt and Gingrich in their Greek lexicon. Paul used the word in 2 Corinthians 4:9 when he wrote, "We are made a spectacle (theater) unto the world, and to angels and to men." The apostle thus figuratively described his sufferings as a production being played out on a stage before the whole world. It should not be difficult to see that the meaning of the word here and in Acts 19:21,31, where it denotes a playhouse of decidedly different significance. The basic meaning of *krino* is to judge. It is used in the New Testament of the judgment of men upon each other (Romans 2:27); the expression of an opinion on some matter (Luke 6:37); the testimony of righteous persons against unrighteous ones (Matthew 19:28) and to criticize, to find fault with (Romans 14:13;) (it is interesting to observe that the word is used in two different senses in the same verse here); a decision a father makes to keep his daughter from marrying (1 Corinthians 7:37); to condemn undue preference for one day above another (Romans 14:5); judging one's own motives (Acts 13:46); judgment in human tribunals (Acts 25:10); and the great judgment at the last day (2 Timothy 4:1.)

This simple induction of New Testament usage of a very few terms—and the list might be indefinitely lengthened—should be sufficient to show that words may and often do have varied significance, depending on the context, and that it is absurd to assume that each Greek word should be translated by the same English word in every instance where appearing.

"When and where was the Hardeman-Bogard Debate conducted, and what is your impression of it?"

April 19-22, 1938, was indeed one of the most significant and important periods in the interests of truth and righteousness in this, the 20th century. This was the week of the *Hardeman-Bogard debate,* a discussion first orally conducted in the meetinghouse of the Fourth and State Streets church of Christ, Little Rock, AR (and arranged by E. R. Harper, then the regular preacher there), and later published in full by the Gospel Advocate Co., Nashville, Tenn.

The themes discussed in that remarkable debate are of the most interesting, vital and important nature: the necessity of perseverance and faithfulness in order to salvation; the identify, marks and establishment of the New Testament church; the proper place of baptism; and, the work and mode of operation of the Holy Spirit.

The chief participants, without peers in their respective communions, were N. B. Hardeman, cofounder and longtime president of Freed-Hardeman College, an educator and college administrator of superb ability, an evangelist of the churches of Christ of national reputation, and an orator exceeding in ability, as a speaker, any other in the land; and Ben M. Bogard, dean of the Missionary Baptist Institute, Little Rock, a veteran Baptist minister, and the acknowledged champion Baptist debator of his day.

These men brought to the polemic platform in Arkansas' capital city, a richness of scholarship, long experience and training, and maturity of mind on the matters discussed the highest degree possible.

The transcript which resulted is undoubtedly the clearest and most perceptive study of the differences between churches of Christ and Baptist churches, on the matters discussed, in existence. It ought to be taught in every Christian school among us; every gospel preacher should master it; it should be in every church library and on the study table of every elder in the church today.

The shocking truth is that some among us today are advocating views, concerning the Spirit's operations, more nearly coinciding with those of Baptist Bogard, than those of brother Hardeman, thus clearly evidencing the extent of the departures now characteristic of some in the churches of Christ today.

In this momentous discussion, Mr. Bogard argued that the Holy Spirit operates *apart* from, and *independent* of, the word of truth—the scriptures. By this he meant that, in the view of Baptists, there is an impact of the Holy Spirit, upon the individual being influenced, which is literal and actual and personal, in *addition* to, and *beyond* that wrought by the word. Such is precisely the opinion entertained by a small segment of brethren today. True, those who subscribe to this

348

view stoutly affirm that they claim no miraculous powers or outward manifestations of such; but, so did Mr. Bogard. He said, "In my debate with Aimee McPherson, I said that we did not need miracles any more. Since we have the word we do not need the direct inspiration from God for God to speak to us or to inspire people now. We do not need that. We don't need to go around opening the eyes of the blind and raising the dead. Our all-sufficient rule of faith and practice is thoroughly established now and the power of men to work miracles has passed away so says that perfect rule." (Page 51.)

Brother Hardeman, in what, to this writer, is one of the most irrefutable arguments ever made (and which I urge the reader to obtain and study in full in the published debate), shows that in both *conversion* and *sanctification* (both with reference to the influence wrought upon the sinner, *and* the child of God), the Holy Spirit's influence is *simply* and *solely* and *only* by means of the all-sufficient and final revelation of truth—the scriptures.

In summary, Brother Hardeman pointed out the conclusions to which his arguments lead: "But how does the Spirit operate? That is the question. My answer, first, last and all the time, is that he influences through the gospel, which is God's power. The word is the medium through which the Spirit accomplishes His work. If that book there were the sinner's heart and this hand were the Holy Spirit (placing hand on book) there is direct and immediate contact; if you put something between, the hand will operate on the book, but this time it is through the medium of this tablet. *That represents the only two ideas that can be had from this proposition.* That represents the difference between Dr. Bogard and me, the difference between error and truth." (Page 21.)

In the final moments of the discussion on the Holy Spirit, brother Hardeman, in his eloquent, precise manner, said: "Only a few minutes remain for review of things already stated. There is not a single step taken by any man from the time he decides to leave the cold, bleak world of sin until he enters the door that stands ajar, but said step is effected either directly or indirectly by the word of God. The Spirit does his part, and he, as always, uses as a medium of contact the word of God which is 'able to make one wise unto salvation' and to thoroughly furnish everyone unto every good work. Our difference is not that of whether the Spirit does or does not operate—it is whether he operates outside the realm of God's will or in harmony with it. I know the man doesn't live who can find a single passage where the Spirit operates distinct—away—from the blessed word, or where there is the slightest intimation of an isolated span or distance intervening between the Holy Spirit's work and that of the word. It simply is not in God's book, and it is futile to fight against it." (Pages 64, 65).

And so also is the conviction of this writer. The view, that the Holy Spirit exercises an influence apart from, and beyond that of the word of God is a new, novel and dangerous doctrine, unheard of in the churches of Christ until the last decade or two. We challenge any man among us to produce a statement from any prominent writer from the inception of the Restoration Movement until 1950 who taught that there is additional guidance and direction through the Spirit, not set out in God's word. Any differences which obtained among brethren, in an earlier day, regarding the *manner* or *mode* of the Spirit's "indwelling" did not extend to contentions urging additional influence. It remained for our day and decade to produce the view that the Baptist Bogard was right in his insistence that there are influences wrought upon us, by the Spirit, in addition to the written word. Such a view is, of course, an impeachment of the authority, totality and all-sufficiency of the sacred writings; and it paves the way for the gross departures of alleged tongue-speaking, the baptism of the Holy Spirit, and special revelations, now increasingly being heard among us. This writer thinks that these unfortunate and fatal trends are logical and natural consequences of the view that the Holy Spirit actually, bodily, and literally resides in the Christian. Were I to accept the view that *deity* is personally in me; and he exercises powers over me beyond the divine revelation of truth set out in the scripture, I would indeed expect some outward, visible manifestation thereof. Strange indeed would it be that such power is present; yet, not outwardly active! Why limit him? "Tongue speakers" are at least consistent in their error.

These disastrous views have resulted from an abandonment of the teaching of the scriptures touching the personality of the Holy Spirit. *He* is a *person;* not, a mere influence. (John 16:13.) A person does not literally abide—nor can he—in the person of another. One person influences another person through moral suasion. Such is the manner by which the Spirit has always acted. "The Spirit *spake* by me." (2 Samuel 23:2.) "The Spirit *speaketh* expressly." (1 Timothy 4:1.) "He that hath an ear, let him hear what the Spirit *saith* to the churches." (Revelation 2:7.) God, Christ, the Holy Spirit, all of them divine *Persons,* are in us as they influence us by Word of truth. (1 John 4:15; Colossians 1:27; Galatians 4:6.) To reject the word is to reject the Spirit who gave the word. (Nehemiah 9:30.)

"Why is sin sometimes referred to as 'missing the mark'?"

Sin is set forth in the sacred writings both as an act and a principle, accordingly as it is regarded as specific disobedience or as a state of sin. Many terms, both in the Old and New Testaments, appear and present these aspects in a variety of ways. Of frequent occurrence in the former is the word *hatah* and rendered in the Septuagint by the Greek word *hamartia,* to miss one's aim, thus to *miss the mark.* It is a figure from the practice of archery—the use of bows and arrows. By an easy transition the word passed from the literal act of failing to hit the target to a figurative significance of erring in understanding, then a bad action and finally an evil deed.

If one shoots an arrow at a target and misses, it is not good sportsmanship to fling aside the bow and admit defeat. The failure itself becomes a challenge to try again.

In a truly wonderful sense the gospel of Christ may be called *The Gospel Of The Second Chance.* Theologians have vainly sought to find some trace of hope for those who spurn the gospel call here in the world to come. All such efforts fail because the period of probation for man is limited to this life. "He that believeth not shall be damned," is our Lord's final word on this subject. (Mark 16:15,16.) Certain destruction awaits those who do not obey the gospel. (2 Thessalonians 1:8-10.) Far better for us is the realization that there is a second chance in this world for all those who turn in penitence to the Lord. (1 John 1:7-9; 2:1.)

Repentance is the price of a new round of shots at the target!

From the far country, slowly, wearily and in shame the prodigal returned. His oft-rehearsed speech begins, "Father, before heaven, and in thy sight I have missed the mark and do not deserve another try. Please suffer me to become one of thy hired servants." The father drowns out these words in a sea of love and devotion. As he rains kisses on the humbled wanderer, he shouts (in effect), "Bring out a bow and give it to him." The elder brother complains, "He had the bow and missed the mark." "Never mind," the happy father answers, *"he has come back to try again!"* How grateful all of us should be that the heavenly Father allows us to come back and try again.

"Brother Woods, should those who have ceased to be faithful and who resist all efforts to restore them be withdrawn from? Is this not impossible since such have already withdrawn themselves from the congregation?"

All who have been baptized into Christ are members of the local church, whether they attend or not. (Acts 2:42-47; Romans 6:1-6.) As such, their actions reflect upon the church locally, whether good or bad. (1 Corinthians 12:12-27.) Those out of duty who are either sick or dead spiritually (1 Corinthians 11:30), are still members of the church and are recognized as such by the community in which they live. Paul instructed the Thessalonian church to withdraw from every brother who walked "disorderly." (2 Thessalonians 3:14,15.) To walk disorderly is to be *out of step* with the rest of the congregation. Those who no longer attend the services from indifference are certainly out of step with the rest of the members and ought to be visited, counselled, warned and, as a final resort, withdrawn from. Fellowship is not limited to the public assembly!

There are many scriptural and sound reasons why discipline ought to be practiced. (1) It is a New Testament doctrine, plainly taught by precept and example. (1 Corinthians 5:1-13; Romans 16:17; Matthew 18:15-17.) (2) it operates for the good of the offender who through its exercise may be brought to realize the error of his way and to repentance and forgiveness (1 Corinthians 5:13.) (3) It guards the church from the contaminating influence of wicked people and those who refuse to do right. (4) It enables the people of the world to see that the church is resolved to keep itself pure and faithful. Were it practiced the church would enjoy vastly greater respect and esteem in most communities today.

"We have a man and wife who have obeyed the gospel but will not locate with one church. They attend here and there on a regular basis. One church in the area will not call on the brother for prayer or ask him to assist at the Lord's table. Is there a book, chapter and verse that states one must locate or be identified with a particular congregation?"

Yes, numerous ones. (Acts 2:42-47; 9:26; Romans 16:1,2; Hebrews 13:7,17.) It is also logical, reasonable and desirable. Faithful disciples will wish to be recognized as members of the congregation, sharers in the blessings and burdens requisite to the work, and in humble submission to the elders who oversee the congregation. (Hebrews 13:7.) My observation over many years of extensive travel among the churches is that those who refuse to place membership are motivated by the desire to avoid responsibility but at the same time to claim the blessings of church attendance. If one can *worship* acceptably with a congregation, one can *work* there also; and dedicated disciples desire the warm, close communion which results from the realization that they are actively associated with others of like precious faith, in the work of the Lord. I have never known any drifter from congregation to congregation who ever made any substantial contribution to the advancement of the cause of Christ. Those who truly love the Lord will wish to join hands actively with the Lord's people, in the Lord's way.

"Would you please explain to us how you have drawn the conclusions from the scriptures that Judas was not present at the time the Lord's Supper was instituted?"

In the *Adult Gospel Quarterly* lesson, the following statement, prompting the foregoing query, appeared: "The Lord's Supper was instituted on the evening before our Lord's death on the cross, and immediately following the observance of the passover feast in the upper room in Jerusalem. (Matthew 26:26-30; Mark 14:22-26; Luke 22:14-23.) All of the apostles except Judas (John 13:21-30) were present when it was instituted."

The conclusion is a necessary one when all of the details of all the writers are carefully considered. It should be noted that none of the biographers of Jesus relates all of the events associated with the institution of the supper and that a full and accurate account may be had only when each detail by each writer is placed in harmonious relationship to the whole. To this end, the following passages in the order given should be read: Luke 22:14-18; John 13: 23-30; Matthew 26:26-30; Luke 22:19,20.

The chronological order of the events of the upper room appears to have been as follows: (1) Jesus and the 12 disciples assembles to observe the Passover feast. (2) After the feast began, contention among the disciples regarding their relative status prompted the Lord to teach an object lesson in humility by washing their feet. (3) The Lord took his place at the head of the table and the feast resumed. (4) He began to exhibit much distress and revealed to the group that one of their number would betray him. (5) The perplexed disciples were greatly confused and Peter asked John, who was reclining at the table near the Lord, to inquire of him who it was who would betray him. (6) Jesus identified the infamous disciple to John as the one to whom he would give "the sop." (7) Jesus handed to Judas Iscariot the sop following which "Satan entered into him." (8) The Lord thereupon bade the wicked disciple to "do quickly" that which he had already purposed. (9) Judas *went out* "immediately" into the night to consummate his vile and faithless scheme. (10) Jesus then instituted the supper, using the emblems remaining from the passover feast. Following the supper, he delivered the discourse recorded in John 14, 15 and 16. From the upper room he went to Gethsemane.

The *sop* was a morsel of bread or meat dipped into the gravy sauce of the sacrifice. It was not unusual for guests, as a special act of recognition, to be thus served by the host himself. Jesus, by this method, revealed privately to John the identity of the infamous betrayer. The use of the definite article with the word "sop" shows it to have been a part of the paschal supper. Immediately following this Judas left the gathering. Thus, either the Lord's supper was instituted before the passover feast; or, Judas had already departed when the supper was instituted. The former is in conflict with plain statements of the narrative; hence, the latter conclusion follows and Judas was not present when the supper was instituted.

Once we received a lengthy and labored effort from a brother who sought to avoid this obvious conclusion with the allegation that there were *two* upper room meetings, the first of which was to observe the Passover, the second to institute the supper; and that the meeting from which Judas departed was the former, being present at the latter! For such a conclusion there is of course not the slightest evidence.

"Is eating on church premises forbidden in 1 Corinthians 11:20-34?"

The Lord's Supper was instituted on the evening before our Lord's tragic death on the cross, and immediately following the observance of the Passover Feast in the upper room in Jerusalem. (Matthew 26:26-30; Mark 14:22-26; Luke 22:14-23.) All of the original apostles, except Judas, were present when Jesus instituted the supper. (John 13:21-30.) Paul, of course, was not there, not having been selected to be an apostle until some years later; but, he received directly from the Lord, by special revelation, the details. (1 Corinthians 11:23-25.) Its design is to commemorate the death of our Lord (1 Corinthians 11:26), and it is to be observed each first day of the week (Acts 20:7).

The Corinthians had corrupted the supper by combining it with an ordinary meal. It is very likely that this resulted from an improper mingling of the "love feasts," in which the saints met and shared their food, with the Lord's supper. (Jude 12; 2 Peter 2:13.) At any rate, they had greatly abused the purpose and intent of the memorial which the Saviour established on the eve of his death, and the situation required immediate correction. There was, indeed, such divergence from the original design of the supper that it was not possible to observe it under the conditions there prevailing.

What led to this corruption the apostle describes in this fashion: "For in your eating each one taketh before other his own supper; and one is hungry, and another drunken." Some had more food than others; these ate before the others; and, thus some were filled and others were hungry. From the fact that the apostle said some were "hungry," and others, "drunken," some draw the conclusion that this means they were getting drunk at the Lord's table, whence they infer that the fruit of the vine used in the memorial feast must have been intoxicating wine! But, this is to read into the passage more than is really there. The meal at which some were "drunken" was not the supper of the Lord, but one of common food; and, it is by no means certain that the word *drunken* here signifies intoxication. It is placed opposite *hungry,* in the text, to describe a state opposed to hunger; and the Greek word is *also* defined by the lexicons "to be filled, plentifully fed." Such is very possibly its meaning here. Moreover, it undoubtedly describes the same action as that which the apostle intended by the word *drink* in the sentence, "What, have ye not houses to eat and to *drink* in?" (I Corinthians 11:22.) Who would possibly conclude from this that Paul is telling the Corinthians that they may imbibe intoxicating liquor at home? It is sinful to drink alcoholic beverages, in *any* quantity, anywhere. The word drunken and the word drink, as used in these passages, may not be properly construed to support the concept of alcoholic use.

There are those who cite this instance in an effort to prove that it is wrong for Christians to eat food on church property, particularly, if the premises are also used for the purposes of worship. But, this is grossly to misapprehend the situation which existed in Corinth, and the criticism which Paul offered. The abuse in Corinthian worship consisted of (1) participating in a common meal in connection with the Lord's Supper; (2) selfishness in eating before others; and (3) a failure properly to understand the nature and purpose of the Lord's Supper. Paul did not condemn the brethren for eating on church property—there is absolutely no evidence in the sacred writings that the church in Corinth owned any property—but for corrupting the worship and for exhibiting greediness and selfishness. Obviously, the apostle is not saying here that it was permissible to eat and drink to excess and to ignore the poorer brethren *at home!* He alluded to their houses as places in which to eat and to drink, because this is where people ordinarily consume food—not in worship! If his statement is to be construed as a positive command to eat and drink *at home,* then it would be wrong to eat and to drink in restaurants or other eating places, or, for that matter, in the homes of relatives or friends.

It is clear, therefore, that the correct understanding of this matter depends on the proper analysis of the situation then existing in the church in Corinth and the purpose which prompted Paul to deal with it. It is a misuse of the passage to cite it as prohibiting "dinners-on-the-ground," or other similar exercises widely practiced by our brethren today. The "love feasts," of the early church were very similar (if not identical) to the "covered dish luncheons" in vogue today in many congregations. I have joyously shared in these bountiful feasts from coast to coast, and from the Great Lakes to the Gulf for many years and I have never observed any resemblance to the corruption which Paul condemned in the church in Corinth. On the contrary, these happy occasions warm the hearts and elevate the spirits of those who generously and unselfishly share their food with others. Members of the church who regularly sit down to eat together do not usually engage in bitterness and back-biting. Congregations would promote a higher level of fellowship and brotherliness by participating in more of these delightful exercises.

"What is meant by Peter's statement, 'Neither lords over God's heritage' (1 Peter 5:3)?"

Those who regard the sacred writings as the total, complete and authoritative expression of the divine will do not question the fact that the church, in its local and congregational aspect, is to have "elders" as *overseers* (Acts 20:28), "deacons" as *servants* (1 Timothy 3:10), and "evangelists' as *preachers* of the word (2 Timothy 4:1). In order properly to discharge these functions those thus designated must be qualified, and the qualifications are clearly recorded and easily understood. The qualifications for elders are set out in 1 Timothy 3:1-7 and Titus 1:5-11; for deacons, 1 Timothy 3:10-13; and for evangelists, the book of 1 Timothy, 2 Timothy, Titus and occasionally elsewhere in the New Testament.

The position I hold on the duties, the responsibilities and the proper functions of elders has often been expressed, and can be presented in the very words which the Holy Spirit used in the revelation of these and all other matters of the divine will. I believe that the elders who "rule" well are to be counted worthy of double honor (1 Timothy 5:17); I believe and teach that it is the duty of all faithful children to God to "obey them that have the rule over you, and submit yourselves: for they watch for your souls . . ." (Hebrews 13:17); and it is my settled and firm conviction that it is a part of the divine plan that bishops (elders) are "overseers" and made such by the Holy Spirit who set out the qualifications which must be characteristic of them as a condition precedent to their appointment. (Acts 20:28.)

It has been said that this is an "authoritarian" concept of the eldership and that those of us who so teach believe that elders are "bosses" of the congregation to whom the members must submit whatever their "edicts" may be. I long ago learned that men often exaggerate and rework a proposition and reply to their perversion of it and thus make up with semantics what is lacking in logic and proof on the original proposition. We think this is an excellent example of this not unusual practice and it evidences an awareness of weakness in dealing with the matters involved. If by an "authoritarian eldership" it is meant that men impose their wills upon the congregation simply in virtue of the fact that they act from powers resident in themselves and because of an investment of "office," I have never believed such and, in a lifetime of preaching, I have never met a man who did. I believe that the viewpoint is a will-of-the-wisp, a figment of the imagination, utterly without reality in the churches of Christ today. I do most stoutly believe that an eldership is empowered by divine right, within the framework of New Testament teaching, to direct the work of the congregation in the discharge of the duties divinely imposed, and that to oppose the

356

plan of God is to oppose God himself. It was the Holy Spirit who said, "*Obey* them that have the *rule over you,* and *submit* yourselves: for they watch for your souls." (Hebrews 13:17.) Those whom we are to "obey" are qualified men, duly and properly selected by the congregation and whose "rule" over us is within the sphere of proper church action.

Elderships are composed of weak, fallible men who do not always function as God wills and some, on occasion, flagrantly violate these principles. Those who thus do are in grave error and of such I offer no defense whatsoever; on the contrary, I would point out that it is grievous sin to "lord" it over God's heritage—the body of Christ. (1 Peter 5:3.) The Diotrephean spirit even now occasionally rears its ugly head and men who falsely pose as shepherds of the flock on occasion seek to use their usurped powers to suppress the preaching of God's word.

I recall but one such experience and it occurred more than 35 years ago. I was in a meeting in a Midwestern state, and had announced a series of themes to be discussed on the remaining evenings of the meeting. An elder approached me privately and informed me that the elders had met, had decided that the theme announced for the final service of the meeting should not be presented and that they were ordering me to desist from its presentation. It was a subject of vital importance, and especially relevant in that area and congregation. Had he said to me, "We question the propriety of this presentation and we would like to discuss the matter with you," I would have listened to their reasons, offered those which prompted my decision to preach on the subject, and in the exchange determined what was right to do under the circumstances. No such reasonable and proper solution of the matter was given me.

I said, in effect, to the elder, "I am here by the invitation of the eldership and am speaking here at your will. I concede your right to decide who speaks here, but this does not include *what* I am to speak. Therefore, I shall do one of two things: I shall speak on the theme and at the time announced; or, on the evening *preceding* I shall announce to the congregation that I have been forbidden by the eldership to preach my convictions and close the meeting. Which shall I do?" They lacked the courage to face the congregation and so they did nothing and I preached on the theme as announced. No man or group of men under heaven may suppress the preaching of the truth. "And they called them, and commanded them not to speak at all nor teach in the name of Jesus. But Peter and John said unto them, Whether it be right in the sight of God to hearken unto you more than unto God, judge ye. For we cannot but speak the things which we have seen and heard." (Acts 4:18-20.)

357

"What should one do who sincerely makes a vow and later learns that it was an improper one?"

Solomon said, "When thou vowest a vow unto God, defer not to pay it: for he hath no pleasure in fools: pay that which thou vowest. Better it is that thou shouldest not vow, than that thou shouldest vow and not pay." (Ecclesiastes 5:4,5.) The Psalmist listed among the characteristics of one who pleases God, swearing to one's own hurt, and changing not. Obligations are to be kept, promises are to be performed, and duties are to be discharged, though such may be vastly more difficult than when first proposed. (Psalm 15:4.) No oath, however, can justify an offence against God or man; such vows ought never to be made and if made, should be repented of, *not performed.* Herod's foolish and wicked vow to Herodias falls into this category.

This *Herod* (a title given to certain rulers in Palestine during our Lord's public ministry) was Antipas, son of Herod the Great by a Samaritan woman named Malthace, one of the many wives of that monarch. He is called "the tetrach" (which means ruler of *the fourth part*) from the fact that he was assigned a fourth portion of the realm of his father, details of which are given by the Jewish historian Josephus. He was first married to the daughter of Aretas, an Arabian king of Petraea, but became infatuated with Herodias, the wife of his half-brother Philip, and eloped with her, though both were married at the time. For this they were rebuked by John the Baptist. (Matthew 14:4.) For this outspoken criticism of the king and his consort, the fearless harbinger of the Lord was "shut up in prison." (Luke 3:19,20.) Herod, at the instigation of Herodias, would have killed him but for fear of public opinion. The people regarded John as a prophet and the wicked ruler was hesitant to risk the disfavor of his subjects at this time by having John slain. The wicked woman with him felt no such restraint; the rebukes she received at the hands of John rankled in her bosom; and she determined to destroy her accuser at the first opportunity. This came on the occasion of Herod's birthday.

"But when Herod's birthday came, the daughter of Herodias danced in the midst, and pleased Herod." (Matthew 14:6.) This "daughter of Herodias" was the off-spring of Philip and Herodias, and her name was *Salome.* Her dancing, a part of the festive entertainment which attended the celebration, greatly pleased the king and, doubtless under the influence of the liquors which freely flows on such occasions, he made a rash and foolish promise which he was soon to regret himself: "Whereupon he promised with an oath to give her whatsoever she should ask. And she, being put forward by her mother, saith, Give me here on a platter the head of John the Baptist." The request originated with the mother who had anticipated just such an opportunity; and it was to be granted "here," *here,* at that moment, and in the presence of the king's distinguished guests. It is very possible that she felt she could achieve her purpose only if she urged its performance at this time; and it may also be true that she wanted the satisfaction of exhibiting her triumph over him who had dared openly to criticize her in the most public fashion.

"And the king was grieved; but for the sake of his oaths, and of them that sat at meat with him, he commanded it to be given; and he sent and beheaded John in the prison. And his head was brought on a platter, and given to the damsel: and she brought it to her mother." The request had a sobering effect on the king; it had not occurred to him that he would be asked to do such a thing. Any hesitancy he had regarding the matter was overcome by (a) the oath and (b) the presence of those who had heard his rash promise. He ought to have remembered two things: (1) one is never bound morally to perform any oath or vow when such requires wrong-doing and (2) he should have told Herodias, Salome, and his guests that the promise was intended to embrace maters of pecuniary value only, and not the commission of crime. He should have said, "I ought never to have made an offer which could be interpreted as unconditional. I had no idea that you would ask for a human life; such is wholly beyond what I intended. I have no right to grant your request, even though the authority so to do is in my hands. It was wholly out of order for me to make an offer which would include such an act, and it would only compound the crime for me to perform it. For these reasons I cannot isue the order you designate. Ask of me anything reasonable, and I shall gladly grant it."

Unhappily, the king was not thus influenced. In full compliance with the wicked proposal, he issued the order for John's execution, and the wilderness preacher was beheaded. When this gruesome object of her hatred was brought before Herodias, did she find in her revenge the satisfaction she sought? Perhaps, for the moment; but, there must have often appeared before her in the lonely hours of the night those sightless eyes of John peering deeply into the innermost recesses of her soul and accusing her of this senseless and shocking murder. And, in the days which followed until her death, she must have heard again and again the voice ringing in her ears recounting her wicked act against him whom she wished so much to silence. Her infamy was ever with her, and she must have experienced remorse which, as brother McGarvey pointedly remarked, "like the fires of hell, never shall be quenched." She and her partners in crime acquired in the act a reputation for wickedness publicized far, far beyond the sin for which the Harbinger rebuked them, *and they must again face John at the judgment!*

"What is the doctrine of reincarnation?"

It is a refinement of the theory of transmigration—a rebirth after death in new forms of life, either of a lower or a higher nature, as determined by one's manner of life—widely held and taught today by Far Eastern religions. It is to be distinguished from the biblical concept of a resurrection to life eternal at the end of the age, because it alleges that one may return to earth with a new fleshly identity rather than that possessed in the earlier earth-life. Those who advocate reincarnation in this country would reject the cruder forms of the doctrine as taught by the Brahmans, the Hindus and some African tribes; nonetheless, they teach that the doctrine is compatible with Christianity and seek to sustain it by citing Matthew 17:1-13 (the appearance of Moses and Elijah on the Mount of Transfiguration), and John 1:19-28 (John's coming in the "spirit and power" of Elijah).

The doctrine is wholly false, being opposed to every basic principle of Christianity. It makes a mockery of the judgment (how can one be judged both as a good and bad person in varying states of this life?), it renders impossible the resurrection, and the doctrine of rewards and punishments, so plainly taught in the scriptures, and it flagrantly wrests the scriptures from which it seeks support.

The coming of Moses and Elijah on the Mount of Transfiguration was not a reincarnation—entrance into new bodies—but a miraculous appearance of these saints for a special and temporary purpose. There is no semblance of evidence that they continued to live on earth in "new bodies," and later abandoned them in death, or that they were ever seen following that remarkable event. Stephen, on the occasion of his martyrdom, besought the Lord to receive his spirit—not to send it into some other body, and Paul expressed the hope of all the faithful that to die is to *go to be with the Lord*! These biblical concepts, so clearly taught in the sacred writings, render impossible the theory of reincarnation.

John the Baptist did indeed come "in the spirit and power of Elijah;" that is, he exhibited the disposition and the courage of that earlier prophet in his stern message of repentance and reformation, but he did not enter into the body of John the Baptist on the occasion of his death, *because he did not die!* The famed prophet was translated to heaven without dying: "And Elijah went up by a whirlwind into heaven" (2 Kings 2:11). John specifically asserted that he was not Elijah (John 1:21). This is made completely clear in the context of John 1:19. A delegation of Jews came from Jerusalem, headquarters of the Jewish religion, to investigate reports being received there regarding one professing to be the Messiah. They approached John the Baptist, not Jesus, with their query. John is called "the Baptist" to distinguish him from other Johns mentioned in the New Testament, and also to indicate the nature of his work which was to baptize people in preparing them for the coming of the Lord (Matthew 3:1-12). His appearance, his preaching and his manner of life were all unique in that day. He was austere of life and uncompromising in preaching and he made it crystal clear that the Jews, who regarded themselves as fully acceptable to God because of their ancestry, were in need of repentance. His ministry attracted much attention and there went out to hear him "all the country of Judea, and all they of Jerusalem" (Mark 1:5).

These Jews asked, "Who art thou?" The construction of the sentence is significant: *su tis ei?* "You, on your part, who do you claim to be?" The pronoun appears first for emphasis. They thus made it clear that they were not asking about his place of origin, his parentage or the time of his birth; they were only concerned about his claims of position in the Jewish community. It appears that thus far they thought that John was the one of whom rumors had spread to Jerusalem.

"And he confessed, and denied not; and he confessed, I am not the Christ" (John 1:20). The emphasis with which John disclaimed all right to the position implied is impressive. Contrary to what his querists had expected, the baptizer shrank from the slightest implication that he was in any sense the Messiah. His words to this end are very emphatic. "He confessed, and denied not." The first statement indicates the readiness with which he answered, and the second, the clear and unequivocal nature of it. Thus, plainly, clearly, decisively, he said, in effect, "I am not the Christ."

"And they asked him What then? Art thou Elijah? And he saith, I am not. Art thou the prophet? And he answered, No" (John 1:21). The view was widely current in that day and area that the prophet Elijah, in his own person, would return to the earth prior to the coming of Messiah. Was John the long expected prophet? they asked (Matthew 11:14; 17:10-13; Luke 1:17). John was indeed the prophet Elijah *in a spiritual sense,* i.e., as the forerunner of the Christ; he called for a reformation of life on the part of the people like Elijah did in preparation for the coming of the kingdom and king; but he was not the prophet in the sense that the Jews understood the matter and as reincarnationists today do. Had John identified himself as the one who was to come "in the spirit and power" of Elijah, (Luke 1:17), this would have been beyond their current powers of apprehension and it was thus useless to attempt it. He simply answered their question by saying, "I am not." This should forevermore settle the question whether John the Baptist was Elijah reincarnated. *He said he was not.* How dare then anyone say he was!

Was he "that prophet" then? Fifteen hundred years earlier, Moses had prophesied of a great prophet to come. Jehovah said to him, "I will raise them up a prophet from among their brethren, like unto thee . . ."

(Deuteronomy 18:18). Jewish theologians mistakenly distinguished between this prophet and Messiah. New Testament writers make clear that the reference is to the same one, our Lord (Acts 3:22; 7:37).

"They said therefore unto him, Who art thou? that we may give an answer to them that sent us. What sayest thou of thyself?" (John 1:22). To this point these Jews had learned nothing of him of whom they had inquired. They knew only of whom he was not! Being completely baffled by him and frustrated in their attempts to discover his identity and without any information to carry back to Jerusalem, they put the question directly, "Who art thou?"

"He said, I am the voice of one crying in the wilderness, Make straight the way of the Lord, as said Isaiah the prophet" (John 1:23). Here, John revealed his mission; his personal identity was of no importance, whatsoever. He was but a voice, a herald, an announcer of him who was to come. By reference to Isaiah's prophecy, he showed that he fulfilled the prediction of one who would come to prepare the way for Messiah (Isaiah 40:3).

Index

Subjects Treated

364

BIBLE VERSES TREATED
Old Testament

GENESIS:
1:1 226, 227, 336
1:11 20
1:20 231
1:26 228
1:28 37
1:30 231
2:7 230
2:28 112
3:4, 5 185
3:6, 7 185
3:9, 10 185
3:10 185
3:13 264
3:16 59
3:19 17, 167
3:21 185, 196
4:3-16 250
5:32: 264
6:3 23
6:4 19, 20
6:5 44
6:13-16 251
6:17 231
6:22 251
7:15 231
7:22 231
8:4 26
9:4 219
11:10 264
11:26 263
11:32 263
12:1-3 176, 184
12:4 263
12:21, 24 20
18:1, 2 180
18:12 44
18:22-23 44
22:1 179
22:14 51
25:8 102, 286
25:17 286
32:28 271
34:15 254
35:9-15 69
35:18 102
38:24 143
46:11 159
49:29, 33 286
49:33-Chapter 50:1-
    3 286
50:1-3 286

EXODUS:
2:2-24 28
3:2 180
3:6 343
3:13-15 51
3:16-22 159
4:24-26 156
4:25 156
6:2-8 51
8:22, 23 163
8:32 278
10:1 278
12:29, 30 180
13:21, 22 252
15:20 159
17:13, 14 219
17:14 269
17:15 51
18:1-4 158
20:1ff 60
20:19 175
22:1 228
22:26, 27 307
23:21 179
24:9-11 233
24:11 233
25:23-30 193
29:1ff 293
32:10 44
33:11 32
33:20 32, 233
33:27 51
34:11-16 306
34:14 82
39:36 193
40:10-13 187

LEVITICUS:
3:17 219
6:2-5 228
6:26 219
8:1ff 293
10:1, 2 251
17:10-14 219
18:21 82
19:18 306
19:26 219
20:7, 8 187
20:14 143
22:16-22 187
22:16-32 187
23:15-17 221
24:5-9 19, 300, 304

NUMBERS:
3:19 159
6:11 187
12:1-16 158
20:14 271
21:14 269
22:31 180
23:19 44
23:19-20 44

DEUTERONOMY:
4:4 250, 298, 335
4:12 233
4:26 89
4:39 112
5:1, 2 67
5:5 175
6:4 291
6:6, 7 295
7:2 306
12:16 219
12:16, 23 219
14:1 198
15:23 219
18:15 159
18:18 362
23:6 306
23:25 19, 193, 304
23:6 306
23:25 19, 193, 304
24:1-4 255
25:5 342
31:16 254
32:50 286

JOSHUA:
2:1, 7 31, 300, 202
10:13 269

JUDGES:
2:17 254
4:17-24 31, 303
6:24 51
11:1-40 31, 303
13:6-13 180

1 SAMUEL:
2:2 82
13:19 271
14:33 220

371

373

374